The Kings of Buddhism

The Kings of Buddhism

Power, Religion,
and Fury in Myanmar

Robert Edward Sterken Jr.

ROWMAN & LITTLEFIELD
Lanham • Boulder • New York • London

Published by Rowman & Littlefield
An imprint of The Rowman & Littlefield Publishing Group, Inc.
4501 Forbes Boulevard, Suite 200, Lanham, Maryland 20706
www.rowman.com

86-90 Paul Street, London EC2A 4NE

Copyright © 2023 by The Rowman & Littlefield Publishing Group, Inc.

All rights reserved. No part of this book may be reproduced in any form or by any electronic or mechanical means, including information storage and retrieval systems, without written permission from the publisher, except by a reviewer who may quote passages in a review.

British Library Cataloguing in Publication Information Available

Library of Congress Cataloging-in-Publication Data

Names: Sterken, Robert Edward, Jr., author.
Title: The kings of Buddhism : power, religion, and fury in Myanmar / Robert Edward Sterken Jr..
Description: Lanham : Rowman & Littlefield, [2023] | Includes bibliographical references and index. | Summary: "This is a political history of two of the most intimate of human concerns - religion and power. The history of religion in Myanmar is fascinating, brutal, and reveals the consequences of entangling the powers of state and religion"-- Provided by publisher.
Identifiers: LCCN 2022052750 (print) | LCCN 2022052751 (ebook) | ISBN 9781538177938 (cloth) | ISBN 9781538177945 (paperback) | ISBN 9781538177952 (epub)
Subjects: LCSH: Buddhism and state--Burma--History. | Buddhism and politics--Burma--History. | Theravāda Buddhism--Political aspects--Burma--History. | Religion and state--Burma--History. | Religion and politics--Burma--History. | Religious pluralism--Burma--History. | Nationalism--Religious aspects--Buddhism. | Nationalism--Burma--History. | Burma--Religion.
Classification: LCC BQ420 .S74 2023 (print) | LCC BQ420 (ebook) | DDC 294.309591--dc23/eng/20230130
LC record available at https://lccn.loc.gov/2022052750
LC ebook record available at https://lccn.loc.gov/2022052751

Dedicated to the people of Myanmar, with hope.

And to
Sayadaw Ashin Arriyawuntha Biwunsa and all religious leaders
who teach peace and tolerance.

"To know the road ahead, ask those coming back."

—Chinese Proverb

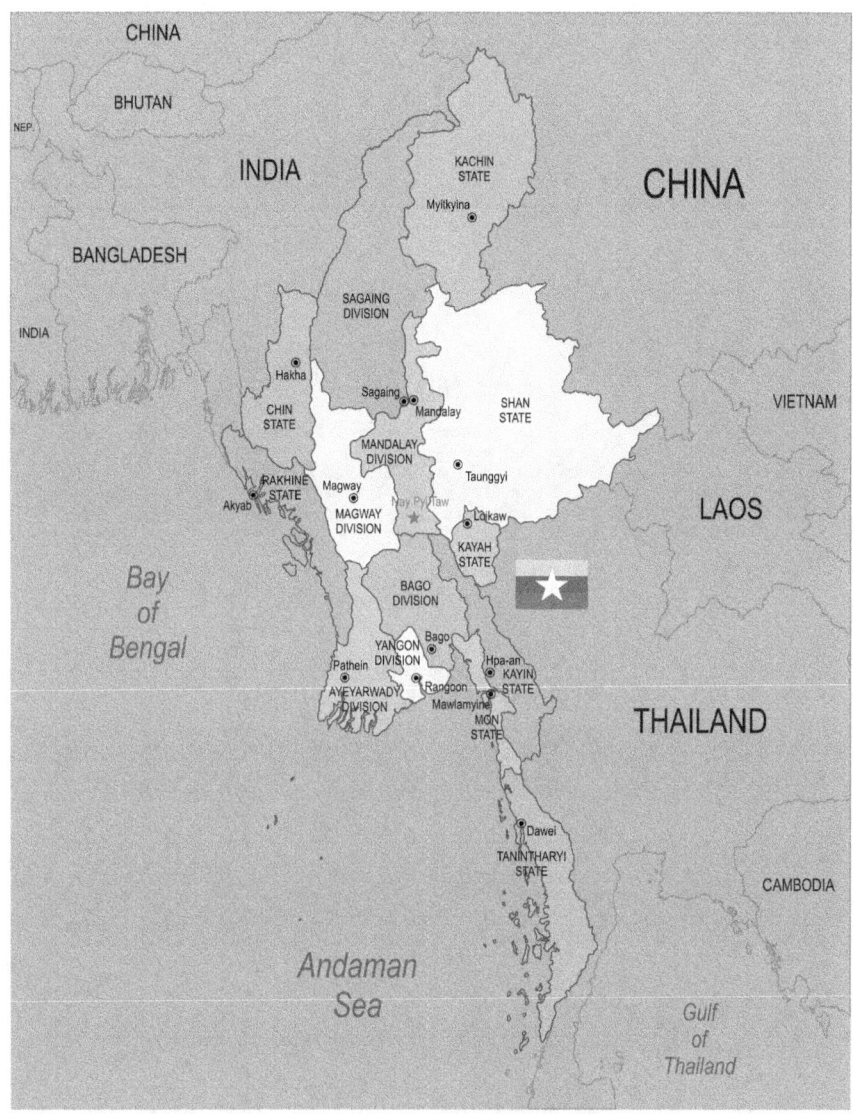

Map of Myanmar. Kosmozoo/ DigitalVision Vectors via Ghetty Images

Contents

Preface: The "Buddhist Country" Myth xi

Acknowledgments xix

A Note on Language and Usage xxv

Cast of Characters xxvii

Introduction: State and Religion Entanglement:
        Controlling, Protecting, and Corrupting Religion 1

1 Nats, Kings, and Government Monks: The Foundations
   of the Myanmar Religious Economy 1057–1824 27

2 The Golden Shore: An Experiment in Religious
   Freedom 1824–1948 47

3 To Be Burmese Is to Be Buddhist: Religious Nationalism in the
   Myanmar Religious Economy 1930–1948 71

4 Saturday's Son: The Religious Economy under a
   Devout Religious Leader 1947–1962 89

5 Going to Moscow: The Religious Economy under
   a Brutal Dictator 1962–1988 109

6 Buddhism, Nat Spirit Wives, and Christian Clerics:
   Religious Convictions in the Myanmar Religious
   Economy 1974–2022 131

7	The Ashokan Road: The Consequences of a Highly Regulated Religious Economy for the State and Majority Religion	159
8	A Different Ashokan Road: The Consequences for Minority Religions, Religious Competition, and Truth	185
Glossary		209
Bibliography		213
Index		237
About the Author		242

Preface
The "Buddhist Country" Myth

Imagine for a moment standing on the main street of downtown Sittwe, the capital of Rakhine state, on the westernmost edge of Myanmar. As the sun sets, street vendors sell savory evening meals to locals. Behind the vendors and Sittwe citizens seated in small pink and green plastic chairs eating their evening noodles is a mix of dense deep green jungle undergrowth and trees. Mostly hidden in that undergrowth, except for the charred remnants of the minarets that tower among the trees, is an abandoned ancient mosque, called the Sawduro Bor Masjid. The eight-hundred-year-old house of worship, today a ghostly reminder of a once-thriving Muslim community, was destroyed in a fire set by rioting Buddhist nationalist monks in 2012 (Holt, 2019, p. 151). The fire burned for hours and destroyed many homes around the mosque. The homes destroyed were owned by Rohingya people who are typically followers of Islam.

Before the 2012 riots, there were nearly one hundred thousand Muslims (nearly half the total population) in the city of Sittwe. By 2021, there were almost no followers of Islam left in the entire city. Since 2012, the Myanmar military has systematically destroyed many mosques and madrasas (religious schools) in Rakhine state. In burning mosques and religious schools, the Myanmar government destroyed more than houses of worship and places of learning. They destroyed the symbolic, religious, social, and cultural elements of a specific religion. The plight of the Rohingya people is the result of a government's attempt to eliminate a religious practice, a culture, and a people. The burned eight-hundred-year-old mosque in Sittwe is the result of nearly one thousand years of government protection of one religion, Theravada Buddhism. The long history of state and religion entanglement supports a dangerous myth.

It is a common and often-repeated myth that Myanmar is a Buddhist country. The historical narrative of the Buddhist country historical narrative is a social construct. Buddhist nationalists claim that their religion is culturally embedded. The ancient and culturally embedded narrative is a social construct that has been fostered and nurtured by those who benefit from it since 1057. The reality is that Myanmar's society hosts a diverse array of religious ideas—animism, Buddhism, Christianity, Islam, Hindu, and others. But one religion holds a monopoly. Myanmar's majority religion is Theravada Buddhism. That religion was selected for the people of Myanmar and protected and supported by the state. All other religious ideas were not tolerated.

The single-story narrative of Buddhism as the religion of Myanmar is far from complete and is harmful and destructive. There is actual harm (burned-out mosques) and danger (ethnic cleansing) wrapped in the Buddhist-nation single story. The myth of the Buddhist-country historical narrative has shaped and reshaped the Myanmar society for almost one-thousand years. The Buddhist country narrative fosters a tolerance of intolerance in the Myanmar society. In the pages of this book, I argue that *all* the people of Myanmar have suffered and continue to suffer under that single story. The narrative of the "Buddhist nation" combined with the powers of the state has led to perpetual conflict, othering, distortion of the Myanmar religious marketplace and corruption of religion and the state.

"MYANMAR HAS ALWAYS BEEN A BUDDHIST COUNTRY"

In the grand ballroom of the Park Royal Hotel in Yangon, I gave a public lecture on June 25, 2016, to a large audience of Myanmar citizens. The Yangon School of Political Science invited me to lecture, and the turnout was oddly robust given the topic. The audience, which included Buddhist monks, had come to listen to an American professor discuss "religion and politics." About fifteen minutes into the presentation, the mostly male and mostly Buddhist audience clearly disagreed with my lecture's central arguments concerning the perils of a close relationship between state authority and religion. After my conclusion, a person stood and politely but firmly said, "Myanmar has always been a Buddhist country, and the government must support and protect Buddhism." Most of the audience nodded in approval. The only smiles or receptive nods I received were from the Yangon School of Political Science faculty and my students, all thankfully seated in the front row. In that lecture, I argued that the ancient and very close relationship between Buddhism and the Myanmar state had harmed Buddhism, the Sangha, the Rohingya people, and Myanmar's minor religions and general population. In short, everyone in Myanmar was hurt by the state's entanglement with Buddhism. I argued that continuing the British colonial policy of state neutrality toward religion would better serve Myanmar's people. Since then, my research and writing has focused on religion in Myanmar, and this book reconsiders that argument in a larger context.

This book takes a fresh and in-depth look at the age-old entanglement of religion and politics. Leaders and citizens in every society struggle with how the twin powers of religion and government should relate. Political leaders frequently seek the powers of religion, so a political leader may pose for a photo with a Bible in front of a church or while bowing and giving gifts to Buddhist monks. Just as often, religious leaders reach for protection and the state's powers (Fox, 2019b). For example, some evangelical Christians in the United States seek to install Christian religious leaders into authoritative positions at all levels of government (Whitehead and Perry, 2020; Brockman, 2020). The late Presbyterian theologian R. J. Rushdoony told his followers to "take back government . . . and put it in the hands of Christians" (Sterken, 2019, p. 109). Today, these Christians are a significant force in U.S. politics and seek to overtake all government institutions (Brockman, 2020, p. 9; Diamond, 1995, p. 246). These religious leaders and their followers argue "that Christians must not only dominate society but institute and enforce biblical law" (Ingersoll, 2015, p. 14). Christianity's control over law and policy in the United States would amount to the state's establishment, support, and full regulation of religion.

Clerics and policy makers from Austin to Yangon would be well served to consider Myanmar's religious economy's history and outcomes. Myanmar's Buddhist nationalists resemble U.S. Christian nationalists in that both seek the protection of their religion (Brockman, 2020; Sterken, 2019; Walton and Hayward, 2014). Myanmar Buddhist nationalists and U.S. Christian nationalists have both held an active and visible presence in politics for decades. Myanmar's Buddhist nationalists (like U.S. Christian nationalists) idealize a society with "real" citizens and "other" noncitizens who do not belong. Like Christian nationalists, Buddhist nationalists wish for a country where "real" citizens—Bamar, native-born, and Buddhist (versus white, native-born, and Christian)—enjoy governmental protection and support of their religion (Brockman, 2020; Fink, 2018). Both nationalist groups seek strong boundaries to separate the in-group from the out-group, and both seek governmental protection and support to maintain political power, status, and privileges (Whitehead and Perry, 2020; Ibrahim, 2016; Fink, 2018). Like U.S. nationalists, Buddhist nationalists equate racial and religious outsiders with criminality, violence, and inferiority (Fink, 2018, p. 274; Whitehead and Perry, 2020, pp. 118–19). With these similarities, religious nationalists in the United States and Myanmar seek similar outcomes, but the religious economies in each country remain significantly different. Christian nationalists only think they want the religious monopoly that Buddhist nationalists have in Myanmar, but U.S. constitutional law disallows extensive government support or regulation of the U.S. religious economy. Therefore, these two religious economies have very different outcomes, as the Myanmar case illustrates. Various religions (individual religious firms) have historically received disparate treatment in Myanmar's religious economy, making it a vivid and important case study. What happens to religion(s) in such a society? What happens when the state protects a religion? What happens to religious and political leaders? Would religion's close entanglement with the state bring the outcomes these religious actors expect? What happens when a society's religious economy is highly regulated? What are the consequences of illiberal religious regulation?

Myanmar provides compelling answers to these questions. In the following pages, I explore these questions by closely examining a country where one religion dominates the society and culture, and where the state supports, protects, and regulates that religion. Excepting the years of British colonial rule, the Myanmar state's powers and the powers of Theravada Buddhism have been highly entangled for centuries—since 1057. I explore historic trends and how interruptions to state-supported religion and the entanglement of powers impact actors in Myanmar.

This book focuses on political rather than theological interests. Of course, theology matters to specific actors, but politics, interests, choices, and consequences make up the focus of this book. The analyses of internal conversations within specific religions are left to scholars of those religions. Using rational choice theory, I examine the structure and results of state–religion policy on the Myanmar religious economy.

AXIOMS

This analysis makes three foundational assumptions. First, I assume that humans regularly seek power to control, promote, and protect their interests, beliefs, and desires. Second, I assume that people have pluralistic religious preferences. This means that, given enough religious liberty, people will individually make religious choices to meet their specific needs and preferences. Humans in Myanmar are as religiously pluralistic as humans elsewhere but lack freedom and religious choices. The restrictions on Myanmar's religious economy have distorted individuals' decisions and religious choices. The status and support given to one religion over the centuries has distorted the religious marketplace and created economic inefficiencies in Myanmar's society, including fewer religious choices and a tolerance of intolerance. Third, I assume that all religious individuals and organizations (religious firms) have goals, desires, and preferences and act upon those preferences within historical and environmental structures. In addition, these religious and political actors use tools—such as divisive racial and religious campaigns—to meet those desires and choices. For example, on July 9, 2020, Myanmar's president U Win Myint attempted to manage the environment and structure of the religious economy when he instructed election officials and ministers to block campaigns, parties, and religious actors from the "misuse of race and religion" in the November 2020 elections (San Yamin Aung, 2020).

FOR THE MYANMAR PEOPLE, WITH HOPE

Myanmar's current illiberal culture (e.g., factions of the Buddhist Sangha, Myanmar's 2008 constitution, citizenship laws, and the military dictatorship) largely results from the historical and present entanglement of religion and state. The twin powers of Myanmar's state and the single-story Buddhist narrative are bound together in an illiberal structure that simultaneously benefits some and remains destructive for many. The research presented here offers Myanmar's people more than a glimmer of liberal hope. In these pages, I share evidence of significant factions that prefer liberal policies in present-day Myanmar. The Theravada Buddhist monastic community in Myanmar, for example, currently includes prominent and outspoken liberal monks who strongly support a liberal peace.

"WESTERN" BIAS: A PREFERENCE FOR LIBERTY

In this work, I share a simple, suggestive, and unique perspective. The entanglement of state and religion is killing the Myanmar people. Literally. My research, teaching, and lived experiences are to blame for the perspective presented in these pages. I do make some bold claims about religion and the state in Myanmar. I believe that my analysis, arguments, and findings are broadly correct, even in the face of the inevitable errors I have made in some of the specifics.

I lived, taught, and conducted research in the bright and optimistic years of 2015 and 2016 in Myanmar and remain in close contact with my Myanmar friends and colleagues. In 2021, for security reasons, we moved our daily communication from Facebook messaging to the encrypted Signal messaging app. My Myanmar friends continue to provide me with

Figure 0.1 Burmese woman. *Source*: hadynyah/ E+ via Getty Images

regular updates and information. I love Myanmar and its people, who are, without any doubt, "the most generous people on earth" (Sterken, 2016, p. 64). Again, I felt compelled to write this book. I have a perspective and an argument that I feel needs to be discussed.

Anonymous reviewers noted my "Western perspective" and biases. No doubt, I have biases. I readily acknowledge my own perspective and very often question my assumptions. It is important to acknowledge that all our interests and expectations influence our perspectives and understandings of history. The desires, hopes, beliefs, and fears of Myanmar scholars permeate their construction of history—just as they do this one. We must each acknowledge our own interests and perspectives (Metro and Aung Khine, 2022, p. 175). My interests and perspective are simple: I hold a preference for religious toleration and liberty.

King Ashoka suggested that we "let all listen and be willing to listen to the doctrines professed by others" (Rahula, 1974, p. 5). It is my hope that in the Ashokan spirit of sympathetic understanding, my perspective and this analysis provide constructive political and policy insight for the people of Myanmar and for others who may consider protecting a religion, regulating a religious economy, or linking the state's powers with those of religion. I hope this work will be read not only by policy makers and graduate students but also by students at Baptist seminaries in Dallas and Yangon, as well as Buddhist monks in Mandalay and Muslim clerics in Chattogram.

Acknowledgments

This book was made possible by many people, and I owe each of them a great debt of gratitude.

I am grateful to the generous people of Myanmar who wrapped me in their protective arms to make sure that I was well cared for and safe. Many kind people in Myanmar made this research and writing possible. The research for this book would not have been possible without the patient and kind support of my colleague and friend, Htoo Htoo Wah. Before I arrived in Yangon, Htoo Htoo Wah had been a Fulbright Scholar in the United States. In the United States, he learned first-hand the difficulties of plunging into a very new culture. Htoo Htoo Wah took care of me. Htoo Htoo Wah introduced me to many Buddhist monks, to Karen and Kachin Christian clerics and schoolmasters, and to researchers. He provided me with access to the archives of the Judson Research Center at the Myanmar Institute of Theology. He patiently sat on the floors of many monasteries and translated hours of my questions for monks. Htoo Htoo Wah and many like him are the foundation of a brighter future in Myanmar.

Myanmar Institute of Theology's president, Rev. Dr. Samuel Ngun Ling, was generous with his time and patient with my questions. Over meals and in his office, he shared so much about Myanmar's people, history, and culture. I am grateful for the access that he provided and the support of the Judson Research Institute. Ohnmar Lwin and Starry Tun assisted this research in so many ways. Ohnmar and Starry set up many monk visits, translated, and took notes while I asked endless questions. They went beyond the role of research assistants and made sure that I had food and was safely tucked into a taxi after late nights on the MIT campus.

Two former Four Eights political prisoners, U Myat Thu and U Myo Aung Htwe, are now political researchers and educators at the Yangon School of Political Science. Each of these generous and kind scholars guided my research and helped me with Saffron monk interviews. They shared their stories and provided me with powerful insights into power and choice in Myanmar's politics. This book would not have been possible without them and two of their YSPS students. Khin Sandar and Than Toe Aung also introduced me to many monks, shared their own stories and political struggles, and provided me with an inside look at the struggles of being considered foreign in one's own land. Khin Sandar and Than Toe Aung took me deep into Myanmar villages, culture, and religion in a way that challenged and reshaped my understanding and perspectives.

The Buddhist Sangha gave me refuge and graciously provided so many lessons. The monks I interviewed taught me so much not only about religion, politics, and the state but also about the struggles of all humans. I cannot name most of the monks I spoke with for reasons of their safety and security, but I can acknowledge the most generous and kind Mayawaddy Sayadaw (Sayadaw Ashin Arriyawuntha Biwunsa). Sadly, Myawaddy Sayadaw was again a political prisoner in 2021 and after being released died while in hiding in the Thai border town of Mae Sot in October 2022. The Saffron monks understand and are willing to share history and politics in a way that only one who has lived and survived under brutal dictators can. Mayawaddy Sayadaw's insights about power and the decisions made by different members of the Buddhist Sangha are central to my reasoning in selecting the rational choice theoretical framework for this book.

The faculty and archival librarians at Yangon University opened many doors and provided me with history and a new understanding of the power of the state. Dr. Chaw Chaw Sein, then chair of the Department of International Relations, graciously spent hours of time in her office explaining power, control, and king law. The insights she gave about state control of the materials taught (even the questions I asked on the exams I gave to YU students) gave me a deeper understanding of the lengths to which a government can go to control its people. Dr. Chaw Chaw Sein also pushed aside the curtain and allowed me to glimpse inside the isolated world of Myanmar's military elite.

My Yangon University students, 2015–2016 Diploma in Political Science (DPS 2nd Batch), provided me with many lessons about life in Myanmar and specifically about the military's use of power to control their lives. Specifically, the study group leader, Ms. Ah Noh, provided me with many contacts in the Christian, Muslim, and Buddhist communities, as well as with lawyers who have recently worked with political prisoners inside Insein Prison. I am incredibly grateful to Ah Noh and her DPS 2nd Batch classmates.

Acknowledgments

The research and dedication of the Fortify Rights team made this work possible. Much of their excellent research is included in the last chapters of this book. The people at Fortify Rights are ardent human rights defenders who believe in the influence of evidence-based research, the power of truth-telling, and the importance of working with individuals, communities, and movements pushing for change. I owe a special debt of gratitude to Fortify Rights CEO Matthew Smith for his time, help, and support. I hope that this book will support the excellent work of the Fortify Rights team.

The brilliant and always professional staff at the U.S. Embassy in Yangon made this book possible. Political and information officers spent time helping me understand the power structures and the issues facing the Myanmar people. Ambassador Derek Mitchell was gracious and generous with his time and provided me with a better understanding of the central and underlying problems facing the people of Myanmar. After meeting with Ambassador Mitchell one afternoon at the U.S. Embassy, I came away thinking how he not only honorably represents the United States but is also making our world a better and safer place. Kristen F. Bauer, Deputy Chief of Mission U.S. Embassy Yangon (Rangoon), set up workshops with members of the Myanmar Parliament and graciously had me to dinner many times at her Yangon home to meet many of the top abbots, Muslim and Christian clerics, educators, diplomats, and political leaders of Myanmar. Ms. Sarah Quinzio, U.S. Embassy cultural affairs officer, set up many interviews and so much more. Mr. Winston Pugh set up many monk interviews including connecting me with Mayawaddy Sayadaw.

The work presented in these pages on the Methodist Church in Myanmar was aided by Rev. Dr. Jeff McDonald, St. Paul's United Methodist Church, and Rev. Fredrick Burns III, Whitehouse United Methodist Church. These Methodist pastors provided me with insights and sources and patiently answered questions. Dr. McDonald and Mr. Burns also provided me with sources for theological and philosophical underpinnings. Dr. McDonald also graciously provided me with contacts at United Methodist archives.

Archival librarians were critical in this work. Ms. Robyn Perdue and Ms. Jan Harp of the University of Texas at Tyler Library graciously received many requests for books, articles, and obscure documents. Archival librarians at Drew University provided many historical documents on the early Methodist efforts in Myanmar. Specifically, Ms. Candace Reilly, Special Collections Associate, Drew University Archive made it possible to continue my research during the travel-restricted months of COVID-19. Ms. Reilly spent hours scanning and uploading documents from boxes in her archives. Ms. Ada Bravo supported this research with hundreds of book orders. This book would be incomplete without the dedication and kind efforts of each of these professionals.

This book would not be in your hands without the hard work and professional excellence of Ms. Ashley Dodge and Ms. Haley White, editors with Rowman & Littlefield. Ms. Dodge was in an editorial meeting about another book on Myanmar when she read the Shan-Style Rice section in the introduction of this book. She saw merit in both my approach and writing and kindly and immediately wrote to tell me so. I am grateful for her kindness, attention to detail, and support. For a writer, there is perhaps no greater reward than having someone understand your work. Ms. Haley White graciously took care of the peer reviews—which is no easy or small task. She reached out to half a dozen busy scholars and worked to make the wait bearable by keeping me informed about the process and sharing reviewer timeline expectations. Haley also shared the excitement of some of the more enthusiastic reviews. I am very grateful for the precise, excellent, and detailed copyediting work of Ms. Jo-Ann Parks.

This book is supported by many scholars, but I owe a special intellectual debt to a specific few. The vast, brilliant, and detailed scholarship of anthropologist Dr. Juliane Schober made this book possible. Her wealth of experience in Myanmar, crisp writing, attention to detail, and sharp analysis blazed the trail along which I merely stumble. Without Dr. Schober's work, I would not understand the larger context of the conjectures of Buddhism in which to place my own Myanmar experiences.

In 2015, I followed two U.S. Fulbright scholars, both celebrated political scientists, to Myanmar. Drs. Donald Eugene Smith and Richard Butwell were among the last U.S. Fulbright scholars to travel to Myanmar in the years immediately before General Ne Win's coup in March 1962. Both professors returned to the United States in the early 1960s and penned brilliant books. As they have done for so many others, these two scholars provided much of the early political history for this analysis.

The recent scholarship of Melissa Crouch, Roman David, Christina Fink, Roger Finke, Jonathan Fox, Nile Green, Anthony Gill, Susan Hayward, Ian Holliday, Nyi Nyi Kyaw, Ronan Lee, Michał Lubina, Donald Seekins, Matthew Smith, Alicia Turner, Matthew Walton, and U Myat Thu made this work possible. Without their work, this book would not have been conceivable.

Several colleagues read all or parts of the manuscript, answered questions, and provided constructive feedback. Several anonymous reviewers gave critical reviews that substantially improved the book. I am grateful to Drs. Greg Bock, Qiao Dai, Paul Djupe, Jesse Dobson, Roger Finke, Tony Gill, Warren Goldstein, William R. Johnson, Neal Katz, Ward Keeler, Randy LeBlanc, Sarah Lee, Nihal Perera, Chaw Chaw Sein, Sarah Sass, Matthew Smith, Marcus Stadelmann, Matthew Stith, Paul Streufert, Amentahru Wahlrab, and Mary Wong for their kind support and for reading, editing, and sending me comments.

My teaching partner, Dr. Matt Stith, supported this research and writing with two years of weekly discussions. I am also grateful to Matt for his careful reading and extremely helpful suggestions and edits.

My running partners, Drs. Sarah Sass and Amentahru Wahlrab, listened to hours and many miles of this book every Sunday for years and provided me with not only scholarly suggestions but support for the writing. This book was made possible by Sarah and Tahru.

Institutional support for this work was provided by the U.S. Department of State, the U.S. Fulbright Scholar Program, the University of Texas at Tyler (thank you to Provost Amir Mirmiran, Dean Neil Gray, Chair Marcus Stadelmann), the Myanmar Institute of Theology, the Yangon School of Political Science, and Yangon University.

None of this book is the fault of those who supported and made it possible. They each did their best to help me get it right. The errors and mistakes are mine alone.

My son, Robert Edward Sterken III, a brilliant lawyer and legal scholar, supported this work with detailed explanations of legal theory and lengthy discussions about the rule of law, human rights, and the role of law in the relationship between religion and the state. Bobby, I am grateful.

My daughter, Alexandra Grace Sterken, a well-read anthropologist, historian, and teacher, walked many miles with me during the writing of this book and patiently listened to arguments and history, all the while asking pointed questions and providing me with support and encouragement. Alexandra Grace spent considerable time in Myanmar and knows well the meaning of "foreigner." Her support made this book possible.

My brother, Michael Joseph Sterken, provided daily support during my time in Myanmar. At the beginning and end of each day (Myanmar is twelve hours ahead) we would visit about all things. Michael would ask tough questions about Myanmar's politics and history, and I would seek answers. Often, he would share information that he had come across. Michael's support made this book possible.

Last, and by no means least, my partner in life, Alison Johnson Sterken, traveled to Myanmar and made the Hledan village in the Kamayut Township our home. Alison made many Myanmar friends, photographed many nat shrines, and visited with nuns. She supported my research in Myanmar, then she suffered as I talked endlessly about it as I struggled to make field notes into sentences and chapters. On those many days when I felt my writing was merely a plodding along in the intellectual paths forged by the great Myanmar scholars, Alison was there to tell me that I could do it and that my perspective mattered. This book would not have been possible without Alison Johnson Sterken.

Grateful I am.
Robert Sterken
2022

A Note on Language and Usage

Is it Burma, Myanmar, or both?

The names given to places are an important part of geographical and cultural identity. The name given to a place/state or people (Rohingya) is a social signal of culture and belonging. What to call a country is complicated and political. Since the early 1800s, the English-language name for the country discussed in these pages was Burma. The people who lived there called their country "Myanma"—in Burmese and typically "Burma" when speaking English.

For centuries, the country's kings referred to themselves as Myanma kings. Thus, they referred to their kingdoms as Myanma country (Thant Myint-U, 2020, p. xi). Over time Myanma became colloquially pronounced "Bama." Hearing the country called Bama, early visiting Europeans recorded the country's name in some variation of "Burma." During the British colonial era, the official English-language name of the country became Burma.

The name of the country became an international question in 1989. A year after the 1988 uprising, when the military junta brutally suppressed a pro-democracy uprising, the military leaders suddenly changed its name to Myanmar. The military, seeking international legitimacy, declared that it was discarding the name handed down from its British colonial past to foster ethnic unity. The military stated that calling the country Burma excluded the country's many ethnic minorities. It was all rhetoric. Within the country, nothing changed. In the Burmese language, "Myanmar" is simply the more formal version of "Burma." The country's name was only changed in English.

While some authors (Thant Myint-U, 2020; Aung San Suu Kyi, 2010) use only Burma, others (David & Holliday, 2018) use Burma when referring to times before 1989 and Myanmar when referencing times after 1989. In these pages, for ease, understanding, and clarity, I use Myanmar as the name of the country throughout, from ancient times to the present. I do not use Myanmar as a political statement.

A NOTE ON THE USE OF THE WORD *FIRM*

Following the work of William Bainbridge, Roger Finke, Tony Gill, Rodney Stark, and many others, I use the term *firm* to refer to religions and religious groups as competing entities that compete for customers in a religious market. A religious firm is an organization that shares religious ideas with people who make rational choices among the available products (religious ideas) that are shared in a given society. The use of the word *firm* is not intended to be disrespectful. Rather, it is meant to place all religions and religious groups in the same light.

Cast of Characters

The Kings of Buddhism: The men who have ruled Myanmar, from King Anawrahta to King Thibaw Min, to modern military dictators, have assumed the role of protectors and promoters of one specific school of Buddhism—Theravada Buddhism. Modern rulers of Myanmar, like Generals Ne Win and Min Aung Hlaing, have cast themselves as Buddhist kings and have courted and controlled Buddhist clerics and Buddhism. In 2021, Min Aung Hlaing portrayed himself as the next in the long line of just and good Buddhist kings, monarchs who protect Buddhism. Soon after his coup, General Min Aung Hlaing undertook major construction projects to insert himself into the Buddhist king lineage. He built three enormous statues of Buddhist kings in northern Shan state. The statues aim to amplify the image of the Buddhist kings while not so subtly allowing the general to associate himself with them.

'Abd al-Khaliq: 'Abd al-Khaliq held the title of mawlwi (Islamic scholar) and was an Islamic missionary in Myanmar during British colonialization. In 1893, 'Abd al-Khaliq wrote the *Sayr-e Barhma* (*Burmese Journey*), in which he detailed the history, language, and religion of the Burmese people. To share his beliefs, 'Abd al-Khaliq translated Islamic works from Urdu into Burmese during the years of British rule.

Anawrahta (1014–1077): Anawrahta turned a small principality in Upper Myanmar into the first Burmese Empire that formed the basis of modern-day Myanmar. Historically verifiable Burmese history begins with his accession to the Pagan throne in 1044. Anawrahta is one of the most famous kings in Myanmar's history. He embraced Theravada Buddhism in 1057.

Ashoka (also Aśoka; 304–232 BCE): Popularly known as Ashoka the Great, Ashoka was an Indian king of the Maurya Empire. King Ashoka (sometimes referred to as emperor) ruled almost the entire Indian subcontinent from c. 268 to 232 BCE and was known as the "ideal Buddhist king." While tolerant of other religions, Ashoka promoted the spread of Buddhism across ancient Asia.

Aung San (1915–1947): Aung San is considered the founder of modern-day Myanmar and is commonly referred to by the title "Father of the Nation." Aung San promoted a liberal democracy and complete separation of state and religion. Aung San and eight of his cabinet members were assassinated on July 19, 1947; they were among the most progressive and promising political leaders of that generation.

Aung San Suu Kyi (1945–): Aung San Suu Kyi is a Burmese politician, diplomat, author, and a 1991 Nobel Peace Prize laureate who served as Myanmar's state counselor (equivalent to a prime minister) and minister of foreign affairs from 2016 to 2021. Suu Kyi is the youngest daughter of Aung San, Father of the Nation of modern-day Myanmar.

Judson, Adoniram (1788–1850): Judson arrived in Myanmar in 1813 before British rule. He and his wife Ann established the first mission of American Baptists. Their work included evangelism and Bible translation. The had very little success until the British arrived.

Min Aung Hlaing (1956–): Min Aung Hlaing is an army general who has ruled Myanmar as the chairman of the State Administration Council since seizing power in the February 2021 coup d'état. The United Nations has reported that Min Aung Hlaing's soldiers have been committing systemic discrimination and human rights violations against minority communities in Rakhine state. Min Aung Hlaing has been widely accused of ethnic cleansing against the Rohingya people. After taking power in the 2021 coup, Min Aung Hlaing ordered the destruction of seventy-six Christian churches, twenty Buddhist monasteries, and one mosque. As a "king of Buddhism," Min Aung Hlaing is also building what he claims will be the largest seated Buddha statue in the world.

Mindon Min (1808–1878): Born Maung Lwin, he was the penultimate King of Myanmar from 1853 to 1878. Mindon is one of the most popular and revered kings of Myanmar. Mindon was known for his Buddhist devotion and religious tolerance. He helped build churches and missionary schools for Christians and mosques for Muslims, and funded a rest house for Burmese Muslims in Mecca. Mindon also asserted the king's role as the protector of Theravada Buddhism.

Myawaddy Mingyi Sayadaw (Sayadaw Ashin Arriyawuntha Biwunsa) (1951–2022): Ven. Arriyawuntha was the Buddhist abbot of Myawaddy Mingyi Monastery in Myanmar. Myawaddy Mingyi was a highly respected abbot who was well known for preaching about justice, democracy, and human rights. He was a dedicated supporter of religious tolerance and interfaith groups in Myanmar and a vocal critic of Buddhist nationalism and military and military-backed organizations and businesses. He was repeatedly imprisoned for confronting the military dictatorship, speaking in favor of tolerance and democracy. Myawaddy Sayadaw publicly criticized Sitagu Sayadaw (see below), who has close ties to junta chief Min Aung Hlaing, for his discriminatory remarks against other religions and for failing to condemn the military's killings of civilians.

Ne Win (1910/11–2002): Ne Win served as prime minister of Burma from 1958 to 1960 and 1962 to 1974, and president of Burma from 1962 to 1981. Ne Win was Burma's military dictator from 1962 to 1988. Ne Win overthrew the democratic Union Parliament of U Nu in 1962. His rule was characterized by a non-aligned foreign policy, isolationism, one-party rule, economic stagnation, and superstition. Ne Win abruptly resigned in 1988 in response to the Four-Eights Uprising.

Saya San (1876–1931): Saya San was a physician, former monk, and the leader of the Saya San Rebellion of 1930–1932 in British Myanmar. Saya San and the rebellion associated with him remain a popular icon to this day.

Sayadaw U Ottama (1879–1939): Sayadaw U Ottama was a highly educated and tolerant Theravada Buddhist monk, author, and leader of the Myanmar independence movement during British colonial rule.

Shin Arahan (c. 1034–1115): The Venerable Shin Arahan was Thathanabaing (keeper of religion) of Myanmar from 1056 to 1115. The monk was the religious adviser to King Anawrahta (and others). He is credited with converting Anawrahta to Theravada Buddhism. Anawrahta's conversion to Theravada Buddhism is considered a key turning point in the history of Theravada Buddhism and religion in Myanmar.

Sitagu Sayadaw (1937–): Sitagu Sayadaw participated in the Four-Eights Uprising and gave a famous sermon, criticizing the government for not acting in accordance with the ten duties of the king. Since his return to Myanmar in the mid-1990s, Sitagu Sayadaw has maintained close ties to the military and delivered a sermon attempting to provide religious justification for the military's mass killing of the Rohingya people. Since the 2021 coup, Sitagu Sayadaw has sought to legitimize Min Aung Hlaing's dictatorship by subtly referring to the general as Myanmar's king.

Sladen, Edward Bosc (1831–1890): Sir Edward Bosc Sladen was a British army officer who served in India and Myanmar. He organized a provisional government in Myanmar and oversaw the surrender of King Thibaw.

U Gambira (1979–): Nyi Nyi Lwin, more widely known by his monastic name U Gambira, is a former Buddhist monk, activist, and a leader of the All Burma Monks' Alliance, a group that helped lead the 2007 Saffron Revolution protests against Myanmar's military government.

U Nu (1907–1995): U Nu, also known by the honorific name Thakin Nu, was a leading and widely respected Myanmar statesman and politician. He was the first prime minister of Myanmar under the provisions of the 1947 Constitution of the Union of Burma, from January 4, 1948, to June 12, 1956, again from February 28, 1957, to October 28, 1958, and finally from April 4, 1960, to March 2, 1962. U Nu was a devout Theravada Buddhist and was seen (and is still viewed) as a respected spiritual leader of Myanmar.

U Thant (1909–1974): Thant was a Burmese diplomat and the third secretary-general of the United Nations from 1961 to 1971. Thant was a devout Buddhist and the foremost Myanmar diplomat. Thant was widely admired and held in (and still holds) profound respect by the Myanmar.

U Wisara (1889–1929): Ven. U Wisara was a Theravada Buddhist monk who died in prison after a 166-day hunger strike against the British rule. U Wisara had been repeatedly imprisoned and tortured by the colonial government for "inciting sedition." Wisara was a key figure in the early organization of the independence movement. The monk is commemorated with the U Wisara Road, a major avenue in Yangon, and the U Wisara Monument in Yangon.

Introduction: State and Religion Entanglement
Controlling, Protecting, and Corrupting Religion

This is a political history of two of the most intimate of human concerns—religion and power. The history of religion in Myanmar is fascinating, brutal, and reveals the consequences of entangling the powers of state and religion. For nearly one thousand years, the Myanmar government has used its authority and power to protect one religion—Theravada Buddhism. Theravada Buddhism, in turn, protected the state, and together these institutions maintained a unique power structure and social order. The entanglement of religion and state powers and the social order it maintained fundamentally altered, and shaped the culture, religion, and structure of the Myanmar society.

Bordering Bangladesh, China, India, Laos, and Thailand, the people of Myanmar host a wide and diverse array of cultures. There are more than a hundred different ethnic groups, each with its own history, culture, and language, within a population of fifty-four million, but state statistics indicate nearly 90 percent of the population practice just one specific religion. Centuries of state protection of Theravada Buddhism shaped the reporting, nature, and practice of religion in Myanmar.

In this analysis, I share a unique narrative, perspective, and the consequences of Myanmar's long state-religion history. This narrative includes the stories of supernatural spirits, ancient kings, the imprisoning, defrocking, and killing of Buddhist monks, proselytizing by Muslim and Christian missionaries, religious nationalism and convictions, brutal dictators, and raw political power. To begin, I beg you to hold and consider one central question: What happens when government supports, regulates, and protects one religion?

This work begins and ends with animism (the belief in spirits concerned with human affairs and considered by scholars to be the earliest form of religion). Spirits called *nats* lived in Myanmar culture long before the arrival of other religions, and these nats are woven into the fabric of this story. One of the consequences of state support of religion is that, in 2021, nat festivals (see chapter 8) hold special significance for Myanmar's LGBTQ community (Baker, 2017). Our story continues with a king's choice to convert to, embrace, and protect one religion. After the king closes the religious economy, we meet the arrival of Christian and Muslim missionaries and swing through colonialism, religious nationalism, democracy, and the violence and fury of iron-fisted military rule.

This is a fascinating history told in a new way and from a quite unique perspective. I frame this analysis in rational actor and economic marketplace terms and theory to provide the reader with a shift in perspective. This reframing is intended to be a conversation changer. I seek to reveal actors, motivations, and, most importantly, the consequences. The unique perspective presented in these pages is controversial. Some have claimed that it is simply a Western perspective. I leave it to the reader to be the judge of that. Others argue that it does not represent the full extent of Theravada Buddhist thought in Myanmar politics. To this argument, I categorically state that this is not a book about Buddhist political thought. Many scholars have explored Buddhist political thought (Walton, 2016a).

The analyses and arguments in this book will offend some and have been outright rejected by others. It will offend and be rejected, in part, because the arguments and history presented in these pages undermine existing power structures and challenge some long-held beliefs about religion and identity in Myanmar. On the other hand, the perspective and arguments presented have been embraced by those who are confident with religious liberty as well those who have long suffered under the existing status quo in Myanmar and elsewhere around the world.

In 2015, the Myanmar government enacted a series of four laws intended to "protect race and religion." These four laws are highly discriminatory against ethnic and religious minorities, as well as against women. Among these four laws, the Religious Conversion Act is the most controversial. To "protect Buddhism," the Religious Conversion law significantly regulates the right to freedom of religion. It regulates an individual's choice of religion. The law gives a government registration board the authority to review and approve (or not) an individual's decision to convert to a different religion. In 2015, factions of Buddhist monks as well as senior clerics on the State Sangha Mahanayaka Committee supported the enactment of these four laws (David and Holliday, 2018, p. 87). These same sects of radical Buddhist monks repeatedly call for government protection of Buddhism. In hate-filled sermons, these monks seek to protect Buddhism from Muslims, who they refer to as "crazy dogs" that are "breeding so fast," "stealing our women, raping them," and "would like to occupy our country" (Beech and Saw Nang, 2019). The same monks instruct their followers to "make your blood boil," and incite conflict and violence toward Muslims and Christians (Beech and Saw Nang, 2019). These factions of Myanmar's Buddhist monastic community embrace violence and seek government support and protection for Buddhism. This is not a recent development. The Myanmar government has supported and protected Theravada Buddhism for centuries—since 1057. This book is focused on uncovering the consequences of centuries of government protection of religion. The consequences include (1) a state-supported religious monopoly; (2) corruption, regulation, and repression of Theravada Buddhists; (3) a tolerance of intolerance, repression, and violence against religious minorities; (4) perpetual conflict and violence; (5) a corrupt and distorted religious economy and competition; and finally (6) a perversion and corruption of truth.

PROTECTING SHAN-STYLE RICE

This analysis is framed in the rational actor approach to understanding religion and politics. This approach uses economic logic and terminology to answer the above questions. The terminology and economic analysis are not meant to be disrespectful to religion. The basic theory is that government policy on religion directly influences religion. Government support and protection of religion corrupts or distorts religion and the religious marketplace. A religious economy or religious marketplace is a social arena wherein religious firms and religious actors compete for members, influence, power, and resources (Gill, 2007, p. 231). The government may distort a religious marketplace, for example, by financially subsidizing one specific religion. Or a government may protect a religion (by excluding other religions), leading to underproduction of other religious ideas—or forced exclusion of religious ideas. Government protection of one religion can lead to changes in the religion, lessening or distorting the qualities of the religion, and privileged access to religious consumers. For example, let us turn to Shan (one of Myanmar's larger ethnic groups) style rice.

For a moment, imagine the beautiful Bogyoke Aung San Market in central Yangon, Myanmar. Known for its British colonial architecture (built in 1926, the British called it Scott Market) and its narrow, red cobblestone streets crowded with shoppers, the Bogyoke market (so renamed in 1948 after Bogyoke [General] Aung San) is a huge, bustling bazaar in central Yangon's Pabedan township. This crowded market hosts vendors who sell nearly everything. Thousands of stalls overflow with glorious and colorful goods and food. Imagine that the market has a popular vendor who sells the most delicious Shan-style rice at reasonable prices. In time, the vendor's Shan-style rice becomes so popular that he becomes immensely wealthy and influential and befriends the market administrator. Due to the success of the vendor, the market administrator favors him with a prime location and reduced rent. The vendor and the administrator share the profits, so each benefits from the other. Because of the official favor and support, the vendor's Shan-style rice costs less to produce, and his competitors go out of business or leave the market. Shan-style rice soon becomes the only option, so customers have no other rice choices. Enjoying the brisk business, wealth, power, and influence, the vendor and the administrator collaborate to undermine competitors and craft regulations that *protect* Shan-style rice. With the rice market all but closed, Shan-style rice becomes the only dish served, and the market is distorted. Like Shan-style rice in this free market metaphor, Theravada Buddhism became the preferred religion of the Myanmar religious market. In both cases, favored people gained special privileges, and competitors were excluded from the market. For centuries, Myanmar has (mostly) maintained a closed and regulated religious market. Theravada Buddhism was protected. What are the consequences of centuries of protection?

How did Theravada Buddhism become the favored religion in Myanmar's religious market? What were the consequences of protecting one religious firm? Using the rational choice theory widely applied in studies of religion around the world, this book explores the history and outcomes of centuries of shared power and favor in a closed regulated religious market. This work sees humans as rational creatures who make decisions based on interests and who typically weigh risks and benefits to achieve the best outcomes. Using rational choice theory, this analysis focuses on the interests of all members of Myanmar's religious economy rather than on religious ideas. Unlike many studies of religion in Myanmar, this book does not mainly concern Buddhism. Instead, it analyzes the interests and outcomes of a religious economy that includes Theravada Buddhism as one of the most important actors. Many scholars have conducted extensive research on Theravada Buddhism in Myanmar and throughout Southeast Asia, but there are few structural analyses of the entire Myanmar religious economic system (Brac de La Perrière, 2009a). A systemic study of Myanmar's religion and politics that excludes Muslims, Christians, nat religions, and other religious firms remains incomplete and does a disservice by effectively writing those religions out of the history of Burma/Myanmar (Crouch 2016a, p, 3). This book focuses on Myanmar's entire religious economy.

A RELIGIOUS ECONOMY AND KEY ACTORS

Scholars of religion and politics have established a robust paradigm with solid theoretical foundations for studying a religious economy (Gill, 2017; Chen, 2014; Haynes, 2013; Ahdar and Leigh, 2013; Hylton, 2011; Green, 2011; Obadia, 2011; Gill, 2007; Stark and Finke, 2000; Finke, 1990; Finke and Stark, 1992; Spiro, 1987). Finke and Stark write,

> Religious economies are like commercial economies in that they consist of a market made up of a set of current and prospective customers and a set of firms seeking to serve that market. The fate of these firms will depend on (1) aspects of their organizational structures, (2) their sales representatives, (3) their product, and (4) their marketing techniques. (1992, p. 17)

While looking at a religious economy, these scholars focus on religions' various actors and on the competition for believers. A religious economy is a conceptualized "marketplace" in a state or society that allows social scientists or historians to examine the dynamics of many actors (Green, 2015; Haynes, 2011). A religious economy comprises people (religious or not) and religious organizations or firms interacting within a social framework of competing interests, groups, and ideologies (Stark, 2007). The conceptualized marketplace includes all the important actors within a given marketplace (Haynes, 2011, p. 7). Religious actors (ministers, imams, monks, clerics, church leaders, and practitioners) and secular actors (people, presidents, dictators, monarchs, and legislators) all have interests, motives, and incentives regarding the religious marketplace (Haynes, 2011; Stark, 2007). For example, some promote their religions and ideas while others manipulate religion for personal and/or public gain. I assume that most actors within any religious economy care about their survival and act accordingly (Haynes, 2011, pp. 1–13). Over decades of brutal rule, since March 1962, Myanmar's military leaders have focused on two goals in the following order: (1) political survival and (2) enriching themselves and those associated with them (Gill, 2007, p. 232). Their decisions on state–religion policy are predicated on these two goals.

Modeling a religious marketplace can clarify our understanding of religious and non-religious actors and of key players' actions while highlighting the social transactions and power structure within a given marketplace (Chen, 2014; Young, 1997; Stark, 2000). An examination of religion in Myanmar in terms of ideas, choices, and opportunities elucidates the interplay of religion and a state that does not give its agency to modernity. I am not arguing that an individual's religion is only a preference, choice, or identity (Mitchell, 2007, p. 352). Rather, this analysis follows the work of other empirically oriented social scientists and argues that the marketplace, choices, preferences, and identities are useful in describing and explaining religiously motivated political behavior (Wilcox, Wald, and Jelen, 2008, p. 878). As noted in chapter 1, Myanmar's founding king clearly chose Theravada Buddhism for himself. Then the king and his appointed religious elite promoted the religion and turned his personal religious choice into a political preference and national identity. The rational choice model offers a unique and different view of Myanmar's history and a robust understanding of the preferences and outcomes of various religious actors, firms, and state policies.

Several actors make up Myanmar's religious economy. The religious actors include *all* the people, citizens, and noncitizens (acting as individuals and subgroups), *all* the religious firms (religions and ideas), and the state (government via a monarchy, military, democracy, etc.). Critically, the economy includes small religious firms (the nat religion, for example) as valid actors (although nat worship may indeed be widespread and robust). In addition, all individuals—even those who are not religious—constitute actors within Myanmar's religious economy. A religious economy has almost as many goals as actors; therefore, the Myanmar economy has quite complex interactions. Different actors represent diverse interests and wield various amounts of power. Some subgroups, like Bamar Buddhists, hold an enormous market share and power. Others, like Karen Christians, hold less power and a smaller market share. In this economy, Myanmar's people are buffeted about by two other major actors: religious firms and the state.

Religious firms and governments remain fundamental institutions in all human societies because both exist in every society, and both often hold considerable authority and power. Throughout history, societies have grappled with the relationship between religious firms and governance. Some societies have opted for no (or virtually no) relationship between religion firms and the state. In contrast, others have chosen varying degrees of entanglement (from superficial connections to a full theocracy to complete regulation). Each institution seems, at first glance, to fulfill distinct functions in a religious economy. Religious institutions typically nurture the spiritual or inner person, while a government usually encompasses a more public and policy-oriented scope and purpose. Some people in Myanmar do not know that difference or believe that any difference is meaningful (David and Holliday, 2018, p. 85). Worldwide, some argue that religion should play an important or even leading role in governing, but others do not see a difference between the spheres of government and religion.

Humans have debated this relationship for centuries. In 1308, the poet Dante argued that humans have two fundamental pursuits: an earthly life and a spiritual life. In his treatise *De Monarchia*, Dante argues that the pope (i.e., religion) should only manage man's spiritual life. In contrast, the king (i.e., the state) should manage the earthly endeavors of man. For Dante, the king's purview did not include the religious market. The Catholic Church so vigorously disagreed that it banned Dante's work in 1585 (Gagarin, 2009). In Myanmar, as elsewhere, the two powerful authorities of religious firms and the state often appear in the same arena and seek to shape, regulate, or control the same issues. These two institutions interact so frequently that scholars have identified one hundred and eleven ways in which states and religious firms regularly become entangled (Fox, 2019b). Again, this analysis is focused on what happens when they become highly entangled.

STUDYING RELIGION AND THE STATE IN MYANMAR

Broadly, analysis of religion in Myanmar and across Southeast Asian societies has been mostly descriptive or relied on classical theorists (Neo, Jamal, and Goh, 2019; Lang, 2004, p. 103). Scholars have largely avoided the application of contemporary sociological theory to their case studies or have attempted to analyze religion in Asia as if the actors and motivations are somehow different from those in other parts of the world. Historians, anthropologists, and political scientists have explored religion and the state in Myanmar's beautiful, rich, and complex society since the British colonial days. Specifically, scholars have explored and described the historical relationship between Theravada Buddhism and Myanmar's politics since the early 1960s (see Badgley, 1963; Smith, 1965; Mendelson, 1975; Maung Maung, 1980; Aung-Thwin, 2005; Schober, 2011; Charney, 2009; Tuner, 2014; Walton, 2016a; David and Holliday, 2018).

Scholars tended to focus, appropriately, on the relationship between Buddhism and the state and on Theravada Buddhism's worldview and internal conversations concerning politics and political actions (Walton and Hayward, 2014; Kawanami, 2016; Walton, 2016b). Some scholars examined Buddhists' beliefs and interests (Walton, 2016a), but fewer scholars have examined the perspectives of minority religions and different subgroups (Crouch, 2018; Cheesman, 2016). Scholars have also examined the fears and anxieties of Myanmar's Buddhists (Turner, 2014; David and Holliday, 2018) and highlighted the many challenges facing religious minorities (Basu, 2018). Compared to these essential works (which I utilize and to which I owe a great debt), this book focuses on a larger picture: Myanmar's religious actors, the state, and choices.

Western scholars have too frequently focused their analyses on the Theravada Buddhist firm and its supporting actors while neglecting minority firms (Carstens, 2018, p. 126; Crouch, 2016a, p. 3; Brac de La Perrière, 2009a). In studying religion and the state in Myanmar, the focus on the Theravadin tradition tends to obscure the many other important actors and other religious firms throughout history and in Myanmar's current religious economy. Although the Theravadin tradition and its supporting actors are absolutely critical in shaping Myanmar's religious economy, systemic studies should consider other actors when looking at the entire structure. Analyses that do not recognize other religious actors miss the full story. The ancient (and present) Myanmar religious economy included many important actors and religious firms—including the nat religion (animism or spirit religion), Islam, Hindu, Christianity, and others. By examining the broader sociocultural environment, this book offers a needed structural analysis of the Myanmar religious economy and its range of actors and religious firms in Myanmar.

In his foundational book *Religion and Politics in Burma*, Donald Smith described and explored the historical relationship between religion and the state until the early days of military rule in the 1960s (Smith, 1965). Contrary to the title, Smith's study devotes little space to minority religious actors, and he addresses minority firms (like Christianity or the nat religion) from the Buddhist actors' perspective. For example, "Nationalist sentiment was clearly present in the Buddhist conviction that Christianity had failed to bring peace to the world and that Buddhism was the only ideology capable of doing this" (Smith, 1965, p. 123–24). Again, this significant oversight ignores the current and historical presence of many other important religious firms and actors in Myanmar. Examining the relationship between one interest group (Theravada Buddhism) and the state, while important, does not tell the full story. Like Smith's book, Michael Charney's work, *A History of Modern Burma*, provides an excellent historical overview and analysis of the relationship between monks and the modern state (Charney, 2009). Smith and Charney detail many historical events and the recurring significant impact of the Buddhist Sangha on politics and government. Still, neither focused on the whole religious economy.

Scholars in the fields of political science, anthropology, and Buddhist studies have extensively examined the conjunctures of Buddhism and politics in Myanmar (Walton, 2016a; Turner, 2014; Schober, 2011; Gravers, 1999). Juliane Schober's vast and extraordinary scholarship focuses broadly on Buddhist narratives and moral authority in colonial and postcolonial contexts as well as on Buddhism's relationship with politics and with the state (Schober, 2011, 2007, 2005, 1997). Schober examines the role of Buddhist institutions in public policy and illustrates how Theravada Buddhists produced and reproduced a narrative of history that intertwines Buddhism with the state (2011). My argument in this book builds upon Schober's findings that present-day "Buddhist conceptions and practices are intimately tied to conceptions of political power in social, economic, and political realm" (Schober, 2011, p. 11). The Buddhists in Myanmar are unequivocally involved in politics and governing.

Alicia Turner's excellent work focuses on the colonial period and argues that the Burmese Buddhists reinvented Buddhism during the colonial period according to their interests, thus reclaiming Buddhism and defining a new narrative (Turner, 2014). Building on Turner's work, I show that the colonial era Buddhist Sangha did change to meet the new and mostly unregulated religious economy's demands. I employ Turner's findings that Buddhist religious actors reformed their ideas about Buddhism and about the politically active role of monks and the Sangha. In chapter 3, I discuss the impact of the religious nationalism of the monks U Ottama and U Wisara as prominent examples of that change because both monks opposed British rule and demanded political change to meet their interests. I detail in chapter 3 how Buddhist nationalism evolved from the Buddhist anti-colonial movement against the neutral and open British religious economy. Without the powers of the king or the colonial government to support Theravada Buddhism, the religious firm broke into factions and had to reinvent itself, redefine its interests, rethink monks' political role, and find a different narrative (religious nationalism).

Recently, Matthew Walton examined Myanmar monks in politics from a political theoretical perspective (Walton, 2016a). Walton's work details the broad traditional elements and foundations of Burmese Buddhists' political thought and concepts. Walton provides a robust and well-considered theoretical understanding of the impact of Buddhist thought on monks who participate in Myanmar's politics and on Myanmar's political leadership and the general population. In part, Walton sought to understand how Buddhist monks in Myanmar theorized their own political participation (2016a, p. 128). To this end, he specifies how Myanmar's monks define democracy, politics, and how they view political action and behaviors. Walton details how monks rationalize, justify, and engage in politics and governance (2016a, p. 150). In chapters 6 and 7, however, I present evidence that disagrees with Walton's claim that "very few monks in Myanmar speak explicitly about politics or democracy" (Walton, 2016b, p. 62). This work builds on Walton's finding that current Buddhist political thought will continue to support an active role in political discourse, supporting my argument that Buddhism (like other religious firms) seeks to promote its interests.

Scholars studying Myanmar have also focused on conflict, violence, and other issues across communities (Cheesman and Farrelly, 2016). Holt (2019), Ibrahim (2016), and Wade (2017) provide comprehensive and excellent analyses of the background of contemporary political violence targeting the Rohingya community. Cheesman's (2015) excellent and comprehensive analysis of the rule of law in Myanmar informs the impact of Ne Win's citizenship laws. My argument in chapters 5 and 8 builds upon some of Chessman's unique observations and analyses.

Much of the analysis and debate within Myanmar and elsewhere focuses on the tenets and precepts (i.e., what Buddhism allows). Political scientists, like Walton, and anthropologists have focused on the worldviews of Buddhist actors in the Sangha (Walton, 2016a; Jordt, 2003). Similarly, Mikael Gravers examines Buddhism's politicized role in Myanmar and suggests that religion increasingly dominates Myanmar's identity politics (Gravers, 2015). I argue that this is not a recent development. The entanglement of politics and religion has significantly affected Myanmar's history since 1057.

Several scholars have examined the political nature of Buddhism (Lewy, 1974). Peter Lehr's book takes a close and detailed look at the rise of militant Buddhism in Sri Lanka, Myanmar, and Thailand (Lehr, 2018). Lehr explores the questions of why militant strands of Theravada Buddhism are on the rise and the roles monks play in militant Buddhist nationalism. Schober, Lehr, and others have shown a capacity for Buddhist political violence (Schober, 2007, p. 52; Lehr, 2018; Jerryson and Juergensmeyer, 2010). These and other studies reveal that Buddhist monks in Myanmar participated in nearly all landmark historical and political moments, along with some smaller moments. Much debate exists about whether monks *should* participate in politics, and scholars know a great deal about Theravada Buddhism's influence on Myanmar political thought. Building on this work, in chapter 6, I explore the impact of religious convictions on Myanmar's religious economy.

While valuable and fundamental, scholarly analyses at the firm level (i.e., the internal makeup of religious and ethnic minority groups) do not adequately explore the system-level structural tensions imposed by a regulated religious market with a prevailing narrative that Theravada Buddhists should exercise unquestioned dominance. The scholarship needs an examination of the full narrative (beyond the Buddhist narrative), foundations, and structures that tightly entangle the Myanmar state with religion. The recent work of Nick Cheesman (2015) and Christina Fink (2018) on structures created in Myanmar law includes the systemic-level examination. Cheesman's excellent analysis provides support and structure for my argument (in chapter 5) that Buddhist nationalism has led to the structured othering and exclusion of specific actors from the Myanmar religious economy.

Fink's work focuses on the experience of religious minorities in Myanmar between 2011 and 2017 in the context of the 2008 Constitution (2018). Fink's analysis resembles the one presented here in that Fink examines the structural components of Myanmar's basic law for underlying inequities (2013). Fink highlights the precarity of Myanmar's religious minorities and argues that neither the constitution nor the state offers reliable protection (2018, p. 274). Noting the "special position of Buddhism" in Article 361 of the 2008 Constitution, Fink provides support for the argument presented here—that the 2008 Myanmar Constitution calls for "extensive state engagement in the religious sphere, and, given historical narratives about Buddhism requiring protection, this could be interpreted as meaning the state can do whatever it likes to support Buddhism" (Fink, 2018, p. 273). To better understand the Myanmar religious economy's structure and outcomes, I employ marketplace and social control theories that work together to delineate my arguments about Myanmar's religious economy.

TWO MAIN ARGUMENTS ABOUT MYANMAR'S RELIGIOUS ECONOMY

In this book, I lay out two main arguments that each build on the other. First, I argue that protection, extensive control, regulation, and favoritism of one religious firm is woven into the historical narrative and structure of Myanmar's religious economy. Religion and the state have been historically entangled *and* the people and religious groups in Myanmar view and act as if the two institutions are separate. Second, I argue that social control, regulation, and favoritism of one religion has corrupted the Myanmar religious economy. State protection of Theravada Buddhism has corrupted or distorted the religious marketplace, Theravada Buddhism, and the larger society. The historical "Buddhist country" narrative and the legal and social structures fostered by that narrative have had substantial and often brutal consequences.

ARGUMENT 1: CONTROL AND REGULATION OF RELIGION

Since 1057, religion has been highly regulated and controlled in Myanmar. Before 1057 the religious economy was open and diverse. Religion in Myanmar has always been understood to be separate from the power of the state. Myanmar's founding king made a rational and personal choice to convert to Theravada Buddhism and then to promote his religious choice to the people. Except during the colonial era, the religious economy of Myanmar has been closed and highly regulated since 1057, and the state has used religion to control and support state interests. Myanmar's kings and modern-day generals have used the power of religion as a tool of social control. Scholars of religion and politics have long studied the use of religion as a tool of social control. That literature helps to clarify the patterns of pressure and the consequences of how various social groups seek to create or maintain a specific power structure or social order (Rousseau, 2003; Stark and Bainbridge, 1997). Individuals, groups, or organizations achieve social control either by persuasion and or force—the carrot or the stick—to seek conformity (Black, 1976). Among other control methods, societies routinely use the two extraordinarily powerful institutions of the state and religion to persuade or force a specific social order. I do not claim that religion is only a tool of social control. Rather, I argue that, among meeting many other needs, religion in Myanmar has served as a state tool of social control and functioned as a powerful force for the promotion of social change (Friedrichs, 1985, p. 361). Governmental and religious institutions use both coercion and persuasion to establish norms and rules that control their society and, critically, each other. The Myanmar government has often controlled and regulated religion, and the majority religion has often sought government protection and support.

The values of authority figures (those with at least some measure of legitimacy) appear in policies, laws, and actions that punish deviation or reward compliance with those values. Social control can be positive and constructive when it justly and fairly upholds society's values and desires (see chapter 6) while respecting the rights and existence of all people. However, social control often exists as a construct of the existing power structure and does not respect the rights and values of minority communities or even the will of the people. This was the case in Myanmar in March 1962 and again in February 2021 when factions of the Buddhist firm supported the military takeovers of democratically elected governments. In opposition to the people's will and out of either disrespect or outright rejection of minorities, authorities may define behaviors and practices as "deviant" to protect and privilege themselves and specific groups (Nyi Nyi Kyaw, 2019; Stark and Bainbridge, 1997). For example, Myanmar's military-controlled parliament defined interfaith marriages as deviant and outlawed them in 2015. Myanmar's marriage policy is a social control measure that protects specific values. When social control measures become unfair and unjust—or when those measures promote or permit the oppression of individuals, groups, or entire societies—people must disrupt existing social control measures and powers. Chapter 6 explores the importance of religious convictions in four cleric-led movements (1974, 1988, 2007, and 2021) that attempted to do just that: disrupt existing social control measures.

Religious institutions and individual clergy must be considered legitimate to maintain social control; otherwise, they generally collapse in failure. Government institutions and political leaders also need legitimacy to succeed (Dahl, 1956). In Myanmar, like in many countries, religion has often been used to manipulate the legitimacy of a government, leaders, or specific policies (Fox, 2016b). On the other hand, governments worldwide seek to further their control by benefiting from religious legitimacy, while religious firms seek to use political authority for individual or group legitimacy and protection. Theravada Buddhism and the Myanmar state have both drawn legitimacy from each other since 1057.

Religious Deviance, State Regulation, and Corruption

Nyi Nyi Kyaw (2019) examined the regulation of "deviant" Buddhist sects and concluded that there has been significant regulation and punishment of deviant Buddhist sects in Myanmar since the 1980s (Nyi Nyi Kyaw, 2019, p. 185). His findings led him to conclude that deviant Buddhist individuals and sects have suffered from the lack of religious freedom. The suffering has been far more pervasive. In Nyi Nyi Kyaw's analysis, "deviant sects" are individuals, factions, or subgroups within mainstream Buddhism that are deemed "deviant" or judged to be theologically wrong by the leaders of the state and majority religion. This raises the conceptual question: who decides what is deviant? While scholars (Perrin, 2001) debate religious deviance, studies of religion and deviance reveal that religious firms tend to be inhospitable to religious deviance (Stark and Bainbridge, 1997, p. 103). Change is hard, especially when it involves power. According to Stark and Bainbridge (1997, p. 104), by far the most common form of deviant religious group is the sect. A *sect* is a religious group within a conventional religious tradition of a society that has a different interpretation or understanding of the religion than do the mainstream believers (Stark and Bainbridge, 1997, p. 104). Within Buddhism and religious firms worldwide, sects (factions) are common. Humans often tend to rethink and reevaluate and to challenge the status quo. Worldwide, sects often serve to invigorate and revive older religious firms (Stark and Bainbridge, 1997, p. 104). The older religious firm, as it loses market share, is replaced by a sect with newer products or greater vigor. This renewal has been suppressed in Myanmar. Older religious firms seek to maintain a monopoly and suppress religious deviance. In Myanmar, the older and established religious Theravada Buddhist firm maintains a monopoly by employing the power and authority of the state. The Buddhist firm's behavior and leadership are controlled by the State Sangha Mahanayaka Committee (see chapters 5 and 6). This state-empowered committee decides which individual clerics, sects, ideologies, and practices are deviant (Nyi Nyi Kyaw, 2019, p. 170). The Mahanayaka Committee uses state power to punish those individuals and sects that they deem deviant. The power to decide who is deviant and to control the internal ideologies and practices of Buddhism has corrupted not only the mainstream Buddhist firm but also the entire religious marketplace. The regulation and suppression of deviant sects did not begin in the 1980s with Ne Win's Mahanayaka Committee; as argued by Nyi Nyi Kyaw (2019) it began in 1057 with Myanmar's first king.

Highly Controlled and Regulated

Comparative data indicate that Myanmar's present-day religious economy is highly regulated (Fox, 2019b). Jonathan Fox and scholars associated with the Religion and State (RAS) Project (a university-based project at Bar Ilan University in Ramat Gan, Israel) have contributed to a surge in cross-national empirical studies of religion as it relates to liberal democracy, the separation of religion and state, and religious discrimination (Fox, 2019b). The RAS project has provided scholars with cross-national data on states' religion policies. Scholars have used those data to sketch an overview of general trends and to examine correlations between states' religion policies. As a result, scholars now understand much better how governments deal with religion and how a state's religion policy influences a religious economy. According to Fox (2016b), governments support religion in fifty-one unique ways, regulate or control religion in twenty-nine separate ways, and restrict religious minorities in thirty-one ways. Myanmar ranks "high" on the RAS Religious Regulation Index, the Religious Minority Discrimination Index, and the Societal Discrimination of Minority Religions Index (Fox, 2019b). The RAS ranked Myanmar "medium" on the State Funding of Religions Index (Fox, 2019b).

	Myanmar	*Southeast Asia*	*World*
Government Regulation of Religion Index: average governmental regulation score over Association of Religion Data Archives (ARDA) researchers' coding of the 2003, 2005, and 2008 U.S. Department of State's International Religious Freedom Reports from 0 (no regulation) to 10 (entirely regulated).	9.1	5.9	3.0
Average social regulation score over ARDA researchers' coding of 2003, 2005, and 2008 U.S. Department of State's International Religious Freedom Reports (0–10; lower means less regulation).	8.1	2.5	4.5

Figure 1. Myanmar's Regulation of Religion (Fox, 2019c).

	Myanmar	Southeast Asia	World
Government Favoritism of Religion Index: average government favoritism score over ARDA researchers' coding of the 2003, 2005, and 2008 U.S. Department of State's International Religious Freedom Reports (0–10; lower means less favoritism).	8.9	5.6	4.6

Figure 2. Myanmar Favoritism of Religion (Fox, 2019c).

Taking into account all of the twenty-nine measurements of the RAS project for the governmental regulation of religion, Myanmar's religious economy is restricted, regulated, and controlled. Notably, a state's *protection and support* for a religion is also a means of social control. Unsurprisingly, the RAS database shows that the Myanmar state strongly favors Theravada Buddhism.

ARGUMENT 2: PROTECTION AND CORRUPTION OF THE RELIGIOUS ECONOMY

Based on evidence of control and regulation, I argue that state protection and support of religion in Myanmar have led to corruption of the religious economy. Evidence of corruption is seen in a state-supported religious monopoly, repression and violence against religious minorities, perpetual conflict, alienation, othering, and the distortion and degradation of the religious marketplace and individual religions. The "corruption" argument has been around for centuries (Koppelman, 2009, p. 27). Early corruption theorists included John Milton, Adam Smith, John Locke, Thomas Jefferson, and James Madison.

Pleasing Their Paymasters

Milton was writing about General Ne Win's (see chapter 5) regime when he warned that state support and protection of religion tends to elevate the state over the religion and subjects the religion to the "political drifts or conceived opinions" of the ruler (Koppelman, 2009, p. 32). Milton wrote, "For magistrates . . . will pay none but such whom by their committees of examination they find conformable to their interests and opinions: and hirelings will soon frame themselves to that interest and those opinions which they see best pleasing to their paymasters; and to seem right themselves, will force others as to the truth" (Koppelman, 2009, p. 32, n. 71).

For Milton, any state influence over religion is a perversion (Milton, 2012, p. 122). Factions (sects) of "government monks" (see chapter 7) in the majority religion in Myanmar have conformed their interests and opinions to meet the needs of their paymasters (Nyi Nyi Kyaw, 2019, p. 179). Not only has the Buddhist firm conformed to the needs of the state, but those Buddhist sects or factions that refused were deemed "deviant" and forced by the state to conform or were forced out of existence (Nyi Nyi Kyaw, 2019, p. 181). Since 1057 this pattern of state control and regulation has reshaped the entire Myanmar religious economy. Over the centuries, many different religions, religious ideas, and "truths" were suppressed by those who held the power of the state.

Incompetent Perversion by the State

In 1689, in *A Letter Concerning Toleration*, John Locke argued that state authority over religion corrupted religion. For Locke, state-supported religion led to coerced worship, and a state-coerced worship would be hypocrisy and hold no religious value. Locke also argued that the state would be generally incompetent in the administration of religion: "The one only narrow way which leads to Heaven is not better known to the Magistrate than to private Persons, and therefore I cannot safely take him for my Guide, who may probably be as ignorant of the way as my self, and who certainly is less concerned for my salvation than I my self am" (Locke, 1689, p. 35). Myanmar's state leaders (see chapters 3, 4, 5, and 7) were roundly incompetent in the administration and regulation of religion. As Jefferson wrote, "religion is too personal, too sacred, too holy, to permit its unhallowed perversion by a civil magistrate" (Cousins, 1958, p. 125).

Buddhists as Servants of the State

In 1786, Thomas Jefferson warned that a close relationship between a government and a religion could reduce the religion to a servant of the state (Cousins, 1958, p. 126). As mentioned above, the control by the State Sangha Mahanayaka Committee has (at times) made the majority religion a servant of the state. Loyal government monks (see chapters 1 and 7) have been servants to the needs of kings and military regimes. Jefferson argued that protecting the integrity and legitimacy of religion meant separating and protecting it from the government (Cousins, 1958, p. 131). Jefferson feared that religious firms working closely with the government risk corrupting religion and losing religious legitimacy. This is precisely how many would describe Myanmar's "government" and Ma Ba Tha monks (see chapters 6 and 7). Echoing Milton and Locke, Jefferson wrote that state-religion entanglement "tends also to corrupt the principles of that very religion it is meant to encourage, by bribing, with a monopoly of worldly honors and emoluments, those who will externally profess and conform to it" (Koppelman, 2009, p. 54; Jefferson, 1779). A thousand years of state entanglement with religion in Myanmar provides vivid evidence that indicates that each of Jefferson's fears and warnings are correct.

The Degrading of Religion

In short, government power controls, corrupts, or even transforms religion. The corruption argument rests on the assumption that religion has value and that it is best when protected from the powers of the state. Justice Hugo Black, writing for the U.S. Supreme Court, explained: "a union of government and religion tends to destroy government and degrade religion. The history of governmentally established religion . . . showed that whenever government allied itself with one particular form of religion, the inevitable result had been that it had incurred the hatred, disrespect and even contempt of those who held contrary beliefs. That same history showed that many people had lost their respect for any religion that had relied upon the support for government to spread its faith" (Black, 1961, p. 431). The alignment of the Myanmar state with Theravada Buddhism has incurred hatred, disrespect, and contempt of those who hold contrary beliefs.

Writing in 1776, Scottish economist and philosopher Adam Smith focused on the corrupting effect of state financial support on religion. Smith argued that if clerics were to receive financial support from the state, "[t]heir exertion, their zeal and industry," were likely to be much diminished (Smith, 1776, p. 608). Smith further argued that "[t]he clergy of an established and well-endowed religion . . . are apt gradually to lose the qualities, both good and bad, which gave them authority and influence." (Smith, 1776, p. 608). Smith wrote that the way to avoid unwanted cleric behavior is "to bribe their indolence, by assigning stated salaries to their profession, and rendering it superfluous for them to be farther active, than merely to prevent their flock from straying in quest of new pastures" (Hume, 1985, p. 791). General Ne Win and the generals who followed him have lavishly supported loyal government monks and in doing so undermined their authority and influence (see chapters 5 and 7).

Factions, Sects, and Conflict

James Madison led the United States to adopt a liberal and neutral disestablishment of religion. Madison was concerned with "differences in political, religious, and other opinions" as the causes of factional (see chapters 3 and 7) disputes (Madison, 1785). While factions are to be expected, Madison argued that government support of one religion led to political factions within that religion. As a direct result of state power,

Myanmar's Buddhist monks are divided into four political factions today (see chapter 7).

Further, government support or protection of one religion leads to political conflict. Myanmar's first prime minister, U Nu (see chapter 4), provides a vivid example of Madison's concern. U Nu sought to promote Theravada Buddhism and then needed to make amends to concerned minority religions by supporting all religions, only to find his government engulfed in conflict from all sides (including the majority religion) over the issue. Madison also denounced the idea that religion should be protected and promoted by the state because it leads to good citizenship. In Myanmar in the 1950s, Prime Minister U Nu sought to employ Theravada Buddhism as an engine of civil policy (see chapter 4). Writing in 1785, Madison warned that such an attempt would lead to "an unhallowed perversion of the means of salvation" (Madison, 1785).

A Distorted Religious Economy: Fears, Intolerance, and Conflict

Political scientists have focused on various aspects of distorted or corrupt religious economies (Gill, 2007). A distorted religious economy lacks freedom, justice, and fairness. Myanmar's regulated religious economy is corrupt because it lacks the rule of law, respect for human rights, religious liberty, and a fair and open marketplace for all ideas. This distorted religious economy increases fear of others, legal inequities, a tolerance of intolerance, and mistrust of others and of the government. It also allows government officials to manipulate and corrupt religion and society (see chapters 5, 7, and 8). Basedau and colleagues examined religious discrimination's influence on armed conflict in sub-Saharan Africa and found that a rise in religious discrimination coincided with a rise in armed conflict—especially theological and religious-identity conflicts (2011). Religious discrimination and violent conflict in Myanmar constitute part of what Basedau identified as "a wider context of problematic state-religion relations" (Basedau, 2017). This discrimination and prejudice are linked to violent conflict with Muslim and Christian groups within Myanmar (Cheesman and Farrelly, 2016; Crouch, 2016a; Ibrahim, 2016; Schober, 2007, p. 52). A religious economic policy based on the theories of liberal peace and an open marketplace of ideas allows for a tolerant society, the inclusion of minority religions, less conflict, and an environment in which religions can flourish.

Corruption of Truth

The regulation of the Myanmar religious economy has distorted the market and discouraged competition. Finke found that "religious deregulation" in the United States created "a religious market where competition was . . . encouraged" (1990). The economist Friedrich Hayek, a disciple of Adam Smith, argues that the religious economy is improved by free-market competition (Hayek, 1989, p. 137). Hayek argued that a religion that served the needs of a society would succeed, and those that did not would go out of business (Hayek, 1989, p. 138–39). The evidence presented here indicates that a state-protected religion distorts or corrupts the entire religious marketplace. In Myanmar, the power of the state supported one religion and religious competition has been largely eliminated. An undistorted market without the corrupting regulation of the state has greater religious diversity and higher rates of religious participation, and the open market has served people in the United States well by liberating and enlivening spiritual affairs (Finke and Starke, 1992). The protection of religion in Myanmar has led to a lack of competition in the marketplace of ideas, to far less religious diversity, and to the corruption of "truth."

A corrupt religious marketplace restricts the participation of minority firms. Mataic and Finke found that "when a state and the dominant religion(s) form an alliance, the state will be under increased pressure to restrict the activities of the minority religions perceived as unwanted religious competitors" (2019). The lack of religious ideas, combined with government regulation of the content of the majority religion, has corrupted and distorted the "truth."

In sum, these corruptions and others are precisely the consequences of thousands of years of state protection of Buddhism in Myanmar. The historical entanglement of Theravada Buddhism and the state has shaped Myanmar's religious economy, created structural inequities, distorted religious practices, reshaped the majority religion, and produced negative attitudes toward factions of Theravada Buddhism. Myanmar's current state religion policies and religious conflicts have deep historical roots that are better understood within the rational choice framework and within the broader intellectual debate about the role of state and religion entanglement.

LIBERTY, PROTECTION, AND THE MARKETPLACE OF IDEAS

Scholars have argued that "thick versions of liberal or constitutional democracy" can reduce violence (Snyder, 2000). Liberal institutions that embrace justice and fairness provide citizens with equal respect and freedom of conscience. Internal conflict resulting from underlying factors (injustice) makes violence more likely. The suppression of minority religious ideas (or a closed religious economy) may yield disunity, turmoil, and even war (Ahdar and Leigh, 2013, p. 70). A society's prospects for avoiding conflict increase significantly with the political system's fairness. When states "restrict religious freedoms, physical persecution and conflict increase" (Grim and Finke, 2010).

In this book, I take a non-neutral stance on Myanmar's question of religion and the state. A liberal and open religious economy is preferred. I work from the foundation that the elements of a liberal religious economy encourage human rights, peace, and religion (Philpott, 2012; VanAntwerpen, 2014). Philpott (2015) writes that a liberal peace has three elements. First, a liberal justification for religious liberty originates in the Enlightenment period with the concepts of individual rights, liberty, equality, and the rule of law. Second, a liberal religious economy must be hosted by actors and institutions that fully embrace justice and fairness. All citizens must be treated with equal respect and have freedom of conscience. This must include allowing individuals to leave or change their religion. Third, a liberal religious economy must uphold the rule of law, respect all humans' rights and liberty, and gain consent of the governed through free and fair elections—and a free marketplace for ideas and religions (Ahdar and Leigh, 2013; Snyder and Ballentine, 1996). Myanmar's people have only briefly glimpsed these three elements of religious liberty and have not enjoyed an entirely free marketplace of ideas since 1057. In Myanmar's history and culture, the concepts of justice, liberty, human rights, and the rule of law have been largely absent or altered.

Is religious liberty possible in Myanmar? I argue that yes, the Myanmar people clearly support it, but if religion and the state remain deeply entangled, then no. Recently, David and Holliday (2018) set out to answer that question. What are the prospects for liberal democracy in Myanmar? They examine Myanmar's political institutions, political culture, constitutionalism, and historical justice and arrive at a bleak conclusion. While acknowledging that Myanmar's citizens could move toward a liberal peace, they assess the chances of this as slim (David and Holliday, 2018, p. 202). I fully agree with their evidence-based assessment that Myanmar's society today comprises both liberal and illiberal factions (David and Holliday, 2018, p. 199). Aung San Suu Kyi has (so far) not been a strong proponent of liberalism, and Myanmar's military has remained a retrogressive and illiberal force. Thus, combined with a "nationalistic, chauvinistic, and xenophobic Sangha," Myanmar's people will likely continue suffering under an illiberal state and an intolerant society (David and Holliday, 2018, p. 200).

Myanmar's illiberal state is the result of the historical entanglement of religion and state. These twin powers bind together in an entangled illiberal structure that is at once mutually beneficial and destructive to Theravada Buddhism and to the larger society. However, my interviews with monks offer Myanmar a glimmer of liberal hope. Of the monks I interviewed, nearly all noted significant illiberal *and* liberal factions within the modern Sangha of Myanmar, including many monks (cohorts of liberals) who strongly and vocally support a liberal peace. As discussed in chapters 6 and 7, the Myanmar Sangha includes prominent and outspoken liberal monks. In chapter 7, I present evidence that Myanmar's Buddhist Sangha is divided into four political factions and is not as "nationalistic, chauvinistic, and xenophobic" as David and Holliday conclude (2018, p. 200).

RESEARCH METHODS

For the study, I employ the *analytic narrative* method (Bates et al., 1998). Although the analytic method has critics (Elster, 2000), researchers have successfully employed it to examine several cases of religious economy (in the United States, across Latin America, and in Russia) and recently to understand reactions to communal violence in Myanmar (Wells, 2016; Green, 2011; Gill, 2007). This book explores Myanmar's religious economy from prehistory to the present, and the narrative method's use of historical description with a theoretical framework reveals the dynamic emergence of politics and policy over time. The narrative method allows this analysis to account for historical events, political issues, and the collective construction of those events and issues (Boswell, 2013).

Each chapter builds on the previous one and uses the narrative approach to show how various Myanmar leaders approach state–religion policy issues and solutions differently. I do this for two reasons. First, I want to clarify that my analysis is not merely a Western application of rational choice and liberal theory to a society in which they do not apply (McKinnon, 2013). In each chapter, I describe people and groups throughout Myanmar's history who made or would have made liberal state–religion policy decisions. Second, Myanmar's powerful narrative of state–religion policy reveals the power, interests, and desires of the storytellers (Walton and Hayward, 2014). The state–religion policy decisions made by ancient kings, colonial administrators, benevolent prime ministers, and brutal dictators shaped and reshaped the contours of the Myanmar religious economy.

With a generous year-long Fulbright grant, I began research for this book in 2015. In 2016 and beyond, I have fortunately had access to several libraries, including monastic libraries and libraries of Buddhist and public universities in Yangon and Mandalay. I enjoyed full access to the archives at Yangon University and records at the Judson Research Institute at the Myanmar Institute of Theology. In addition to textual sources and historical documents, this book resulted from interviews with fifty-four Myanmar monks, a few nuns, numerous Myanmar government officials, many members of Myanmar's national and regional parliaments, university faculty and academic leaders at Yangon University and at the Yangon School of Political Science, U.S. Ambassador Derek Mitchell, Kristen F. Bauer, Deputy Chief of Mission in Myanmar, numerous political officers in the U.S. Embassy, and many practitioners in intergovernmental and nongovernmental organizations. These interviews, especially those with monks and other clerical leaders (including Imams and Anglican, Methodist, and Baptist ministers), provided valuable insights into Myanmar's state–religion policy and, critically, the divisions and interests in the Buddhist Sangha and the state's profound influences on religion. I spent many hours interviewing monks (sometimes full days) about the Sangha's issues and influence on the state and about the state's influence on the Sangha and on individual monks. In each interview, I guided the conversation with questions and took notes as the monks (and others) spoke with me. I also had two Myanmar research assistants who took notes and helped with translation. In this book, I give the names of specific monks (and of other clerics and leaders) when given permission and for individuals widely known and covered in the media. Otherwise, for their safety and security, I do not name individuals.

Faculty at Yangon University, the Myanmar Institute of Theology, and the Yangon School of Political Science arranged interviews for me with monks, political leaders, and clerics. In most cases, those faculty members assisted by translating and generously taking notes while I asked questions. The leadership at the U.S. Embassies in Yangon also arranged meetings and interviews. I worked closely with the U.S. Embassy Deputy Chief of Mission, Kristen F. Bauer, and her staff during full-day workshops with members of Myanmar's Parliament. These workshops allowed me to ask many policy makers questions about state–religion policy.

The U.S. Embassy in Yangon asked me not to visit certain monks (U Wirathu, for example), but I did visit a wide range of monks—from well-known and established Buddhist scholars and monastic leaders to monks who did not remotely describe themselves as political actors or leaders. Many of Myanmar's monks are active on social media (specifically Facebook), and I learned much from their posts and from the posts of Myanmar's state officials. I attended many public sermons (often in the streets of Yangon and Mandalay) and religious ceremonies in Yangon, Mandalay, and across the country in monasteries and homes. The interviews, experiences, and other information provide a rich understanding of the impact of Myanmar's religious economy. I have analyzed data from interview notes, field notes, and books and documents given to me by monks and faculty members. I also rely on the rich and deep wealth of work of anthropologists, historians, and political scientists to provide a more complete understanding of Myanmar's state–religion policy and religious economy.

CHAPTER OUTLINE

This book provides a practical and systemic case study of Myanmar's religious economy. To meet that goal, the book is organized and written at both macro and micro levels. Each chapter is focused on the macro historical entanglement of religion and includes microlevel elements, brief "religious biographies" of the key individual actors, providing life and context for larger ideas and discussion. The religious biographies of both revered and hated men and women (Myanmar's state and religious actors) provide insights and an analysis of each person's impact on religion. Chapters include brief religious biographies of these key actors: (1) Kings Ashoka and Anawrahta; (2) Christian and Muslim missionaries Adoniram Judson and 'Abd al-Khaliq; (3) political "agitators" Sayadaw U Ottama, U Wisara, and Saya San; (4) Prime Minister U Nu; (5) General Ne Win; (6) United Nations Secretary-General U Thant, U Gambira, and Myawaddy Mingyi Sayadaw; (7) Aung San Suu Kyi. Religious biographies were drawn from historical and archival research and personal interviews.

Each step of this narrative builds on the previous and includes animism, Buddhism, Christianity, Islam, nat worship, and other religions as we consider five important sub-questions: (1) What is the impact of a liberal policy on religion? (2) What is the impact of religious nationalism? (3) What happens when a devout and beloved person of faith seeks to employ the powers of the state to support religion? (4) What happens when a ruthless dictator micromanages religion? (5) What roles do religious convictions play in maintaining and disrupting existing power structures? Our dance ends where it began with animism and intimate prayers (along with consequences and answers) in a village north of Mandalay with ancient Nats accepting gifts of bananas, coconuts, alcohol, and cash.

Chapter 1 (Nats, Kings, and Government Monks: The Foundations of the Myanmar Religious Economy 1057–1824) opens by examining the ancient prehistoric Pyu people, the diversity of religions during the pre-Myanmar centuries, and the profoundly influential founding king of Myanmar. The important foundation of nat worship is introduced, and nat worship remains a constant throughout the book as it has in Myanmar's culture. This chapter examines the historical and complex political link between King Anawrahta's choice to select, promote, and protect Theravada Buddhism and the state of Myanmar. Myanmar's religious economy has pluralistic foundations, and I show that the early decision to support one religion dramatically changed and shaped Myanmar's religious economy. This chapter concludes with a discussion of the impact of "king-law" on the modern Myanmar religious economy.

Chapter 2 (The Golden Shore: An Experiment in Religious Freedom 1824–1948) explores the historical relationship between the state and religion from colonial times to 1948 (British rule in Myanmar lasted from 1824 to 1948). This chapter focuses on Britain's deregulation of Myanmar's religious economy. The British opened the religious marketplace and allowed minority religious firms to proselytize, share ideas, and recruit followers. The numbers of followers of Muslim and Christian firms grew substantially in market share during the colonial years. The abrupt liberal change in the religious economy forced changes in the Theravada Buddhist firm and, in part, catalyzed Buddhist nationalism. I argue that the British era fostered in the people of Myanmar a liberal understanding of the role of religion in Myanmar politics.

Chapter 3 (To Be Burmese Is to Be Buddhist: Religious Nationalism in the Myanmar Religious Economy 1930–1948) explores religious nationalism and colonial state–religion policy. How did religious nationalism develop in the colonial era and what roles did it play in the colonial religious economy? By examining key religious nationalists and historical events, this chapter details the impact of religious nationalism on four important aspects of the colonial-era religious economy: a controversial British state–religion policy, the breakdown of colonial-era social control, the definition of a national identity, and the building blocks of the coming independent nation. Buddhist nationalism of the 1930s not only fostered independence but also created a sense of who belonged as a citizen and who was labeled as foreign, setting the foundation for much of the conflict facing the Myanmar people since 1962.

Chapter 4 (Saturday's Son: The Religious Economy under a Devout Religious Leader 1947–1962) examines Myanmar's religious economy from General Aung San's interim government in 1947 through Myanmar's first prime minister, U Nu. The early years of Myanmar's independence were marked by both inclusive and tolerant state-religion policies. What happens in a religious economy when a beloved and devoted religious leader holds political power? General Aung San and U Nu held quite different views on the appropriate role of the state in the religious economy. Aung San sought a neutral state–religion policy, but U Nu fully engaged the state's powers to regulate the religious marketplace. This chapter explores the effects of U Nu's liberal and illiberal state–religion policies and highlights the outcomes of a devout and deeply religious political leader who sought to use his religion to promote the health and well-being of his country. What happened when a beloved, devout person of faith sought to align state power with one religion? I show evidence that the people of Myanmar unequivocally understood the entanglement of religion and the powers of the state.

Chapter 5 (Going to Moscow: Religion under a Brutal Dictator 1962–1988) examines Myanmar's religious economy under the military regime led by General Ne Win. From 1962 to the Four Eights Uprising in

1988, Ne Win and his military government made sweeping and dramatic changes to Myanmar's religious economy. First, they declared liberal state–religion policies—they would not support the Buddhist firm as the state religion—then the military moved to micromanage every aspect of the Myanmar religious marketplace. Ne Win sought to eliminate minority religions and firmly control and regulate the Buddhist firm. Nat worship was outlawed and denigrated. Christian and Muslim missionaries were forced out of the country, and nearly every aspect of the Buddhist firm came under some form of government control. Ne Win's military government promoted, regulated, and manipulated the Buddhist firm to meet the goals of his government and tried to regulate and control the entire religious economy.

Chapter 6 (Buddhism, Nat Spirit Wives, and Christian Clerics: Religious Convictions in the Myanmar Religious Economy 1974–2022) examines religious convictions and the participation of clerics and Buddhist subgroups within Myanmar from 1974, 1988, 2007, and 2021. The Myanmar state has long attempted to prohibit the participation of clergy in politics. This chapter examines the impact of the Buddhist firm on the struggle for liberal democracy. Religion has played an important role in the disruption of state control and repression. I argue that the history of the impact of religion on Myanmar politics indicates a vital role for religious convictions in governance. Contrary to earlier research, I offer a more optimistic assessment of Myanmar's future (even after the 2021 coup). This chapter concludes with a look at extreme Buddhists and asks an important question: are the fruits of religion sweet or bitter?

Chapter 7 (The Ashokan Road: The Consequences of a Highly Regulated Religious Economy for the State and Majority Religion) presents the consequences of nearly one thousand years of state protection of one religion. The consequences include a state-supported religious monopoly, regulation, and repression of Theravada Buddhists. In this chapter we discuss the first two (of six) consequences: (1) a state protected and supported religious monopoly; (2) corruption, regulation, and repression of Theravada Buddhists. This chapter includes a religious biography of Aung San Suu Kyi and the consequences of Buddhist and state entanglement. This chapter presents the findings of extensive interviews and fieldwork in the framework of the "rational actor" theoretical approach. Findings include four political factions within the Theravada Buddhist firm. Those four political factions are (1) government monks, (2) Ma Ba Tha monks, (3) Saffron monks, and (4) Pure or passive monks.

Chapter 8 (A Different Ashokan Road: The Consequences for Minority Religions, Religious Competition, and Truth) wraps up the final three consequences: (3) repression and violence against religious minorities, (4) perpetual conflict and violence, (5) a corrupt religious marketplace (the lack of competition has created a distorted religious economy), and finally (6) an incompetent perversion or corruption of truth. This chapter includes a look at modern-day nat worship and argues that religious regulation has suppressed and altered nat worship participation and belief. However, contrary to supply-side theory and state suppression, nat worship has survived, thrived, and adapted to meet the needs of the Myanmar people.

LIMITATIONS AND QUESTIONS

Of course, limitations and questions remain. Quantitative data are needed and could, for example, elucidate the illiberal and liberal factions within Myanmar's society. It would help to know the number of people who worship nats. It would also help to know how many times Myanmar's Buddhist Sangha has been purged. As Bruce Matthews noted, Michael Mendelson's efforts to determine the number of monks in the Buddhist firm were stymied by lack of data. Mendelson's point that "the situation in regard to statistics is a little short of disastrous" remains all too true today (Matthews, 1995, p. 409).

This work should at least add an important structural dimension to the discussion of Myanmar's religious economic policy and answer the overarching question: what happens when a religion is protected? As argued in the concluding chapter, Myanmar's trouble with religion, Buddhism's trouble with the Myanmar government, the 2017 genocide and mass exodus of Rohingya people from Myanmar, and the disunity, turmoil, and prolonged war with ethnic minority groups result in large part from the history and structure of Myanmar's state–religion policy that began with King Anawrahta in 1057. The next chapter explores the diversity of Myanmar's ancient religious economy until critical decisions and precedents were made by a king and his appointed government monk.

1

✛

Nats, Kings, and Government Monks

The Foundations of the Myanmar Religious Economy 1057–1824

Imagine the deep greens of the grass and trees in the heat of a sunrise as it melts away the mists in the middle reaches of the Irrawaddy River Valley. At the center of Myanmar is the brown and muddy Irrawaddy River. During the Iron Age, the Irrawaddy River was home to the empire of the Pyu people. On these fertile and well-irrigated lands sit the remains of three ancient cities: Halin, Beikthano, and Sri Ksetra. These cities were home to the Pyu people, who flourished in what is today Myanmar for more than a thousand years—between 200 BCE and 900 CE (Stargardt, 2016; Moore, 2009, p. 101). Some of their palace citadels, burial grounds, city walls, and brick Buddhist stupas still stand today. These cities were founded by Tibetan-speaking people who migrated south into the Irrawaddy River Valley from the present-day Chinese province of Yunnan (Stargardt, 2016; Aung-Thwin, 2005). The Pyu people had a striking capacity to assimilate and reinvent Indic influences. In art, architecture, and literature, the Pyu created new ways of understanding and practicing the religions of their Indic neighbors (Stargardt, 2016, p. 365).

Myanmar's current religious economy derives from the ancient pre-Burma Pyu civilization (200 BCE–1050 CE). A look at the foundation of Myanmar's religious economy illuminates several important state–religion consequences. The beginning story describes the closure of the open Pyu religious economy and the founding of a state religion. The earliest settlers in present-day Myanmar enjoyed religious pluralism (Aung-Thwin, 2005; Niharranjan, 1946, p. 151; Hudson, 2008, p. 555). They lived in a religiously diverse society and had the freedom to worship or not. This changed in 1057. The Pyu's religious practices and the changes that occurred in 1057

Figure 1.1 Bagan, Myanmar. *Source*: AdrienC/ Moment via Getty Images

still profoundly impact Myanmar's religious economy and entire society. Today, monks commonly give sermons on the streets of Yangon or Mandalay that reference Buddha along with King Ashoka (304–232 BCE), King Anawrahta (Sanskrit Aniruddha, 1014–1078 CE), and the Venerable Shin Arahan (1034–1115 CE).

A MONK WHO BUILT THREE STUPAS

In Myanmar's closed and highly regulated religious economy, a Buddhist monk recently built three stupas. On September 12, 2015, in the Hlaingbwe township of Myanmar, a locally revered Buddhist monk, Myaing Kyee Ngu Sayadaw, built a stupa on the grounds of a Baptist church. Eight months later, on April 23, 2016, he had another one built on the grounds of the Saint Mark Anglican Church. On May 3, 2016, the monk built a third stupa on the grounds of a mosque in a nearby Muslim village. Building these mound-shaped structures, which Buddhists use as a place of meditation or worship, violated basic property law and constituted overt aggression against the Muslim and Christian residents of Hlaingbwe township (McConnell and Goodrich, 2016; Mendelson, 1975, p. 123).

In April 2015, the Myanmar government's Ministry of Religious Affairs announced that it would investigate the matter. The Minister of Religious Affairs, Thura U Aung Ko, thought it best not to rush because "it would take time to look into the conflict as not to jeopardize the country's volatile peace" (Ye Mon and Aung Kyaw Min, 2016). The Minister of Religious Affairs then noted that the Myanmar State Sangha Maha Naryaka Committee (a government-appointed body of high-ranking Buddhist monks that regulates the Sangha [Buddhist community] in Myanmar) also thought it best not to rush. One commnity member, who asked not to be named due to the sensitivity of the situation, said that the monk "is building the stupas for missionary work. He [the monk] said there were many stupas beneath the church compounds dating back to King Ashoka" (Mon, 2015). U Ashin Wirathu, the monk *Time* magazine called "The Face of Buddhist Terror," (Beech, Meikhtila, and Pattani, 2013) stepped in to ask the Christian and Muslim communities to remain calm.

On May 11, 2016, Myanmar's Minister of Religious Affairs met with the Christian community and apologized for the construction of the stupas but did not apologize to the Muslim community. Then, government officials met with local Buddhist leaders and asked them to refrain from taking any action against the monk. When asked how the Sangha would handle the monk's aggressive stupa building, a Sangha committee member said, "We don't know how to decide on these issues because the new government hasn't told us to take action and neither did the previous government" (Ye Mon and Aung Kyaw Min, 2016). In the end, the stupas remain. Bishop Saw Stylo of St. Mark Anglican Church "donated" the land for the new Buddhist stupas (Ye Mon and Aung Kyaw Min, 2016). A senior monk described the monk's longing to build stupas as a dream. "Whenever he gets a dream to build pagodas in any place—he accomplishes it," Bishop Stylo said. "And all the places he has dreamed of are in Christian church compounds. We pray that he doesn't dream anymore of building more pagodas on our Christian properties" (Ye Mon and Aung Kyaw Min, 2016).

The building of three stupas encompasses many actors in Myanmar's modern religious economy. The monk who built the stupas constitutes a rational actor and a religious representative (missionary) who supports the interests of Myanmar's dominant religious firm (Theravada Buddhism). The monk even invoked the ancient King Ashoka (268–232 BCE) from the dominant historical and primordial narrative about Myanmar's religious economy. The monk represents a religious firm or an organization that shares religious ideas (Epstein, 2018; Gill, 2007). The minority Christian and Muslim religions (upon whose grounds the stupas were built) are important actors in Myanmar's religious economy because they too supply or meet religious marketplace demands. The Myanmar government officials who reacted slowly and favored the monk and his firm helped shape the religious marketplace. The monk, minority religious firms, government actors, and citizen bystanders acted and reacted within the context and structure of a specific religious economy. The construction of those three stupas on the properties of minority religious firms and the reactions (official and unofficial) of all involved actors encompass the central theme and questions of this book.

The founding narrative is powerful in the present religious economy. When asked about religion in Myanmar, faculty members of Buddhist universities and prominent public universities in Yangon and Mandalay, as well as members of the Myanmar Parliament, commonly reference *Rajadhammasangaha*, or "king law" (Yaw Mingyi, 2004; personal communications, 2016). The histories and ideas of these ancient kings and monks are not merely part of the past: they constitute the living narrative of Myanmar's present religious economy (Leider, 2009). The kings and Buddhist monks of ancient Myanmar made decisions about the religious economy that people still follow today. These ancient decisions are still important not because of their age, but because they are often repeated. The historical narrative acts as a tool of regulation and social control. The ancient history of state–religion policy, often retold in present-day Myanmar, is an important modern instrument of power. Those who seek to maintain the existing power structure argue that religion (specifically Theravada Buddhism) is entangled with the state because it is primordial (Fox, 2018, p. 34). Theravada Buddhism is ancient and culturally imbedded within the identity of the people of Myanmar. It is argued that the Buddhist religious identity became relevant in politics so long ago that no one can point to why or when. Thus, the protection of Theravada Buddhism is relevant today because it was long ago. This primordial narrative has embedded conflict, injustices, and generations of violence throughout the centuries of Myanmar's history.

The stories we tell matter. The state–religion policies of ancient Burmese kings affect present-day Myanmar. Early policy decisions get repeated because they serve a purpose (function) for those who repeat them. Myanmar's state and religion have a serpentine and nonlinear history with a spiral of ancient decisions remade and recounted into the present norm. It is quite common to read that the people of Myanmar do not make a distinction between the religious and secular domains (Carstens, 2018, p. 126). History reveals a quite different reality. Those who wield power have controlled and shaped the historical narrative about the domains of religion and state authority. The promotion of the myth that there is no meaningful distinction maintains a specific power structure.

This chapter explores the establishment and founding of Myanmar's religious economy. Of course, Myanmar's long history is also complex, as many have written (Thant Myint-U, 2020; Charney, 2009; Smith, 1965; Cady, 1958). This chapter aims not to recount that history but rather to detail the historical foundations of Myanmar's religious economy. What decisions in those early years shaped and continue to shape Myanmar's religious economy? The ancient history, what Aung San Suu Kyi calls the "pre-Buddhist days," is critical to the overall narrative (Aung San Suu Kyi, 1991). Buddhists often correctly point to the early days of King Anawrahta's rule as the beginning of Theravada Buddhism in Myanmar. Still, the history of Myanmar's religious economy covers time before Anawrahta much beyond the story of Theravada Buddhism.

THE BEGINNING OF THE MYANMAR RELIGIOUS ECONOMY

The Pyu People

Myanmar's current religious economy began in a kingdom about 125 miles north of present-day Mandalay in the city of Tagaung (Aung Htin Muang, 1967). The city was built on a long-standing trade route between China and India that passed through northern Myanmar. From Tibeto-Burmese tribes came the earliest settlers, known by the Burmese term *Pyu*. The Pyu people journeyed from the southern slopes of the Tibetan mountains to northern Myanmar over a two-hundred-year period, around 128 BCE. In the Irrawaddy River basin, they built three walled cities with moats: Halin, Beikthano, and Sri Ksetra (Stargardt, 1991). From the remains of the Pyu people, archeologists have discovered texts and other iconography indicating that they derived their religious and intellectual history from India (Aung-Thwin, 2005).

The Pyu people practiced several religious ideas, including nat worship (Aung-Thwin, 2005, p. 34; Mendelson, 1961, p. 578). The burial terraces in Sri Ksetra show that religions with Indic inspiration became widespread among Pyu (Stargardt, 2016, p. 357). Archaeologists have found evidence of religious diversity among Pyu relics, including the widespread presence of animism, Tantrism, Buddhism, Mahayana Buddhism, and Hinduism (Ibrahim, 2016, p. 5; Aung-Thwin, 2005, p. 31; Stargardt, 1991; Mendelson, 1975). The Pyu people clearly had pluralistic religious preferences, practicing various religions, and allowing individuals to make religious choices that met their specific needs and preferences. That liberty appears in their diverse worship choices. Among the Pyu people's religious practices was nat (spirit) worship. The worship of nats developed out of Burmese folk religion, and many people in Myanmar still practice it today (Spiro, 2011; Nu, 1988; Brac de La Perrière, 1989; Moe, 2015). The Pyu worshiped many nats. As a pluralistic belief, multiple gods, or spirits (instead of only one) met the various needs of nat worshipers. The Pyu had not one religion to meet their spiritual needs; they had many.

Nat Worship and the Mahagiri Siblings

Nat worship originated with the Pyu out of a form of animism, which involves worshiping spirits called nats, the "spirits of earth and sky, rain and wind, whirlpool and whirlwind, of mountains, rivers, and trees, of jungles, and even of villages and houses" (Hall, 1955, p. 13). For example, the Pyu would worship the nats of a tree or a lake. Nats could be impersonal or local, and stories of thirty-six unique nats eventually became part of the whole country's religious economy. The thirty-six nats held distinct personages with individual histories and were widely worshiped (Spiro, 2011; Aung Htin Muang, 1958). Among the nats who came into existence, the most important are the nat siblings called Mahagiri Nats (DeCaroli, 2004; Temple, 1991; Spiro, 2011; Nu, 1988). Among the most revered nats, the Mahagiri siblings highlight a specific problem for early Myanmar kings and a critical reshaping of the religious economy.

The Glass Palace Chronicle of the Kings of Myanmar recounts the legend of the Mahagiri siblings (Pe Maung Tin and Luce, 1921). The brother, Min Mahagiri (Lord of the Great Mountain), and the sister, Shwe Myet Nha (Lady Golden Face) are still revered Myanmar nats who, like many nats, were once human and suffered tragic deaths before transforming into supernatural beings (Fink, 2013, p. 10; Nash, 1960). Min and his sister lived under a non-Burmese (Pyu) king, and all accounts portray them as handsome and well-liked young people. Min was a blacksmith famous for his incredible strength (he could wrestle a full-grown elephant) and gentle character. His sister, Shwe Myet Nha, was lovely and quite strong. Their king envied Min's strength and worried Min might usurp the throne. After some time, the king "commanded his ministers, saying, 'This man will rob me of my prosperity. Seize him and do away with him!'" (Pe Maung Tin and Luce, 1921, p. 45). Min learned of the king's plan and, fearing for his life, ran away to live deep in the jungle.

The Pyu king worried that Min might return, so he took Min's sister as his queen for protection. Years later, the king said to the queen, "Thy brother is a mighty man. Send for him straightaway, and I will make him governor of a town" (Pe Maung Tin and Luce, 1921, p. 45). The queen sent for her brother. Min believed that he could safely return because his sister was queen and because the king asked for his service. Upon his return, the jealous king had Min seized, bound to a saga tree, and burned to death. Hearing her brother's cries, the queen said, "Because of me, alas, my brother hath died!" She then threw herself into the flames and also died. After their death, the siblings became supernatural spirits and dwelt in a saga tree. The jealous king ordered the tree to be cut down and floated down the Irrawaddy River. Downriver, the Burmese king Thinligyaung of Bagan (344–387) had the tree pulled from the river. Next, he had images of the siblings carved into it and enshrined the Mahagiri nats on Mount Popa (Temple, 1991; Nu, 1988).

Over time, many people in these pre-Buddhist days started worshiping the Mahagiri nats as guardian spirits. At home, many people found comfort and value in presenting coconut offerings to Mahagiri nats (Fink, 2013, p. 11). The stories and powers of nats served the people, so nat-worship flourished. Eventually, the people who worshipped nats came to believe that the spirits had power (dominion) over certain groups of people and over specific objects and geographic areas. As guardians, the nats protected all people and territories that recognized them. While Pyu people worshipped nats, the religious economy in neighboring India welcomed a new religious firm, Buddhism.

Ashoka: The Ideal King Protects Buddhism

Considered one of the most significant figures in Indian history, the Indian King Ashoka is frequently mentioned by Myanmar's Buddhist monks today (personal communications, March 2016). Emperor Ashoka is revered and emulated as the archetype ruler in Myanmar (Lubina, 2021, p. 14). Feeling remorse for establishing his vast empire through bloody conquest (his conquest caused the deaths of about 100,000 people), Ashoka converted to Buddhism (Mendelson, 1975, p. 400). The personal choice of King Ashoka to convert to Buddhism is viewed by historians as a significant and important moment in world history (Thapar, 2004). Scholars debate the details of Ashoka's decision to convert to Buddhism (Strong, 1983). Some argue that the king's conversion to Buddhism was gradual. Over a period of several years, he was influenced by a combination of earlier Indic religions and guilt. Others argue that a guilty (due to his violent and despotic rule) and suffering King Ashoka converted in a more sudden moment of enlightenment (Thapar, 2004, p. 180). However long his conversion took, most scholars agree that he made a personal choice to convert to Buddhism because of a guilty conscience (Lamotte, 1988, p. 252). The version of Buddhism of King Ashoka was quite different from the Theravada tradition later found in Myanmar. Like most Indians, Ashoka's version of Buddhism was heavily influenced by earlier Indic religions (Strong, 1983, p. 160). During his long reign, Ashoka ruled according to Buddhist principles, widely promoted the religion, and became what many see as the ideal Buddhist king (Bechert, 1973, p. 87). Notably, however, King Ashoka did *not* close India's religious economy. Ashoka did not exclude other religious firms in his empire. Hinduism and other religious firms flourished along with Buddhism under Ashoka (DeCaroli, 2004).

With King Ashoka's support, Buddhism flourished in India, and he sent missionaries (firm representatives) far and wide to help people convert to Buddhism (Niharranjan, 1946, p. 84). Over time, the religion spread throughout the world. With state support, followers of the Theravada tradition spread the religion from India to Sri Lanka in the third century BCE (Berzin, 1996). In Sri Lanka, the missionaries successfully converted King Devanampiya Tissa to Buddhism. King Tissa supported the Buddhist religion by building a monastery, which became a central institution that promoted a version of Buddhism (Theravada Buddhism) that became the main religion in Sri Lanka.

King Ashoka is now considered the model king of the Buddhist literary tradition; Buddhist sermons and texts note the great care he took to enshrine the Buddha's relics in thousands of pagodas. In Buddhist literature, the Buddha himself commented on meritorious action taken by the Indian King: "King Dhammasoka will put [the parts of] my bones, my skin, and my flesh at the places where I lived in 84,000 reliquaries and zeidi" (Leider, 2009, p. 339). Indeed, many stupas, pagodas, and stone inscriptions across Southeast Asia indicate Ashoka's support of Buddhism (De and Chirathivat, 2018).

Ashoka also established another important precedent for the religious economy. In addition to promoting Buddhism, Ashoka also formalized state–Sangha relations by taking responsibility for the well-being of the Buddhist monastic community. Ashoka established the precedent of a Buddhist sociopolitical order, known as the "Two Wheels of the Dhamma" (Keyes, 2007, p. 148). King Ashoka's sociopolitical precedent makes the ruler responsible for the perpetuation and protection of the teachings of the Buddha (Keyes, 2007, p. 148). This sociopolitical relationship gave the state enormous power over the entire religious firm. Ashoka had a duty to act and, if necessary, the power to protect the "purity of the Sangha" (Bechert, 1973, p. 86). Historical inscriptions include Ashoka's "schism edict," which gave him the authority to purge the Sangha. Buddhist communities parallel other religious communities in that many (if not all) religious firms split into factions over disagreements. Naturally, disagreements occur over myriad issues: who is admitted to the Sangha, how to apply monastic rules, leadership, the existence of monastic properties, and, critically, interpretations of the Buddha's teachings. King Ashoka gave himself (the state) the authority to judge disagreements and bring harmony to the Buddhist religious community. This authority included the enormous political power to expel those monks unwilling to live according to Vinaya's rules as defined by the king/state. This action by the state became known as the "Śāsana reform" (Bechert, 1973, p. 86), which gave the state ultimate authority to purge monastic communities. Ashoka adamantly supported and controlled the Buddhist firm, and he sent representatives of Buddhism far and wide.

Theravada Buddhist Representatives Travel Widely

Ashoka sent the monk Mahinda to Ceylon Island, present-day Sri Lanka, to share the ideas of the Buddhist firm. Mahinda founded a thriving monastic community where the Pali Canon was first written (Keown, 2000). Mahinda's monastery in Ceylon and other missions from Ashoka spread Theravada Buddhism's ideas to the Pyu people in the north-central part of Myanmar (Keown, 2000). With the Pyu, Buddhism gained its first foothold in Southeast Asia. Over time, many Pyu people of all social classes—from the ruling elite to laborers and farmers—chose to practice Theravada Buddhism (Ibrahim, 2016, p. 5; Aung Htin Muang, 1967, p. 11). The religion met the spiritual needs of many Pyu people. Chinese historians noted that the Pyu people, as devout Theravada Buddhists, wore silk–cotton cloth instead of real silk because making silk involved taking life. The Pyu people built many monasteries, and children shaved their hair and became novices at the age of seven. Chinese historical records indicate that the Pyu had a great white statue of the Buddha one hundred feet tall, before which people made oaths and in which the Pyu king lit incense and took an oath to rule his people with justice (Aung Htin Muang, 1967). The trading networks linked the Pyu people to the rest of Southeast Asia, China, and India. Through these trade routes and connections, Buddhist firm representatives (monks) carried the Theravada Buddhist religion based on the Pali Canon to other parts of Southeast Asia's religious market. In the Pyu community, they found an open market with people who widely shared their ideas.

The Open Religious Economy of the Pyu People

The Pyu had an open and unregulated religious economy that did not force people to practice one specific religion. Like many people around the world, the Pyu commonly practiced a combination of religious beliefs. Archaeologists have discovered that many Pyu people practiced non-Theravada routines, such as ceremonial cattle sacrifice and regular alcohol consumption (Aung Htin Muang, 1967). Compelling evidence of Hindu and Mahayana Buddhism has been found in the ruins of the Pyu city of Sri Ksetra (Mendelson, 1975, p. 35; Aung Htin Muang, 1967). The Pyu's religious practices resulted from interactions between pre-Buddhist nat-like practices and, later, Buddhist influences from India (Aung-Thwin, 2005, p. 30; Stargardt, 1991; Mendelson, 1975, p. 33). In the religious marketplace of Pyu cities lived an eclectic group of monastics called Ari monks.

The Ari Monks

Among the Pyu lived the Ari monks, a religious subgroup (Mendelson, 1961, p. 578). Ari monks practiced a rich and interesting blend of religious ideas that combined elements of Mahāyāna Buddhism, nat worship, Hinduism, and other folk-religion practices (Coedes, 2015). The Ari also presided over many nat spirit festivals (Aung Htin Muang, 1958). Not much more is known about the Ari, but the Burmese king's courts described them in less than favorable terms (DeCaroli, 2004, p. 151). The founding Burmese king clearly did not like the Ari monks, who are described as heretical Buddhist forest-dwelling monks who regularly consumed alcohol, engaged in sexual relations, and ate after noon (Coedes, 2015; Mendelson, 1975, p. 36; Aung Htin Muang, 1967). The *Glass Palace Chronicle* states that Ari monks worshipped Naga (serpent) and made the fatal mistake of falsifying (holding a different interpretation of) the Buddhist texts (Mendelson, 1975, p. 36; Mendelson, 1961). The Ari monks had an antagonistic relationship with Myanmar's founding king, Anawrahta, so this description raises some suspicion (DeCaroli, 2004, p. 152; Mendelson, 1975). Whether the Ari monks were as King Anawrahta described remains a matter of debate. However, people do not debate the precedent the king established, giving himself and the state significant power and authority over religion. The state could now decide who to keep and who to purge.

The First Myanmar King Inherits a Liberal Religious Economy

In the waning years of the Pyu city-states, the region became unstable; several struggles ensued for the throne, for power, and for changes in control. When Anawrahta was a young boy, his father had to give up the throne and become a monk (Aung Htin Muang, 1967). When Anawrahta came of age, he successfully challenged the man who forced his father from the throne. He offered the throne to his father (now a monk), but his father declined. Anawrahta was a strict disciplinarian and a strong and charismatic leader who penalized even slight disobedience with death. He quickly established a large army whose exploits appeared in legends and folktales throughout Southeast Asia and beyond. Anawrahta unified the entire Irrawaddy valley for the first time in Myanmar's history (Aung Htin Muang, 1967). Even with his military success, Anawrahta was unhappy with his new kingdom's religious economy. His new kingdom's people widely worshiped nats and "coexisted and or coalesced with various religions of Indian origin, including several Hindu sects and both Theravada and Mahayana Buddhism" (Niharranjan, 1946, p. 149; Smith, 1965, p. 12). Scholars call this blending or fusion of different religions and practices from diverse sources *syncretism* (Leopold and Jensen, 2005, p. 14).

Anawrahta had three concerns about this pluralistic liberal religious market. First, he disapproved of the common fusion or blending of Hindu, Mahayana Buddhism, and native folk religions (Mendelson, 1975; Aung Htin Muang, 1967). Second, his power was challenged by the nats (Fink, 2013, p. 11). Third, he resented the religious prestige and authority of the Ari monks (DeCaroli, 2004; Aung Htin Muang, 1967). In the first ten years of his reign, the young king addressed each of these religious concerns.

KING ANAWRAHTA AND SHIN ARAHAN CLOSE THE MYANMAR RELIGIOUS ECONOMY

Using reward and punishment as social control tools, King Anawrahta took four steps to regulate his new kingdom's religious economy and to solve what he saw as his kingdom's religious problems. Following Ashoka's example, Anawrahta entangled religious and state powers (Aung-Thwin, 2012, p. 83). Specifically, the founding Burmese king linked the support and protection of one religion with the legitimacy of the state, and thus his legitimacy. To create this link, Anawrahta first dealt with the nats. Second, he purged the Ari monks. Third, he largely eliminated religious diversity and the theological divisions within his chosen religion of Theravada Buddhism. Fourth, and critically, the king financially linked the state to Theravada Buddhism to further control his religious economy (Aung-Thwin, 2012, p. 84; Aung-Thwin, 1979). These four actions established a highly regulated religious economy along with structural precedents and policies that people still, to some degree, follow in Myanmar today.

King Anawrahta's Nat Problem

The nat religion met the specific needs of many people and flourished in Anawrahta's young kingdom (DeCaroli, 2004). Even with the introduction of other religious ideas, strong nat beliefs remained in the culture and were often combined with new religious ideas from India and elsewhere. King Anawrahta found that Theravada Buddhism had significant competition from nat worship and Brahminical Hinduism on one side and Mahayana Buddhism on the other (Niharranjan, 1946, p. 150). But Theravada Buddhism had something the other religions did not: a devoted king and the resources of the state (Niharranjan, 1946, p. 150).

The powerful nats represented a challenge to Anawrahta's authority. The nats held dominion over people and territory, so they held power and control that King Anawrahta desired (Fink, 2013, p. 11; Moe, 2015, p. 126). In short, the powers of the nats rivaled those of the founding king. At first, King Anawrahta tried to eradicate nat-worship by ordering the destruction of all nat shrines (Moe, 2015, p. 126). Fearing the king, people removed their nat shrines from public, but they kept them within their houses. The indigenous and ancient nat religious firm was too firmly established to completely eradicate (Smith, 1965, p. 14; Niharranjan, 1946, p. 150).

Making a substantial first step toward closing his new country's religious economy, King Anawrahta changed nat worship. First, he created a new nat (and thus changed the religion) by adding a new spirit to the existing thirty-six (Aung Htin Muang, 1958). The king announced that this new spirit, Thagymin, would be the guardian god of Buddhism and act as the head spirit (Smith 1965, p. 14). To further harness the nats' powers, Anawrahta had images of all thirty-seven nats sculpted into wood and then chained in a cave to signify that he held their powers under his firm control (Fink, 2013).

Like many future state leaders, Anawrahta used religion to shape his image and power. Recognizing the nats' success and popularity, Anawrahta employed the spirits to further reshape the religious economy. He promoted nat worship and Buddhism by allowing nats in Buddhist places of worship. State policy supported the convergence of animist beliefs with Theravada Buddhist beliefs. Anawrahta shaped the religious marketplace by helping people make a switch: "Men will not come for the sake of new faith. Let them come for their old gods, and gradually they will be won over" (Smith, 1965, p. 14).

With the nats under control and ensconced in Buddhist temples, Myanmar's founding king turned to remedy his two other concerns about the religious economy. Serendipitously, a young Theravada Buddhist monk named Shin Arahan arrived in Pagan from the lower region of the country. The young monk and the king would forge a powerful partnership that shaped Myanmar's religious economy for centuries (Aung-Thwin, 1979; Mendelson, 1975).

King Anawrahta's Ari Monk Problem

Upon arrival, the young firebrand monk Shin Arahan presented himself to King Anawrahta as a strict and "pure" Theravada Buddhist. Arahan vigorously disapproved of any other religious ideas—even variations of Theravada Buddhism (Luce and Ba Shin, 1970). Interestingly and unsurprisingly, some scholars offer evidence that the variation of Theravada Buddhism that Arahan practiced included elements from the Hindu religion (Mendelson, 1975).

In 1057, not long after he arrived in Pagan, the devoutly religious young monk converted King Anawrahta to his "pure" version of Theravada Buddhism from the version the deviant Ari monks practiced (Niharranjan, 1946, p. 76). After learning about Theravada Buddhism from Arahan, Anawrahta said, "Master, we have no other refuge than thee! From this day forth, my master, we dedicate our body and our life to thee! And Master, from thee I take my doctrine" (Niharranjam, 1946, p. 78). King Anawrahta chose his faith—Theravada Buddhism. With his newfound faith, Arahan by his side, and religious zeal, King Anawrahta set out to change, regulate, and control his kingdom's religious economy. The king and Myanmar's first government-monk (a monk who exhibited loyalty to the state) became perfect partners, and each had his own source of power (Mendelson, 1975, p. 283). The monk found a ruler who provided him with the power, status, and prestige he needed to promote his religious ideas. From the monk, the king gained the legitimacy and power of religious authority to help rule his kingdom and to legitimately force the Ari monks and the entire Pagan religious economy to change.

The king soon made Arahan official, appointing him *Thathanabaing* (primate or highest-ranking clergy) of the Pagan empire. The Thathanabaing (literally "owner or keeper of the religion") advised the king; however, since a Theravada Buddhist monk "theoretically had nothing to do with politics or things of this world, [the king] was really the political power, the only permanent power" (Furnivall, 1946, p. 200). The king ruled with the support of his government monk (Mendelson 1975, pp. 53–57).

In his new position, Arahan (like King Anawrahta) was a ruthless and strict disciplinarian. The monk did not tolerate any departure from his interpretation of Theravada Buddhist practices. In short, Arahan did not approve of the Ari monks and labeled them heretics. Arahan labeled the Ari monks as a deviant religious group. Of course, it is likely that the Ari monks were simply a faction within the existing Sangha whose practices were not considered orthodox by Shin Arahan (Mendelson, 1975, p. 36). Anawrahta and Arahan saw a Sangha that needed purification, and they had political and religious reasons for purging the Ari monks. With King Anawrahta's authority, Arahan proceeded to "persecute the heretics" (Aung-Thwin, 1979, p. 673).

Using state power, the monk executed the leaders of the Ari monks and then conscripted lower-ranking monks into the king's military service. The king and the monk eliminated the Ari-monk religious ideas from the marketplace and set a precedent by intervening in Sangha affairs and reforming the religion. The king and his appointed keeper of religion made a religious choice for the Myanmar people. The king ruled on interpretations of the tenets of the religion, on monastic rules, and on the organizational structure of the Sangha. The king decided important matters (Bechert, 1970, p. 87). With this enormous power, śāsana reform (the purification of the Sangha) has become an unsurprisingly endemic and common cycle in Myanmar's history (Mendelson, 1975, p. 50–53; Bechert, 1970, p. 88).

King Anawrahta and Shin Arahan Establish a State Religion

After the Ari monks were purged, the king and his religious partner, the monk, further reshaped the religious marketplace using education to promote their religious product and eliminate other religious ideas. Under the king's authority, Arahan sent monks he had trained to villages and communities throughout the kingdom to establish Theravada Buddhist monasteries and schools. These monasteries and schools provided foundational Theravada Buddhist literacy for generations of students. Villagers depended on monks for schooling and spiritual guidance, and the monks relied on villagers for food and basic needs, which yielded unprecedented levels of Buddhist knowledge and practice of Theravada Buddhism across Anawrahta's religious economy. Over time, the available options (i.e., the number of religious firms) in the religious marketplace narrowed to only Shin Arahan's version of Theravada Buddhism (with tolerance of nats for practical reasons). Shin Arahan served as the head of the Buddhist Sangha under four Pagan kings, from King Anawrahta to King Alaungsithu in 1115. Next, King Anawrahta financially linked the state to Theravada Buddhism (Aung-Thwin, 2012, p. 84).

Financially Linking the State and Religion

Support of religion often means control of religion (Fox, 2016a) because support (especially financial support) is often a tool of control. One of the most effective ways to regulate a religious economy is by financially supporting religion (Coşgel and Miceli, 2009; Demerath, 2001; Grim and Finke, 2010). King Anawrahta's support made Shin Arahan and Theravada Buddhism highly dependent on and accountable to the king, who gained the influence and power he lacked over independent and free Ari Buddhists (Fox, 2016a, p. 455). To deepen his control and influence, the king built temples, pagodas, and monasteries across Pagan and many remain today (Hudson, 2008, p. 554). Of course, the gifts of land, temples, and monasteries left the Sangha indebted to the king. However, the Sangha's accumulation of property also created a problem for Myanmar's kings (Aung-Thwin, 1979, p. 672).

With wealth and time, the Buddhist firm grew powerful. Weber termed this Sangha-owned land system "monastic landlordism" (Cady, 1958, p. 257). Although the king still owned the properties, he could not simply reclaim them because they had been donated to the Buddhist firm. The Sangha held the power. To solve this problem and regain some of the land and wealth in a socially acceptable manner, Myanmar kings regularly initiated King Ashoka's policy of śāsana reform (Aung-Thwin, 1979, p. 672). The king's enormous power to purge the monastic community gave the state full control of the religion and the entire religious economy. A purge gave the king control of wealth, land, and resources once held by the religion, along with the authority to eliminate entire monasteries and those he considered rebels, pretenders, or political opponents. The king could merely say the Sangha (or a specific subgroup) no longer followed the Vinaya (the rules and procedures that govern the monastic community, or Sangha) to make reform ideologically justifiable (Aung-Thwin, 1979, p. 672).

Financial support, along with the śāsana reform power, kept the Buddhist firm under state control. The kings—from Ashoka to Anawrahta to the last Burmese king, Thibaw—supported and controlled the religious economy and, specifically, Theravada Buddhism. These kings' policies and actions have become a codified part of the culture (see the "special position of

Buddhism" in Article 361 of the 2008 Myanmar Constitution) taught to generations of Myanmar students (Fink, 2018, p. 273). In the present, since February 2021, Myanmar rulers, following this precedent, have eliminated twenty Buddhist monasteries they deemed deviant. King law is an integral part of Myanmar governing culture today. Importantly, Bagshawe (Yaw Mingyi U Hpo Hlaing, 2004) translated Rajadhammasangaha, (king law) a text that was composed to educate the young King Thibaw, in December of 1878.

King Law: Supporting and Protecting Buddhism

When King Mindon died in 1878, his prominent advisor U Hpo Hlaing authored a book called the *Rajadhammasangaha* (a compendium of king law; Yaw Mingyi U Hpo Hlaing, 2004). The word *raja* means "monarch" or "ruler," but the term *dhamma* (in Pali) has several meanings. Here, it means "law" or "things as they should be" (Huxley, 2007, p. 26). In this usage, the word *sangha* means "a collection." Thus, the *Rajadhammasangaha* is a "collection of king law." *Rajadhamma* records the values and norms of the Pali Buddhists regarding the ethics and practices of kings. It has become a revered Buddhist social contract between the government and the people (Huxley, 2007, p. 27). The king-laws in the *Rajadhamma* were deeply entrenched in Myanmar's culture for well over two thousand years by the time U Hpo Hlaing recorded them (Huxley, 2007, p. 28).

Today, monastic and public schools and universities in Myanmar teach this king-law. Secondary students study a moral code, titled Lawkathara-Pyo, written by a Buddhist monk, Kandawminkyaung Has Ya Daw. Students memorize moral virtues for laypeople and royal virtues for kings or rulers. These virtues emphasize order, unity, and the absolute authority of the king's order (Chaw Chaw Sein, personal communications, March 2016). Students at Yangon University in the 1970s and 1980s were required to learn king-law and many of those students are in positions of leadership in Myanmar today (Chaw Chaw Sein, personal communication, April 6, 2020). To complete their core course requirements in 2016, students at Mandalay and Yangon University had to pass an examination in which they recounted large passages of the *Rajadhammasangaha* (Sterken, 2016).

The monarchy system collapsed under British colonial rule, but the deep-rooted virtues and religion remain. Myanmar's modern history is filled with generals who employ the tenets of this king-law. The coup leader in 2021, General Min Aung Hlaing, rose unremarkably in a hermetically sealed world with the Myanmar military elite (Thant Myint-U, 2020, p. 132). In that sealed-off world, he learned king-law and, like generals before him, acted as if he were king. Following the generals before him, Min Aung Hlaing has evoked Myanmar's royal past to legitimize his own rule. Seated in power in the capital, Naypyidaw, the "seat of kings," Myanmar's generals attempt to evoke the traditions and authority of the royal past. There are many physical references throughout Naypyidaw to the king-law narrative of history. In 2005, the military government erected giant statues of three of Myanmar's most famous kings, Anawrahta, Bayinnaung (1551–1581), and Alaungpaya (1752–1760). These kings tower over the military parade grounds and serve as the backdrop of many photos of Myanmar's military leaders (Cockett, 2015, p. 69).

The Duties of the Kings of Buddhism

The social contract in the king-law is detailed, difficult to read, and exhaustive, but it encompasses important values, norms, and guiding principles about regulating the religious economy. The *Rajadhamma* includes "Ten Duties of Kings," "Seven Safeguards Against Decline," "Four Assistances to the People," "Twelve Practices of Rulers," "Six Attributes of Leaders," "Eight Virtues of Kings," and "Four Ways to Overcome Peril." In her book *Freedom from Fear*, Aung San Suu Kyi outlined the critical importance of the *Rajadhamma's* "Ten Duties of Government"—specifically, that a government governs best "through the observance of the dhamma" (Aung San Suu Kyi, 1991, p. 169). The *Rajadhamma* states that a good king and government adhere to and practice those teachings, laws, customs, and duties. Suu Kyi wrote, "When the king does not observe the dhamma, state functionaries become corrupt, and when state functionaries are corrupt, the people are caused much suffering" (1991, p. 171). Suu Kyi also wrote that "the Ten Duties of Kings are widely known and generally accepted as a yardstick which could be applied just as well to modern government as the first monarch of the world" (1991, pp. 169–73).

The *Rajadhamma* references religion thirty-five times, detailing the state's duties and responsibilities toward Buddhism. Four examples from the Rajadhamma exemplify its impact on the religious economy. First, U Hpo Hlaing wrote: "King Mindon hoped to be regarded and honoured as the supporter of the religion in a quite special way, beyond all other kings" (2004). If we look at the essentials, we see a rule instituting a basic disposition to preserve Myanmar's culture and its peoples' traditions. Second, in the section on "Burma's Native Democracy," Hpo Hlaing included seven rules for "not causing decay" in society that directly relate to regulating the religious economy (2004). The last two rules—respecting spirit guardians and protecting the monkhood—express a state–religion policy. The power to protect includes the power to shape and control. Third, in the section on finances and the treasury, the king-law details specific instructions for governmental spending. In those instructions, "the King [is] expected to provide without fail monthly and yearly support to monasteries, pagodas, scriptural publications, to monks, novices, devout laymen and thila shins [nuns]" (Yaw Mingyi U Hpo Hlaing, 2004). As noted above, financial support constitutes a significant state power. Finally, the text notes in several places and in several ways that kings should "take care of the religious order" (Yaw Mingyi U Hpo Hlaing, 2004). The king laws set down in the Rajadhamma codify expectations and an entangled relationship between Theravada Buddhism and the government. The state is expected to regulate the religious economy in a way that protects and supports Theravada Buddhism, and this expectation encoded the illiberal culture of a closed religious marketplace in Myanmar.

CONCLUSIONS

Why has Theravada Buddhism historically enjoyed a huge share of Myanmar's religious market? State protection and support enabled the Theravada Buddhist firm to emerge completely triumphant and wipe out even the memory of its rivals (Niharranjan, 1946, p. 151). In short, the decisions about the religious economy made during the Pagan period still shape Myanmar's people and politics. Myanmar's religious economy is founded on a structure, culture, and narrative that began in the ninth century under Pagan kings. In support of a state religion, kings during the Pagan period built more than ten thousand Buddhist stupas, temples, and pagodas, more than two thousand of which remain today. Theravada Buddhism became the dominant religious faith for people of the Pagan kingdom and remains so today. Some kings from the Pagan period are today memorialized via imposing statutes in the present capital of Naypyidaw. Historians commonly view the success of King Anawrahta and Shin Arahan as a critical turning point in the history of Theravada Buddhism. The powerful king's partnership with the pious Theravada monk is widely credited with saving the Theravada school, which had been declining in India (DeCaroli, 2004, p. 151). Anawrahta "was the first king to establish Burmese rule over much of the country," wrote Aung San Suu Kyi, "He was also the man who did the most to promote Theravada Buddhism among the Burmese" (1991, p. 46).

King Ashoka supported Buddhism, but also allowed other religious firms to operate freely in India. The result of this market freedom is that the people of India have largely chosen to practice the Hindu faith, and there are also large populations of Muslims, Christians, Sikhs, Buddhists, Jains, and Animism (Majumdar, 2018). In contrast, in the founding of Myanmar, King Anawrahta selected, promoted, and supported Theravada Buddhism and used the state's power to regulate and reshape the Pyu religious economy. The Pyu history and Anawrahta's decision to support a religion and to regulate the religious economy highlight religion's effects upon Myanmar politics and the effects of politics on religion. The seamless connection between religion and the state was created and nurtured by

Myanmar's kings. Entanglement was a decision of social control made by and for the benefit of the state.

The Pyu civilization included religious pluralism. As noted in the previous chapter, religious preferences are pluralistic; people need and want different religious ideas. Some Pyu people choose nats, some choose Hindu, and others choose variations of Buddhism. Gradually, however, the Pyu people, Ari monks, nats, and a culture of religious pluralism came under the state's control. The pluralism and open religious marketplace that the Pyu civilization enjoyed for more than a thousand years had closed, either vanquishing or altering the religious ideas of the Ari monks, nats, and other Indic religions.

Myanmar's early history established precedents for the religious economy. Broadly, Anawrahta designated a state religion by officially selecting, supporting, and establishing Theravada Buddhism. The king and his religious partner started the pattern of a ruler who held secular and religious authority. Anawrahta made it clear that no religion controlled the state and that the state controlled Theravada Buddhism. That power and control allowed kings to close and regulate the religious economy.

As another powerful tool of social control, Anawrahta clarified that Burmese kings could select the top monks and purge the religion. If a king did not like something about the religious community, he could purge the community and reshape it to fit his needs and desires. With this power, Anawrahta and the kings who followed undermined the independence of the chosen religion and assumed the power and responsibility of shaping the behavior and practices of the Buddhist Sangha.

Anawrahta took steps to limit the religious marketplace and to change the very content of religions. The king used his authority to reshape the nat religion by adding a head nat and to reshape Theravada Buddhism by including nats in Buddhist temples. As Milton, Locke, and Jefferson argued, a state that can regulate its religious economy can reshape or corrupt the content and product of its religious firms (Gill, 2007, pp. 47–53; Cousins, 1958).

Since Anawrahta, Myanmar kings and generals have used Theravada Buddhism to gain legitimacy. Supporting and controlling the religious marketplace gave kings a powerful source of legitimacy. Burmese kings, with leading monks as partners, supported the Theravada Buddhist religious firm and product by building temples and monasteries, by acquiring and honoring relics of the Buddha, and by implementing monastic purges and reforms. Kings and monks both expressed real power and authorized or legitimized the other's political actions. Myanmar's generals have tried to employ this power but have not had the king's level of success.

The people of Myanmar's kingdoms had few choices of religious ideas in the Pagan religious marketplace. The king-controlled Theravada Buddhism, which readily helped normalize the king's legitimacy and compliance with his rule (Hurd, 1999, p. 381). Burmese kings' politics often required dealing with and bestowing favors upon the Sangha to secure popular legitimacy for their decisions. The legitimacy of both the king and the Buddhist Sangha was derived from the state religion.

The king's financial support (especially when combined with the power to purge) dramatically altered and regulated the religious economy. The new state-supported firm took over minority firms (nats), and others (Hindu) were put out of business. With financial support (building tens of thousands of temples, monasteries, and stupas), the state gained and maintained control over a religious firm. Myanmar's people came to expect the government to support and control the dominant religion. Ruler support led to the entanglement of the Buddhist firm and the state. The Buddhist firm used the power of the state to protect Buddhism. In return, the Buddhist firm legitimized the ruler. The entanglement of power established a state religion (Lewy, 1974, p. 28).

King Ashoka, King Anawrahta, Shin Arahan, and subsequent rulers established precedents that became entrenched and widely followed historical values in Myanmar's society and government. Myanmar's rulers (kings and modern generals) appear to have ruled on the idea that the merit they earned through moral acts (building pagodas and protecting the Buddhist firm) would outweigh any immoral deeds they committed. Following King Ashoka, the ends justify their actions, and their devotion, protection, and support of Theravada Buddhism made up for their actions.

The relationship between Burmese kings and the Sangha depended on the balance of power. A stronger king could control the Sangha more and a wealthier Sangha could influence the king more (Mendelson, 1975, p. 53). Over time, these relationships, precedents, and values shaped the Myanmar people's values and norms regarding government (rulers or kings). Anawrahta and almost all subsequent kings and governments took control of the religious economy. Myanmar's kings, from Anawrahta to King Thibaw (1878–1885), assumed the responsibility and power of being Theravada Buddhism's noble patron. These governing authorities promoted Theravada Buddhism, and it flourished while most other religious ideas withered.

These historical values and norms gradually became entrenched in Myanmar, along with a widespread acceptance of Theravada Buddhism. Many kings and kingdoms between Anawrahta (1044) and King Mindon (1853) established values and norms for the government and the monastic community and for overseeing the structure and integrity of Myanmar's religious economy. King Mindon, one of Myanmar's most popular and revered kings, further highlighted the state's relationship with Theravada Buddhism in 1868 by having a 729-page book, the *Pali Canon*, inscribed in marble. Today, each stone slab (or page) is individually housed in its own small stupa in the Kuthodaw Pagoda at the foot of Mandalay Hill. Burmese kings gave the Theravada Buddhist firm a special status and prominence that it still enjoys today. Thus, Myanmar has had a mostly closed and highly regulated religious economy since 1057, when Anawrahta and Arahan teamed up to capture the market. Due to this state-created dominance, the most important individuals, events, institutions, religious ideas, and places in Myanmar's history have been identified with Theravada Buddhism, excluding all other religious firms.

Did Theravada Buddhism win the hearts and minds of the Pagan people over other religious ideas? Yes and no—many Pyu people chose Buddhism, but the religious marketplace closed in 1057, and the king chose for the people. Evidence indicates that Theravada Buddhism has maintained its cultural dominance through the power of the state—not by the people's choice. After 1057, the people of Myanmar had far fewer choices. The specific version of Theravada Buddhism supported by the king and the state-appointed and supported leadership of the Buddhist firm enjoyed a near complete religious monopoly. While the religious preferences in the society were clearly pluralistic, the king and his "keeper of religion" established an extremely high level of regulation. Together, they reshaped the options in the religious marketplace and corrupted the religious economy.

Deep historical factors structured Myanmar's religious economy to favor one specific religion. Ashoka and Anawrahta's state-religion policy provides the model for today's rulers of Myanmar and set the norm for the relationship between the Buddhist firm and the state (Lubina, 2021, p. 118). From 1057 forward, religion and nationality became one phenomenon. People who lived under Anawrahta and successive kings were socialized to see Theravada Buddhism as the central feature of their religious, social, cultural, and political existence because their religious economy held few choices. The kings, the Buddhist firm, and the larger Myanmar moral community suppressed any religious deviance. After centuries of this socialization, many of Myanmar's people have difficulty separating the state from Buddhism (Neo, Jamal, and Goh, 2019, pp. 1–4). For Myanmar's followers of Theravada Buddhism, the religion has a social and political function along with a spiritual function. For many Myanmar people, this ancient religion–state entanglement came to mean that a citizen of Myanmar is Buddhist.

What if King Anawrahta had decided, like Ashoka, to allow other religious firms to exist and to freely operate? What choices might the Myanmar people have made? Would nat worship flourish? What would have happened in Myanmar if the state had taken an open, liberal, and neutral approach to its religious economy? An answer to this question began to emerge in November 1885, when Colonel Edward Bosc Sladen, the British chief political officer, entered Mandalay's royal palace to receive King Thibaw's submission.

2

✦

The Golden Shore
An Experiment in Religious Freedom 1824–1948

Imagine, for a moment, the beautiful city of Mandalay. Founded in 1857 by King Mindon on the east bank of the Irrawaddy River about 450 miles north of Yangon, Mandalay was Myanmar's last royal capital. Mandalay holds the stunning Kuthodaw Pagoda (mentioned in the previous chapter) where King Mindon supported Theravada Buddhism by having the entire Pali Canon inscribed in marble and housed in ornate white stupas. Scholarly and devoutly Buddhist (he spent most of his adult life in a Buddhist monastery before ascending to the throne), Mindon became one of Myanmar's most popular and revered kings. Mindon ruled Upper Myanmar in the peaceful years before the British colonized Upper Myanmar. During his reign, Mindon was highly involved in Upper Myanmar's religious economy. As king, he purged the Buddhist monastic community, required all monks to vow to adhere to the Vinaya code of discipline, and over three years, produced a new edition of the Pali Canon (Prebish, 2004). Importantly, while clearly supporting Buddhism, Mindon temporarily opened the religious market in his kingdom to a Christian missionary and to a small group of representatives of Islam known as the Panthays (Keck, 2016, p. 45; Purser, 1911, p. 117). In the 1860s, the Muslim inhabitants of Yunnan—the southwestern Chinese province that borders Myanmar—began migrating to Mandalay for safety and security (Yegar, 1966, p. 76). King Mindon allowed the Panthays to settle in the community and to work in his court as jade assessors (Maung, 2007, p. 52). King Mindon also permitted building a mosque on land he granted to the Panthays (Keck, 2016, p. 55; Maung, 2007, p. 54). After Mindon died in 1878, his son, Thibaw, succeeded him. King Thibaw would be Myanmar's last king.

THE EXPEDITION TO UPPER BURMA—EX-KING THEEBAW BEING REMOVED FROM HIS PALACE AT MANDALAY TO THE BRITISH SHIPS

Figure 2.1. Vintage engraving of Third Anglo-Burmese War, Defeated King Thibaw Min escorted by British soldiers from his Palace at Mandalay, 19th Century. *Source*: duncan1890/DigitalVision Vectors Via Getty Images

ABRUPT SHOCK TO THE RELIGIOUS ECONOMY

In a series of three wars beginning in 1824, the British colonized Myanmar. The last kingship in Myanmar abruptly ended in Mandalay in the late afternoon of November 29, 1885, when Colonel Edward Bosc Sladen, the British chief political officer, entered the royal palace and received King Thibaw's submission (Sladen, 1849). Several hundred British soldiers unceremoniously escorted the king and his royal party (including Supayalat [Thibaw's queen and half-sister] their three young daughters, other close family members, several ministers of state, and servants) in an ox-drawn cart to a steamship on the Irrawaddy River (Thant Myint-U, 2001). Burmese kings had traditionally traveled in pomp along this road south of the city: "The Burmese populace, men and women watched him along the course and, lamenting and grieving their loss, cried, 'They are taking away our King,' and kept on wiping away the tears from their eyes" (Chain, 2015, p. 24). British rule and the departure of the last king brought many changes and challenges to Myanmar's people and to religions of the land. Under British rule, the religious economy that had for centuries fully supported Theravada Buddhism collapsed. British rule allowed Baptist, Muslim, Methodist,

Catholic, Hindu, Baha'i, and other missionaries to widely share their beliefs in a land once monopolized by the Theravada Buddhist firm. What did abolishing a state religion mean for the larger society, the Buddhist community, minority religious firms, and religious participation?

British rule forced three substantial structural changes in Myanmar's religious economy. First, the British administrators encoded a uniform rule of law that applied to all people—including the Buddhist Sangha and its hierarchy. Second, the British adopted a liberal and neutral stance to religion, thus empowering previously repressed religious minority groups. British rule allowed Muslim, Christian, and other missionary entrepreneurs to compete with a weakened Buddhist establishment. As discussed below, Baptist, Muslim, and Methodist missionaries (and representatives of other Christian groups and of Baha'ism and Hinduism) arrived in Myanmar almost immediately after King Thibaw's fall (Egreteau, 2011, p. 35). In the years just before and during British rule, two missionaries, Adoniram Judson Jr. and 'Abd al-Khaliq, shared their religious beliefs with Myanmar's people. Third, the colonial rulers established and promoted a secular education system. In Myanmar's precolonial religious economy, Buddhist monastic schools offered primary education for all Burmese young people and that education supported the Buddhist religious firm. Under colonial rule, the Buddhist Sangha's educational objectives, worldviews, and political goals collided with those of the British, and British attempts to reform education in Myanmar highlighted Theravada Buddhism's monopoly in the religious economy and largely led to the rise of Buddhist religious nationalism. These three profound structural changes to state–religion policy (a uniform rule of law, a neutral stance toward religion, and secular education) ignited the fires of religious nationalism in Myanmar for the first time. Many Burmese people saw these policy changes as an attack on their culture, on their traditional values, and specifically on Buddhism (Turner, 2014, p. 2).

RULE OF LAW AND LIBERAL NEUTRALITY

The King Is an Absolute Sovereign

Before British colonization, individual kings had ruled Myanmar and established the rules and laws of the land. Ann Hasseltine Judson, one of the first American Baptist missionaries in Myanmar, noted in 1822 that the King of Myanmar "is an absolute sovereign, and is regarded as the sole lord and proprietor of life and property in his dominions; and without the concurrence of any, his word is irresistible law" (Judson, 1823, p. 2). As discussed in chapter 1, the king's authority and legitimacy depended upon how much leading Buddhist monks and, to some degree, the Myanmar people accepted his rules and laws. Under Myanmar kings, the Buddhist Sangha operated within a well-regulated hierarchy. As noted in chapter 1, the king appointed the most senior Buddhist cleric/primate, called the *Thathanabaing*. In turn, the Thathanabaing appointed regional officials and other lower-ranking monastic leaders. This arrangement gave political authority to the Sangha and legitimacy to the king. Under this monastic hierarchy, social control of the entire country was vested with the king and his appointed Buddhist monks. Schisms, factions, minority religions, and leaders were ignored at best and, at worst, severely repressed.

With the king's approval, the Thathanabaing held authority over top appointments, disputes in the Sangha, punishing monks who violated the Vinaya, interpreting the Vinaya, and generally maintaining order and discipline in the monastic community. He enforced disciplinary decisions with law enforcement officers appointed by the king. This power relationship served the Sangha, the Buddhist religion, and the king, but did not allow for an open marketplace of religious ideas. The king enjoyed legitimacy derived from religion and social control of the Myanmar society, and the Sangha enjoyed the promotion, protection, support, and legitimacy offered by the king—along with monopolistic power over the religious marketplace.

With the support of the king, Buddhism and the appointed Sangha were the legitimate and favored religion in the country while other religious firms and communities struggled to exist. This arrangement (state–religion policy) between a religion and the king gave the Buddhist Sangha and the king substantial influence and power over Burmese society. With the deposition of King Thibaw, British rulers immediately disrupted that power structure. British administrators imposed a legal system with laws enforced fairly equally against all people and took a neutral or "liberal" position toward religion, neither supporting nor controlling Buddhism or any other religion. Under the British, the Sangha no longer oversaw the civil or criminal behavior of the monastic order, and monks became subject to laws, police, and courts just like any citizen (Smith, 1965, p. 47).

Liberal/Neutral State–Religion Policy

In response to the 1857 Sepoy Rebellion in India, Queen Victoria moved to avoid a troubling entanglement with religious matters in the British colonies. An 1858 proclamation outlined the imperial policy of respect for all religions:

> Firmly relying ourselves of the truth of Christianity, and acknowledging with gratitude the solace of religion, we disclaim alike the right and the desire to impose our convictions on any of our subjects. We declare that it be our royal will and pleasure that none be in any wise favoured, none molested or disquieted, by reason of their religious faith or observances, but that all shall alike

enjoy the equal and impartial protection of the law; and we do strictly charge and enjoin all those who may be in authority under us that they abstain from all interference with the religious belief or worship of any of our subjects on pain of our highest displeasure. (Smith, 1965, p. 42)

Burmese Buddhists, especially Sangha members, did not see the British queen's policy position as neutral. In fact, British state–religion policy was not entirely liberal or neutral. Crouch points out that British rule in Myanmar codified the customs and traditions of local religious communities (2016a, p. 69). A few years after annexing Upper Myanmar, the British imposed a system of personal law for Muslims nearly identical in substance to the law constructed by colonial authorities in British India (Crouch, 2016a, p. 69)

After centuries of favoritism and support, the British neutral state–religion policy appeared overtly hostile to Buddhism. The Sangha saw the British authorities' lack of support as an injury to Buddhism because of Buddhism's continuous need for protection and support. The Sangha members widely believed that monks would decline into immoral behavior without state support and authoritative oversight. Many Buddhists saw the state as ultimately responsible for the śāsana's health and for preserving Buddhist teachings (Turner, 2014, p. 28; Braun, 2013, p. 66).

The British rule over Myanmar brought an abrupt shock to the state's religious economy. The British disrupted a religious marketplace that was monopolized by the king and by Theravada Buddhism, creating a new "liberal" or "open" economy in which any religion could, in principle, compete with Buddhism. This change in state–religion policy left Buddhism's structure in Myanmar in a severe crisis (Woodward, 1988, p. 71). Turner sets the scene:

> In the decades after the fall of the monarchy to the British in 1885, Burmese felt the ground shifting under their feet. Everywhere they turned, their colonial condition seemed to be characterized by decline. Knowledge of the Buddha's teachings was slipping away before their eyes. Boys no longer learned the basics. They abandoned studying in the monasteries to attend government schools to pursue a lucrative career as a clerk. The monks no longer held the same respect and felt that their world was sliding into decay. (2014, p. 1)

The turmoil from these changes would raise questions about this British approach to religion. Scholars have pointed to the British administration's withdrawal of state support for Buddhism and for the existing Sangha leadership as a failure of the colonial government (Smith, 1965; Mendelson, 1975). These scholars argue, correctly, that British rulers wholly and abruptly disrupted the order of the Sangha and of the existing social structure (Turner, 2014, p. 2). As noted in chapter 1, state-controlled Theravada Buddhism had been a central and guiding feature in Myanmar since 1057, and the policy change degraded Buddhism and the regulation of the religious marketplace.

The neutral state–religion policy of colonial rulers (which did not support or promote Buddhism) had profound effects. Colonel Sladen wrote, "The worst of it is, that the members of all these sects divide themselves socially as well as religiously, and the domestic relations of life have in many cases been materially disconcerted" (Mendelson, 1975, p. 180). Without the state's power and support, the Sangha split into factions around various leaders, understandings of Theravada Buddhism, or interpretations of the Vinaya. Since 1057, state power and authority had artificially suppressed these factions.

On the one hand, the British state–religion policy was a failure. The British gave up a significant power that kings and monks had long utilized—using Buddhism as a tool of legitimacy and social control. The British state–religion policy dramatically changed the religious marketplace and the status of Buddhism in Myanmar. One British administrator wrote, "The Burman cannot conceive of a religion without a Defender of the Faith—a king who appoints and rules the Buddhist hierarchy. The extinction of the monarchy left the nation, according to the people's notions, without a religion" (Smith, 1965, p. 45). Myanmar's people experienced the collapse of state-supported Buddhist structures of power and authority. For many who enjoyed Buddhism's market monopoly, that was a policy failure. If the goal was to regulate, promote, and protect Buddhism, its power structure, and its social order, the new British state–religion policy had failed. Buddhism and its leadership struggled under British rule (Turner, 2014).

If regulating religion and promoting Buddhism were not goals, however, then perhaps the British state–religion policy was not a failure. The British open religious marketplace had succeeded for the missionaries of non-Buddhist firms who could suddenly freely share their religious products in Yangon (Rangoon), Mandalay, and elsewhere.

In turn, these structural changes had three profound effects on Myanmar's religious economy. First, they fractured the structure and leadership of the Buddhist Sangha, forming schisms or factions in the Buddhist Sangha. Second, minority religious firms found new opportunities in the open religious market. Smaller religious firms established missionaries and began sharing their ideas throughout the country. Third, without state support, the Buddhist monastic education system and the religious economy it supported faced profound changes.

1. SCHISMS AND FACTIONS IN THE BUDDHIST FIRM

Until the arrival of the British, the Theravada Buddhist Sangha observed a strict hierarchy and power structure. Monks followed the rules (Vinaya) established and interpreted by kings and superiors. However, Buddhist scholars note that viewing the Sangha as a "monolithic institution" is incorrect because "historically, it comprises diverse communities that distinguish themselves through local teachings, practices, language, and ethnic diversity" (Schober, 2007, p. 54). Like all human organizations, the Sangha had and still has various opinions, practices, and teachings. Madison summed it up this way: "As long as the reason of man continues fallible, and he is at liberty to exercise it, different opinions will be formed" (Madison, 2003, p. 90). Until the colonial era, kings suppressed dissenting opinions by purging uprisings, schisms, or factions within the Sangha. Factions (a dissenting group within a larger one) are common and inevitable. Humans often collaborate around ideas and then break with those original ideas into subgroups supporting others or a variation of ideas. Buddhism, Islam, and Christianity each have many divisions throughout the world. Schisms are part of being human, and, as Madison wrote, the "causes of faction are sown in the nature of man" (Madison, 2003, p. 90). Individuals have vastly different perspectives, life experiences, circumstances, and opinions. Religious firms constitute factions or alliances of people with similar values and beliefs. Individuals or subgroups within an alliance often find that they no longer share the same beliefs or interests of the group. Madison again summed it up well:

> A zeal for different opinion concerning religion, concerning government, and many other points, as well of speculation as of practice; an attachment to different leaders ambitiously contending for preeminence and power; or to persons of other descriptions whose fortunes have been interesting to the human passions, have, in turn, divided mankind into parties, inflamed them with mutual animosity, and rendered them much more disposed to vex and oppress each other than to co-operate for their common good. (Madison, 2003, p. 90)

The removal of the king's support and direct control of Buddhism left the Sangha in its natural state—broken into factions (Taylor, 2005, p. 271). Because King Anawrahta appointed Shin Arahan as primate and owner of the religion, the king-approved Sangha regulated the religious economy, including many Buddhist monks who may have differed in ideas, practices, and beliefs. The British refused to follow Ashoka and Anawrahta's precedent of appointing the Buddhist leadership.

After years of indecision, the British did not appoint or reappoint a Thathanabaing in Upper or Lower Myanmar (Mendelson, 1975, p. 180). British Lieutenant-General Albert Fytche wrote, "The English government, while tolerating every form of religion, will not appoint spiritual heads, or enforce the canons of any religious sect by the secular arm" (Smith, 1965, p. 44). After the last king-appointed Thathanabaing died, the British refused to appoint a new primate. Sir Hugh Barnes, the lieutenant governor of Myanmar, summed up the British policy:

> We English, you must remember, have our own religion, our Christian religion, in which we firmly and devoutly believe; and though, in accordance with the wise policy enjoined by the Great Queen Victoria in Her Majesty's famous Proclamation of 1858, we abstain from imposing our convictions upon others and molest no one in the observance of his Religious Faith; and though we extend to all religious communities alike the equal and impartial protection of the law, and refuse to favour one rather than the other; that is the whole extent of our obligation, and no Religion but our own can claim from us anything more. Therefore, you must clearly realize that we cannot interfere in the internal affairs of the Buddhist Hierarchy, and that it is not our business to interest ourselves in the selection of its chief. These are matters for the Buddhist community alone. You must understand that we do not appoint your *Thathanabaing*. We merely ratify the selection made by the monks themselves, and we grant our official recognition of it for the purposes of administrative convenience only and because the recognition is prerogative which the people expect the ruling power to exercise, and one which has come down to us from the Kings of Burma. (Mendelson, 1975, p. 185)

The Sangha could not agree on a successor, factions naturally arose, and the colonial government refused to support any of them. The monks comprising the Sangha were angry and confused with their new freedom and responsibility. They had never selected their own leadership, had never voted to select leaders, and could not understand why British rulers were so fearful of naming a Thathanabaing. For the Sangha (at that time and later) and for some historians, this British state religion policy was an "undermining of the Sangha" (Turner, 2014). The policy had destroyed a long-standing norm in the religious economy. The British policy was, in fact, an opening of the marketplace of religious ideas. One British court summed up the opening of the marketplace, writing, "It is not the policy of the Government to interfere in matters of religion, and it would be utterly contrary to every British tradition to lay down that there should be but one Buddhist sect in Burma, and that every Burman who wished to embrace a religious life should accept the dogmas laid down by the Thathanabaing" (Mendelson, 1975, p. 188).

This British state–religion policy had immediate consequences within the Sangha leadership. Describing the new state–religion policy's impact, Fytche added that "schisms have crept in since the establishment of our rule, which threaten to disorganize the ecclesiastical structure" (Smith, 1965, p. 44). The neutral policy was not blind to the shift in power. The British recognized the power and control that comes from appointing monastic leadership. Colonel Edward Sladen, a British officer in charge of provisional government in Upper Myanmar at the time, recommended that Britain appoint a Thathanabaing to maintain "social order" (Mendelson, 1975, p. 180). To argue for an appointment, Sladen wrote, "We have studiously refused to recognize the Buddhist ecclesiastical code. The result is that the power of the priesthood to regulate church affairs is almost nil, their influence for good has vastly deteriorated, and Buddhism is broken up into numerous sects and schisms, without and beyond all ecclesiastical control" (Mendelson, 1975, p. 180).

2. SMALLER RELIGIOUS FIRMS SEEK MARKET SHARE

Before British rule, Myanmar's marketplace of religious ideas mostly excluded other religious ideas. As noted in chapter 1, Myanmar has always had diverse cultures and people. More than 135 ethnic groups live in Myanmar, each with its own culture, history, and language (Matthews, 1995, p. 287). The country comprises seven states, each named after a minority ethnic group: Chin, Kachin, Karen, Karenni, Mon, Rakhine, and Shan. According to the Myanmar Ministry of Religious Affairs, Myanmar's religions include Buddhism (approximately 89 percent), Islam (4 percent), Christianity (4 percent), and other religions (3 percent) such as Hinduism, Bahai, and native nat worshippers. Although these Myanmar government statistics are gross estimates, they point to a remarkable religious plurality for a country that has historically supported only Theravada Buddhism. While Theravada Buddhism is and has been the dominant religion, Islam and Christianity also have a long history in the country (as has the nat religion discussed in chapter 1). Scholars have largely ignored Myanmar's Muslim population (Crouch, 2016a, p. 3). Still, Muslims are widely dispersed geographically and include highly diverse ethnicities, religious practices, socioeconomic backgrounds, and social and political integration (Farrelly, 2016, p. 102). Several unique Muslim groups exist throughout the country: the Rohingya, the Panthay, the Malays (who immigrated from Bangladesh, India, and Pakistan), the Zerbadee, and the Kaman (Farrelly, 2016, p. 102). In addition to Buddhists and Muslims, the Myanmar religious market includes the Chin people (traditionally animists, but today they are mostly Christian) and the Mro and Khami peoples, who practice a mix of animism, Buddhism, and Christianity.

Myanmar's current state–religion policy reflects centuries of state-supported Buddhism mixed with the direct legacy of British colonial policy. The British policy of neutrality toward religion and its ruling strategy of empowering minority ethnic groups to control minority populations allowed significant changes in Myanmar's Christian and Muslim communities. The British laissez-faire state–religion policy allowed minority religions, rather than only Theravada Buddhism, to thrive in Myanmar's religious economy (Woodward, 1988, p. 57). Christian and Muslim missionaries traveled to Myanmar seeking new followers in the British-made open market.

Islam in Myanmar's Religious Marketplace

Muslims follow or practice Islam. Like Christianity, the Islamic faith emerged in the Middle East. The Prophet Muhammad revealed the faith in 610 CE, and it has reached every corner of the earth through its rich history and following. The religion's diversity testifies to its strength and indicates it has proven viable by meeting many humans' spiritual needs across time and around the world. Citizens from various backgrounds in Myanmar have practiced Islam for centuries. During the Konbaung dynasty (1752–1885), for example, people who practiced Islam served as troops loyal to the Buddhist kings (Farrelly, 2016, p. 104). The political and economic elites of the Islamic faith were, in fact, critical in shaping and creating modern Myanmar society (Keck, 2016, p. 58). In short, Islam is a long-established firm on the Myanmar religious market.

Depending on the source, the Rohingya Muslims (who practice a form of Sunni Islam) migrated to Myanmar's Rakhine state, previously called the Kingdom of Arakan, in the fifteenth century, or they instead emigrated from Bangladesh in several waves during the colonial era (Basu, 2018, p. 5). Both appear to be true (Crouch, 2016a). According to the government census, about 4 percent of Myanmar's population practices the Islam Sunni sect. However, the country's non-Buddhist populations have been frequently noted as significantly underestimated in Myanmar's government census (another outcome of centuries with a closed religious economy). Further, the Myanmar Ministry of Religion excludes the Rohingya from the 135 ethnic groups because the Myanmar government considers them illegal immigrants from Bangladesh. The Rohingya name refers to the place they have called home for generations. *Rohang* derives from the word *Arakan* (the former name of Rakhine State) in the Rohingya dialect, and *ga* or *gya* means "from" (Albert and Maizland, 2020).

The politically disputed status of the Muslim people in Myanmar is the result of centuries of a closed religious economy. As discussed in chapter 5, the Myanmar state's promotion and protection of Buddhism has created an untenable situation for minority religions. For centuries, Muslims lived peacefully alongside Buddhists in an independent kingdom in Rakhine. Historians found evidence of a Muslim presence along the Arakan coastlines in the ninth and tenth centuries, when Arab traders and proponents of Islam first arrived in the region (Crouch, 2016a).

In 1784, the Rakhine state was conquered by the Burmese before falling under British rule in 1826 (Basu, 2018, p. 6). Scholars argue that the current tensions between Muslims and Buddhists began under British rule with a large-scale immigration of mostly Muslim farmworkers from Chittagongs, a port city on the southeastern coast of Bangladesh (Green, 2015, pp. 175–204). Ample evidence shows that large-scale immigration led to social and economic problems and conflict. Importantly, however, the Burmese religious marketplace also saw a considerable influx of new religious ideas and entrepreneurs as a direct consequence of British rule. The Rakhine state has been a part of Myanmar since 1948, but the Rohingya people who have lived there for centuries are not considered citizens of Myanmar because they are not Buddhist. Undoubtedly, there are economic causes for the tensions between Muslim people and Burmese Buddhists, but historical evidence also reveals religious and cultural factors (Mendelson, 1975; Schober, 2011). People have often seen Islam as a threat to the Buddhist religious firm.

Rakhine's marketplace of religious ideas has been quite diverse, a place where large Muslim communities in Central Asia neighbor the Buddhist communities in Southeast Asia. Historically, an array of cultures, languages, ethnic groups, and religions have converged in the state of Rakhine. In a British census of 1891 of the area with most of Myanmar's currently recognized territory, Muslim people were subdivided as Shaykhs, Sayyids, Moghuls, Pathans, Arakanis, Panthays, Shan Muslims, Turks, Arabs, and Choulias. Many Arakan Muslims born of marriages between Indian Muslims and Burman Buddhists were registered as Shaykhs in the census. By 1921, more than 500,000 Muslims lived in Rakhine (Simba, 2013).

During British rule, many thousands of Hindus, Muslims, Nepalis, and Tamils migrated to Myanmar to work as farmers, laborers, merchants, and members of the British administration (Beyer, 2016, p. 132). Evidence shows that the British were not entirely neutral toward religion. With British rule came an influx of Indians into Myanmar. The British favored Indian administrators over Burmese and thus set the stage for decades of ethnoreligious conflict. The Indian immigrants included Chettiar from southern India, who allegedly impoverished farmers in Myanmar through predatory lending practices. With British land support, Tamil Hindu Chettiar moneylenders funded the construction of the Nattukottai temple in Rangoon in 1860. In 2020, the stories Buddhists tell about Hindu Chettiar reflect decades of resentment and animosity. Chettiars are one of the most vilified people in Myanmar's history, and people in present-day Myanmar often bitterly recall stories of "Chettiar money lenders" from India (Cockett, 2015, p. 32).

In planning the new capital city in Rangoon, the British administrators again violated their neutral state–religion policy by reserving land specifically for religious institutions (Pearn, 1962, p. 133). The Buddhist religion had long received gifts of land and gold from the monarch, but the British supported an American Baptist Church, an Armenian Church, two Chinese temples, a Shi'a mosque, and a synagogue with tax-exempt land grants (Cockett, 2015, p. 16; Pearn, 1939, p. 183). The British changed the religious marketplace by providing actual shop space for religious entrepreneurs in Yangon (Rangoon). Muslim missionaries were among the most active and aggressive participants in the newly opened Burmese religious economy.

Green (2015) recently highlighted the first known primary Urdu source on Islam (the *Sayr-e Barhma*) in colonial Myanmar. The *Sayr-e Barhma* ("Burmese Journey") was written by the Muslim cleric 'Abd al-Khaliq in 1893. Although little is known about him, Green found that 'Abd al-Khaliq held the title of *mawlwi* ("Master," or a highly qualified Islamic scholar) and was an Islamic missionary in Myanmar during British colonialization (2015, p. 189). In Myanmar, 'Abd al-Khaliq shared his religious beliefs and sought to shape public opinion about Islam and Buddhism. In his writing, 'Abd al-Khaliq detailed the history, language, and religion of the Burmese people. He absolutely clarified his belief in Islam's superiority and his hope that the Burmans would convert (Green, 2015, p. 189). 'Abd al-Khaliq saw Buddhist beliefs as a corrupted echo of Islam along with "a great need among this community for a guide (hadi) who can show them the difference between idolatry (shirk) and monotheism (tawhid) and so show them the faults of their own religion and make them Muslims" (Green, 2015, p. 190). To share his beliefs, 'Abd al-Khaliq and other missionaries translated Islamic works from Urdu into Burmese during British rule (Green, 2015, p. 196).

In his writings, 'Abd al-Khaliq recounts vigorous public debates about religion spurred on by the open religious economy of the era. Christian missionaries and Muslim religious leaders used public debate to challenge other religious ideas (Green, 2015, p. 187). In a robust example of an open and liberal marketplace, 'Abd al-Khaliq debated religious ideas with the Thathanabaing ("Controller of the Religion") in Mandalay from 1889 to 1890 (Green, 2015, p. 198). Green states that "the available evidence affords no certainty as to whether the debate ever actually took place," but "there is no reason to doubt that some form of such a debate did take place" (Green, 2015, p. 200). Accompanied by a Hindu scholar, 'Abd al-Khaliq posed a dramatic question on the day of his debate with the Thathanabaing: "Let us see whether the Thathanabaing will convert to your religion (mazhab) or not" (Green, 2015, p. 200).

As noted above, many Muslims lived in Myanmar even before missionary 'Abd al-Khaliq was sent to the country. However, his work shows that the liberal and neutral British state–religion policy allowed the religious entrepreneur 'Abd al-Khaliq to freely share his Islamic religious ideas with the Burmese Buddhist. 'Abd al-Khaliq and Islam directly benefited from the collapse of the precolonial religious economy that supported the institutions and authorities of Theravada Buddhism (Green, 2015, p. 197).

Christianity: Catholics and Baptists in the Religious Marketplace

Christianity is the religion of choice for well more than three million people (about the population of Arkansas) in present-day Myanmar, especially among the Karen, Chin, Kayah, Kachin, and Kayin peoples (Gravers, 2013). Christianity (specifically Baptists and some Methodists) is the second-largest religion in the country, practiced by 3,172,479 (6.2 percent) people (again, this may be underreported). Christianity has not been entirely excluded from Myanmar's religious market, and Christian representatives may have first introduced their religion to Myanmar's people as far back as the eleventh century. A common bias among Western Christians is that the Christian religion first came to Southeast Asia via Western missions in the sixteenth and nineteenth centuries (Ruppell, 1999, p. 435). However, archaeological evidence indicates that representatives of Christianity may have entered Myanmar's religious market in the ancient Pagan kingdom (England, 1998, p. 95). Evidence also shows that Christian merchants traveled from India to Myanmar and shared their religious ideas around 1500 (Gillman and Klimkeit, 1999, pp. 312–13). Catholic representatives probably made the first formal missionary efforts in Myanmar (Moffett, 2005, p. 330). However, Myanmar's people did not readily accept Christianity, possibly due to the closed religious market (a market heavily dominated by Buddhism) or possibly because the newly introduced religious ideas did not resonate with them. The Catholic representatives set up a mission in 1613 but immediately encountered problems with the closed marketplace (Moffett, 2005, p. 330).

In 1692, two Catholic priests arrived in Bago to share their religion. Foreigners had the freedom to worship as they chose—but not to convert people to another religion. The king had the priests arrested for attempting to convert people to Christianity, then bound and exposed naked to mosquitos, and finally sewn into sacks and thrown into the Bago River (Purser, 1911, p. 88). The religious economy was clearly closed. By the king's decree, no Burmese person could change their religion or be anything other than a Buddhist or nat worshiper (Purser, 1911, p. 91). By the early 1800s, Catholic representatives had "abandoned direct evangelistic work among the Burmese" (Purser, 1911, p. 93). In 1813, however, subsequent Christian missionaries arrived in Yangon and found more success than the Catholic priests.

In addition to several others across the country, Yangon in 2021 has two large Christian institutions of higher education: the Karen Baptist Theological Seminary and the Myanmar Institute of Theology (known initially as the Baptist Divinity School). These two Baptist institutions began in 1845 and 1927, respectively, under a liberal and neutral British state–religion policy in the Yangon district of Insein on what is now known as Seminary Hill, eventually graduating thousands of Christian ministers, teachers, and community leaders. Faculty and students at both institutions are proud of their connection with Adoniram Judson Jr. and his wife, Ann, two reformed Baptists from America whose life's work was to share Christianity with the people of Myanmar (Hayami, 2018, p. 251; Brackney, 1998, pp. 122–27). A few miles south of Seminary Hill on the campus of Yangon University, the large Judson Church, named in 1920, stands in honor of Adoniram Judson (James, 2002, pp. 1–28), and the Myanmar Institute of Theology hosts the Judson Research Center (a center focused on interfaith research). Each July, Myanmar's Christians celebrate Judson Day, commemorating Judson's arrival in Myanmar. On July 13, 1813, religious entrepreneurs Ann and Adoniram brought their religious ideas to Myanmar's religious marketplace. Although Judson's life in Myanmar is the subject of important debates, his work illustrates a critical element of the religious economy under British colonial rule.

Judson was born on August 9, 1788, in Malden, Massachusetts; his father worked as a Congregationalist pastor. By many accounts, Judson was a brilliant student with a gift for language (early in his life he published the introductory textbook *Elements of English Grammar*; Brackney, 1998, pp. 122–27). Judson went to the College of Rhode Island (later Brown University) at sixteen years old and entered Andover Theological Seminary in 1808. At Andover, Judson became known for his devotion to the Bible and his decision to start a missionary career. In his last year at the seminary, Judson read *Star in the East* by Claudius Buchanan, a minister of the Church of England who served as chaplain at Fort William College in Kolkata (Calcutta), India. Buchanan's sermons and writings expounded the need to "combat immorality and convert the unsaved" (Chancey,

1998, p. 507). Judson's wife, Ann, wrote that Buchanan's sermon "first led his thoughts to an Eastern mission" and later recounted that "the subject harassed his mind from day to day, and he felt deeply impressed with the importance of making some attempt to rescue the perishing millions of the East" (Judson, 1823, p. 6).

To prepare for his mission, Judson read Symes's (1827) *An Account of an Embassy to the Kingdom of Ava*. Upon reading Symes—a British Army officer who reported on Myanmar in 1797—Judson learned that "the Birmans are Hindoos: not votaries of Brahma, but sectaries of Boodh" and that "images of the supreme Boodh" were worshiped (Symes, 1827, p. 33). Ann Judson further noted, "The Burmans are Boodhists or a nation of atheists" with "no eternal God" (Judson, 1823, p. 33). Writing in the language of religious economy, one of Judson's biographers concludes that "a civilized society in the East that was completely pagan and without the Word of God held forth a great opportunity in the mind of Judson" (Anderson, 1956, p. 56).

In the years before the British arrived, Judson struggled to share his religion. When Adoniram and Ann settled in Rangoon in 1813, they planned evangelistic and church-building ministries but soon realized the enormity of that goal. American Baptists found no simple or easy entry into the Burmese religious market. Judson studied the market, finding it closed to Christianity by the king. Anyone embracing Christianity faced a harsh sentence by the Burmese government (Purser, 1911, p. 96). Undeterred, Judson dedicated himself to learning Burma's language, history, and customs while studying Theravada Buddhism for years before attempting public ministry (Martin, 2002, p. 1). In his study, Judson found that Christianity and Buddhism shared many tenets (Dingrin, 2009). After six years, Judson baptized his first Burmese convert (a man named Maung Nau) in 1819 (Wayland, 1853, p. 87).

Wishing to avoid the fate of the Catholic priests, Judson understood that he needed the Burmese king's approval and support to successfully share Christianity. After seven years in the country, Judson traveled to Ava, the capital city, in 1820 to visit with King Bagyidaw. In a series of meetings, Judson asked the king for permission to publicly teach Christianity. He also asked Bagyidaw to remove the death sentence given to Burmese who changed religions (Purser, 1911, p. 91). The Burmese kings (who had lived for centuries with a closed religious marketplace) saw religion and their people as one and the same. King Bagyidaw's questions to the Christian missionary imply that he thought that the people who embraced Christianity might not be real Burmese. He directly asked Judson, "Are Judson's Christians real Burmans? Do they dress like other Burmans?" Judson replied that they do (Maung Shwe Wa, 1963, p. 42).

King Bagyidaw refused both of Judson's requests, and the missionary's sharing of Christianity became painfully slow. Over the next twelve years, Judson converted only eighteen Buddhists to Christianity. Although her

Figure 2.2. Ann Hasseltine Judson, the first American woman to be a missionary visits Burma in the early 1800s. *Source*: traveler1116/DigitailVision Vectors via Ghetty Images

husband blamed the king, Ann Judson saw another reason for their slow success. The Burmese Buddhists simply felt their religion sufficiently met their needs. Ann wrote, "We often converse with our teachers and servants on the subject of our coming to this country, and tell them if they die in their present state, they will surely be lost. But they say, 'Our religion is good for us, yours for you'" (Knowles, 1854, p. 137). While unable to share Christianity in the closed marketplace, Judson (like 'Abd al-Khaliq) spent time translating his beliefs into the Burmese language. He published an English–Burmese dictionary and an English to Burmese translation of the entire Bible (Brackney, 1998, p. 122). Overall, Burmese kings prevented the widespread public sharing of religions other than Buddhism. The history of the missionary pioneers in Myanmar fully reveals their anxieties about the treatment of religious converts and about the danger to themselves (Purser, 1911, p. 98).

In 1826, the British won the war over Burma and thus changed the fate of Judson's religious firm. As noted, the British granted land for a church in Yangon (Rangoon). The British liberal and neutral state–religion policy allowed Judson and his fellow Christians to preach as they wished. Under British rule, Judson and his colleagues enjoyed years of rapid growth for Christianity. Within a few years of British rule, the number of Burmese Christians, on average, doubled every eight years for the next thirty-two years. Judson had the most success with the Karen people. Reverend Judson died in 1850, leaving a legacy of sixty-three Baptist churches and around seven thousand Christian converts (Rogers, 2007, p. 14). Other missionaries followed and found significant success, establishing a Karen Theological Seminary in Moulmein in 1845 and the Baptist Judson College in Rangoon in 1875 (Cockett, 2015, p. 31). With this success, Judson and the Baptists turned to help the Methodist firm enter Myanmar's market (Thoburn, 1892, p. 298).

More Christianity: Methodists Enter the Religious Marketplace

The Methodists followed Bishop James Mills Thoburn (1836–1922) and were hosted by the Baptists in Yangon (Rangoon; Leigh, 2011, p. 3). Thoburn was an extraordinarily successful Methodist missionary in India in the 1870s. Early in the 1870s, Bishop Thoburn rapidly expanded the Methodist firm across India and Malaysia (Oldham, 1918). In 1879, Thoburn expanded the Methodist missionary work from India into British-controlled Lower Myanmar (Harwood, 1955, p. 16; Thoburn, 1892, p. 298). Writing about the first Methodist invitation to Rangoon, Thoburn recalled that "our own work in Myanmar was thrust upon us, rather than sought by us" (1892, p. 448). Thoburn began mission work in Calcutta, India, in 1874 and "very soon came into contact with a person who had lived in Rangoon, and who lost no time in writing to their friends in that city of the new work which we were beginning in Calcutta" (1892, p. 449). Because the Lower Myanmar's religious market was open, "the result was that [Bishop Thoburn] received immediate and urgent invitations to go to Rangoon" (Thoburn, 1892, p. 450). In 1878, at the Rock River Conference in the United States, Methodists raised funding for a mission to Myanmar (Methodist Church, 1964). Later that year, Bishop Thoburn joined Methodist missionary Robert E. Carter in Yangon (Rangoon). Within two weeks, the two Methodist representatives secured "a valuable plot of land . . . on which to build a church and parsonage" and "organized a church of sixty or seventy members, started a Sunday-school operation, held our first Quarterly Conference, had licensed one local preacher, . . . and had commenced street-preaching in three different languages" (Thoburn, 1892, p. 450).

After the British took full control of Myanmar in 1885, the British Army chaplain Joseph H. Bateson saw an opportunity for the Methodist firm in the country's upper region. Chaplain Bateson encouraged Methodists to begin work there, and the Wesleyan Methodist Missionary Society did so in 1887 (Leigh, 2011, p. 10; Harmon, 1974, p. 359; Purser, 1911, p. 105). Historian Michael Leigh perfectly captured the Methodist firm's market entry: "The Upper Burma Mission began as most corporate projects do—with a gleam in an enthusiast's eye, a feasibility study and a campaign to persuade the Board" (Leigh, 2011, p. 20). Reverend W. R. Winston was the Methodist firm's enthusiastic entrepreneur, and the Mandalay religious marketplace was the gleam in his eye (Leigh, 2011, p. 20). Reverend Winston would need a roof over his head and was offered space with Chaplain Bateson (Leigh, 2011, p. 22). In another break with their neutral state–religion policy, colonial authorities had given Chaplain Bateson an abandoned Buddhist monastery to house his mission (Green, 2015, p. 199; Harwood, 1955, p. 11).

Bishop Thoburn returned to Myanmar in 1889 to check on his firm's work. Pleased with the success, he wrote that "we have a small but energetic and devoted church in Rangoon" and that "in all the Methodist world no church of equal membership can be found which has undertaken and accomplished more than has been done by this little band of Christian believers" (Thoburn, 1892, p. 453). In 1889, Bishop Thoburn encouraged further Methodist investment, writing that "both of our Missionary Societies should come to their aid quickly and in the most liberal spirit (1892, p. 454). Over time, Christianity enjoyed enormous success within the Karen and other ethnic groups of Myanmar. Among the many minority ethnic groups, especially among the Karen, Christianity "satisfied a great national religious need" (Poe, 1928, p. 60).

Although Christians constitute a minority religious firm, they play an integral role in Myanmar's religious economy. Christians established hospitals and schools, provided aid to the displaced, and supported the civil and social rights of religious and ethnic minorities (Rogers, 2015,

p. 60). In 2013, Baptists marked the bicentenary of Reverend Judson's arrival in Myanmar, and Catholics celebrated their firm's five hundredth anniversary in the country one year later. On May 24, 2014, Myanmar reached the final stage when the country's first saint, Isodore Ngei Ko Lat, a lay catechist from Karenni state killed by rebels on May 25, 1950, was declared "Blessed" (Gheddo, 2014). In June of 2018, Myanmar had thirty-one Methodist churches and gospel centers across the country. Accordingly, thirty-one full-time preachers, including twenty-one ordained Methodist ministers, served 3,270 Myanmar Methodists.

The success of Christian religious firms in British-ruled Myanmar led to conflict. After the British took control of Lower Myanmar, many hill tribes, especially the Chin, Karen, and Kachin, became Christians (Leigh, 2011, p. 10; Sakhong, 2003, p. 106). Karen Christians then helped the British suppress Buddhist rebellions after the fall of King Thibaw. The British state–religion policy of neutrality removed the Buddhist religion's king-appointed leadership and Buddhism's favored status, which it had enjoyed for centuries. Thus, among the many people identified as Buddhists, these losses led to widespread resentment toward the British, foreigners, and Karen Christians (Keenan, 2011, p. 13; Matthews, 1995, p. 301).

The success of Christian firms in British Myanmar brought conflict and long-term consequences for sharing Christianity. The arrival and success of Christian representatives under colonial rule prompted many Burmese to view missionaries as allied with the British. The hostility toward British rulers was also directed at Christian missionaries (Walton and Hayward, 2014; Moe Nyunt, 2008, p. 104). The people's resentment toward the religious firm extended beyond its association with colonial rule and its religious ideas to include resentment toward the schools that Christians established. In addition to their evangelistic work, Christian missionaries provided Christian instruction, English-language training, and secular education for children (Hellman-Rajanayagam, 2020, p. 244; Loomis, 1953). The Baptist, Methodist, and Anglican Churches established and supported several schools, including the Karen Baptist Theological Seminary (as mentioned earlier), the Baptist Divinity School, and the Methodist English High School (commonly known today as Dagon 1 High School; Matthews, 1995, p. 301). Until British colonial rule, education played a significant role in controlling and regulating the country's religious economy. During the colonial years, British policy dramatically changed the Burmese educational system and sparked religious nationalism (Mendelson, 1975, p. 159).

3. RELIGIOUS EDUCATION AND A CLOSED RELIGIOUS ECONOMY

For centuries, Myanmar's education system has supported and regulated its religious economy. Each generation of boys (few girls were permitted an education) learned a specific Burmese culture and history, and they learned how to read and about Buddhism from monks in Buddhist monasteries (Schober, 2007). This education "was key to Burmese acculturation and foundational for preserving the Buddha's words and his Śāsana [teachings of the Buddha] in the world—it created civilized Burmese and ensured the future of Buddhism" (Turner, 2014, p. 45).

Until the British era, schools had a specific focus: preserving and teaching Buddhism and a specifically Burmese history and culture. According to Mendelson, "writer after writer, whatever his opinion of monastic education, has repeated the opinion that to it, and it alone, has been due the preservation of Burmese culture until very recent times" (1975, p. 150). The central purpose consisted of teaching and preserving Buddhism (Turner, 2014, p. 49). The method of education—reading and copying text—aimed at "paying respect to the Buddha and his teachings" (Turner, 2014, pp. 51–53). Buddhist monasteries and education had a link so strong that the contemporary word for a school (*kyaung*) is the same as for a monastery (Turner, 2014, p. 49).

The first thirty years of the twentieth century marked a turning point in Myanmar's religious economy, largely due to structural changes in the Buddhist education system and its content. With British rule, the Burmese had a choice. The marketplace of ideas opened, and parents and community leaders (including the Sangha) could choose a public and secular lay education with unique expectations, objectives, and values, or they could choose a Buddhist monastic education with its own values. Most chose secular lay education. Before the 1890s, most Burmese boys received education in the country's Buddhist monastic schools (Turner, 2014, p. 46). In 1891, there were 2,434 Buddhist monastic schools and only 757 lay schools scattered across the country (Mendelson, 1975, p. 159). By 1938, the country had 5,255 lay schools and only 976 monastic schools remaining (Mendelson, 1975, p. 159).

These dramatic changes in the education system brought about four significant changes in the Burmese religious economy. First, it created widespread fears and anxiety about losing the influence, status, and market share of the Buddhist firm's values, ideas, and traditions. Buddhists worried about the moral climate and the loss of discipline in their society. Second, that general fear and anxiety motivated some people who practiced Buddhism in Myanmar to "*save* Buddhism" by establishing associations (Turner, 2014). In the decades to come, those Buddhist associations, in turn, became powerful in shaping politics and policy. Third, educational access for girls improved dramatically. The number of girls enrolled in school rose 61 percent from 1911 to 1921 and another 82 percent from 1921 to 1931 with the expansion of lay schools (Ikeya, 2011, p. 55). These newly educated girls and boys suddenly had the power to fight for liberal values, democracy, and, ironically, liberation from the British rulers who had supported the lay schools. Their liberal education helped them recognize their exploitation by the British and realize innovative ideas about government (Cady, 1958). In 1920, 1936, and 1938, Rangoon University students met on campus at the U Chit Tea Shop to begin a series of national strikes to protest the British, marking students' entry into national politics (Sterken, 2016, p. 113). Fourth, as boys left Buddhist monastic education to attend lay schools, individual monks and the broader monastic community felt a loss of power, respect, and status. This loss of power and status led to a notable change within the Buddhist Sangha. Politics changed religion. The Buddhist monastic community had long believed that monks must not participate in politics (Walton, 2016a; Mendelson, 1975, p. 195; Smith, 1965). The decline in Buddhism and the abuse suffered under colonial rule led some monks to reinterpret the rule supporting that belief, and they took political action to protect Buddhism (Walton, 2016a).

CONCLUSIONS

The British colonial experiment with religious freedom in Myanmar highlights several important outcomes and consequences of the state–religion policy (Van der Veer, 2001, p. 5). Centuries of state support for Theravada Buddhism clearly dampened the religious options within Myanmar, and people had few choices until the colonial era. The monopolized religious market suddenly became deregulated when the British abolished the state religion and lowered the entry barriers for new religious firms. Those new firms realized significant immediate and long-term success in the numbers of churches, schools, and converts. Theravada Buddhism became one religious firm among several in a religious economy that it had formerly dominated. Individuals could debate, freely convert (or not), and choose religions. The Christian Bible was translated into Burmese, and people openly debated Christian and Islamic ideas with Buddhists. A person could become a Buddhist or Christian, convert to Islam, or choose no religion. Myanmar, and specifically the city of Yangon, became a remarkably liberal and tolerant place. Under the neutral state religion policy, many religious ideas were shared. A synagogue was built in Yangon in 1854 that still stands today. There was a robust Bahá'í community. The Bahá'í firm teaches that all religions have worth and seeks a unity of all people. The Bahá'í religious ideas arrived in Myanmar in 1876 when two firm missionaries, Jamal Effedi and Sayyaid Mustafa Rumi, arrived to share (Cockett, 2015, p. 22). These two missionaries saw much success in converting Buddhists to the Bahá'í faith. During the colonial era there were about forty-seven thousand practicing Bahá'í in Myanmar (Cockett, 2015, p. 22). Baptists, Hindus, Jews, Methodists, Muslims, and Sikhs built places of worship under the British policy of religious neutrality (Cockett, 2015, p. 16). The market was equally open for all religious firms and people. No firm was favored, supported, or protected. Religious vitality grew within the colonial era's open marketplace.

The British state–religion policy was not neutral, but it was *substantively neutral*. Laycock defines a substantively neutral state–religion policy as one that neither "encourages nor discourages religious belief or disbelief, practice or nonpractice, observance or nonobservance" (Laycock, 2007, p. 54). The British administrators minimized their interference with religion and attempted to leave religion as an individual choice. The British authorities minimized (but not entirely) how much they encouraged and discouraged religious participation. Religion became a private choice for everyone, and the government did not coerce or persuade religious participation. In a shocking break with the past, the British allowed small religious firms to flourish (Islam and Christianity) or wither (as many worried Buddhism would do). Religions could stay the same, change (as Buddhism did), or fade away. In the colonial era's open religious economy, a religion's survival depended on peopleacting voluntarily rather than on the support of the state (Laycock, 2007, p. 54).

The "Burmans consider the Buddhist faith the very raison d'être of their state. The wearers of the yellow robe were proverbially the conscience of the people, the custodians of literature and learning, the educators of youth, the champions of the moral order" (Cady, 1953, p. 150). The British liberal policy led to removing the state religion and the custodians of education, social welfare, and the transmission of history and culture. For centuries, Buddhism and its institutions led these critical areas of life. With British rule, the government assumed responsibility for implementing, funding, and regulating those critical functions. When British administrators took this power and responsibility from the state religion, they opened the religious marketplace and displaced a significant source of cultural responsibility and power. The anxiety and unrest caused by this laissez-faire British policy was destructive but ultimately constructive (Turner, 2014). Until the British, Buddhism (with state power) had functioned as a tool of social control and a stabilizing "virtue-inculcating institution" (Ahdar and Leigh, 2013, p. 75). Without a state religion, individuals and groups could foster their own virtues, values, civic health, and spiritual well-being—or not. With religious freedom came the power of choice and the burden of responsibility.

The open market also forced the dominant religion to change. British rule deprived Buddhist monasteries of state support. Without that support, the livelihoods of thousands of monks and nuns depended directly on the support (or lack thereof) of private people. Myanmar's British occupation and the abolition of a state religion sparked a major crisis for the Buddhist religious firm that had so long depended on state support and protection. The monastic leadership fell into disarray, and the Sangha broke apart into many factions based on various interpretations of the Buddha's teachings, of the Vinaya, and of local beliefs and customs. Many students abandoned Buddhist monastic schools for government-supported schools or Christian schools. With the freedom to choose and make their own decisions, many of Myanmar's people and the Buddhist monastic community set about saving Buddhism (Turner, 2014, p. 2). Thus, they created voluntary private associations to forge a stabilizing and virtue-inculcating "moral community" (Turner, 2014, p. 3). The Buddhist firm adapted to the demands of the liberal religious economy.

Religions unable or unwilling to compete with other religious firms by adapting to market forces and to believer demands will fade away or loudly call for government protection and support. Like for-profit firms supported by the state and shielded from competition, religious firms that rely on the state also run the risk of becoming lazy monopolies. In 1780, Benjamin Franklin wrote, "When a Religion is good, I conceive that it will support itself; and when it cannot support itself, and God does not take care to support, so that its professors are obliged to call for the help of the Civil Power, 'tis a sign, I apprehend, of its being a bad one" (Franklin, 1997). Here, Franklin restates an idealized version of the free religious market: "Religions flourish [or not] according to the zeal of their adherents and the appeal of their dogmas" (Chen, 2014, p. 214). Less than ideally, however, Myanmar's religious economy had only one firm that had been supported, regulated, and protected via the state's power for centuries. As a result, enormous barriers existed for new missionaries seeking followers, including many people's reluctance to convert religions because they associated Buddhism with their national identity. After centuries of only one religion, choosing a religion (other than Buddhism) presented more than a religious question; it also concerned culture and nationality. Would someone still be a citizen if they converted to Islam or Christianity? For many Burmese people, converting to another religion seemed to mean also rejecting their Buddhist culture, history, and larger society. An early Catholic missionary wrote, "They do not understand how one can embrace a foreign creed without losing one's nationality. Such a [person] has become a foreigner ('Kala') which means that he has become a Christian" (Maung Kaung, 1930, p. 73; Cockett, 2015, p. 38). In addition, "Their noteworthy historical past gives the Burmese a distinctive national pride. . . . The Burmese, therefore, see no reason why they should listen to the White Westerners preach about their religion. Thus, the historical heritage of the Burmese is a challenge to the Christian Gospel" (Von Der Mehden, 1963, p. 11). Centuries of state favoritism provided (and still provides) significant advantages to the Theravada Buddhist firm. The British provided non-neutral affirmative action and help for the new religious firms in the form of office space in Yangon and Mandalay (Chen, 2014). Perhaps states should consider affirmative action policies to remedy past market inequities for historically disadvantaged religions?

There is much discussion in the literature about the hostile nature of the missionaries toward Buddhism in Myanmar (Purser, 1911, p. 98). Aung Htin Maung wrote, "American missionaries in their writings presented a monstrous picture of the people to whose country they had come uninvited" (Aung Htin Maung, 1967, p. 9). While certainly uncivil, a free and open religious economy expects the representatives of one firm to express passion for their ideas and hostility toward other religious ideas. In an open religious market, a firm's representatives often are intolerant, passionate, and even condescending in their belief in their religion's superiority. Both Judson and 'Abd al-Khaliq absolutely saw their beliefs as superior, and both missionaries passionately hoped to convert many people. As Judge Learned Hand quipped, "Tolerance ends where faith begins" (Smith, 1990).

Finally, one common measurement in analyses of an open religious economy is *citizen participation* in organized religion (Stark and Finke, 2000). Religious economy theory suggests that closed markets restrict choice (clearly so under Myanmar's kings). Closed economies are also said to foster widespread religious apathy and lower rates of participation in religions. That does *not* appear to have been true for the Myanmar people from 1054 to 1885, when Colonel Sladen deposed the last King. Conversely, religious freedom can support robust rates of religious participation (Gill, 2007). The British deregulation of the religious economy clearly fostered success for minority religious firms, but it also left many people without a moral compass (Turner, 2014). To fill that void, Buddhist associations turned to religious nationalism, and "to be Burmese is to be Buddhist" became the mantra of private associations that spearheaded independence and the reformation of a national identity. How did Myanmar's leadership (British and beyond) of Myanmar manage a religious economy that included the power of religious nationalism?

3

✣

To Be Burmese Is to Be Buddhist

Religious Nationalism in the Myanmar Religious Economy 1930–1948

Imagine climbing barefoot up the steep and narrow steps leading to the base of the stupa at the ancient Shwesandaw Pagoda in Bagan. At the top (328 feet high) of one tall pagoda, a stunning sunrise (or sunset) highlights countless surrounding temples. Today, the pagoda's symmetrical structure is painted white, and bell-shaped stupas appear for many miles across Bagan's plains. Built in 1057 by King Anawrahta, the Shwesandaw Pagoda enshrines hair relics of the Buddha and supports the Theravada Buddhist religious firm. During the British colonial era, the Shwesandaw Pagoda became the site of a clash in which the British regulation of the religious economy provoked a spark of religious nationalism (Khin Maung Nyunt, 1970). The clash concerned whether shoes could be worn at religious Buddhist sites. Before entering a temple or pagoda, Buddhists remove their shoes and other foot coverings (Edwards, 2006, p. 199). Historians frequently mark the "shoe question" as the beginning of religious nationalism and the end of colonial rule in Myanmar (Cady, 1958). However, the clash over shoes did more than spark revolution; it encompassed social control and regulation of the religious marketplace by the British, along with the use of religion to disrupt social control. Over time, religious (Buddhist) nationalism had an enormous impact and major influence on Myanmar's religious economy. This chapter explores the origins of religious nationalism and its impact on Myanmar's religious economy during the colonial era. During that time, religious nationalism helped disrupt British control and restructured Myanmar's religious economy through a fusion of national and religious identities.

Figure 3.1. Shwesandaw pagoda. *Source*: Punnawit Suwuttananun/ Moment Via Ghetty Images

RELIGIOUS NATIONALISM IN MYANMAR'S RELIGIOUS ECONOMY

Religious nationalism has had (and continues to have) an extraordinary impact on Myanmar's religious economy. However, examining this story and its impact requires a clear definition of religious nationalism. First, scholars define *nationalism* as the doctrine "that the political and the national unit should be congruent" (Gellner, 1983, p. 1). Nationalists contend that a culturally or historically distinctive group of people constitutes the legitimate sovereign and that the state should reflect the interests and values of that group while protecting that distinctive group. Policy decisions by nationalist leaders aim to fulfill the cultural or religious identity of a specific group. In turn, *religious nationalism* is the "fusion of nationalism and religion such that they are inseparable" (Rieffer, 2003, p. 225). In Myanmar, religious and national identities reinforce and reify each other. Buddhist nationalists tend to divide Myanmar's society into two distinct groups: those who subscribe to Theravada Buddhism (and thus dominate the political, economic, and social order) and those who do not. Myanmar's Buddhist nationalists idealize a society of "real" citizens and without the "others" (noncitizens who do not belong). Buddhist nationalists tend to favor a society in which "real" citizens, Bamar, native-born, and Buddhist, enjoy government protection and support.

Scholars typically identify the colonial era as the beginning of Buddhist nationalism, but it began in 1057 when King Anawrahta linked the state with one specific religious firm (Nemoto, 2015, pp. 221–23). Over the centuries, a cultural framework of myths, traditions, symbols, and historical narratives became the foundation for Buddhist nationalism, which became something beyond Theravada Buddhism. Namely, this religious nationalism identified specific social groups, provided a framework for a defined community (who belongs and who does not), and defined a historical framework for understanding the nation (Brubaker, 2012, p. 6). Ethnic groups like Rohingya, Mon, Shan, Kachin, Karen, Indian, and Chinese, who had lived in the country for centuries, were thought of as "others" and as foreigners. A shared state-supported religion and a shared narrative of a Buddhist history led to Buddhist nationalism (Win Kanbawza, 1988, p. 271). For many Myanmar people, Buddhism has come to define the nation—and that sense of national identity supports the Buddhist firm above all others (Smith, 1965, pp. 82–83). How did religious nationalism develop in the colonial era and what roles did it play in the colonial religious economy? Religious nationalism had four important effects on the religious economy of the colonial era. First, it forced an important change in the controversial British state–religion policy. Second, it disrupted the social control of the colonial era. Third, it came to define national identity. Fourth, it provided the building blocks dominated by the Buddhist firm for the coming independent nation.

RELIGIOUS NATIONALISM AND THE COLONIAL STATE–RELIGION POLICY

Scholars show that religious nationalism often influences public policy (Grzymala-Busse, 2015, 2016). Religions tend to hold moral authority, and a specific religion (such as Theravada Buddhism) that claims to represent the broad national interest can enormously influence policy debates (Grzymala-Busse, 2016). In 1919, Buddhist nationalism was used to influence the British state–religion policy regarding the wearing of shoes at Buddhist monuments (Schober, 2011, pp. 73–75).

The "Shoe Question" in Regulating the Religious Economy

The British shoe policies (policies such as wearing shoes in temples) reflect the complexities of the state's role in the religious economy. In an attempt to stay neutral (and/or protect British and European status) and refrain from regulating the religious economy, British authorities first established a policy that regulated religious actions. Prompted by religious nationalism, however, they sought to remedy that mistake and then finally decided to (mostly) stop regulating the Buddhist shoe question.

The shoe question was not new to Myanmar's people. In 1892, the Buddhist monk Okpo Sayadaw shocked his nation when he marched up the stairs of the Sandawshin Pagoda in his sandals (Turner, 2014, p. 121). People saw the monk's dusty sandals on the steps and terraces of the pagoda as demeaning and highly disrespectful to the Buddha. The monk wore his sandals on the pagoda to provoke a public debate about what really mattered in the Buddha's teachings. He successfully provoked a debate, but the emotional debate about the disrespect of wearing shoes at a pagoda obscured his intended point (Turner, 2014, p. 122). The monk's act was meant to galvanize, for the broader public, the link between shoes and respect for the Buddha and the teachings of the Buddha. Wearing shoes anywhere on or around a pagoda appeared gravely disrespectful and destroyed the Buddha's teachings (Turner, 2014, p. 122). Shoes were disrespectful and viewed as a threat to the Buddhist religious firm. Thus, with their shoes and boots on, the British traipsed into the middle of this public and emotional religious debate.

State–Religion Policy Regarding Respect at Religious Sites

From the beginning of their colonial rule in Myanmar, the British did not remove their shoes at Buddhist monuments (Turner, 2014, pp. 120–21). The precedent for their exemption from the requirement began with the stationing of British troops at prominent pagodas during the three wars. The stated justification for Europeans wearing shoes in Buddhist sacred sites was that "Europeans remove their hats while Asians remove their shoes" (Turner, 2014, p. 123). Whether they actually removed their hats remains unanswered (Seekins, 2013, p. 149).

British Regulation of Behaviors at Religious Sites

In 1875, Buddhist leaders in Rangoon protested that Muslims wore their shoes at Buddhist pagodas. The British authorities agreed that Muslims should not wear their shoes at a Buddhist pagoda. Regulating the religious marketplace, British administrators allowed each subgroup to show respect in a manner traditional to that specific group. Ostensibly about religion, the classifications the British used for each subgroup really encompassed perceptions of race (Seekins, 2013, p.149). British authorities reasoned that Europeans traditionally remove their hats as a show of respect, and Buddhists and Muslims traditionally remove their shoes. Thus, to remedy the problem of Muslims wearing shoes in Buddhist sites, the British commissioner decreed, "those persons, whose creed required them to show respect by taking off their shoes, should take off their shoes on entering a pagoda" (Turner, 2014, p. 123). Thus, according to the government, each person entering a pagoda should show respect according to their own tradition. This government policy sought to minimize the state's interference with religion. However, this policy involving race, religion, hats, and shoes did, in fact, constitute a state regulation of religious acts in Buddhist pagodas. This state–religion policy seems to have satisfied all parties for about twenty-five years.

In 1906, the Young Men's Buddhist Association (YMBA) was founded specifically to address religious and social issues. This association provided a popular forum for monks, students, and intellectuals to discuss Buddhism and nationalist concerns. The YMBA's membership comprised mostly young British-educated elites, and the group formed as a reaction to the Buddhist firm's perceived crisis in Buddhism. The YMBA promoted a combined religious and national identity and allegedly coined the phrase "To be Burmese is to be Buddhist" (Schober, 2018, p. 66; Slater, 1951, p. 35). Identifying nationalism with religion harnessed Buddhist fervor to mobilize popular support (Schober, 2018, p. 67). In 1916, the YMBA forced the colonial government to again address the shoe issue (Turner, 2014, p. 124).

1916: British Ban the Shoe Discussion

Signs posted at the entrances of pagoda grounds encouraged everyone to remove footwear on sacred Buddhist monuments. The bottom of each sign, however, included an exemption allowing Europeans to wear shoes (Schober, 2011, p. 73). The British law allowed that "permission should be granted to prohibit persons other than Europeans . . . from ascending the pagoda platform with their shoes on" (Seekins, 2013, p. 149). In 1916, Buddhist leaders and religious nationalists once again decried the shoe-policy exemption as a threat to their religion (Seekins, 2013, p. 148; Edwards, 2006, p. 204; Smith, 1965, p. 87). Representatives of the Buddhist firm felt that anyone who wore shoes on sacred ground had committed a sin and that the British policy was not neutral—they felt it was, in fact, hostile toward Buddhism (Turner, 2014, p. 127). U Thein Maung, a lawyer and activist leader in the YMBA, protested to the trustees of the Shwesandaw Pagoda about the sign at its entrance: "no one but English and Americans is allowed to wear shoes" (Seekins, 2013, p. 149). The British government refused to change the policy. In 1917, Governor of British India Sir Archibald Douglas Cochrane kept his shoes on while visiting earthquake-hit Shwemawdaw Pagoda in Pegu. The governor's shoes upset local Buddhists, who complained to the YMBA. In May 1918, the YMBA held its national meeting at Jubilee Hall in Rangoon and passed a resolution completely banning footwear in all Buddhist monuments (Smith, 1965, p. 87). The state again sought to regulate the religious marketplace by banning public discussion of the religious issue, proclaiming a "truce to all public discussion on the subject" for "public tranquility" during the war (Seekins, 2013, p. 151; Smith, 1965, p. 87). The attempt to silence the religious discussion failed.

1919: The British Concede and Opt Out of Religious Regulation

Members of the YMBA and the Buddhist Sangha published papers, pamphlets, and books protesting the state's continued regulation of the footwear issue. One revered member of the Buddhist firm, Ledi Sayadaw, published the book *On the Impropriety of Wearing Shoes on Pagoda Platforms*, which fueled the public discussion and provided religious reasons for changing the state's policy (Smith, 1965, p. 88). In October 1919, angry Buddhist monks attacked a group of Europeans who wore shoes while visiting a pagoda in Mandalay, prompting a state–religion policy change. The colonial government needed to remedy a problem of its own making after the regulation of religious actions at Buddhist sites created and then intensified religious nationalism and unrest.

The government finally conceded and presented a new policy. The state would no longer make decisions about appropriate behaviors at religious sites; instead, the decisions would fall to the firm representatives of each religious site. The trustees of each pagoda would establish the rules for the grounds and monuments (Smith, 1965, p. 89). To reestablish a neutral policy toward that religious issue, state authorities decided that "it is not for the Government to lay down what observances should be followed by persons entering the religious edifices of others" (Seekins, 2013, p. 151). The state would not regulate the shoe issue. Buddhists would enjoy religious liberty at pagodas, with two exceptions in which British authorities saw a state interest. First, they limited religious liberty for public safety and security reasons. The government required that managers post signs clarifying expected behaviors and, specifically, where visitors must have bare feet. Second, government officers, soldiers, or police could, in the line of duty, enter while wearing shoes for safety, security, and public order (Smith, 1965, p. 89). The shoe–religion issue marked the first public expression of an anti-colonial political sentiment, but other grievances and actions quickly followed.

RELIGIOUS NATIONALISM AND THE DISRUPTION OF COLONIAL SOCIAL CONTROL

The shoe controversy, structural concerns (stemming from the state's lack of support for Buddhism), and the decline in monastic education sparked political action by monks (Mendelson, 1975, p. 198). Within this context, the Buddhist firm became a significant force in disrupting colonial social control, and Buddhist monks became the first nationalists in the struggle against colonial rule (Smith, 1965, p. 85). The Buddhist Sangha served as a supportive community for those in the Buddhist firm and as a source of leaders, political advocates, and political actors.

The Buddhist religious firm held (and still holds) strong theological commitments, and its leaders felt obliged to ensure that state policies respected, protected, and promoted Buddhism. In short, the Buddhist firm sought to ensure its own survival. By influencing the British shoe policy, the firm disseminated and enshrined its religious values to thus fend off British secularization and potential new religious competitors. Centuries of widespread support from the state and from citizens gave the Buddhist firm legitimacy and moral authority. Fusing religion with the nation reinforced the moral authority of the Buddhist firm and transformed it into a potent political force (Grzymała-Busse, 2015, p. 45; Schober, 2007, p. 55). People saw monks as impartial and credible representatives of the nation. The authority of the monks allowed representatives of the Buddhist firm to mobilize society to shape policy in ways that favored their religion. The Burmese monks U Ottama and U Wisara inspired nonviolent Buddhist nationalism, but the ex-monk Saya San turned away from the nonviolent struggle of the 1920s and staged an armed rebellion against colonial rule. These members of the Buddhist firm used religious nationalism to align against the British state. U Ottama, U Wisara, and Saya San used religion to influence and mobilize their society and to profoundly reshape the nation-state and the foundation and structure of Myanmar religious economy.

Sayadaw U Ottama and U Wisara

Today, Myanmar citizens consider U Ottama (1879–1939) the father of the country's independence movement (Smith, 1965, p. 95). He has been called a "cosmopolitan revolutionary" and "the Gandhi of Myanmar" (Solomon, 1969, p. 209). In addition, "U Ottama did for nationalism in Burma part of what Gandhi did for it in India by transforming an essentially political problem into a religious one" (Mendelson, 1975, p. 199). Importantly, U Ottama became the first of thousands of monks who fought against British colonial rule and against later governments. U Ottama's background, cross-cultural education, and transnational experiences gave him a unique understanding of oppressive and illiberal colonial rule and policies.

The Education of a Rebel Monk

U Ottama was born in Rupa village in Sittway, Arakan, on December 14, 1879. From an early age, he resolutely worked toward getting an education (Mendelson, 1975, p. 200). He attended a local village school from age five, but at age nine he persuaded his parents to send him to an Anglo-Burmese school in Akyab. He excelled and was frequently at the top of his class. A Christian priest noticed his academic potential and enthusiasm for learning, so he asked the parents of U Ottama for permission to take him to India for further studies. However, U Ottama's parents refused. His mother dreamed that her son would be a monk, so she withdrew him from school and set him under the tutelage of monks in a Sittway monastery (Mendelson, 1975, p. 201). After learning the Pali text and scoring highest on his examinations, U Ottama caught the attention of a wealthy Shan woman who sent him to Kolkata (Calcutta) for further studies. U Ottama was "obsessed with the idea of acquiring and spreading knowledge," and excelled in the Calcutta schools (Mendelson, 1975, p. 201). At twenty, Ottama fulfilled his mother's dream and became an ordained monk. After his ordination, Ottama returned to India and studied at Hindu College for four years. In April 1904, he studied law and political science at Cambridge University with U May Aung (also spelled Oung) in England (Saw Mra Aung, 2015). May Aung (January 6, 1880–June 5, 1926) was a Burmese legal scholar, judge, and the first law professor at Rangoon University (Aye Kyaw, 1993). May Aung was known as an expert in Burmese Buddhist law and as a founder of the Young Men's Buddhist Association (Aye Kyaw, 1993). U Ottama traveled widely (England, France, Germany, India, Japan, Netherlands, Singapore, Sweden, Demark, Norway, the United States, and many more) and served as a professor in several universities. He knew nine languages fluently: Pali, Sanskrit, Hindi, Bengali, Nagari, Tibetan, Japanese, English, and French (Saw Mra Aung, 2015). Both May Aung and Ottama were empowered with a liberal education. With a thirst for knowledge, Ottama plunged into learning philosophy, history, and concepts of representative government (Fink, 2013, p. 13). As a scholar of religion, U Ottama could openly accept other religious beliefs. For example, after his election as the president of the Hindu Mahasabha, he carefully avoided allowing Buddhist religious appeals to become a divisive force (Bhattacharya, 2004, p. 23). Ottama spent several years in India working closely with Mahatma Gandhi's nonviolent approach, political goals, and methods of supporting citizens' rights in the Indian National Congress. He often spoke in Hindustani and promoted unity among Muslims, Hindus, Christians, and Buddhists (Smith, 1965, p. 97). His education and experiences gave him a unique understanding and the tools and skills needed to disrupt British state control. Ottama's background allowed him to combine Buddhist nationalism with a broader struggle against the British.

Political Agitators in Yellow Robes

Ottama frequently traveled to Japan, where he worked as a professor of Pali and Sanskrit at the Tokyo Buddhist Academy. While teaching, he also studied Japanese culture and authored the book *Biography of Japan* (Lewy, 1972, p. 29). From Tokyo, Ottama penned an open letter in 1912 to the British government requesting funding to establish a university in Myanmar (Aye Kyaw, 1993, p. 86). British authorities in India allocated about $60,000 to establish Yangon (Rangoon) University (Aye Kyaw, 1993, p. 13), supporting the scholar-monk's clear interest in promoting education.

In Myanmar, Ottama campaigned to disrupt existing British–Burmese politics with fiery Buddhist nationalist sermons against colonial authorities (Ba, 2007). He gave speeches across the country advocating the nonpayment of taxes and, following Gandhi, peaceful noncooperation with the British. A charismatic leader, Ottama attracted a large following of mainly Buddhist monks who organized publications, demonstrations, and protests. Colonial authorities labeled politically active monks as "political agitators in yellow robes" and swiftly responded with force, using police to break up protests.

While arguing against Myanmar's separation from India, Ottama demanded home rule (Ottama, 1931). U Ottama's version of Buddhist nationalism was framed within his understanding of Myanmar's connection with India (Sana Aiyar, as cited in Dizikes, 2019). At the time, other prominent Myanmar nationalists, such as U Wisara, defined their nationhood in Buddhist religious terms to demand the separation of Myanmar from India. U Ottama insisted that since India was the birthplace of Buddhism, Myanmar was inextricably linked with India (Sana Aiyar, as cited in Dizikes, 2019).

The monk's religious sermons gave the struggle for independence a Buddhist foundation. Ottama clearly linked the promotion and protection of the Buddhist religious firm with the struggle for independence (Solomon, 1969, p. 219). Thus, they used religious nationalism to challenge British authority and social control. Ottama argued that those in political bondage could not achieve deliverance through suffering. He directly linked Buddhism with the disruption of the existing power structure and political independence, arguing that "Pongyis [monks] pray for Nirvana but slaves can never attain it, therefore they must pray for release from slavery in this life" (Lewy, 1972, p. 29).

Upon his arrest in 1921 for one of his speeches, Ottama became the first monk in British Myanmar to be imprisoned specifically for speaking against the colonial authorities. His offense was calling upon Sir Reginald Dorman-Smith, the lieutenant governor, to return to Britain. From 1921 to 1927, Ottama spent more time in prison than outside prison for his anticolonialist religious–nationalist political activities. To protest his detention, he went on a hunger strike and later died in prison in 1939. Historian John Cady dubbed Ottama "the first martyr of Burmese nationalism" (Solomon, 1969, p. 218).

Ottama was, of course, not alone. In the 1920s, another prominent and fiery monk, U Wisara, joined Ottama's work to disrupt the existing social order. Both monks faced multiple imprisonments and torture by the colonial government for inciting sedition. Wisara was imprisoned several times for delivering anti-colonial speeches. After his second arrest for anti-colonial speeches, the British authorities transferred Wisara to a prison in India. Upon release, he continued to call for change. He was arrested, placed in a Yangon prison, and forced to wear plain clothes instead of his yellow robes. The British authorities sought to remove his religious authority and legitimacy. The monk refused to eat until he could wear his yellow robes, but prison authorities unsuccessfully tried force feeding him to keep him alive. One hundred and sixty-six days into his hunger strike in 1929, Wisara died at age forty-one in the Yangon prison.

The Saya San Rebellion and Religious Nationalism

Ottama, Wisara, and other groups of Buddhist monks established small associations of monks in villages across Myanmar. These associations comprised a far-reaching religious–nationalist network that provided a structure for local governance and a space for the Myanmar people to articulate concerns and grievances. Rural leaders used these religious nationalist organizations to voice their grievances about taxes, rising costs, and high rent rates and to provide a structure for village governance. By 1924, these religious nationalist associations existed in nearly every village in Myanmar (Taylor, 2006). After the worldwide depression hit Myanmar in 1929, farmers lost their homes and land as rice prices plummeted, and their taxes became impossible to pay. Into this suffering stepped a charismatic former monk and healer, Saya San, who led an attempt to disrupt the existing social order of colonial rule. By December of 1930, via the local village associations and the monks who led them, Saya San used a populist political strategy to organize a massive and violent anti-colonial resistance. Saya San may be the first populist in Myanmar's history because he clearly used his charisma to mobilize a mass movement in pursuit of political power (Kenny, 2018, p. 1).

Saya San led a series of uprisings from 1930 to 1932 that the British dubbed the Saya San Rebellion and that scholars widely regard as a pivotal event in Myanmar's history and one of Southeast Asia's largest anti-colonial movements (Smith, 1965; Mendelson, 1975; Aung-Thwin, 2011, p. 2). For a full historical analysis of the Saya San Rebellion, see Maitrii Aung-Thwin's excellent book *The Return of the Galon King* (2011). Using the local network of monk-led village associations previously established by Ottama, Wisara, and others, Saya San organized peasant supporters and promised he would restore the Burmese monarchy, revitalize the Buddhist religion, and expel the British (Aung-Thwin, 2011, p. 2).

Saya San was born on October 24, 1879 in Upper Myanmar; his parents, Kyaye and Daw Hpet, named him Yar Kyaw. Like Ottama and Wisara, young Yar Kyaw spent his youth studying at the local Buddhist monastery. After leaving the monastery, Yar Kyaw worked as a carpenter, as a fortuneteller, and as a traditional medicinal healer. At this point, he took or was given the name Saya San, which derived from his role as a medicinal healer, or *se saya* (Aung-Thwin, 2011, p. 4). In the early 1920s, Saya San became a local village representative in Moulmein and was elected in 1924 to chair a commission examining the alleged abuse of villagers by British government tax collectors. Between 1928 and 1930, Saya San listened to peasants' grievances and recruited people into the village associations. Under the leadership of local and traveling monks, these village associations provided the structure for Saya San's attempt to disrupt colonial authority.

The catalyst for the Saya San rebellion consisted of a mix of domestic struggles, colonial rule, and a global economic downturn (Adas, 1974). According to Adas (1974), the peasant revolts at least partially resulted from unmet economic expectations of the peasant farmers. Colonial-era farmers had benefited from a robust global rice economy early in the century. Still, the crashing world markets brought by the Great Depression left farmers with economic hardships and grievances (Adas, 1974).

Saya San blamed the British for the economic difficulties and for the general decline of Buddhism, and he employed religious images and language to call for a rebellion against colonial rule. Saya San employed Buddhist nationalism and nat traditions to press for change. As discussed in chapter 1, the nats (spirits) have played a vital role in Myanmar's religious culture since pre-Buddhist times and have since become woven into Buddhism. Saya San mixed nat faith with Buddhism to inspire the rebellion, saying, "Do away with the heathens, Oh Nats, so that our glorious Buddhist religion may prosper" (Von der Mehden, 1963, p. 155). In letters and speeches, Saya San linked his rebellion with religion: "Protect and help our religion, O ye greater and lesser Nats of this world and of all worlds. O Monastery Nats and Village Nats, O Tree Nats and Country Nats . . . O ye four great Nats who guard the world . . . deliver us quickly from the unbelievers and their government. Grant to us liberty, and to the Galon King dominion over this land" (Solomon, 1969, pp. 222–23). Saya San wrote, "Since the British deposed King Thibaw . . . they have deceitfully striven to destroy the Sutta (teachings of Buddha), Abidhamma (ethical philosophy), and Vinaya (monastic code of conduct). [I] act not merely with the desire to treat kindly all rational beings, but with a keen desire to advance the interests of the religion ... and appeal for help ... to promote the interests of the religion" (Solomon, 1969, p. 222). Inspired by religious nationalism, peasant rebels armed mostly with swords and sticks attacked the British in December 1930. The British authorities quickly curbed the monk movement by trying to shutter village associations and arrest the leaders of the movement.

Saya San's deliberate use of language and symbols of religious nationalism contributed to the emotional power and long-lasting impact of the rebellion. The narrative of Saya San's rebellion came to represent a peasant uprising motivated by local and global economic grievances and a call to reinstate Buddhism as the favored firm in Myanmar's religious economy. Saya San's efforts and the revolt did not yield immediate success, but the rebellion solidified the foundation of Buddhist nationalism in Myanmar (Fink, 2013, p. 15). The British authorities executed Saya San on November 28, 1931. Still, religious nationalism and the infrastructure of the village associations provided rebels with the inspiration and organizational structure needed to continue the rebellion for nearly two more years. By the time British forces violently ended the rebellion in 1932, more than ten thousand rebels had been killed and nine thousand imprisoned (Aung, 1967, p. 292).

The political actions and deaths of Ottama, Wisara, and Saya San heightened Buddhist nationalism and anti-colonialist sentiment among the Myanmar people. Today, Ottama is widely considered a national hero of modern Myanmar. In a Gandhian way, he transformed a primarily political issue—home rule and independence—into a religious issue that broadly appealed to people who had not received an education. Both Ottama and Wisara have been honored with memorials. These two monks and Buddhism became intertwined by establishing a state and a nation and by directly shaping the religious economy. The British had named a road in Yangon after a British lieutenant, Voyle, who died in the Second Anglo-Burmese War in 1852, but Myanmar authorities renamed Voyle Road in 1940 to honor Wisara, and a monument to Wisara was unveiled at a crossroads near the western gate of the Shwedagon Pagoda in 1943. Today, Myanmar's official histories sympathetically present Saya San as a compassionate and motivated peasant leader who sought to improve farmers' livelihood by appealing to their nostalgia for precolonial times (Aung-Thwin, 2011, p. 219). Myanmar's people celebrate Saya San via a street and a memorial hall named after him in Yangon, and a Burmese banknote immortalizes his likeness. The Saya San rebellion still today evokes sentiments of Buddhist nationalism. He still constitutes a figure of national unity and continues to shape Myanmar's religious economy by linking Buddhism with national identity.

Saya San and the rebellion he sparked demonstrate the political power of religious nationalism. The deliberate use of nat and Buddhist symbols and ceremonies by Saya San had a substantial and long-term impact on the religious economy of the country. Buddhist nationalism became a critical component for disrupting the existing order and a significant marker of culture and identity for many Myanmar people (but not all, of course). Saya San, Ottama, and Wisara furthered a specific narrative about Myanmar's religious economy. That narrative successfully disrupted colonial control, emphasized the historical relationship between kings and Buddhism, and linked the dominant religious firm with the national identity. The link of Buddhism with national identity gave the Buddhist firm a dominant position in Myanmar's religious economy. Other religious firms could not compete and were viewed as outsiders and foreigners. To be Burmese was to be Buddhist, and all other religions were excluded (Slater, 1951, p. 35). Myanmar's religious economy was effectively closed to all other religious firms.

RELIGIOUS NATIONALISM AND NATIONAL IDENTITY

In July 1938, the year before Ottama died in prison, Buddhist monks clashed with members of the Muslim firm. The Buddhist firm clearly saw the Muslim firm as a threat after Shwe Hpi, a Muslim writer, published a book in 1931 that criticized Buddhism. Shwe Hpi's book went mostly unnoticed until excerpts appeared in a novel published in 1938. Upon reading these excerpts that criticized Buddhism, some members of the Buddhist firm wrote letters and articles urging action against the author. The Buddhist firm claimed that Shwe Hpi's book constituted a "grave menace to the Buddhist religion and to the larger society" (Smith 1965, p. 110). Monks of the Buddhist firm attended a mass meeting at the Shwedagon pagoda to address this menace and resolved to punish Shwe Hpi.

The monks' resolution also warned the British that, if the government did not act, "steps will be taken to treat the Muslims as enemy No. 1 who insult[ed] the Buddhist community and their religion, and [steps will be taken] to bring about the extermination of the Muslims and the extinction of their religion and language" (Smith, 1965, p. 110). In anger and protest, the Buddhist firm marched in downtown Yangon (Rangoon), clashed with police, attacked Muslims, and looted and destroyed Muslim shops and businesses. The protest quickly spread to other cities and villages, and Buddhist monks played a leading role in instigating and directing rioters (Smith, 1965, p. 111). The Buddhist firm used monasteries as armed strongholds and sanctuaries for people sought by the police. British authorities noted that Buddhist monks' revered status in their communities made them "the greatest political force in Burma" (Smith, 1965, p. 111). As a result, the Buddhist firm made substantial gains in the religious economy. Buddhist nationalism encompassed more than an anti-British or pro-Myanmar sentiment and a movement for independence. It created nationalism based on perceptions of a common race, language, and—most importantly—religion. Buddhism coalesced with nationalism and dramatically altered the religious economy. The nation was not seen as comprising diverse peoples, languages, and religions. For many people, Buddhism had become the most critical identifying symbol for the nation, which, of course, excluded every other religious firm and group and marginalized minority religious firms. This was especially true for Muslims, many of whom descended from immigrants who came to the country during the British period. Buddhist nationalism essentially crowded Muslims, Hindus, Christians, and other non-Buddhist religious firms out of the religious economy.

RELIGIOUS NATIONALISM AND THE BUILDING OF THE MYANMAR STATE

Buddhist nationalism and the tools of social and political protests used by Saya San, Ottama, and Wisara inspired activists and students involved in the independence movement. These political leaders and many others played an essential role in disrupting colonial control and in laying the foundation for the state of Myanmar. Monk political parties, known in Pali and popularly as Sangha Sammeggi, formed in the early 1900s. The General Council of Sangha Sammeggi brought together monks, who became known as *political pongyis*, or political monks. The monks used their status and authority (and the power of religious nationalism) to disengage from and oppose British secular authority. The Buddhist clerical actors and the authority of the religious firm provided the leadership, organization, and legitimacy needed to challenge the British colonial government. Religious nationalism gave authority to Ottama, Wisara, and Saya San. As representatives of the Buddhist firm, they and many others had political influence in part through the power of religious nationalism. The activities of the Buddhist firm generated an anti-colonial movement that propagated a combination of nationalism and Buddhism. Most nationalist politicians in Myanmar adhered to this mixture of political and religious beliefs to varying degrees. In the coming decades, Myanmar's government and political parties would depend on the Buddhist firm for support and legitimacy (Grzymała-Busse, 2015, p. 65). The Buddhist religious firm offered a coherent identity for the fledgling nation-state. Religious nationalism abetted the formation of a Buddhist national identity, and the power and legitimacy of the Buddhist firm itself supported social control and social disciplining that facilitated the widespread socialization and promotion of the Buddhist national identity.

Religious nationalism created a narrative of history and identity in early modern Myanmar in which the Buddhist firm disrupted the existing political order and came to dominate the Myanmar religious market. The result is that one religious firm, Buddhism, became a dominant source of national identity and a tool used to unite and define the nation and its citizens and noncitizens. The idea that "to be Burmese is to be Buddhist" led to the common belief that only Buddhists constitute real citizens, and all non-Buddhists remain outsiders.

CONCLUSIONS

Throughout Myanmar's history, the Buddhist religious firm has dominated the culture and religious economy while functioning as a moral and integrative force in the society. Religious nationalism—the fusion of national and religious identities—became critical in shaping the colonial era's religious economy. In the leaders of the British era, the Buddhist firm challenged government policy, authority, and social control and unified citizens to create an increasingly aggressive nationalist movement. The Buddhist firm members effectively challenged the colonial government's state–religion policies and authority to reshape the religious marketplace for the next century.

Religious nationalism forced an important change in a controversial British state–religion policy: the shoe policy. Religious nationalism emerged as an important strategic political tool that was effectively utilized by the Buddhist firm. In short, religious nationalism inspired and empowered the Buddhist firm and other Buddhist religious associations to change public policy. The Buddhist firm became central, and religious nationalism came to directly influence state–religion policy.

Buddhist nationalism served to disrupt colonial-era social controls. Although they paid a high personal price for their actions, Ottama, Wisara, and Saya San changed the political course of their country, and the representatives of the Buddhist firm contested the legitimacy of the state. The religious nationalism these men initiated ultimately rejected British colonial rule. Religion was used to mobilize popular sentiment for the Buddhist firm and to transform the existing political order.

For Myanmar's people, Ottama, Wisara, and Saya San possessed the social capital and legitimacy needed to facilitate their goals and to challenge British authority. These charismatic leaders framed an identity, shaped political action, and mobilized the Myanmar population to undermine the legitimacy of the existing state. Religious nationalism legitimized the nonviolent and violent disruption of colonial authority. The Buddhist firm provided the essential inspirational and organizational structure (i.e., associations) that allowed communication across villages and cities. Religious nationalism also provided widespread solidarity based on a common purpose (to preserve the Buddhist firm) and the leadership needed to organize and sustain the mobilization.

Buddhist nationalism defined Myanmar's national identity. Buddhist nationalism appealed to the basic human desire for identity and belonging. In the challenge to colonial authority, Buddhist nationalism provided identity, meaning, and legitimacy for disrupting the political order. As discussed previously, the Buddhist history provided a basic cultural narrative that reinforced belief in a common religion, provided shared historical memories, and built solidarity among the followers of Saya San, Wisara, and Ottama.

The Buddhist firm's framing of nationalism and identity evoked symbols and emotions that resonated widely—so widely that Saya San's rebellion continued for two years after his death. For members of the Buddhist firm, the Buddhist historical narrative gave meaning to the conflict with the British and to their lives and the difficulties they and their religion faced after losing state support of Buddhism. Since British rule, many people (including Saya San, Wisara, and Ottama) saw a threat to Buddhism. These leaders employed a robust narrative of Buddhist nationalism that promoted the idea that the nation should support and protect the Buddhist firm. Buddhist nationalists claimed that a resurgence and protection of the Buddhist firm was vital for preserving the nation. A common anti-colonial slogan, "Amyo, Batha, Thathana," (which roughly translates to "race, language, and religion!") declared the need to protect a specific identity. Buddhism became the widely accepted national identity. U Ottama created a national identity that combined belonging and citizenship with religion. During the fierce struggles of Ottama, Wisara, and Saya San (and bloody battles), national and religious identities merged to forge a powerful framework of religious nationalism. National identity became inseparable from religious identity. Buddhist nationalists cultivated negative images of non-Buddhists and depicted those deemed "foreign" as disloyal and in opposition to the state, peace, and unity. One consequence of linking religion and national identity was a policy and thinking in Myanmar of the need to convert or make non-Buddhist and non-Burmans into good Burmese citizens. Muslims and Christians would be asked (forced) to covert to Buddhism. By linking national identity with Buddhism, these leaders distorted the religious economy, created an untenable situation for citizens who did not follow the Buddhist religion, and laid the foundation for state corruption of the Buddhist firm.

The Buddhist nationalists not only rejected the British colonial government, but also sought to exclude all culture and religion deemed "foreign." The reality of the diverse population of the country that included many different indigenous ethnic groups and religions was rejected, but it could not be ignored. The Chin, Christians, Karen, Kachin, Mon, Muslims, Shan, and others were depicted by Buddhist nationalists as foreigners in need of "Burmanization." The Buddhist nationalists sought a culturally homogenous state in a country where such did not exist. Seeking a culturally and religiously homogenous state set the society up for perpetual conflict—wars that are continuing still.

Finally, Buddhist nationalism helped establish a social movement toward self-determination that aided in building the Myanmar state and thus reshaped Myanmar's religious economy. The conflicts between Saya San, Ottama, Wisara, and the British authorities placed the Buddhist firm in a critical role regarding the nation. Ottama and the other Buddhist nationalists established a religion-based identity and a shared understanding that justified, inspired, and legitimized their rebellious movement. The Buddhist nationalism narrative allowed for the identification and articulation of the problem with British rule. As Ottama argued, those in political bondage could not achieve deliverance from suffering. With the context and causes of the problem identified, Ottama and Saya San offered solutions. Their solutions included independence from the British and the restoration and protection of the Buddhist firm. These religious nationalists framed their solutions in terms of what their country "once was" and what it "should be." In other words, the citizens of Myanmar and the state once were Buddhist and should be Buddhist again. In this framing, the Buddhist firm reestablished itself within the foundation of the coming independent nation and, in doing so, excluded other religious firms. With important long-term consequences, they reinforced the Buddhist firm's dominance and made all other firms "foreign." Buddhist nationalism provided legitimacy to only one religion in Myanmar's religious marketplace. The rejection of British and foreign cultures also included minority religious firms. Minority firms, such as Christian, Muslim, Hindu, and others (even the native nats) would soon find it nearly impossible to compete for followers in Myanmar's religious economy. These findings suggest the need to explore two broad questions in the following pages. In the early post-independence years (1948–1962), how did Buddhist nationalists align with and against the state? When did the state and religious nationalists work together? The next chapter examines the motives, steps, policies, and methods that a beloved religious leader, Prime Minister U Nu, took to promote, entangle, and align state power with the Buddhist firm.

4

✠

Saturday's Son

The Religious Economy under a Devout Religious Leader 1947–1962

Imagine walking the bustling streets of downtown Yangon. Once called Rangoon, the city now displays impressive British colonial architecture (Association of Myanmar Architects, 2012). As noted in earlier chapters, Myanmar became a colony in 1824 and remained under British control until 1948. During those years, the British built remarkable buildings, and many of those beautiful structures still stand today. However, in recent years, they show an increasing need for maintenance (Girke, 2015; Rush, 2015). Yangon's public spaces, streets, and buildings have hosted the unfolding of British rule, world war, military rule, and an ongoing struggle for democracy and peace. Unfortunately, the regulation of the religious economy by the Myanmar government has perpetually undermined this struggle for both democracy and peace.

One of the most impressive colonial-era buildings, the Jubilee Hall, no longer stands on Shwedagon Pagoda Road in Dagon Township. The Myanmar military destroyed it about thirty years ago. The beautiful Gothic-style building, located near Shwedagon Pagoda, hosted many important historical milestones during the colonial era. In Jubilee Hall, U Ottama (see chapter 3) gave a fiery speech against the governor of British Burma, Sir Reginald Craddock, called "Craddock, Get Out!" (Aung, 2020). At Jubilee Hall in 1947, the Anti-Fascist People's Freedom League (AFPFL), led by Bogyoke (General) Aung San (1915–1947), drafted the country's first constitution (Smith, 1965, p. 230).

The 111 members who assembled in Jubilee Hall to draft Myanmar's foundational law decided that their constitution would support and require a liberal and open religious economy. Some in the assembly pressed to establish the Buddhist firm as the state religion, but that idea was vehemently rejected by General Aung San, who wrote, "Freedom of conscience should be established," and "the State should remain neutral on religious questions" (von der Mehden, 1961, pp. 169–70). Many who gathered at Jubilee Hall felt that favoring the Buddhist firm in the religious economy would face resistance from people who belonged to minority religious firms. They argued that state support for Buddhism would be divisive and exclude minority communities that Aung San was desperately trying to pull together.

On May 23, 1947, a draft of Myanmar's new constitution included this clause: "The Union shall observe neutrality in religious matters" (Smith, 1965, p. 231). With that sentence, the newly independent state apparently took the liberal approach of allowing an open and unregulated religious marketplace. However, those who sought to favor the Buddhist firm included another sentence in the draft that let the new state support and regulate the religious economy, stating that the Union "may, however, extend material or other assistance to religious institutions" (Smith, 1965, p. 231). That sentence would have allowed the state to assist (fund) and control religious firms and Myanmar's religious economy. Funding and support often constitute a means of control (Fox, 2016a).

The British briefly interrupted centuries of state support for Buddhism, but those who sought to recognize Buddhism as the state religion continued fighting for state support of their firm. The critical question of state involvement in Myanmar's religious economy was under debate when General Aung San and his leadership team were brutally assassinated on July 19, 1947. On a rainy July day in Yangon in a beautiful Victorian-colonial building called the Secretariat (once the seat of the British government), General Aung San and six respected leaders worked during a cabinet meeting to build a secular, inclusive, and independent Myanmar state. Like the country itself, the assembled cabinet members came from widely diverse backgrounds. Aung San, his brother Ba Win, and journalists Deedoke U Ba Cho and Thakin Mya all identified as Burmese Buddhists. Mahn Ba Khaing was a Karen scholar who identified as an ethnic Pwo Karen and a Christian. Sao San Htun identified as a Shan from Mongpon. Sayagyi U Razak worked as a scholar, teacher, and high school principal, as well as a national and regional leader who followed the Islamic faith (Myat Htoo Razak, 2007, p. 7).

After the assassinations, Jubilee Hall became a place of mourning as Aung San and his comrades lay in state in the hall for the next six months. Thousands of Myanmar people came to mourn their nation's founder, General Aung San (father of Aung San Suu Kyi), whom they still revere for his heroic efforts to liberate and unite all the Myanmar people as a single entity. Although many revere him as the architect of modern

Myanmar, the nation does not yet adhere to his preferred neutral state–religion policy.

General Aung San and those who supported his drafting of the 1947 constitution sought to remove state favor, support, and regulation of religion from Myanmar's religious marketplace. Aung San said, "We must draw a clear line between politics and religion because the two are not one and the same thing. If we mix religion and politics, then we offend the spirit of religion itself" (Win, 1988, p. 276). Few members of the

Figure 4.1. U Nu, his hands folded in prayer, participates in the 1961 ceremonies marking the death anniversary of the Buddha. *Source*: [public domain/artist unknown]

dominant religious firm (who sought to align their firm with state power) supported this state–religion policy.

After British rule, many Buddhist firm leaders sought power and favor from the state, but many also sought a liberal and open religious economy. From 1948 to 1962, the people of Myanmar enjoyed a sustained period of liberal democracy. In the late 1940s and early 1950s, each step toward aligning the state's powers with the Buddhist firm faced calls for a neutral state–religion policy from within Buddhism and, more often, from minority religious firms. Some in the Buddhist firm worked diligently to overturn General Aung San's liberal and neutral state policy and to align Buddhism with state power, but that same firm would later fight against the state and its control of Buddhism. This chapter examines the motives, steps, policies, and methods that a beloved Myanmar leader, Prime Minister U Nu, took to promote, entangle, and align state power with the Buddhist firm. What happened when a beloved, devout, and earnest person of faith sought to align state power with his religion?

PRIME MINISTER U NU AND STATE ALIGNMENT WITH ONE RELIGION

While General Aung San lay in state in Jubilee Hall, those who promoted the Buddhist firm's alignment with the state adopted this sentence into their draft of the constitution: "The state recognizes the special position of Buddhism as the faith professed by the great majority of citizens of the Union" (Smith, 1965, p. 231). That sentence in the 1947 constitution reinforced the historical link between Buddhism and the state. However, it did not declare Buddhism the state religion. Myanmar's 1947 constitution broadly established a neutral and secular government.

After Aung San's assassination, his friend U Nu (1907–1995) took his place as the prime minister of the newly independent Myanmar. Nu sought to build a nation-state on a foundation of liberal principles. Initially, Prime Minister Nu retained Aung San's secular state–religion policy. Interestingly, given his status as a holy man, he did not reference Buddhism or religion in his speech and moved to adopt the 1947 constitution (Butwell, 1963, p. 90). It remains unclear when and why Nu's official interest in state support and regulation of the religious economy changed. Still, his personal interest in religion appeared in his early years (Mendelson, 1975, p. 263).

Saturday's Son, Nats, and Buddhism

By almost all accounts, U Nu was an extraordinary individual and an able politician who led Myanmar through its early years of independence as its first prime minister (Schober, 2011, p. 79). Nu was "a handsome man with gentle searching eyes" who "seemed to fascinate all who met him" and had a sincere religious faith (Butwell, 1963, p. 63). Indian Prime Minister Nehru noted, "It is not that Nu is religious that is so eye-catching but the earnestness of his convictions" (Butwell, 1963, p. 65). Others, more recently, have written that Nu "lacked an understanding of [his] own sociocultural milieu and the majority of the Buddhist population" (Kawanami, 2016, p. 34). Nu's speeches, histories, biographies, and political actions strongly indicate otherwise. Nu believed that, as prime minister, he should act as a "promoter of faith" in the manner of past Myanmar kings. In many ways, he succeeded in that role (Butwell, 1963, p. 65).

Saturday's Son

U Nu was a Buddhist who also believed in and called upon the ancient Myanmar nats (Nu, 1988, p. 8). Nu was born on Saturday, May 25, 1907, to U San Htun and Daw Saw Khin of Wakema, Myanmar (Butwell, 1963, p. 3). Some people in Myanmar believe that a child born on a Saturday will have an extremely strong (some say difficult or stubborn) character and a tendency to be serious, hot-tempered, dangerous, unique, and disciplined (Butwell, 1963, p. 3; Htoo Htoo Wah, 2020). To propitiate the nats, San Htun and Saw Khin named their Saturday son Nu, meaning "gentle or soft" (Butwell, 1963, p. 4). Nu titled his autobiographical novel *Saturday's Son* (Nu, 1975), a nod to this mythology.

In *Saturday's Son*, Nu (1975) recounted his turbulent life until 1962. From his early youth, Nu regularly challenged the status quo (Butwell, 1963, p. 5; Nu, 1975) and became an unruly child who regularly drank alcohol (Butwell, 1963, p. 5). Becoming involved in politics at the age of thirteen, he participated in the first university student strike against British rule. He attended Myoma High School in Yangon, built as part of a nationwide movement by Myanmar nationalists to counter the perceived drawbacks of the British colonial education system (Aye Kyaw, 1993).

Nu underwent a personal transformation at age eighteen, inspired to live a life of virtuous deeds and service (Butwell, 1963, p. 5). Nu credited this change to the influence of Buddhism, which gave him "a new sense of values" and the urge to strive for Buddhist ideals (Butwell, 1963, p. 5). Nu came to adamantly believe in the guiding and healing power of Buddhism.

Nu went on to earn a BA from Rangoon University in 1929, and, after a few years of teaching, Nu returned to Yangon University in 1934 to study law. While studying law in 1936, Nu was elected as president of the student union and his friend, Aung San, as his secretary. Not long after that election, the university expelled Nu and Aung San for an article published in the student union magazine. University administrators considered the article, "Hell Hound Turned Loose," defamatory. Their expulsion sparked a robust round of student protests that forced the university to readmit Aung San and Nu (Aye Kyaw, 1993, pp. 67–68). The expulsion of Nu and Aung San and the widespread student protests pushed both men to national fame. Nu and Aung San were prominent figures in the movement that led to Myanmar's independence from Britain in 1948. Although Aung San was a nationalist who believed the state should remain neutral toward religion, his friend, U Nu, was foremost a Buddhist with a deep interest in furthering Buddhism.

Nu's Belief in Nats

A devout and pious Buddhist, Nu's religious faith also included a belief in nats (Butwell, 1963, p. 61; Spiro, 2011, p. 138). Many people in Myanmar (of all religions) believed in nats (Nu, 1988, p. 7; Spiro, 2011, p. 61). While prime minister, Nu regularly retired to Mount Popa, the ancient center of the nats, for long retreats to meditate and make policy decisions based on his nat beliefs (Spiro, 2011, p. 61). Prime Minister Nu and his cabinet leadership team, including the president and his entire cabinet, made annual official ceremonial offerings to nats (Spiro, 2011, p. 61). Prime Minister Nu also ordered the construction of two national shrines of the Mahagiri nats, one for Upper and one for Lower Myanmar, at the cost of 100,000 kyats. Later, the government announced its decision to build only one shrine on Mount Popa (Spiro, 2011, pp. 60–61).

Nu sought to support nats by proposing the planting of vast coconut plantations. Nu explained in a party speech that Mahagiri nats (see chapter 1) enjoy coconuts, so his political party and the country would succeed by incurring the favor of nats (Spiro, 2011, p. 60). Early in Nu's administration, the location of a new Student Union building for Yangon University was under consideration. Prime Minister Nu opposed constructing the building adjacent to Inya Lake because that location would require removing trees that housed nats (Butwell, 1963, p. 71). Nu approved of the final location of the building on the campus only after a careful survey of the preservation of the tree homes of the nats (Butwell, 1963, p. 71).

Delivering a speech in July 1987 at the dedication of the Center for Burma Studies at Northern Illinois University, Nu detailed his personal beliefs about nats (Nu, 1988). Nu related to the Northern Illinois University audience that the Mahagiri nats had explicitly helped his ill mother-in-law and with a large-scale construction problem during his time as prime minister (Nu, 1988, p. 7). As Nu described it, the Myanmar government constructed a dam in 1955 in the Meikhtila district near Mount Popa, where the Mahagiri nats live. As construction was completed and the date was set for the dam's formal opening, government engineers found that the dam was leaking (Nu, 1988, p. 8). After several engineers failed to repair the dam, Nu called a friend who agreed to make offerings to the Mahagiri nats and formally request that the nats stop the leak. As Nu said in his speech, some engineers doubted that the Mahagiri nats could help where they had failed. Therefore, engineers were dumbfounded when a sudden, heavy rainfall filled the dam and soaked the land, revealing the disappearance of the leak (Nu, 1988, p. 8).

Nu believed in nats. He asked the Northern Illinois University audience, "Do the nats help human beings? . . . I feel it should be answered thus: nats help some persons sometimes" (Nu, 1988, p. 8). In the 1950s and 1960s, critics and scholars thought Nu might not really believe in nats, but instead only used the nat belief as a means of social control (Spiro, 2011, p. 139; Butwell, 1963, p. 71). His speech in 1987 seems to indicate otherwise. Nonetheless, together with Buddhism, Nu also attempted to use nats as an instrument of political integration (Spiro, 2011, p. 138).

An Emerging Buddha

Some in the Buddhist firm considered U Nu a literal Buddha-in-the-process-of-becoming (Schober, 2011, p. 81; Smith, 1965, p. 264; Butwell, 1962, p. 9), and Nu was frequently referred to as a modern bodhisattva—an emerging Buddha (Taylor, 2015, p. 235). Myanmar's kings, in part in return for their protection and support of the Theravada Buddhist firm, often came to be granted the semi-divine status of an emerging Buddha. The idea that a ruler could be a bodhisattva is found in Theravada Buddhist scriptures (Lewy, 1974, p. 27).

Nu passionately believed that practicing Buddhism had completely changed his character and way of life (Butwell, 1963, p. 64). His religion was central to his identity and how he lived. After his election as prime minister, he said he planned to hold the post for only a short while because he wanted to spend his life in the further practice of Buddha's teachings (Nu, 1975, p. 215). As prime minister, Nu frequently touted Buddhism's importance as a unifier and reformer of Myanmar (von der Mehden, 1961, p. 167). The deep devotion of Prime Minister Nu to Buddhism appears evident in his speeches, activities, and public policy. In a 1951 speech at Yangon University, Nu told the students that "apathy to religion was the cause of at least 80 percent of Myanmar's troubles" (Butwell, 1963, p. 137; von der Mehden, 1961, p. 171). Nu saw practicing Buddhism as a moral prerequisite for public office (Schober, 2011, p. 79), and he enthusiastically used state power and his authority to promote a Buddhist welfare state and the Buddhist firm in Myanmar. Because of his honesty, integrity, and devotion to Buddhism, Nu sought to control, regulate, and manage Myanmar's religious economy. His state–religion policies led to political and religious factionalism, conflict and revolt from minority groups, and even violent protests from those within his beloved

Buddhist firm. A closer look at Nu's life and his leadership in Myanmar illuminates his motives and the problems a devoutly religious leader faces when aligning state power and policy with religion.

Nu's Motivations for Promoting Religion

U Nu held deep, fervent, and nuanced reasons for wanting the Buddhist firm to become Myanmar's state religion. First, he cared about the spiritual well-being of all humans. Nu felt that the government should care for its people's health and well-being, and for Nu, this included their spiritual well-being. Like many believers, Nu argued that the state must help its people understand, learn, and see the truth—as he understood it. As the religion had done for him, Nu's government attempted to use the Buddha's teachings to rehabilitate criminals (Butwell, 1963, p. 70). He wanted to help Myanmar's people escape the cycle of rebirth (Smith, 1965, p. 265). Like many clerics worldwide, Nu believed that people would look to those in authority and follow a religious firm the government promoted. According to Nu, the state must help those who practice Buddhism to fulfill the wishes of Lord Buddha (Smith, 1965, p. 266). Following the example of early Myanmar kings, Nu also tried to bring non-Buddhists into the Buddhist firm through state-supported cultural exchanges that promoted Buddhism in Myanmar and many countries around the world. As an individual, Nu zealously shared the Buddhist faith with everyone he met. From his household staff to leaders of other countries, Nu sought to convert non-Buddhists. Indian Prime Minister Nehru (who described himself as a "Hindu agnostic") reported that "Nu has even tried to convert me to Buddhism" (Butwell, 1963, p. 65). Myanmar's first prime minister sent Buddhist representatives to ethnic states to spread Buddhism (Kawanami, 2016, p. 32).

Second, Nu sought to promote and protect the Buddhist religion, so it could meet the desires of the majority of the Myanmar population. In a speech, Nu stated his desire to align the Buddhist firm with the state to meet "the desire of the overwhelming majority of Buddhists" (Smith, 1965, p. 263). For the Myanmar people who practiced Buddhism and worshiped nats, Nu's support of Buddhism and perpetuation of nat beliefs promoted the democratic legitimacy of his leadership and his government. As with Myanmar's early kings, supporting the Buddhist firm enhanced Nu's popularity, power, and authority (Butwell, 1963, p. 72). Nu also sincerely believed that the nats (specifically the Mahagiri nats) would help his political party and government succeed (Spiro, 2011, pp. 60–61).

Third, for Nu, the state also helped keep "unrestrained monks" in line with the rules from the Vinaya. Like Myanmar's kings, Nu felt that the state should regulate the behaviors of Buddhist clerics. Alignment with state authority was meant to promote the ideas, beliefs, and expected behaviors of those in the Buddhist firm. Some indications show that Nu wanted to "severely" control the Buddhist monastic community. Mendelson (1975) reports that Nu would have preferred to impose a *thathanabaing* ("keeper of the religion," see chapters 1 and 2) on the Buddhist order and then carried out regulatory measures (such as registering monks) to control the Sangha (Mendelson, 1975, p. 262).

Fourth, Buddhism could hinder the "aggressive ideologies" of Islam and communism (Smith, 1965, p. 149), and state support for Buddhism was needed to regulate the spread of Islam and communism (Smith, 1965, p. 149). Nu used his office's powers to shield the Buddhist firm from communist influences while aligning his government's socialist goals with Buddhism (Ford 2017, p. 26; Butwell 1962, p. 8). Prime Minister Nu sanctioned (or directly arranged for) the publication of a series of articles by a British-born monk, Francis Story, that "presented effective anti-communist arguments" (Ford, 2017, p. 27). In his speeches, Nu frequently noted that Buddhism absolutely condemns greed and that a socialist policy structure would allow Buddhism to thrive (Butwell, 1962, p. 8). Each activity and policy had at least tacit approval from Prime Minister Nu and from the Myanmar Parliament (von der Mehden, 1961, p. 171).

Finally, as a practicing Buddhist, Nu sought to make Buddhism the state religion to acquire religious merit. Making Buddhism the state religion would, Nu thought, constitute a meritorious deed, and Nu's personal desire for religious merit to advance his own spiritual life likely motivated his overt political support for the Buddhist firm (Smith, 1965, p. 265).

PERPETUATION, PROMOTION, AND PROPAGATION OF THE THERAVADA BUDDHIST FIRM

Back to Religion Movement

U Nu's speeches often referenced Buddhism, nats, and his delight in religious activities (Nu, 1988, p. 7). His political actions and policy choices closely related to his Buddhist and nat beliefs (Schober, 2011, p. 79; Butwell, 1963, p. 137). Nu frequently and publicly called for a "Back to Religion" movement (von der Mehden, 1961, p. 170). Agreeing with the advice he received from Nehru, Nu promoted a programmatic Buddhist revival (1947–1958) to further Buddhist nationalism (Schober, 2011, p. 79). Nu supported and began practicing the U Ottama and Saya San (see chapter 3) Buddhist nationalist tradition (Smith, 1965, p. 121). Nu deferred to the Buddhist firm in policy matters and developed elaborate programs to promote Buddhism. With Nu's support, Buddhism and nat worship became a central component of post-independence national identity (Smith, 1965, p. 121). In a speech, Nu proclaimed that "all activities directed towards the stability of the Union and the perpetuation of independence are steps toward the propagation of the Sāsana" (the teachings of the Buddha; von der Mehden, 1961, p. 170).

Prime Minister Nu established U Ottama Day, an annual celebration that kept Buddhist nationalism alive, and erected statues of U Ottama and U Wisara (see chapter 3). In January 1962, the Ministry of Religious Affairs opened the U Ottama Gardens and declared Ottama as Myanmar's "great nationalist leader" (Smith, 1965, p. 121). Under Nu, many people in Myanmar saw Buddhism and nationalism as synonymous with citizenship. As an unintended result of Nu's promotion of U Ottama's Buddhist nationalism, religion came to define those who belonged and those who were labeled as outsiders or foreign.

Administrative Oversight: The Ministry of Religious Affairs

Prime Minister Nu aligned state power with the Buddhist firm in incremental policy steps. In 1950, early in his administration, Prime Minister Nu sponsored the Pail University Act to "purify" Buddhism. This legislation established the Buddha Sāsana Council to study and propagate Buddhism and to supervise all monks. Later in 1950, Nu and the Myanmar Parliament created the cabinet-level post of Minister of Religious Affairs and the Ministry of Religious Affairs to support a Buddhist revival in Myanmar and to focus on implementing legislative acts concerning religion (Smith, 1965, p. 148). The Ministry of Religious Affairs works toward the "purification, perpetuation, promotion and propagation of the Theravada Buddhist Sāsana and the promotion of Myanmar traditional customs and culture" (https://www.mora.gov.mm). The creation of the Ministry for Religious Affairs entangled state power with the internal affairs of the Buddhist firm and gave the Myanmar government the bureaucracy needed to regulate and administer the religious practices of Buddhists (Schober, 2011, p. 81). The Ministry of Religious Affairs also had the authority to regulate minority religions.

The Ministry of Religion gave the state a mechanism for bureaucratic oversight that could regulate the Myanmar religious economy. The Ministry of Religion was intended to support and protect religion, but it also provided the state with bureaucratic power and policy tools to control religion. For example, the Ministry of Religion set up examinations for the monastic community and established a Buddhist University—both responsibilities allowed the state to regulate the Buddhist firm. Nu also used state funding to rebuild pagodas, temples, and monasteries long neglected during the colonial era.

The Ministry of Religious Affairs and other sub-agencies (such as the Buddha Sāsana Council) were created to promote a Buddhist revival that would halt the expansion of Islam and communist ideas (Smith, 1965, p. 148). Nu's attorney general, Chan Htoon, argued that Buddhism's ideas had slowed the expansion of Islam in Myanmar in the fifteenth century. In contrast, Hindu and Mahayana Buddhist countries had failed to stop Islam (Smith, 1965, p. 149). Chan Htoon argued that only Buddhism could prevent conquest by the "aggressive ideologies" of Islam and communism (Smith, 1965, p. 149). Nu needed state power to regulate and control the marketplace of ideas, and Chan Htoon declared that state authority and support were needed to promote the Buddhist firm's ideas and to "make history repeat itself" by stopping the spread of Islam and communism (Smith, 1965, p. 149). Chan Htoon did not support a free and open marketplace of ideas. He believed that Myanmar's people must be protected from "aggressive ideologies," and Buddhism must be protected, or they would succumb to alien ideologies. In a 1951 speech, Minister of Religious Affairs U Win declared that the government had accepted the role of promoting the Buddhist faith (Smith, 1965, p. 151). In the same speech, U Win said the government had several religious construction projects planned. The Myanmar government would renovate temples and pagodas and build a grand space to convene the Sixth World Buddhist Council (Smith, 1965, p. 152). Like King Anawrahta, Nu used construction to support and promote Buddhism. Nu modeled his behavior under the "king law" (see chapter 1) as a moral Buddhist ruler and a protector of Theravada Buddhism; he was committed to being the main patron of the Buddhist firm.

State Construction to Support Religion

Architecture is intricately tied to religious and political power (Wilson, 1988). Myanmar's kings built thousands of temples, stupas, and pagodas. Likewise, U Nu's government supported Buddhism and nat worship with large-scale construction projects. Physical structures, such as stupas and churches, shape the social, religious, and political relationships of a society. Prime Minister Nu ordered the construction of two national nat shrines: a Great Cave to host a two-year international Buddhist meeting and a large-scale coconut plantation for the Mahagiri nats (Spiro, 2011, p. 60). Shrines, monuments, pagodas, and buildings (such as the Great Cave) indicate religious support and, more importantly, the legitimacy and power of the individuals who help build them. The Buddhist and nat construction projects overseen by Myanmar kings and U Nu dominate Myanmar and provide those religious ideas with state-supported market space. State-constructed monuments influence Myanmar's people and religious economy. Because they are physically present and constantly seen, Buddhist structures in Myanmar lead the Myanmar people toward a specific historical narrative through a Buddhist/nat understanding of their culture. The architecture of the state-constructed religious monuments and buildings shapes Myanmar's religious economy and influences how people define in- and out-groups.

In the early 1950s, Nu and the Myanmar Parliament began planning, building, and supporting the country's hosting of the Sixth World Buddhist Synod. From 1954 through May of 1956, Prime Minister Nu hosted the Buddhist firm for a series of state-sponsored meetings in Rangoon (Butwell, 1962, p. 8). The historic two-year meeting of monks and Buddhist dignitaries ostensibly aimed to coincide with the Buddhist firm's 2,500-year anniversary. Following precedents set by Myanmar's kings, Nu used the meeting to attempt to control behavior within the Buddhist firm. Since the Buddha's death, these grand meetings had convened to rejuvenate Buddhism, purify the Pali canon, and help spread the Buddha's teachings (Mendelson, 1975, p. 277). Prime Minister Nu's state-sponsored meeting demonstrated his devotion to Buddhism and the Myanmar state's support of Buddhism. The two years of meetings illustrate the power of Buddhist nationalism and the government's effort to gain popular support and legitimacy by supporting the Buddhist firm (Ford, 2017, p. 36; Mendelson, 1975, p. 263). The preparation of the Sixth Great Buddhist Synod began in early 1952 when Prime Minister Nu ordered the construction of the venue, called the Maha Pasana Guha or Great Cave. The Great Cave seated five thousand clergy and ten thousand laypeople (Mendelson, 1975, p. 277). The construction of the Great Cave visually demonstrated the state's power and authority and clearly signaled the patronage and promotion of the Buddhist firm by the state (Blackburn, 2007, p.194).

Supporting the Buddhist meeting taxed the government's limited resources, thus reinforcing its significance as a show of support for Buddhism. The Myanmar Parliament established a government agency, the Buddha Śāsana Council, in 1950 to protect, manage, and support the affairs of the Buddhist firm. The state-controlled Buddha Śāsana Council oversaw the administrative details of the religious meeting (Schober, 2011, p. 80), and the council's budget for the event included state and private funding of approximately $6 million (in 1955 USD). The council used those funds to establish a printing press for the Buddhist firm and to build a hospital, library, and lodging for meeting attendees. The funding also provided for administrative offices and the construction of a human-made cave to resemble the one that hosted the first council after the Buddha's death (Ford 2017, p. 36). The venue (the Great Cave) still exists in Yangon as a popular tourist site, and it still hosts Buddhist meetings, honors ceremonies, and official disciplinary actions against members of the Sangha (Ashin and Crosby, 2017, p. 200).

Nearly three thousand members of the Buddhist firm gathered in the Great Cave to discuss internal matters, disputes, and policy questions related to the Buddha's teachings (Wei Yan Aung, 2019). Clearly showing their full support for the Buddhist firm, Myanmar's president, Dr. Ba U, and Prime Minister Nu attended the opening ceremony of the 1956 meeting. In a speech to representatives of the Buddhist firm, the prime minister expressed his intention to amend the constitution to make his country's dominant religion the state religion.

Following the prime minister's lead, three Buddhist monastic associations, the Maha Thawthuyana Association of Rangoon, the Yahn Nge (Young Monks) of Mandalay, and the Arakan Thawthuyana Association passed a joint resolution demanding that the Buddhist firm be declared the official religion of the state (Smith, 1965, p. 233).

A Constitutionally Established Religion

At the meeting's conclusion, the Buddhist firm sent copies of their resolution to make Buddhism the state religion to state authorities, including Prime Minister U Nu and the minister of religious affairs. Further, Buddhist firm leaders personally lobbied reluctant government officials to make Buddhism the state religion. Although Nu understood the perils of state alignment with the Buddhist firm, as a devout member of the Theravada Buddhist faith, he regarded his declaration of state support for Buddhism at the 1956 meeting as an unconditional promise he was honor-bound to keep (Smith, 1965, p. 234). Nu kept his promise and, over time, became the chief sponsor of a constitutional amendment that made Buddhism the state religion.

In 1959, the Buddhist firm's Union Presiding Monks Association passed another resolution calling for Buddhism to be the state religion. In the 1960 elections, Nu presented himself as a "devout Buddhist ruler and the defender of the faith" (Smith, 1965, p. 236; Kawanami, 2016, p. 35). During the election, Nu's opponents shrewdly highlighted the dangers of entangling religion with state authority. Arguing for a liberal and open religious economy, Nu's opponents opposed selecting Buddhism as the state's official religion (Smith, 1965, p. 239). An eleven-page statement from Nu's opponent's party argued that myriad social and political evils accompanied the entanglement of religion and politics (Smith, 1965, p. 239). They argued that such a policy would cause widespread discrimination against minority firms and that a liberal and free religious economy could prevent religious persecution and various other issues. In the 1960 elections, one political party (the Stable Anti-Fascist People's Freedom League) argued that making Buddhism the official religion would cause the entire Myanmar society to suffer. A state-declared religion would, they argued, lead to state control of that religion, discrimination against minorities, and religious persecution. The party's official statement argued that "making Buddhism the state religion would greatly weaken national solidarity by undermining the confidence of the ethnic and religious minorities" (Smith, 1965, p. 239).

Nu's opponents clearly understood the perils of an official state religion, but they did not oppose all state support (including unofficial support) for Buddhism. The party published a list of ten ways the Myanmar state could and should advance the Buddhist firm, including the following: making Buddhism a compulsory subject for Buddhist students (not all students), providing material support for monks, providing for state-supported primary schools in Buddhist monasteries, and promoting Buddhist missionary work (Smith, 1965, p. 240).

Although a few monks in the monastic community campaigned against him, U Nu enjoyed widespread and robust support within Myanmar and within the Buddhist firm (Mendelson, 1975, p. 263; Butwell, 1963, p. 224). Buddhist monks rallied support for him, succeeding in towns and small villages across Myanmar. The Buddhist firm thought that making Buddhism the state religion would mean greater success, power, and prestige for Buddhism and for their monastic community (Smith, 1965, p. 243). Thus, in his first eighteen months in office, Nu primarily focused on making Buddhism the state religion (Butwell, 1962, p. 4). Just as he motivated Myanmar's revival of the Buddhist firm after independence in 1948, the prime minister became the chief sponsor of the constitutional amendment to officially support Buddhism (Butwell, 1962, p. 4).

Nu had worked hard to align the state's authority and power with the Buddhist firm, but even as he celebrated success, two immediate and important concerns remained. First, Nu worried about the Buddhist monastic community's ability to handle the responsibility of state power and religious authority. Would the monastic community use these twin powers appropriately for the good of all Myanmar people or only for the Buddhists? Second, Nu worried about the "fears and anxieties in the minds of non-Buddhist citizens of the Union" and admitted that some of their fears were legitimate (Smith, 1965, p. 267).

U Nu's Concern for Minority Religious Firms

In speeches and meetings, U Nu voiced some concerns about the impact of state–religion entanglement that his friend General Aung San had raised in 1947. Nu told the Buddhist firm's leadership that state support for one religion could severely impact the unity of the newly independent nation. He voiced further concerns that people who did not follow the Buddhist faith worried about religious freedom, citizenship, and the financial and market advantages granted to the Buddhist firm compared to minority religious firms (Smith, 1965, p. 233).

In 1957, Nu held a series of meetings with representatives of several minority religious firms—Islam, Christian, and Hindu—to discuss his plan to support and protect the Buddhist firm. The minority firms had reservations about Nu's proposed policies. Christians and animists (nats) in Kachin state reacted with violence and protests. Massive crowds marched with banners and shouted their disagreement with Nu's proposal of selecting the Buddhist firm for state favor and support (Smith, 1965, p. 245). Muslim, Hindu, Nat, and Christian representatives forcefully voiced their apprehensions and growing dissatisfaction with Nu's state–religion policy. In 1960, Nu appointed a State Religion Enquiry Commission to consult and interview leaders of the Buddhist, Christian, Muslim, and Hindu firms (Kawanami, 2016, p. 39). The State Religion Enquiry Commission found that the minority religions opposed a state religion and the majority religion favored establishing Buddhism as the state religion (Kawanami, 2016, p. 39). In early 1961, the mostly non-Buddhist Kachins joined the dissatisfied populations with a revolt inspired (primarily) by the state–religion policy (Butwell, 1962, p. 6). Reassured by the State Religion Enquiry Commission that the majority supported a state religion, U Nu decided to go forward with the State Religion Promotion Bill. In August 1961, the Myanmar Parliament debated this constitutional amendment: "The State recognizing Buddhism as the faith professed by the great majority of the citizens of the Union declares Buddhism the state religion" (Kawanami, 2016, p. 39).

In August 1961, as the Myanmar Parliament debated Nu's constitutional amendment to make the Buddhist firm the official state religion, five men (a Kachin MP, a Muslim, a Christian, and two others) filed a suit in the Myanmar Supreme Court to stop Nu's proposed changes to the Myanmar constitution. Their lawsuit asserted that adopting Buddhism would promote discord and undermine national unity, and, interestingly, that the government was building nat shrines and promoting Buddhism to secure and legitimize state power (Smith, 1965, p. 263). In August 1961, the Myanmar Supreme Court dismissed the case, stating that the questions were not for the court to decide and were instead political questions to be decided by the Myanmar Parliament.

Myanmar's minority religious firms and associations argued that entangling state power with religion would have serious consequences for the country. In following the principles of a liberal religious marketplace, the Burma Christian Council (which represented the Anglican, Baptist, and Methodist firms) stated that each religious firm had a responsibility to support and promote itself (Smith, 1965, p. 249). Another association, the National Religious Minorities Alliance (comprising Baptists, Muslims, nat worshipers, and even some Buddhists from the Shan and Kachin states), argued that selecting Buddhism as the state religion would violate the spirit of General Aung San's Panglong agreement (Smith, 1965, p. 251).

The State Religion Act was made law on August 26, 1961 (Mendelson, 1975, p. 350). This act made Buddhism the official state religion and formalized the government's role in Myanmar's religious economy. The Myanmar Parliament added four subsections that burdened the government with protecting and preserving the Buddhist firm:

> Buddhism being the state religion of the Union, the Government shall:
> (1) promote and maintain Buddhism for its welfare and advancement in its three aspects: pariyatti, patipatti, and pativedha,
> (2) honor the Tiratana (Three Gems): Buddha, Dhamma, and Sangha,
> (3) protect Buddhism in its above-mentioned three aspects and the Tiratana from all dangers, including insults and false representations made by words, either spoken or written, or by other means,
> (4) maintain and preserve the Tipitaka Pali texts, the commentaries, and sub-commentaries thereof, as re-examined and recited at the Sixth Buddhist Council. (Kawanami, 2016, p. 40)

In establishing Buddhism as the country's official religion, Nu burdened the newly independent government with protecting and promoting Buddhism while protecting, regulating, and overseeing the minority religious firms. Myanmar gained the responsibility of regulating the marketplace of religious ideas and behaviors. Minority firms and groups felt threatened, and Nu felt the need to reassure and protect them. Members of the Christian firm in the Chin and Kachin states began an armed revolution against Myanmar in response to Nu's declaration of Buddhism as the state religion (Sakhong, 2003, p. 164). The Muslim firm and the Islamic Council declared their opposition. The Islamic Council predicted that making the Theravada Buddhism the state religion would make those who practiced other religions "second-class citizens" (Kawanami, 2016, p. 41). State support of the majority religion led to conflict and disunity.

Interestingly, Nu regarded national unity, not the promotion of Buddhism, as his most important task as Prime Minister (Butwell, 1963, p. 34). However, his favor of Buddhism significantly divided and dissatisfied minority religious firms (Butwell, 1962, p. 9). Opposing factions within the Buddhist firm and between the many different religious and ethnic groups became the single most important political problem of Nu's time in office (Butwell, 1962, p. 9). To address the divisive problems after establishing Buddhism as the state religion, Nu attempted to further control the Myanmar religious economy to protect the minority religious firms of the country and address the fears of those without state support.

U Nu's Attempt to Regulate Equity

To address fears and inequalities in the religious marketplace, U Nu introduced another constitutional amendment. In September 1961, Nu attempted to pass an amendment protecting the rights and privileges of minority religious firms. For Nu and the representatives of minority religious firms, state support for one religious firm necessitated additional state support and regulation in other areas. To promote equity in the religious market, Nu attempted to promote, protect, and further regulate Myanmar's religious economy. Nu sought to grant specific protections (for example, the right to also teach minority religions in state schools) to the minority religious firms. For example, Nu planned to allow Islamic studies for students of that faith in state schools (Smith, 1965, p. 273).

To protect the minority religions, Nu proposed another constitutional provision (Fourth Amendment): "The Union government shall protect the religions from all dangers including insult and false representation made by words either spoken or written or by other means" (Smith, 1965, p. 270). In a radio address to Myanmar's people, U Nu said that his proposed changes to the constitution would prevent bloodshed, internal strife, and the destruction of the union (Smith, 1965, p. 274).

U Nu Ultimately Makes Everyone Unhappy

The Buddhists immediately saw U Nu's attempts at equity in the religious marketplace as a sinister threat to their firm. Confirming his fears about the monastic community's ability to handle their newly established state powers, an angry and militant group of about one hundred yellow-robed Buddhist monks immediately confronted Nu, protesting at the prime minister's residence (Butwell, 1963, p. 226).

Monks held press conferences and declared that they would sacrifice their lives in the struggle against Nu's proposals for equity in the Myanmar religious economy. The Union Sangha League led the Buddhist firm's opposition, giving this warning: "Should the bill be passed with the support of the MPs, the sins of the fourth amendment would greatly outweigh the merits of making Buddhism the state religion" (Smith, 1965, p. 272). On the day of the vote, some five hundred monks picketed the Myanmar Parliament, which was protected by about two thousand police officers armed with bayonets and automatic weapons (Butwell, 1963, p. 226). Although the Buddhist firm's members protested and withheld "merit" to threaten government officials, the Myanmar Parliament unanimously voted to pass the amendment (Butwell, 1963, p. 226).

Nu's two constitutional amendments on the religious economy (establishing Buddhism as the state religion and guaranteeing freedom of religion for minority religious firms) were passed in August and September 1961, respectively. In the months that followed, Myanmar's people suffered from escalating religious violence (Charney, 2009, p. 104). The minority religious firms protested, and much of the Buddhist monkhood was upset. The All Burma Sangha Association staged a demonstration in protest. The Shwe Wa Yaung Sangha Organization in Mandalay declared their opposition to the fourth amendment. Some in the Buddhist firm argued that the amendment gave more rights and privileges to minority religious firms. Monks marched to the Shwedagon Pagoda and pledged to "give their lives for the protection of the Buddha sasana" and to fight the Bill unto death (Kawanami, 2016, p. 42). Nu had placed the burden of regulating the religious marketplace squarely onto his government and created factions and conflict.

The following month, in October 1961, Myanmar's home minister, Dr. E. Maung, gave the Muslim religious firm approval to build three mosques in the North Okkalapa township (in eastern Yangon). The representatives of the Buddhist firm led a series of anti-Muslim riots in the township to protest the state's approval of building places of worship for the minority religious firm. When the Myanmar government maintained approval for building the mosques, about fifty monks staged a sit-in and occupied one partially constructed building. After two weeks in the building, the monks (aided by a large crowd) demolished the construction site and set fire to another mosque (Smith, 1965, p. 279). Two Islamic people and two Buddhist people were killed when the state police fired on the crowd to prevent further rioting. The police arrested 371 people, including 92 monks who acted as direct representatives of the Buddhist firm (Butwell, 1963, p. 226). The Buddhist firm declared the government responsible for the violence and labeled Nu a "bogus Buddhist" (Butwell, 1963, p. 226).

In late November 1961, to ease religious conflict and promote peace, Nu's government directly supported the Buddhist firm through the construction of 60,000 sand pagodas across Myanmar. On November 26, the Ministry of Religious Affairs announced that, "to avert impending dangers and to achieve complete peace and tranquility in the Union," sand pagodas would be built in all district towns. This government directive supporting the Buddhist firm specifically ordered that "pagodas should be nine cubits in height, and the umbrellas of the pagodas should also be in nine rings either in brass or iron." Lastly, the government directed the pagoda sites be completed "between 6 a.m. and 8.24 a.m. on Saturday, December 9" (Charney, 2009, p. 104).

CONCLUSIONS

The U Nu era in Myanmar reveals three important consequences of state–religion entanglement. While fervently supporting the Buddhist and nat firms, Nu and his government also attempted to support minority religious firms. Nu's government not only tolerated, but also sought to protect minority religious firms via laws. Nu's attempts to promote, regulate, and control the religious economy led to critical problems for his administration, for the Buddhist and minority religious firms, and for the Myanmar people.

First, although some Buddhist firm members will claim otherwise, a liberal religious economy is not unfamiliar to the people of Myanmar. General Aung San and his diverse leadership team clearly embraced a religiously neutral and secular government. Perhaps that decision was partly due to the neutral state–religion policy of the British. Without General Aung San's assassination, the liberal and neutral secular government he promoted in the 1947 drafts of the constitution could have changed the lives of Myanmar's people. Had Aung San lived, religious firms and ideas could have flourished or wilted on their own merit. The Buddhist firm would have been forced to continue as it had under the neutral state–religion policy of the British. Instead, the Buddhist firm gained market protection, and all its beliefs and leadership fell under the control of the Myanmar government.

Second, the attempt of a devout and beloved religious leader to rule through religion had failed. After General Aung San's death, Nu and Myanmar's leaders, specifically leaders of the Buddhist firm, sought to manage, improve, and control their society through their religion and by regulating the religious economy. Religious leaders worldwide often believe their religion holds the answers for proper conduct and for a well-functioning society (Fox, 2008). Most accounts show Nu as a sincere and devout Buddhist (who also believed in nats) who genuinely felt that his country's people would benefit if Buddhist and nat ideas were supported and followed. Nu's efforts to promote Buddhism and nats meant that his government faced hostility from his own religion and grave political factionalism and secessionist movements among Myanmar's minority groups and religious firms.

Prime Minister Nu faced hostility from all sides (Charney, 2009, pp. 104–6). Attempting to support, control, and regulate the religious marketplace, Nu failed most conspicuously at the task he regarded as most important: achieving national unity (Butwell, 1962, p. 9). Nu sought to rule as kings had in Myanmar's precolonial past, but he did not (or could not) force a unified monastic community, nor could he manage the religious economy in a way that pleased all religious firms. Thus, the Buddhist firm played "fast and loose" with the government, and minority groups protested (Mendelson, 1975, p. 26).

Prime Minister Nu burdened his government with regulating ideas and religion. Nu's administrations (1948–1956, 1957–1958, and 1960–1962) contentiously tried to regulate the entire religious economy and to control the dominant religious firm, ultimately losing support from and control of Buddhist and minority firms. In the end, his government collapsed. The effort of the sincere and earnest religious leader to manage the religious economy ended with U Nu being labeled by some as "bogus Buddhist" and in nationwide conflict.

Third, and perhaps the most critical outcome for Myanmar's people, Buddhism became more central to citizenship. Prime Minister Nu sought a return to religion and promoted Buddhism to a place of honor and patronage, a place it held under Myanmar's kings. Thus, Buddhism became the foundational element of nationhood, and people with other religious beliefs became outsiders. Under Nu's leadership, the Myanmar society came to define itself in the mold of U Ottama and Saya San Buddhist nationalism. Buddhism became synonymous with national identity.

The conflict and tensions U Nu created in the religious marketplace opened the door for a military government (Schober, 2011, p. 82). With the collapse of his government, Nu temporarily gave power to General Ne Win. Under Ne Win, the army brought about order, and Nu returned to power in 1960 via a national election—only to be ousted two years later by a Ne Win–led military coup in 1962. Ne Win imprisoned Nu from 1962 to 1966. Minority firm unrest, largely because of the constitutional establishment of Buddhism as the state religion, provided pretext for General Ne Win's coup. Chapter 5 explores the Ne Win era (1962–1988). How did General Ne Win and his authoritarian government reshape Myanmar's religious economy? How did the Buddhist and minority firms fare under strict authoritarian control?

5

✟

Going to Moscow

The Religious Economy under a Brutal Dictator 1962–1988

Imagine for a moment flying into Yangon International Airport. As your flight approaches Myanmar's busiest airport, known by locals as Mingaladon Airport, you lean against your window and scan the cityscape below. In this area of northern Yangon, in addition to the ubiquitous white taxis inching along in the traffic below, you might spot the campus and buildings of the Myanmar Institute of Theology or the open areas of the park of the community of Insein. As your pilot banks to line up with runway 21, you might catch a glimpse of Insein Prison (pronounced "insane"). Prisoners commonly call Insein Prison the "darkest hell-hole in Myanmar." In the 1980s, the Myanmar military commonly threatened monks, clerics, students, and other political activists with the phrase "going to Moscow," which meant going to Insein Prison (Kongrut, 2016). The notorious prison stands out from the air and is easily identifiable by its size and distinctive shape.

Insein Prison has been used to defrock and torture Buddhist monks who challenge the military, imprison Catholic missionaries who aid protestors, and violently repress political dissidents (Seekins, 2011, p. 131). The prison is shaped like a pendulum wall clock with a round face and a rectangular attachment where the pendulum would swing (Ma Thanegi, 2013, p. 47). Inside the prison's main entrance is a tall pillar with an image of Buddha on top (Ah Noh, personal communication, April 2, 2021). Inmates and guards say that if a released prisoner looks back at the Buddha while leaving the prison, they will one day return to prison. Every day after the political prisoners line up in the hallway, they are counted and required to repeat a Buddhist prayer in unison, sentence by sentence

Figure 5.1 The infamous "Insein Prison" is located in Yangon (Rangoon), the old capital of Burma (Myanmar). *Source*: Joe and Clair Carnegie / Libyan Soup

(Ah Noh, personal communication, April 2, 2021; Ma Thanegi, 2013, p. 51). Built by the British in 1887, Insein Prison was constructed in the circular design created by the renowned eighteenth-century British philosopher Jeremy Bentham (Foucault, 1995, p. 200). While Bentham was an advocate of the separation of church and state, freedom of expression, and individual legal rights, his prison design became a tool of repression of those very rights (Atkinson, 1972, p. 210). Bentham's panopticon (a circular prison with cells arranged around a central well) design (also used by the Nazis at Sachsenhausen concentration camp in Germany) was created to enable a small number of guards to monitor all inmates without the inmates knowing if they were being watched (Foucault, 1995, p. 201). The effect of Bentham's prison design is to induce in the inmate a state of conscious and permanent visibility. Insein prisoners believe or assume that they are always under surveillance, which ensures an automatic functioning of power and compliance (Foucault, 1995, p. 201; Ma Thanegi, 2013, p. 105). Insein Prison is not just a collection of buildings; it is itself a structure of power, surveillance, a tool of oppression and social control (Semple, 1993, p. 3–4).

Since General Ne Win took control in March 1962, Insein Prison has become notorious around the world for its brutally inhumane conditions and torture (Ma Thanegi, 2013, p. 53). In Insein, Ne Win imprisoned hundreds of thousands of his political opponents, including students, Buddhist monks, and political activists (Ma Thanegi, 2013, p. 19). Many died in the prison from neglect and poor health (Ma Thanegi, 2013, p. 53). A sentence to Insein Prison "could be tantamount to a death sentence" because of the living conditions (Ma Thida, 2017, p. 122). While Insein Prison has been an effective and brutal mechanism of Myanmar's ruling military's violent repression, Bentham's prison design provided guiding principles for Ne Win's totalitarian state (Semple, 1993, p. 3). Ne Win's military government embraced, employed, and widely used Bentham's principles of power, control, and surveillance as mechanisms to suppress and regulate Myanmar society and the religious economy. In his book *Nineteen Eighty-Four*, George Orwell provided a phrase for Ne Win's surveillance, regulation, and repression: "Big Brother is always watching" (Larkin, 2011, p. 71). Following the brutal and repressive regime in Moscow, General Ne Win ruled the Myanmar religious economy with an iron fist (Silverstein, 1992).

WEDNESDAY'S BRIGHT SON

While Ne Win and U Nu were vastly different people and quite different leaders, both men were sensitive to and focused on religion's political potential and powers. Unlike U Nu, General Ne Win's personal views of Buddhism were largely (it appears that he was not devoted to any religion) kept to himself (Taylor 2015, p. 236). While U Nu's Buddhist faith was widely known and admired, Ne Win was seen as a superstitious rather than a religious person (Schober, 2011, p. 13). However, at different points in their political careers, both Ne Win and U Nu perpetuated the mythic claims of descent from Buddhist royalty (Schober, 2011, p. 95). Both men used the Buddhist firm as a foundation for authority and political legitimacy. Ne Win attempted to maintain an image of a devout Buddhist (Matthews, 1995, p. 291).

Ne Win was born in the small village of Paungdale, about two hundred miles north of Yangon, on Wednesday, May 24, 1911 (there is some debate about his birth date and time; he died December 5, 2002; Taylor, 2015, p. 8). At birth, his parents named him Shu Maung. His mother, Daw Mi Lay, was a strict disciplinarian with an intense spirit, and his father, U Po Kha, had a friendly and easy outgoing personality (Taylor 2015, p. 11). Neither of his parents was particularly religious. Unlike most other Buddhist parents, they did not provide Shu Maung with the customary rite of passage of time spent as a novice Buddhist monk (Taylor 2015, p. 11).

Shu Maung went to local schools in Paungdale and then to a National High School in Pyay (Taylor, 2015, p. 15). In 1930–1932, while the Saya San Rebellion raged (see chapter 3) across the countryside, Shu Maung attended Yangon University. The twenty-two-year-old college student was more interested in the Yangon nightlife than in studying and, consequently, was unsuccessful in the second year with the exams needed to continue studying medicine. In 1932, Shu Maung left the university without a degree and took a job as a postal clerk in Yangon.

While working as a postal clerk, he joined the nationalist Dobama Asiayone (We Burmans Association) and, in 1941, accompanied Aung San as one of the famed "thirty comrades" who traveled to Hainan Island for military training by Japan (Taylor, 2015, p. 19). During the training, Aung San selected Shu Maung to be a leader in the Burmese nationalist movement. While in training, twenty-seven of the Thirty Comrades adopted new names. Aung San suggested the new name idea. New names were intended to protect their families should authorities discover their activities and give them a sense of pride in their collective mission to bring about Myanmar's independence (Taylor, 2015, p. 35). Shu Maung adopted the name Ne Win, which means "bright sun" (Taylor, 2015, p. 35).

After training, Ne Win returned to Myanmar as an officer in the Burma Independence Army, where he soon became a lieutenant colonel, and he was quickly promoted to higher posts. After U Nu became prime minister, General Ne Win became chief of the armed forces' general staff and supreme commander. As noted above, in 1962, as tensions with minority ethnic and religious groups increased, Ne Win seized power and abruptly brought an end to Myanmar's brief experiment with liberal democracy. For the next twenty-six years, Ne Win and his military advisers withdrew from the world and sought to control and micromanage the Myanmar religious economy. His government would become defined by policies that protected the Buddhist firm and restricted minority religious communities. What happened to the religious economy of Myanmar under a brutal authoritarian government?

GENERAL NE WIN AND THE MYANMAR RELIGIOUS ECONOMY

On March 2, 1962, General Ne Win seized power, and the very next day he abolished the constitution that included U Nu's two (see chapter 4) religion amendments. The coup and Ne Win's abolishment of the constitution ended the discussion about religion and the constitution and brought an abrupt end to the protests by Buddhist monks. In the days and months after the coup, the Buddhist firm fell silent (Mendelson, 1975, p. 355). Ne Win immediately ordered a series of brutal, repressive, and illiberal policy choices for the Myanmar people. He smothered democracy, imprisoned thousands of political and religious leaders, dynamited the Yangon University student center, swiftly replaced U Nu's administration and the Myanmar Parliament with a military dictatorship, and his government made sweeping, radical, and repressive changes to Myanmar's religious economy (Schober, 2011, p. 82).

The broad macroeconomic policies of the Ne Win era focused on the maintenance of a socialist economy. Socialism is a political and economic theory of organization characterized by social ownership of the means and fruits of production. For Ne Win, social ownership meant that his military government owned and managed almost every aspect of the society. The military took over 129 private schools (many Christian). The students were required to attend a government-mandated curriculum consisting of vocational and agricultural training. Although socialists around the world disagree on the type, degree, and necessity of government social control and regulation, Ne Win's strategy was to create an extensive government structure to control almost every aspect of Myanmar's society, including religion. The Myanmar military took control of all the major means of production, including the Burma Economic Development Corporation, the State Agriculture Marketing Board, and the State Timber Board. Ne Win's rigid command of Myanmar's economy caused dramatic price increases and countrywide shortages in foods and consumer goods, and created a flourishing black market—and had similar effects on the country's religious economy (Badgley, 1962, p. 24).

In May 1962, Ne Win established the Central Security and Administration Committee (SAC), a comprehensive structure for governing Myanmar. The SAC was composed of lower-level SACs set up in the states, divisions, districts, townships, and villages of the country (Butwell, 1972, p. 902). Local SACs were given extensive administrative responsibilities, ranging from administering exit visas to the regulation of educational and medical facilities (Leigh, 2011, p. 180). SACs were required to micromanage the country's religious firms. This extensive governing structure was to replace the British-style parliamentary democracy that Ne Win saw as a failure (Butwell, 1972, p. 906). Where U Nu's liberal democracy and federalism had allowed for disagreement and divisiveness, Ne Win's centrally controlled authoritarian government would not allow divisiveness and intended to bring about order. The military government would eliminate (by force if necessary) partisan, ethnic, ideological, policy, and religious disagreements and divisions (Butwell, 1972, p. 906).

With a declared aim of maintaining order and national unity, Ne Win took steps to reverse U Nu's state–religion policies. In a decree that appeared to be liberal, Ne Win stated that his government would maintain a neutral state–religion policy and would not support one religion over others (Charney, 2009, p. 109). However, rather than open and deregulate the religious economy, Ne Win extended government control, regulation, and interference in the religious marketplace to a far greater degree than the policies implemented by Prime Minister U Nu (Schober, 2011, p. 83). Where U Nu had promoted an open and tolerant religious economy, Ne Win's "Burmese Way to Socialism" focused on heavy-handed (brutal) government management of the Myanmar religious economy. Ne Win sought to eliminate some religious firms and to regulate and control others.

To manage the regulation, Ne Win divided the Ministry of Religious Affairs into two separate agencies: the Ministry of Religious Affairs and the Department for the Promotion and Propagation of the Śāsana (Buddhist teachings). A more accurate translation of the ministry's name, thathana ye wungyi htana, is Buddhist Mission Ministry, not Ministry of Religious Affairs (the latter of which is the official translation; Fleming, 2016, p. 3). One sub-agency's mission was to regulate all minority religious firms, and the other's mission was to promote, support, and regulate the Buddhist firm (Matthews, 1995, p. 295). Using the Ministry of Religious Affairs bureaucracy and the SACs, all religious expression and religious firm liberty were severely limited (Leigh, 2011, p. 10). Under General Ne Win, the entire Myanmar religious marketplace and all religious firms were isolated and micromanaged by a brutal dictator and his "yes-men" (Leigh, 2011, p. 177).

The changes in state–religion policy in Myanmar (from the British colonial secular-neutral to U Nu's Buddhist-religious-state to Ne Win's authoritarian regime) profoundly affected the Myanmar religious economy. Under Ne Win, Myanmar's government attempted to control nearly every aspect of the religious economy. Both the majority and minority religious firms suffered greatly under General Ne Win (Fleming, 2016; Crouch, 2016a, p. 87; Leigh, 2011, p. 177). Ne Win sought to eliminate certain religions and micromanage and control nearly every aspect of those religious firms allowed to remain in Myanmar. Buddhist nationalism became a centerpiece for belonging and citizenship and forced citizens with non-Buddhist affiliations to be labeled "foreign" (Matthews, 1995, p. 291). It was not feasible to portray nat worship as foreign, so Ne Win attempted to suppress nat worship in the Myanmar religious economy.

NE WIN'S REGULATION OF MINORITY RELIGIOUS FIRMS

Ne Win's government applied a confessional policy on religion (meaning that the Myanmar state officially protected and promoted a specific religious firm—Theravada Buddhism). Ne Win's confessional state–religion policy meant that minority religious firms suffered, were marginalized, and were suppressed. Under General Ne Win, nat worship was the first to suffer suppression, then the Christian and Muslim firms were deemed foreign, then marginalized, and finally violently excluded from the Myanmar religious market.

General Ne Win and Nat Worship

For nearly one thousand years, nat worship (animism) has been an integral part of the religious economy of Myanmar (Enno, 1994, p. 43). Nat worship may not be appropriately labeled a minority religious firm in the Myanmar religious economy. Nat worship was and is common in Myanmar, and the actual number of people who practice animism is unknown. As noted in chapter 1, nat worship and propitiation has been part of Myanmar's religious economy since the Pye people—or as one Buddhist monk declared, nat worship began "at the beginning of the universe" (Smith, 1965, p. 177). Although additional research is needed to determine the full extent of nat worship today, every August hundreds of thousands of pilgrims from all over Myanmar descend on the village of Taung Pyone (about ten miles north of Mandalay) to commune with nats (Htun, 2016).

During the Nu era, nat worship enjoyed full government approval and support. U Nu's belief was that nat propitiation was justified with specific Buddhist texts (Smith, 1965, p. 173; Nu 1988, p. 9). Under U Nu, nat worship was not only supported but also practiced by the Myanmar government. In 1951, Prime Minister Nu hosted a sacrificial offering to the nats at his official residence. Before the ceremony, the Minister of Religious Affairs, U Win, sought Buddhist firm approval (Smith, 1965, p. 173). The monk leadership approved, declaring that the worship of nats "can be conducive to the achievement of the country's prosperity and advancement" (Smith, 1965, p. 173). The support of the Buddhist firm for the nat ceremony was recorded, broadcast over the radio, and published in a booklet titled *Union of Burma Procedure for Propitiation of Guardian Spirits* (Smith, 1965, p. 173). While the Buddhist firm had (and still has) mixed views on nat worship, both nat propitiation and lively nat festivals, with the full participation of government officials, were common and remain so today (Smith, 1965, p. 175). Some members of the Buddhist firm disagreed with Nu's support and propitiation of nats and felt that U Nu was practicing "bogus Buddhism" and had "disfigured" the Theravada Buddhist firm (Smith, 1965, p. 177). Taking the opposite approach to U Nu, Ne Win's government actively opposed the nat religion.

While General Ne Win's personal belief in nats remains unclear, he frequently turned to magical protections (Matthews, 1995, p. 301; Spiro, 1982, p. 140). Upon assuming control in 1962, Ne Win's government immediately launched a determined attack to end nat worship (Taylor, 2015, p. 237; Spiro, 2011, p. 62; Smith, 1965, p. 296). Ne Win's government sought to push nat worship entirely out of the Myanmar religious marketplace (Spiro 2011, pp. 62–63). Some in Ne Win's government viewed the practice of the nat religion as "backward" (Spiro 2011, p. 63). One member of Ne Win's military government complained that the Myanmar "people are still worshiping nats while rockets have been orbiting the earth" (Spiro 2011, p. 63). Ne Win's government opposed nat worship both for what they saw as "magical habits of thinking" and that the worship of nats encouraged the spending of capital in nonproductive channels (Spiro 2011, p. 62).

Ne Win's government implemented four policy changes to eliminate the nats from the Myanmar religious marketplace. One of his first acts was to cancel U Nu's plans for the government-funded construction of a nat shrine at Mount Popa (Spiro, 2011, p. 62). Second, the government published many articles ridiculing nat worship in popular magazines (Smith, 1965, p. 296). Third, the government sponsored several theater productions at Buddhist festivals that depicted nat worship as a foolish, ignorant, and superstitious custom that had nothing to do with Buddhism (Smith, 1965, p. 297). Finally, the government banned the production and showing of movies with nat themes or stories (Spiro, 2011, p. 62). General Ne Win's government "issued a decree prohibiting the production of any film depicting nats, ghosts, witches, etc. as part of the Revolutionary Government's efforts to remove the obscurantist influence of superstitious beliefs on the people" (Ho, 2009, p. 306). Ne Win's efforts to stop the practice were largely unsuccessful, as the Myanmar people continued to regularly practice the appeasement of nats (Anonymous, 2019a; Htun, 2016; Spiro, 2011, p. 264). His efforts to regulate the Christian firm were much more substantial and effective.

Ne Win and the Christian Firms

Ne Win's policy of violent repression and regulation of minority religious firms (and the promotion of Buddhism as the de facto state religion) is key to understanding the Myanmar religious economy. In an attempt to suppress them, Ne Win and his government frequently portrayed all Christian firms as "foreign" (Sakhong, 2003, p. 201). Since the country's earliest days, the people of Myanmar have, in fact, entertained many religious ideas. As noted in chapters 1 and 2, the Myanmar religious marketplace had hosted a range of Christian firms and ideas for centuries. Scattered throughout Lower and Upper Myanmar were robust congregations of Anglicans, Baptists, Catholics, and Methodists (Leigh, 2011, p. 9). Since the sixteenth century, Catholic missionaries had been in Myanmar and had enjoyed substantial success during British colonial rule. Baptist missionaries, led by the Judsons (see chapter 2), enjoyed success among the Chin, Karen, and Kachin (Sakhong, 2003, p. 106). Although first expelled by King Thibaw, the Anglican firm returned with the British and established churches in Mandalay, and the Methodists set up shop in Yangon. The Christian faith was not new or foreign in 1962.

Ne Win and others claimed that the Christian faith was an outcome of colonialism. Anglican, Baptist, and Catholic missionaries had enjoyed much proselytizing success under the liberal and neutral state–religion policies of the British. The success of the Christian firms coincided with the British policy, but the relationship between the colonial government and the Christian firms was often not close and always complex. The Christian firms enjoyed the colonial government's liberal state–religion policy, but the religious representatives and the government officials were not always close or operated with the same expectations (Leigh, 2011, p. 41; Sakhong, 2003, p. 85). The British state–religion policy had, in fact, allowed the Christian missionaries to work in Myanmar. Still, for the most part, the Christian firms were not direct representatives of the colonial government (Hellman-Rajanayagam, 2020, p. 244; Leigh, 2011, p. 42). The colonial government's main concern was profiting from natural resources and trade. The primary purpose of the religious firms was to convert the Myanmar people to Christianity (Leigh, 2011, p. 74).

During the British colonial era and beyond, Christian missionaries found it to be more challenging to proselytize those Myanmar citizens who were already adherents to one (or more) of the so-called universal religions—such as Buddhism, Hinduism, Islam, or Judaism (Leigh, 2011, pp. 10–11). By contrast, nat and Chin spirit worshipers made the personal decision to join the Christian firms in the tens of thousands (Leigh, 2011, p. 11; Sakhong, 2003, p. 106). As Leigh notes, people who had not been exposed to universalizing religions were found to be more receptive and open to conversion to different religious ideas (Leigh, 2011, p. 18, n.51).

The success of the Christian firm among the non-Buddhist Karens, Kachins, and Chins (combined with the perception that Christians were linked with British colonial rulers and Ne Win's Buddhist nationalism) led Myanmar's Christians to be commonly labeled as foreign. For many Myanmar Buddhists, the Christian firm, of any denomination, was considered to be controlled and funded by foreign entities (Leigh, 2011, p. 176; Matthews, 1995, 301). Broadly, those who joined the Christian firm became outsiders and were associated with the United States, various European states, and especially the British. Ne Win's government contributed to the othering of Christians and was openly hostile to anything and anyone deemed "foreign." In May 1963, Ne Win declared in a speech that "no foreigner can ever be a friend of Burma," and the following year, he expelled all foreign teachers and professors (Leigh, 2011, p. 13; Matthews, 1995, p. 297).

Ne Win's regime engaged in a policy of "Burmanization" (a euphemism for xenophobia) and "nation-building" through the aggressive promotion of the Buddhist firm and of an unwritten policy of "one nation, one race, and one religion" (Fleming, 2016, p. 3; Leigh, 2011, p. 177). A direct result of Ne Win's Buddhist nationalism was that those who adopted the Christian faith were considered and treated as foreign because of their non-Buddhist religious affiliation. Believing in Christianity meant forsaking one's nationality. The success of the Christian firm among non-Buddhists led to an association or linking of the Christian firm with ethnic secessionism and rebellion (Matthews, 1995, p. 304). Those who adopted the Christian faith were not considered true Myanmar citizens.

From March 1962 to May 1966, Ne Win's government placed increasingly tighter controls on all the representatives and activities of Myanmar's Christian firms. All religious firms and activities (including Buddhism) came under close scrutiny and tight regulation. Ne Win's government nationalized Christian firms' schools, destroyed Christian properties, censored all Christian firm communications, tightly controlled firm finances, stopped proselytism, booted all missionaries, and ultimately created a government-controlled monopoly for the Buddhist firm in the Myanmar religious economy.

Destroying Christian Properties: Under the Ministry of Religious Affairs, Ne Win's government restricted the building of Christian infrastructure. All schools and hospitals owned and operated by Christian religious firms were nationalized (Matthews, 1995, p. 288). The military increased its occupation of predominantly Christian areas (Chin, Kachin, and Naga) and systematically destroyed Christian churches, schools, and other properties (Fleming, 2016, p. 4; Fink, 2013, p. 237). In 1966, Ne Win nationalized 129 Methodist schools. All students were required to follow the same government-mandated curriculum, which focused primarily on agricultural and vocational subjects (Leigh, 2011, p. 174).

Censoring Communications: General Ne Win's censors closely monitored all Christian missionary correspondence, publications, and speech. In 1964, Methodist Reverend Edward Bishop was threatened with a trip to Insein Prison when he criticized the government's treatment of foreigners in a private letter home (Leigh, 2011, p. 176). After Bishop was warned that any criticism of Ne Win or his regime could land him in Insein Prison, he avoided leaving even the imprints of such thoughts on the backs of air-letter envelopes (Leigh, 2011, p. 177). Ne Win's government monitored and limited the materials they published, restricted the hosting of public lectures, restricted who they invited into the country, and finally, above all, halted all missionary outreach (Matthews, 1995, p. 295).

Financial Oversight and Regulation: The Ministry of Religious Affairs required all minority firms to regularly report all activities and report complete and detailed financial records. Ne Win's government went to significant efforts to ensure that minority religious firms were not financially supported with funding from outside Myanmar (Matthews, 1995, p. 295).

Ending Proselytizing: The military government ordered an end to proselytizing activities among all the non-Buddhist firms (Leigh, 2011, p. 180). The military made it a crime to attempt to convert someone from one religion, belief, or opinion to another (Matthews, 1995, p. 294).

Leaving for Good: In March 1966, Ne Win's government announced that all missionaries must leave the country by May 31, 1966 (Leigh, 2011, p. 185). All foreign Christian missionaries were expelled from Myanmar, and any remaining properties and mission schools became the property of the Myanmar government. On May 6, 1966, one Catholic missionary was reported to have been imprisoned for lending his car to dissidents (Leigh, 2011, n 74, p. 188). By early May 1966, most of the Christian firm's representatives had closed shop and departed. The remaining fifty-eight American missionaries, fourteen British, and a small number of Catholic missionaries left Myanmar by the end of the month (Leigh, 2011, p. 185). Marking the end of the Christian firm's mission in Myanmar after 153 years, the phrase "leaving for good" was written on the passports of missionaries as they departed (Leigh, 2011, p. 185). With the close of their Myanmar offices, after a century and a half of proselytization, the Christian firm had managed to convert about 3 percent of Myanmar's entire population (Tegenfeldt, 1968, p. 19). With implied finality stamped in their passports, the Christian firm's missionaries were driven out of the Myanmar religious marketplace. For the Myanmar citizen Christians who remained, Ne Win did not allow them to leave the country for further studies, meetings, and conferences. He maintained a campaign of religious regulation against all Myanmar Christians, removing Christian missionaries and the complete isolation of Myanmar Christians from worldwide support.

Muslims under General Ne Win: "This Is a Buddhist Country! Go Away!"

During the eras of Aung San and U Nu, the young Myanmar government recognized all religions and all the people of its diverse population as citizens. Citizenship laws (such as the 1948 law) before General Ne Win's regime did not record or in any way depend on a person's ethnic identity (Holt, 2019, p. 61). General Ne Win's xenophobia and support for an extreme Buddhist nationalism slowly reshaped the lives of those who practiced non-Buddhist religions and has created a society that is in perpetual conflict. Ne Win quickly drove the Christian missionaries out of his country. They held passports and had a place to go. The Muslim people, who were also considered foreign, but had lived in Myanmar for centuries, posed a different kind of problem. Myanmar was their home. In a speech in 1982, General Ne Win declared, "The foreigners who had settled in Burma at the time of independence have become a problem" (Kin, 1983, p. 94). To address his problem, Ne Win instituted a series of policies in the 1960s and 1970s that redefined human rights and the citizenship status of the Rohingya and other Muslim groups. People who were followers of Islam were expelled from the army and all Myanmar government positions (Matthews, 1995, p. 291). The position of Muslims in society was changed to the status of foreigners (Kin, 1983, p. 95). The legacy of independent Muslim heroes such as Sayagyi U Razak (see chapter 4), who was assassinated along with General Aung San, was no longer celebrated.

Ne Win and his military administration altered the very understanding of basic human rights, and with the reinterpretation of rights in place, he set about defining who was a citizen and who was not. Article 15 of the Universal Declaration of Human Rights states that all humans have a right to a nationality. If you are born on this planet, you have a right to be a citizen of a country. Article 18 declares that all humans have the right to freedom of religion, and that right includes the freedom to choose and change religions or beliefs. Teachers at the Kachin Theological College in Myitkyina (see chapter 6) understood these rights as globally accepted. One teacher, Jan Nan, explained, "[W]e had ties to the ideas of Martin Luther King, his ideas on nonviolent resistance. Social rights and civil rights became part of our vocabulary. Some teachers gave after-school classes at their homes, for discussions about injustice" (Thant Myint-U, 2020, p. 115). Ne Win did not want to respect these basic rights or even allow the people of Myanmar to speak of them. Ne Win's government refused to even allow the use of the words *human rights*. For decades, the Myanmar Institute of Theology in Yangon has held an annual fundraising foot race event to promote human rights awareness. Government officials refused to allow the race organizers to call the race the "Run for Human Rights," so they called it the "Run for Human Dignity" until 2015 (Sterken, 2016, p. 98). From 2015 to 2020, the event was allowed to be named "Run for Human Rights."

Along with references to the rights, Ne Win's military government discarded the traditional and long-established principle that human rights exist for *all* humans. A human right is commonly defined as a right that humans have simply because they were born on this planet. The state does not grant human rights, and they are universal and inherent to all (except in specific situations and according to due process). The principle of universality is absolutely critical and essential to the existence of human rights. There is a growing body of research that human rights are not just Western (Mende, 2021, p. 39). Nonetheless, Ne Win's government redefined this fundamental principle and, in doing so, reshaped and regulated the Myanmar religious economy.

In the 1960s, the Myanmar government determined that human rights existed only insofar as they were expedient for the state (Cheesman, 2015,

p. 99). For Ne Win, all rights were conditional, and the state set the conditions. Nick Cheesman identified this fundamental alteration and named the Myanmar government's redefinition "sovereign cetana" (Cheesman, 2015, p. 99). Sovereign cetana, as defined by Cheesman, is a principle of law and order used in Myanmar to qualify, delimit, and withdraw human rights in response to state policy imperatives (Cheesman, 2015, p. 99). As a dictator, Ne Win declared that he and his government had the authority to determine an individual's legal rights and status. Ne Win redefined basic human rights to fit his government through military domination (Cheesman, 2015, p. 107). When a person failed to meet certain conditions, the Myanmar state denied that citizen the basic human rights accorded to all who are born on the planet (Cheesman, 2019, p. 880). Under Ne Win, rights derived from cetana were dependent upon the state. Human rights were not universal, but were conditional privileges bestowed on certain people and denied to others (Cheesman, 2015, p. 110). General Ne Win's government bestowed rights only on designated citizens. Withdrawal or denial of citizenship meant withdrawal and denial of basic human rights. Foreigners, as defined by General Ne Win, did not have human rights.

To designate citizenship, the government set up a national registration agency. This department scrutinized citizenship records and declared that citizenship would be granted to indigenous people whose communities were deemed to be present in Myanmar before 1823, the year before the British established their colonial rule in Lower Myanmar (Holt, 2019, p. 46; Ibrahim, 2016, p. 5). The military then launched a nationwide operation to register and verify the status of citizens and people they viewed as "foreigners." As Ibrahim (2016, p. 5) noted, where people may or may not have lived in the 1820s is irrelevant to citizenship today, but Ne Win's government disregarded that human right (like others). At General Ne Win's direction, in 1978, soldiers used the operation as an excuse to assault and terrorize Rohingya. They destroyed homes and confiscated Rohingyas' national ID cards. Without the cards, the Rohingya are stripped of citizenship documentation and hundreds of thousands fled to Bangladesh. Ne Win's regime considered them "foreigners" and enacted a law that established a hierarchy of citizenship.

In 1982, General Ne Win's military government enacted legislation that embedded the concept of a "national race" into Myanmar law. The law (which is still in place today) embedded a narrow definition of citizenship and allowed the Myanmar government to discriminate against various groups, such as the Rohingya. Citizenship came to be based on ethnicity, and the Rohingya are no longer recognized as citizens. Denied citizenship in their country, this subgroup of followers of Islam became outsiders and a prime target for violence and hate (Ibrahim, 2016, p. 47).

The 1982 law denied hundreds of thousands of Myanmar people their basic human rights (Lee, 2019, p. 242). Guided by Buddhist nationalism, the Ne Win government began forcing Muslim citizens of Myanmar to leave the country. The Myanmar military conducted a series of brutal ethnic cleansing operations against followers of Islam, looting and destroying mosques and villages. One Muslim man described Ne Win's soldiers destroying a Koran and taunting those followers of Islam who were in tears saying, "Don't cry! This is not a Muslim country. This is a Buddhist country! Go away!" (Fink, 2013, p. 240).

The military regime gave names to each murderous and destructive operation. In 1959 the operation was called Shwe Kyi (Pure Gold), and then in 1966, it was labeled Kyi Gan (Crow), followed by Ngazinka (Conqueror) and Myat Mon (More Purity) in 1967 and 1971 (Habiburahman, 2019, p. 68). In 1973, General Ne Win launched operation Major Aung Than (Millions of Successes), and then in 1974, the military continued to terrorize the Muslim population with operation Sabae (Purify) (Habiburahman, 2019, p. 69). The names of these Ne Win-led operations were meant to both indicate the operation's mission objective and bestow accolades on those who carried out the massacres and destruction.

Hundreds of thousands of Muslim refugees fled to Bangladesh. Ne Win's definition of citizenship left the Myanmar religious economy in a state of fragmented conflict. Relations between those who identify as Buddhist Burmans (about 60 percent of the country's population) and those who identify as non-Buddhist minorities (the remaining 40 percent) are artificially strained and fragmented. Ne Win's extreme version of Buddhist nationalism defined religious minorities as foreign threats to "race and religion." His government sought to protect the Buddhist firm from Islam and used being a follower of Buddha as a test for being a citizen. Ne Win "Burmanized" the Myanmar religious economy by depriving followers of Islam (and other religious minorities) of their basic religious rights and also of their right to exist in the religious marketplace. Ne Win's regime created a religious economy where only those who identified themselves as Buddhists belonged and were considered true citizens. The minority religious firm had no place in Myanmar. The ruthless general did not stop with the Christian, Muslim, Hindu, and nat firms; he also micromanaged and regulated the Buddhist firm.

NE WIN'S REGULATION OF THE MAJORITY RELIGIOUS FIRM

Ne Win's government inherited a Buddhist firm that was sharply divided into several different factions (see chapter 2 and Mendelson 1975, p. 242). The factions and divisions within the Buddhist firm made controlling the monastic leadership and the larger community difficult. U Nu and Ne Win feared this loss of control, albeit for different reasons (Taylor 2015, p. 236). Both leaders followed the example set by Myanmar's kings and sought to organize, regulate, and micro-manage the Buddhist firm. Much had changed during the British era. The Myanmar people had welcomed liberal structures and democratic concepts of governing. Thus, following Saya San and proclaiming himself king did not present itself as a viable political possibility for Ne Win. An alternative was for the brutal military general to govern as king. His dictatorship (and perhaps the one in 2021) is better understood in this context.

Ne Win as King: Protecting Religion

Ne Win identified his political and religious authority with that of King Anawrahta (Matthews, 1995, p. 414). The ruthless dictator and his army assumed the role of the crown. Following the ancient kings who traditionally built a pagoda in their honor to stand as a relic of their rule, Ne Win had the Maha Wizaya Pagoda constructed in his honor. Adopting the ancient king's precolonial pattern of governing, General Ne Win centralized control of the Buddhist firm under the guise of protecting religion. In his policies and speeches, Ne Win proclaimed that "the Government must protect and cleanse the Sangha" and that "the Government must remove the Sangha from politics" (Matthews, 1995, 415).

Appearing at first to take a liberal approach to the religious economy, the Ne Win government publicly removed state support of the Buddhist firm and declared that it supported freedom of religion (Charney, 2009, p. 109). In 1962, all Buddhist religious holidays were suspended, the ban on animal slaughter ended, and proselytizing activities among the non-Buddhist minorities halted (Matthews, 1995, p. 288). However, the military government's actual state–religion policy tightly controlled and highly regulated nearly every aspect of the Myanmar religious economy.

After the coup in 1962, the Buddhist firm was suspicious of and silent about General Ne Win and his regime (Mendelson, 1975, p. 355). That silence did not provide the military government with the symbols of support and legitimacy it needed to govern with at least some degree of legitimacy (Matthews, 1995, p. 414). Ne Win quickly realized that it could become both politically powerful and threatening if the Buddhist firm was not controlled. Monks held significant moral authority and could lead opposition movements, and General Ne Win's fear of the firm turned out to be well founded.

Ne Win's Policies and Actions Protecting and Controlling the Buddhist Firm

Acting on his need for legitimacy and his fears of the Buddhist firm's authority and power, Ne Win's regime established firm control over the Sangha. With the Buddhist firm under his command, he then routinely used religious nationalism as a tool of social control. Ne Win implemented extensive controls on the leadership and members of the Buddhist monastic community. As if managing prisoners in Insein, Ne Win's government sought to regulate and control nearly every aspect of the Buddhist firm. His regime monitored individual monk and Buddhist firm political activities, communications, the status of high-profile monks, properties, finances, proselytizing, entrance examinations and registration, and monk discipline, and promoted a Burman version of Buddhism.

State Monitoring of Monk and Firm Political Activities and Communications: As in Insein Prison, Ne Win had the Buddhist community under constant surveillance and monitoring. His regime placed military intelligence agents, disguised as monks, in the Buddhist firm's monasteries and universities to monitor political activity, loyalty to the government, and discussions of political matters, and to report any meetings with political activists. The monk intelligence agents reported any suspicious activity to the military and were known to urge other monks to refrain from any involvement in politics and policy making (Fink, 2013, p. 230). In an attempt to further control the Buddhist firm's activities, the military also attempted to put intelligence monks on monastery governing committees (Fink, 2013, p. 231). Monks who were found to be disloyal to Ne Win and his regime were defamed and often disrobed (Schober, 2011, pp. 84–85). If a monk began to enjoy widespread popularity or to gain generous support from politically influential donors, Ne Win's government would target that monk and his monastery for a purge and he would be disrobed. The state controlled the intellectual discussions and actions of the Buddhist firm. Many clerics were silenced and disrobed. Ne Win ordered about eighty highly popular monks to be disrobed (Schober, 2011, p. 84). The surveillance and monitoring of individual monks and the Buddhist firm also provided Ne Win with potential loyal "government monks." A government monk is both loyal and willing to support and promote state policies. Loyal monks (like Shin Arahan in chapter 1) were promoted to leadership positions within the Buddhist firm and the state-controlled council of monks (Fink, 2013, p. 230).

Buddha's Tax—Properties and Financial Control: Financial support was used to control the Buddhist firm. Ne Win's government used direct gifts and donations, and financial oversight and control to reward loyal government monks. The Buddhist firm leadership was financially bound to Ne Win's regime. Ne Win relied on these loyal senior monks to keep younger monks in line with his decisions and policies. He rewarded loyal clerics with lavish properties and substantial financial support. During Ne Win's era, his top generals provided financial support for individual monks, the building of new monasteries, the restoration of pagodas, and the bestowing of lavish gifts to loyal monks (Schober,

2011, pp. 83–84). During Ne Win's era and beyond, many monks were unable to turn down the financial support and consumer luxuries given to them by the top military men.

Ne Win's regime organized the administration of the Buddhist firm to mirror the state's regulation and control of the larger political and economic domains. Buddhist institutions were indirectly administered by the military (Schober, 2011, p. 84). The state closely monitored Buddhist financial affairs and donations. This state control meant that donations made to the Buddhist firm were directed only to loyal monks who worked under the patronage of the state (Schober, 2011, p.84).

Ne Win's military government simultaneously expanded the Buddhist firm's infrastructure by building monasteries, pagodas, and stupas while destroying Muslim, Nat, Hindu, and Christian properties. In Muslim communities, Ne Win's policy was to tax the local followers of Islam to fund the construction of Buddhist infrastructure. Habiburahman (called Habib), a Rohingya, recalls his parents paying a "Buddha's tax" (Habiburahman, 2019, p. 41). Ne Win's soldiers regularly patrolled and harassed Habib's Muslim village of Mylmin (between Chin and Arakan State). In the early 1980s, the military announced that every villager was required to help build a pagoda for the Buddhist firm. One member of each family was required to participate in the actual construction work and each family was required to make a donation (Buddha's tax) of one thousand kyats toward the construction project (Habiburahman, 2019, p. 41).

The military was forcing the construction of a pagoda on a nearby mountaintop, at the exact location where a congregation of Christians had regularly gathered for many generations for worship. Habib recounts an outraged Christian villager with important questions: "Destroying our place of worship is totally unacceptable! There are vast forests around here, so many places where they could have built this pagoda. What is all this supposed to mean? That they want to make the country Buddhist and to trample all other religions underfoot? Doesn't making Christians, Muslims, Hindus, and animists pay for their religion go against their principles?" (Habiburahman, 2019, p. 41).

The answer to the villager's questions is that Ne Win's regime was controlling and regulating the religious marketplace. The "Buddha tax" and the building of a Buddhist place of worship on a Christian site of worship put a financial burden on the Hindu, Muslim, and Christian villagers, pushed the Christian firm further out of the marketplace, and pulled the Buddhist firm under the financial control of the government. What appeared to be the support and protection of the Buddhist firm was state control and micromanagement of the power and structure of the firms that were present in the Myanmar religious economy.

Ne Win directly employed monks to proselytize among animists and Christians (Schober, 2011, p. 83). The government employed and directed monks who exhibited loyalty to Ne Win's military; they were sent to establish monasteries to Chin, Kachin, and Naga areas via the department for the Promotion and Propagation of the Sāsana (Fleming, 2016, p. 13). These communities reported incidents of forced conversion (Schober, 2011, p. 83).

Ne Win's State Administration of Internal Buddhist Affairs

To further control and harness the Buddhist firm's power, Ne Win's government established a council of monks called the State Sangha Mahanayaka Committee (Ashin and Crosby, 2017, p. 200; Taylor, 2015, p. 236). This council, or Supreme Council of Abbots, was administered under the Ministry of Religious Affairs and was charged with controlling and regulating internal monastic affairs (Schober, 2011, p. 83). Ne Win created a separate Ministry of Religious Affairs and created the department for the Promotion and Propagation of the Sāsana. A more accurate translation of the ministry's name, thathana ye wungyi htana, would be Buddhist Mission Ministry, not the Ministry of Religious Affairs (the latter of which is the official translation; Fleming, 2016, p. 3). The ministry was instituted to protect, promote, and propagate the Ne Win regime's version of Burmese Buddhism. The government-appointed body of Buddhist monks was established to oversee and regulate the Buddhist firm. The state-controlled and centralized administration of the Sangha reduced the significance of once-powerful monastic factions.

Ne Win's regime determined the council's agenda and the outcome of nearly every decision, and did not tolerate any dissent in policy formulation (Schober, 2011, p. 83). The council was charged with centralizing the administration of all of Myanmar's Buddhist institutions and personnel. It managed and controlled the properties of Buddhist firms; selected the monastery leadership; revised and managed Buddhist training, curriculum, and examinations; and oversaw the registration of all Buddhist monks. The registration of monks, nuns, and novices provided the state with an effective tool of control. Registration was intended to help remove monks from politics and reduce the number of factions within the Buddhist firm, but it also allowed for the micromanagement of internal affairs (Schober, 2011, p. 83). Registration was to establish proper ordination and membership within one of the council-approved factions or lineages (Mendelson, 1975, pp. 341–42). Registration also allowed the Ministry of Religious Affairs, in conjunction with the council, to identify and keep track of the locations and behaviors of all clerics. Many of the clerics in the Buddhist firm realized the implications of Ne Win's registration campaign and were reluctant to comply (Taylor, 2015, p. 237; Mendelson, 1975, p. 341). This reluctance was reflected in low participation rates by members of the monastic community (Schober, 2011, p. 83).

The State Sangha Mahanayaka Committee was granted the power to take disciplinary action against monks who were charged with Vinaya (a set of disciplinary rules and guidelines for monks and nuns) transgressions (Schober, 2011, p. 85). To oversee the regulation and conduct of the Sangha, the council appoints a court that deals with internal religious matters. If a monk or nun is accused of a criminal offense (as defined by the criminal code and the Department of Religious Affairs) or is involved in a civil dispute, they will be tried in secular courts (Ashin and Crosby, 2017, p. 200). For religious matters, such as heresy and malpractice, the council appoints a special court (vincchaya) that tries Buddhist monastics (Ashin and Crosby, 2017, p. 200). The leadership of the state-appointed council oversees a religious court system that has the full authority of the state and its law enforcement agencies, even for purely religious matters (Ashin and Crosby, 2017, p. 200). Cases of heresy and monastic malpractice are heard and decided in trials held in the Great Cave (see chapter 4) built by Prime Minister U Nu. With state oversight and authority, the council's courts oversaw the excommunication of clerics. The council's courts often cooperated with the civil judiciary to investigate civil and/ or criminal infractions by monks who were often ordered to be disrobed (Schober, 2011, p. 84).

The council, courts, and registration of all monks gave Ne Win immediate and significant control over the Buddhist firm and its representatives. These tools allowed Ne Win to eradicate the Buddhist firm's potential involvement in political affairs (Charney, 2009, p. 119). The dictator assumed the role of Myanmar's king-rulers and used the council and courts to purge and purify the Buddhist firm of those who were not loyal and supportive. The state council, courts, and monk registration not only protect and promote the Buddhist firm, but also stifle factions, innovation, and dissent. It is important to note that these tools were not always effective in controlling the Sangha. In chapter 6, the religious and moral convictions and actions of the Buddhist firm are explored. Despite his control, in 1974 and again in 1988, the Buddhists rebelled against the Ne Win regime's policies and power. While monitoring and attempting to control every aspect of the Buddhist firm and individual monk's behaviors, General Ne Win also promoted a specific version of Buddhism.

Ne Win's Regime Promoted a Burman Version of Buddhism

Ne Win promoted a Burmanized version of Buddhism. This Burman version of Buddhism promoted by the dictator's military ran contrary to the ideas and notions of Buddhism held by many ethnic minority

Buddhists. Ne Win refused to allow Mon and Shan monks to distribute literature or take Buddhist examinations in their native languages (Fink, 2013, p. 241). Shan monks were prohibited from holding their traditional funeral arrangements and ceremony for a famous monk (Fink, 2013, p. 241). The state imposed a Burmese-style architecture on the Shan temples and attempted to impose a homogeneous Burman-Buddhist culture on other ethnic minority citizens. The power of the Myanmar state over the Buddhist firm and the promotion of a version of Burmese Buddhism was at odds with the country's minority Buddhists and all the relativist approaches of modern global Buddhism (Ashin and Crosby, 2017, p. 204). The dictator corrupted and distorted the religion and the broader religious economy, and in August 1988, the Myanmar people rebelled.

Ne Win's Burmese way to socialism, protection, regulation, and micromanagement of the religious economy ended with a pro-democracy uprising in 1988. Ever superstitious, Ne Win ordered the Myanmar currency, the kyat, to be based on denominations divisible by nine. With this policy, he wiped out the savings of millions of Myanmar people—including the accounts of the Buddhist firm. Monks and students led the nation in what came to be known as the Four Eights Uprising (August 8, 1988). In the wake of the most peaceful uprising that plunged the country into chaos, Mr. Ne Win formally retired. As General Ne Win recedes into history, his repressive legacy remains. In 2021, General Min Aung Hlaing, who served under Ne Win in the 1970s and 1980s, seized power in a coup d'état after overthrowing the elected government led by former State Counsellor Aung San Suu Kyi. Like Ne Win, Min Aung Hlaing imposed brutal military rule and martial law and immediately imprisoned leading monks in Insein Prison. The religious convictions of Myanmar's clerics have been critical in shaping the country and are explored in chapter 6.

CONCLUSIONS

Like the Insein prison, Ne Win managed the Myanmar religious economy with brutality, constant monitoring and surveillance, and state control and regulation. Ne Win used religion and religious firms as a tool of power, surveillance, oppression, and social control. While U Nu (see chapter 4) embraced liberal democracy and diversity, Ne Win launched violent all-out assaults on minority groups. U Nu sought to promote Buddhism and all other minority firms, and Ne Win controlled and manipulated every aspect of the religious economy to meet the needs of the state.

Between 1962 and 1988, the dictator violently repressed minority religious firms and created a religious marketplace that supported and protected only Theravada Buddhism. Christians and Muslims were labeled foreign. Nat worship was denigrated. The Ne Win military waged campaigns of intimidation and violence against Muslims and Christians with the forced relocation and destruction of Christian cemeteries, violent attacks on houses and places of worship, and maintaining a policy of coerced conversion to Buddhism. Ne Win's regime radically altered the Myanmar religious economy by suppressing nat worship and perpetrating gross human rights violations, sexual violence in Muslim and Christian places of worship, and the torture of clerics, church workers, and civilians.

Ne Win's government not only attempted to regulate and restrict Animism, Christianity, and Muslims in the Myanmar religious marketplace; he also manipulated and corrupted the majority religion—Theravada Buddhism. Following Myanmar's kings, Ne Win used religion to build support and legitimacy for his dictatorship. Ne Win feared religion as a challenger to his authority and micromanaged the internal affairs of the Buddhist firm. By protecting and supporting Buddhism, Ne Win controlled and limited the power and authority of the religion and its clerics. Ne Win found that protecting and supporting the Buddhist firm was a useful means of rule and control. Yet, his incentive to protect and support the majority religion was undermined when that religion encroached on his authority and control.

The use and protection of Buddhism by the government for political purposes directly affected Myanmar's entire religious economy by introducing uncertainty and concern about the citizenship status of non-Buddhists. The U.S. justice Sandra Day O'Connor noted that when a government supports and protects a particular religion, it "sends a message to non-adherents that they are outsiders, not full members of the political community, and an accompanying message to adherents that they are insiders, favored members of the political community" (Lynch v. Donnelly, 1984). Ne Win made religious faith a principal component of national identity in the 1982 citizenship law and, in doing so, alienated those citizens who chose a different or no religion.

Ne Win's government distorted the practice and growth of religion with policies that used religion to determine citizenship and by defining what constitutes an officially recognized religion. Government protection and intervention in Myanmar during General Ne Win's administration nurtured a specific Burman version of Buddhist nationalism that distorted the broader religious economy and escalated to a countrywide crisis. By August 1988, General Ne Win's state–religion policies had so dramatically distorted the Myanmar religious economy that they had set into motion recurring conflict and bloodshed. In 1974, 1988, and again in 2007, Myanmar's religious firms reacted to the regime-made conflict. The religious convictions of the monks and clerics that Ne Win attempted to keep out of politics proved to be critical in reopening and reshaping the religious economy and larger society. Chapter 6 explores the role religious convictions play in politics and in a religious economy. Are religious convictions emancipatory or repressive?

6

✣

Buddhism, Nat Spirit Wives, and Christian Clerics

Religious Convictions in the Myanmar Religious Economy 1974–2022

Imagine for a moment the hot, dusty, and bustling streets of Myitkyina, the capital city of Kachin state, in the far north of Myanmar. The city name means "near the big river," as it is located on the banks of the Irrawaddy River. Since ancient times, the city of Myitkyina has been an important point of trade between Myanmar and China. During the British colonial era, Roman Catholic and Baptist missionaries enjoyed proselytizing success among the peoples of Kachin state.

The American Baptist missionary George J. Geis arrived in Myitkyina in 1892 and by 1894 reported, "During the past year we have had many tokens of the Lord's blessings resting upon our work. Never have more Kachins come to us, and never have they shown a greater interest in the gospel message. Hundreds from the distant north as they came down to Myitkyina on bamboo rafts have for the first time heard the story of Jesus" (Geis, 1894). A few years later, in August 1897, a French missionary, Bishop Alexandre Cardot (born January 10, 1857, died October 18, 1925), founded a Roman Catholic convent called the Sisters of St. Francis Xavier in Myitkyina.

Today, the citizens of Myitkyina adhere to a diverse range of religious beliefs, from Buddhism, Christianity, Islam, Hinduism, to the ubiquitous nat worship. Most of the Kachin who live in Myitkyina are practicing Christians. About half of the Christians are Baptists and the rest are a mix of Anglican, Catholic, and Methodist. In 2015 there were more than fifteen Christian churches in Myitkyina (Cockett, 2015, p. 116). In late February 2021, in the streets of Myitkyina, as elsewhere across Myanmar, the military brutally cracked down on millions of citizens as they protested their country's most recent military coup. The military had seized control on February 1, 2021, following a general election, which Aung San Suu Kyi's National League for Democracy party won by a landslide. Early in the morning on February 28, police and soldiers intensified their crackdown with brutal violence that led to eighteen deaths and scores of wounded nationwide that day.

On the evening of February 28, the citizens of the city of Myitkyina gathered in the streets to protest. As anti-coup protesters peacefully marched with signs that read "Justice and democracy will prevail," the military and police forces positioned themselves behind riot shields and pointed assault weapons at the protestors. Between the weapons and the protestors walked a forty-five-year-old nun, Sister Ann Rosa Nu Tawng, of the Sisters of the St. Francis Xavier congregation. Acting on the strength of her convictions, determined, and undeterred by fear, Sister Nu Tawng pleaded with the leaders of the security forces.

The military and police officers ordered her to leave and yelled that she was in grave danger. The Catholic nun insisted that she would not leave and was ready to die, replying, "I have prepared myself that I will give my life for the Church, for the people, and for the nation" (Gomes, 2021). Sister Nu Tawng then kneeled with her hands clasped in prayer between the assault weapons and the protestors and pleaded with them not to shoot the unarmed Myitkyina citizens. "Just shoot me if you want to," said the nun, adding, "the protesters have no weapons, and they are just showing their desire peacefully" (Gomes, 2021).

"It felt like a battle zone," later said Sister Nu Tawng (Gomes, 2021). The nun was hit in the leg and chest and suffered minor injuries as the protesters ran and hid. A brave nun, with the moral compass of her religious convictions, helped those Myitkyina protesters escape bullets, beatings, and arrests, and the images of her courageous and prayerful kneel were shared worldwide.

Sister Nu Tawng was not the only religious figure to stand between the Myanmar military and the pro-democracy protestors. In March and April 2021, Buddhist monks took the same action and marched in front of protestors to shield them from violence. On May 25, 2021, Cardinal Charles Maung Bo, the archbishop of the Catholic Archdiocese of Yangon, wrote "An Earnest Appeal . . . as a group of faith leaders—not as politicians" to record "our anguish at the attack on innocent civilians, who sought refuge in Sacred Heart Church, Kayanthayar, Loikaw" (Bo Maung, 2021). Calling attention to the "great human tragedy," Cardinal Bo brought it to the military regime's attention that "the places of worship as a cultural property of a community are covered by International Protocols. Churches, hospitals, and schools are protected during conflict through the Hague

Conventions" (Bo Maung, 2021). Taking a moral stand against the military, Cardinal Bo said, "[L]et us remember the blood that is spilled is not some enemy's blood; those who were wounded are the citizens of this country. They were not armed; they were inside the church to protect their families. Every heart in this country weeps for the death of the innocent people. . . . This needs to stop" (Bo Maung, 2021).

The virtues and actions of these clerics came together in support of democracy and against the violence inflicted on the Myanmar people by the military regime. These clerics brought the virtue-enhancing propensities of religion to cultivate a change in the actions of the Myanmar military and in the governance of their society. The voices and actions of religious actors have been, since 1057, an important role in shaping Myanmar's history and politics. This chapter examines the value-inculcating role of religion and the role of religion in support of political action and in the disruption of social control. The Theravada Buddhist firm has served as an arbiter of legitimacy and support for the movement to democracy by leading and making it easier for the Myanmar people to participate.

FOSTERING VALUES: RELIGION AS THE CONSCIENCE OF THE STATE

There is a long-standing conversation within the Theravada Buddhist firm about monk involvement in politics (Walton, 2016a; Mendelson, 1975; Smith, 1965). Although some monks believe that monastic involvement in politics is inappropriate, it is clear from Myanmar's history that many others have decided to engage in political matters. The question of cleric involvement in political matters is also debated worldwide (Ahdar and Leigh, 2013, p. 76). Do religious morals, voices, and ideas have a place in Myanmar's political conversations?

In 1796, the U.S. president George Washington declared that "religion and morality enjoin" to "cultivate peace and harmony" (Washington, 1796). Washington argued that the voices of religion held a vital role as an "indispensable support" of politics and policy. For George Washington, it was important for religious voices to join the chorus of others (political parties, business firms, debating societies, and associations, etc.) to contribute to the political discussion. Religious firms foster values. As Prime Minister U Nu said, religion could serve a distinctive role in enhancing the inculcation of virtue and social responsibility. In fact, Nu did not see another way: "I don't see how we can improve ourselves and others without strong devotion to our beliefs" (Butwell, 1963, p. 65).

The values, practices, and teachings of religious firms often serve to inform and strengthen a society (Eberle, 2002, p. 5; Hall, 1992–1993, p. 88). The religious firms of Myanmar have been a constant source of transcendent values—values based on enduring principles. Myanmar's majority religion has helped to shape what is considered to be acceptable behavior and what is not. Kings Ashoka and Anawrahta, working together with the Buddhist firm, provide moral guidance and ruling precedents in politics and governing in Myanmar today. The models of behavior of Myanmar's kings and the government support for Buddhist monks help us to understand the military response to the revolutionary movements discussed in this chapter.

The Buddhist firm has shaped the society's goals, and monks in protests have articulated "critiques of contemporary politics from ethical perspectives" (Schober, 2011, p. 100). Worldwide, moral and religious teachings often shape societies and have important and lasting public and political effects (Leiter, 2014, p. 13). Max Weber made this argument in *The Protestant Ethic and the Spirit of Capitalism* (Weber, 2001). World history is replete with examples of the actions of citizens who were motivated by their religious convictions to support or oppose governments and laws (Lewy, 1974; Eberle, 2002, p. 5).

The voices and teachings of Myanmar's religious representatives have often been important in the outcomes of events. For example, U Ottama's (see chapter 3) moral discourse was remarkably influential in the independence movement. His moral reasoning resonated with and established a Buddhist nationalist identity that helped propel the nation toward independence (and conflict). Ottama's convictions and narrative about Myanmar's history moved the public to action (Schober, 2011, 103). Citizens joined in associations to promote and save Buddhism (Turner, 2014). Ottama's moral judgments were widely respected as legitimate, and the monk provided a picture of what was possible for the people of Myanmar. Ottama's status and integrity as a religious and public figure provided him with the credentials and foundation to shape the future of his country. U Ottama lived in such a way that his life, and even his death, became the embodiment of a larger religious narrative that shaped his country. Ottama's religious convictions were, as Rev. Dr. Martin Luther King Jr. argued, neither "the master or the servant of the state, but rather the conscience of the state" (King, 1963). King, often quoted by Aung San Suu Kyi, argued that people of faith "must be the guide and the critic of the state, and never its tool (King, 1963). The Buddhist firm has guided and facilitated political and social change by providing legitimacy, ideological justification, and the social cohesion for revolution.

STATE SUPPRESSION OF RELIGIOUS VOICES

Buddhism is woven deep into the fabric of Myanmar's society. Since 1057, the Buddhist firm has been a key actor in life and politics in Myanmar, and those who identify as Buddhist see Buddhism as an essential guide for all of life (Crouch, 2016a, p. 186). Generally, Buddhist monks and the Sangha are revered. The Sangha and the monks hold considerable influence "in whatever area they choose to exert it, including politics" (Smith, 1965, p. 186). Myanmar's widely respected and influential clerics have not been allowed to vote in elections since 1936 (Crouch, 2016a, p. 187).

Since 1962, the Myanmar military government has enacted a series of laws that seek to disenfranchise religious firms for politics and governance. Myanmar's 2008 Constitution prohibits the mixing of religion and politics. Section 364 states, "The abuse of religion for political purposes is forbidden" (David and Holliday, 2018, pp. 51–53). Myanmar's 2008 Constitution also prohibits monks and other religious clerics from voting or forming political parties. Hundreds of thousands of clerics are not allowed to vote. Individual clerics (who are registered and issued a cleric card by the state) of any religion are deprived of their political rights. Christian pastors are required to register at their respective conventions. Karen Christian pastors, for example, register through Karen Baptist Convention and then each cleric is issued a card by the state. No registered clergy are permitted to vote (Htoo Htoo Wah, personal communication, May 2021).

There is a tendency in Myanmar, and elsewhere, to argue that religious individuals and religious firms must be excluded from politics and matters of governing. It is one thing to argue that clerics and religious organizations may not employ the powers of the state (as the Buddhist firm has done in Myanmar) and quite another to say that they must be barred from all political participation. Clerics tend to be opinion leaders in their communities. These people of faith are often respected leaders in their local public spaces. The status of Myanmar's clergy (along with their values) has made them significant and important contributors to political discussions and revolution.

Myanmar's minority and majority religious firms and clerics constitute a significant subgroup of the population. Myanmar's kings and generals enacted these rules as a tool of social control to restrict the value-inculcating and influential power of the majority religion. Monastic disenfranchisement represents a violation of the basic human rights of monks and nuns. Importantly, military control and disenfranchisement of the Theravada Buddhist firm has *not* meant the lack of political influence. Many Buddhist monks who fight for tolerance, justice, human rights, and democracy argue that their exclusion from the formal political processes has opened important opportunities for indirect political influence (personal monk interview, November 2015). They maintain and employ their religious values and authority by not being "tarnished" by direct governing and political party activity (personal monk interview, March 26, 2016). They are not beholden loyal "government monks" (personal monk interview, March 26, 2016). The Myanmar military regimes have tried brutally and routinely to suppress religious voices, but at important points in history these voices have been very influential.

Factions of the majority religion in Myanmar fostered Buddhist traditions and inculcated the principles of human rights, social responsibility, social justice, equality, and a willingness to work for democracy. In an essay titled "In Quest of Democracy," Aung San Suu Kyi wrote, "Members of the Buddhist Sangha [Buddhist firm] in their customary role as mentors have led the way in articulating popular expectations by drawing on classical learning to illuminate timeless values. But the conscious effort to make traditional knowledge relevant to contemporary needs was not confined to any particular circle—it went right through Burmese society from urban intellectuals and small shopkeepers to doughty village grandmothers" (Aung San Suu Kyi, 1991, p. 168).

Since the 1930s, leaders in the Theravada Buddhist firm have been critical actors in fostering the virtues and principles that promote and support democratization. Many Theravada Buddhist monks provided legitimacy and liberal values and principles, and mobilized opposition to military rule and policies in 1974, 1988, 2007, and 2021. Since U Ottama's political agitation in the 1930s, many Buddhist monks have also supported numerous student-led protests and called for liberal constitutional changes. The actions of these monks and factions of the Buddhist firm have been an important force in facilitating social change, providing the ideological justification for change, and supporting protests and revolution. Conversely, Myanmar clerics' religious convictions have promoted religious repression, intolerance, discrimination, and the persecution of those with whom they disagree. Are the fruits of religion sweet or bitter? The Buddhist firm has at four key points in recent history provided legitimacy and the guiding principles that emboldened millions of people to attempt to overthrow the existing political order.

THE SWEET FRUITS OF RELIGION: RELIGION AND REVOLUTION

The religious economy of Myanmar has been the domain of elites. For centuries, kings ruled. Then after the colonial era, a small group of elites in the Myanmar military tightly regulated religion and oppressed the people. With the introduction of modern political ideologies, especially those supporting democracy, the people began not only to participate in politics but to demand self-rule and respect for human rights. In the 1920s and 1930s, British professors introduced liberal political ideologies to many Myanmar students, including U Nu and Aung San (Hellman-Rajanayagam, 2020, p. 250). Over time, those ideas came to undermine not only the ability of British colonial rule, but also the Myanmar military.

As illustrated in chapter 5, the Myanmar military's regulation of religion has been one of its most frequently used tools of social control. Insein Prison was (and still is) used to punish those who deviated from the military's expectations. Since March 1962, the military regimes of Myanmar have exercised brutal social control that was broken by landmark uprisings that inculcated and nurtured liberal thought and human rights and promoted democracy. The Buddhist firm disrupted existing social control (Wahlrab, Sass, and Sterken, 2019, p. 245; Lewy, 1974). The majority religion in Myanmar abruptly disrupted social control when it promoted justice, human rights, and democracy, and protested the oppression of the Myanmar people.

Since 1962, religious firms and clerics have facilitated and supported four major landmark political movements: The U Thant funeral crisis (a series of protests triggered by General Ne Win's reaction to the death of U Thant), the Four Eights Uprising (nationwide pro-democracy protests), the Saffron Revolution (nationwide protests led by the Buddhist firm), and the February 2021 coup. Religion was important in each of these landmark events and each event led to changes in Myanmar's religious economy. Led by clerics and students, these four events propelled the Myanmar society away from authoritarian rule toward a liberal democracy. In each event, religious firms, religious convictions, and clerics were key in disrupting the social order of military rule. Although so far their efforts have been unsuccessful, it is clear that millions of Myanmar citizens understand and desire a democracy.

1974: THE U THANT FUNERAL CRISIS

U Thant is one of the most celebrated citizens of Myanmar. U Thant's life of service exemplifies the role religion can play in inculcating civic virtues and personal and social responsibility. Thant's political leadership is a prime example of religion (Buddhism) in action (Dorn, 2007, p. 179). U Thant's strong devotion to his beliefs shaped his approach to decision making and governance (Dorn, 2007, p. 176). He once said, "I have been trying to concentrate, to contemplate, to mediate and to eliminate all hatred, all anger, all bitterness from my being, to detach myself from mundane things and to achieve emotional equilibrium. Of course, it is very difficult to achieve. But this is my way of life" (Whitman, 1974). It is easy to see why he was close friends with U Nu and hated by General Ne Win (Thant Myint-U, 2008, p. 311). His values aligned with the former and clashed with the latter. In death, his values were celebrated by the Myanmar people and shunned by General Ne Win.

The Philosopher

Traditionally in Myanmar, children born on Friday are given names that begin with the letters Th. Furthermore, in a Myanmar tradition, a child born on a Friday is thought to be peaceful, giving, and a hard worker (Ah Noh, personal interview, April 21, 2021). These characteristics were evident in the life and work of U Thant, who earned the nickname "The Philosopher" in his university days. Thant was born in the Irrawaddy delta village of Pantanaw on Friday, January 22, 1909. His father, Po Hnit, was a prosperous rice miller who had been educated in Kolkata (Calcutta) and could communicate well in English. His mother, a deeply religious woman, imbued Thant with a lifelong devotion to Buddhism and meditation (Firestone, 2019). Thant's parents provided him with protective guidance and a set of values that deeply influenced his behavior, decisions, and relationships. Thant enjoyed retelling a story about a time when he was a child and his parents sent him to London. In planning the trip, his parents repeatedly warned him about the evils of the city. On arrival in London, young Thant ordered fish and chips at the Lyons Tea shop. After taking his order, the server said, "with pleasure," and the young man, frightened, replied, "No. No, no pleasure" (Whitman, 1974). Like many Myanmar youth, Thant spent some time in a Buddhist monastery; however, unlike U Nu, formal religiosity was not an outward trait in his studious character.

Thant's father ignited in him an early interest in reading. A voracious reader, at the age of twelve, young Thant was reading classics in English by authors such as William Shakespeare, Lord Byron, and Arthur Conan Doyle (Firestone, 2019, p. 1) As a second-year student in Pantanaw National High School, he was intent on a career in journalism (Trager, 1961, p. 32). While in high school, he successfully published the first of many English-language articles to appear in Burmese publications.

In 1926, after graduating from high school, Thant enrolled at the University of Rangoon, where he continued reading English literature and took courses in history and philosophy (Firestone, 2019, p. 2). Thant studied Oriental Studies (Pali and Burmese), history, (with a focus on East Asian history and the history of Burma) under world-renowned British professors, Daniel G. E. Hall (1955), John S. Furnivall (Furnivall, 1929), and Gordon Luce (Hellman-Rajanayagam, 2020, p. 250;

Peacock, 1934, p. 284). Thant became close friends with John Furnivall. Furnivall was an outspoken advocate for access to higher education to prepare the Myanmar people for self-rule (Boyd, 1999, p. 427). Furnivall, who owned an English bookshop in Yangon, influenced Thant's literary interest and introduced the young philosopher to British Fabian socialism (Firestone, 2019, p. 1). Fabian socialists argued that state support (collectivism) was necessary if people were to prosper. Furnivall encouraged young Thant to follow a moderate form of Burmese nationalism that would lead to slow and gradual transition to independence and to reject what he considered the destructive revolutionary doctrines of Marxism (Pham, 2005, p. 324).

Many Yangon (Rangoon) University students were influenced by the liberal and anti-colonial thinking of their professors. The rich intellectual environment of Rangoon University in the late 1920s and 1930s produced a substantial number of liberal thinkers who would become intellectual and political leaders in Myanmar and, like U Thant, on the world stage (Hellman-Rajanayagam, 2020, p. 253). At a speech at the university in 2012, U.S. president Obama noted, "It was here at this school where opposition to colonial rule first took hold. It was here that Aung San edited a magazine before leading an independence movement. It was here that U Thant learned the ways of the world before guiding the United Nations. Here, scholarship thrived during the last century and students demanded their basic human rights" (Obama, 2012). In those intellectually rich university days, Thant and U Nu (see chapter 4) developed a close friendship. Nu and his classmate, Aung San, joined Thant and others to resist British rule and build a democracy in their country. From January 1948, when Myanmar became independent from Great Britain, to March 1962, the country and most of its leaders attempted a bold experiment with a democratic system of government (Charney, 2009, p. 72). The young leaders faced the challenge of governing a country with deep religious, political, and ethnic divisions. U Nu asked U Thant for his help.

In 1948, while organizing Myanmar's first fully independent government, Prime Minister Nu invited Thant to become secretary of the Ministry of Information (Selth, 2018, p. 5). Thant left a teaching position in Pantanaw to join his old friend U Nu. Thant's farewell remarks to his students included these words: "In this world, try to be both good and able. If you do not become able men, at least try to be good men. The country has no use for able but bad men" (Dorn, 2007, p. 145). To the people of Myanmar, Thant was to become a celebrated example of what he preached: able and good.

Working closely with Nu, Thant's political career began a quick ascent. Over the next decade, Thant occupied a series of high-level appointments and traveled widely with and on behalf of Prime Minister Nu (Firestone,

2019, 2). In 1952 he traveled to New York as a member of the Myanmar government's United Nations delegation. Five years later, in 1957, Thant was appointed Burma's permanent representative to the United Nations. Thant took on the UN acting secretary general post in November 1961, after the death of Dag Hammarskjold in an airplane crash in Africa in September 1961. Had U Thant been in Myanmar at the time of General Ne Win's 1962 military coup, he would have been arrested and imprisoned along with U Nu.

A Modern Monk's Religious Convictions

In 1962, Thant was elected to a five-year term as the UN secretary general by a unanimous vote. Thant's leading role as a global peacemaker can be found in numerous histories (Firestone, 2013, p. 1060). His list of accomplishments includes guiding the United Nations through a decade (1961–1971) of global conflicts and diplomacy that included the American war in Vietnam, the Cuban Missile Crisis, the Arab-Israeli six-day war, and the cold war between the Soviet Union and the United States (Firestone, 2019). After the Cuban Missile Crisis, U.S. president John F. Kennedy said, "U Thant has put the world deeply in his debt" (Kennedy, 1969, p. 23). Ever the calm diplomat, Thant stood fast in his opposition to the war in Vietnam (Firestone, 2013, p. 1062).

Thant's life was rooted in Buddhism. Thant felt that Buddhism "as a religion is superior to other religions, but this conviction does not blind me to the fact that there are hundreds of millions of people who believe otherwise" (Dorn, 2007, p. 152). In his memoirs, Thant wrote, "Buddhism teaches, above all, a universal compassion to be extended to all living beings, irrespective of their status, race or creed" (Dorn, 2007, p. 152).

Figure 6.1. United Nations Secretary General U Thant meeting with President Lyndon B. Johnson. Cabinet Room, White House, Washington, D.C. United Nations Secretary General U Thant speaking and gesturing. *Source*: LBJ Library. Photo by Yoichi R. Okamoto. Serial Number: C8692-2A.

Worldwide, Thant held the reputation as a person free from corruption and selfish motives. He said that his Buddhist foundation enabled him to cope and thrive in the difficult and high-tension years as head of the United Nations. As secretary general of the United Nations, Thant approached global problems and decisions mindful of his Buddhist upbringing: "I was trained to be tolerant of everything except intolerance. I was brought up not only to develop the spirit of tolerance, but also to cherish moral and spiritual qualities, especially modesty, humility, compassion, and, most important, to attain a certain degree of equilibrium" (Selth, 2018, p. 5). The secretary general began each day with at least fifteen minutes of meditation. "I try to shut myself off from all senses and concentrate on my inner self," he explained (Whitman, 1974). "You think on what is good in life, good thoughts, good deeds. It is difficult to explain exactly, but it is like your New Year's resolutions every day" (Whitman, 1974). Robert Muller, director of the office of the secretary general, described Thant as a "modern monk" (Dorn, 2007, p. 146).

Brian Urquhart wrote, [Thant's] Buddhist self-discipline concealed the irritation and frustration that anyone else in his position would often have given vent to. He never lost his temper or showed impatience. In moments of unusual stress, he would tap his foot rhythmically, his only display of emotion" (Urquhart, 2013). Thant wished that spiritual convictions were part of the larger culture in the United Nations: "I always listen to political and economic speeches. I never hear a spiritual voice in the United Nations, even though I am a spiritual person above everything else" (Dorn, 2007, p. 176). Thant's religious convictions mattered in his work and to the people of Myanmar.

U Thant's Funeral Crisis: A Step toward Democracy

U Thant died in November 1974 (Whitman, 1974). Leaders and citizens from every corner of the world mourned his passing and celebrated his gentle life of peace. In a statement, U.S. president Gerald Ford said "[a]bove all" U Thant was "a man of peace" (Ford, 1974). Thant's body was laid in state in the UN General Assembly building before being returned to Myanmar for burial. Thant was one of the most famous public servants of his time. He had worked tirelessly to bring peace and well-being to people around the world.

While the world's leaders celebrated Thant's life, the dictator in his home country, General Ne Win, refused to allow any recognition or state honors for the man of peace. U Thant's life and work had been dedicated to the promotion and protection of human rights and peace. In life and in death he was a symbol of the values and principles that Ne Win suppressed with violence. Ne Win refused to allow government recognition or even to allow a representative of the state to meet the family and casket at Mingaladon Airport (Selth, 2018, p. 7). Instead, the secretary general's oak casket was loaded into a battered local Red Cross Volkswagen van and driven to the abandoned Kyaikkasan racetrack grounds to allow the Myanmar people an opportunity to pay their respects before the burial (Thant Myint-U, 2008, p. 312).

The steadfast refusal of the Ne Win government to honor Thant's life extended to where the diplomat would be buried. Ne Win also refused to allow the celebrated diplomat to be interred near the famous Shwedagon Pagoda (Thant Myint-U, 2008, p. 311). Then the government claimed that Thant's body was illegally brought into the country and that legal charges might follow. Charges were not filed, but the government only granted approval to bury Thant in Kyanndaw Cemetery, a small private cemetery, without state honors. The way in which Thant's death was received by the Ne Win regime sent waves of unrest through Myanmar. Buddhist monks and students demanded that the government honor Thant and build a suitable mausoleum. The government refused.

At the abandoned racetrack, Thant's casket was laid in a pavilion. In an act of propitiation to the nats, a plate of green coconuts and bananas was placed at the head of the casket (Selth, 2018, p. 8). More than fifty thousand mourners walked by to pay their respects. The UN representatives laid a wreath and held an unofficial ceremony at the racetrack grounds, and all flags on UN buildings in Myanmar were flown at half-mast (Selth, 2018, p. 7). During the ceremony, students seized the casket and took it to the Rangoon University Convocation Hall. A few days later, the students, with the support of Buddhist monks, carried Thant's body to a crudely constructed mausoleum they had built on the site of the student union building that Ne Win had blown up in 1962.

Ne Win, belatedly acknowledging popular demand, proposed a new burial site and mausoleum in Cantonment Park, at the foot of the Shwedagon Pagoda. Thant's family agreed with this arrangement. In the early morning hours, Thant's casket was retrieved from the students' mausoleum and escorted under heavy guard to a site just below the Shwedagon Pagoda. U Thant was quietly reburied with only his relatives and representatives of the United Nations allowed to attend.

The disrespectful treatment of U Thant by Ne Win set off waves of protests and riots. Thousands of citizens took to the streets. They burned effigies of Ne Win and demanded an end to military rule (Charney, 2009, p. 138). Ne Win sent in soldiers to close the university and cut all international communications with the country. From all over the country, a mass movement of Buddhist monks traveled to Yangon (Selth, 2018, p. 8). Students and monks rioted and protested across the country. The military and police opened fire on the protestors, killing and wounding many monks who were protesting with students (Selth, 2018, p. 13). The protests continued intermittently for the next two years (Charney, 2009, p. 139).

The participation of the Buddhist firm in the Thant riots confirmed Ne Win's fears of the threat of the power of the monastic community. The Buddhist firm had shown during the U Thant crisis that it was a powerful and important force. A few years later, in 1979, Ne Win once again set out to "purge" the Buddhist firm of impure monks; he successfully imposed a national registration system on Buddhist clerics (Nyi Nyi Kyaw, 2019, p. 175). Ne Win's regulation of the majority religion led to the disbanding of factions (sects) and defrocking of individual monks (Nyi Nyi Kyaw, 2019, p. 177; Charney, 2009, p. 140). Hundreds of Buddhist monks, including forty senior monks, were disrobed.

Thant's religious convictions and extraordinary life provided the spark, principles, and justification for revolution. The student and monk riots in 1974 were important steps toward disrupting and directly challenging Ne Win's legitimacy and authority. Ne Win, however, remained violently determined to impose a highly centralized and tightly regulated religious and macroeconomic system with fear and authoritarian rule. In the early 1980s, Ne Win appointed General Sein Lwin—later known as the "Butcher of Rangoon" for his brutal suppression of demonstrations and the killing of monks and students—to serve as minister of Home and Religious Affairs. General Sein Lwin's central task was to reign in the Buddhist firm (Nyi Nyi Kyaw, 2019, p. 176). To control and regulate the Buddhist firm, the forty-seven-member State Mahanayaka Committee (see chapter 5) was formed. The committee allowed the state to take disciplinary action against an individual cleric or monastery or an entire sect (Nyi Nyi Kyaw, 2019, pp. 179–83). The government assigned retired military officers to handle the financial affairs of Buddhist monasteries, and established village, township, city, and district level government-appointed Sangha councils (McCarthy, 2008, p. 300). Highly respected monks were and are routinely arrested, disrobed, and imprisoned.

Under Ne Win, Myanmar became one of the poorest countries in the world. His regulation and control of minority and majority religions led to suffering and malaise. The religious and economic suffering that resulted from Ne Win's rule brought the Myanmar people to another watershed moment in August 1988.

RELIGIOUS CONVICTIONS IN THE FOUR-EIGHTS UPRISING

In 1988, corrupt and violent rule and mismanagement of the economy finally caught up with Myanmar's military regime. Ne Win's economic program, called the "Burmese Way to Socialism," had turned Myanmar into one of the poorest countries in the world. People were so poor that many were unable to continue to support the Buddhist monastic community with food and offerings. Ne Win's superstitious decision to demonetize Myanmar's currency destroyed the people's savings overnight, causing a riot of discontent that later erupted in mass demonstrations.

The Myanmar people had reached their breaking point and on August 8, 1988, massive protests shook the foundations of the country. Millions and millions of people from all walks of life—often led by Buddhist monks—took to the streets to demand change. Muslims, Christians, and ethnic minorities marched side by side with Buddhist monks. It was a multiethnic and inclusive fight for democracy and human rights. All citizens shared the same unfortunate fate under the repressive authoritarian government of Ne Win. The movement was a step toward a liberal peace—democracy, human rights, and rule of law. Ne Win responded to the protest with violence. The military brutality was severe; an estimated three thousand people were killed. Ne Win's violence did not stop the protests. Religion played a significant role in the mobilization of millions of protestors.

The Buddhist Firm and Mobilization

The leadership and institutions of the Buddhist firm played a key role in the Four Eights Uprising. Although the Buddhist firm has long held reservations about its involvement in political activities, it does hold both the resources and skills necessary for political mobilization. Religious firms (both minority and majority) and their clerics are often widely respected and have a high profile. The hierarchy of the monastic community in Myanmar develops leadership skills in clerics. Running a large monastery develops both leadership and civic skills. Monks organized security patrols and took over administration of some localities, particularly around Mandalay. The social networks and physical space of the monasteries proved useful for political meetings and shelter from the military. In many cities, including Yangon, monasteries were transformed into fortresses to protect and organize the struggle for democracy. Monks formed independent associations and allowed citizens' strike committees to operate out of monasteries. Buddhist leadership organized a group called the Radical Buddhist Monks United Front (Lintner, 2009). The group organized and led protests from a monastery in Mandalay. The Buddhist firm set out to establish a democracy and to "wipe out political and religious persecution and build a prosperous Burma" (Lintner, 2009, p. 31).

To the surprise of many, Ne Win stepped aside, and the military promised to hold general elections once order had been restored. Convinced that their own National Unity Party would win, the military regime made a major miscalculation. The Buddhist firm came out in support of democracy and a new party, the National League for Democracy (NLD), was established by Aung San's daughter, Aung San Suu Kyi, and her colleagues. Wherever Aung San Suu Kyi campaigned, tens of thousands of people showed up and cheered. On July 20, 1989, the military, afraid of losing control and power, placed Aung San Suu Kyi and the NLD leadership under house arrest in their respective homes in Yangon. Hundreds of NLD activists were sent to Insein Prison (see chapter 5) as the army moved to consolidate its grip on the nation.

Religion and Legitimacy: The Alms Bowl Boycott

An election was held on May 27, 1990, and the NLD won a decisive victory, capturing a wide majority of the popular vote. The military did not expect such sweeping NLD support and refused to hand over power. The Buddhist firm protested. On August 8, 1990, thousands of monks marched in protest. Tens of thousands of citizens came out into the streets to offer food and support to the monks. Soldiers nervously watched and then opened fire. A seventeen-year-old novice was hit, as were nine other monks and two nearby citizens. The military brutally beat fourteen monks. The event triggered open rebellion by thousands of Buddhist monks (McCarthy, 2008, p. 302).

The Buddhist leadership decided to invoke a religious boycott. They would boycott the military by refusing offerings from military men and their families. The "alms bowl" boycott not only denied the regime desperately needed legitimacy, but it also denied the military and their families the ability to gain "merit" (McCarthy, 2008, p. 302). The military ordered the Buddhist firm to revoke the boycott, arrested over four hundred monks, and destroyed some monasteries. The regime leaders claimed that these actions against the Buddhist firm were in line with king law (see chapter 1) and the authority and actions of the purification of the religion and monks of Myanmar's ancient kings (McCarthy, 2008, p. 302).

Myanmar's military regime then issued a decree (Order 7/90) detailing the proper conduct of Buddhist monks. Monks were to obey the orders of the State Mahanayaka Committee and not participate in politics (Nyi Nyi Kyaw, 2019, p. 178). If they failed to obey and participated in politics, then they would be prosecuted and removed from the monastic community. Predictably, these actions by the state divided the Buddhist firm, and it broke into factions. Groups of monks resisted the military and were placed under surveillance, arrested, defrocked, and imprisoned. Others joined the ranks of loyal "government monks" and supported the military. Those who loyally supported the military were rewarded with large donations, lavish facilities, and gifts of consumer goods (Fink, 2013, p. 229).

The student-led and Buddhist clergy supported the Four Eights Uprising propelled the country toward liberal democratic rule. The violence perpetrated by the soldiers allowed the top brass of the military to reconstitute as a junta known as the State Law and Order Restoration Council. Although the ruling junta plunged the lives of the Myanmar people back into poverty, silence, and fear, the uprising was successful in three critical ways. First, the Four-Eights Uprising nurtured the emergence of the National League for Democracy party. The NLD would grow to become a powerful force. Second, the uprising ignited in Myanmar's citizens the duty of participation. Democracies require citizen participation. Third, as stated by Aung San Suu Kyi, the uprising made "[t]he entire nation's desires and aspirations . . . very clear. There can be no doubt that everybody wants a multi-party democratic system of government. It is the duty of the present government to bring about such a system as soon as possible" (Aung San Suu Kyi, 2010, p. 197). Instead, a military junta would violently rule the country for the next two decades. Aung San Suu Kyi would be under house arrest for the next eighteen years until, once again, religious clerics led protests for democracy and human rights in what became known as the "Saffron Revolution."

2007: SAFFRON MONKS AND THE PRINCIPLES OF DEMOCRACY

In 2007, the moral convictions and political courage of the Buddhist firm helped to shore and strengthen the foundations of a democracy. The moral convictions of the monks and nuns of the Theravada Buddhist firm surfaced once again in September 2007. Myanmar's saffron-robed monks employed Gandhi's nonviolent methods to protest a repressive military regime. In 2007, the continued mismanagement of the macro economy by the regime and the suffering of the Myanmar people proved to be a tipping point for action by many in the Buddhist firm.

In response to recommendations from the International Monetary Fund, the military abruptly stopped all government subsidies for natural gas. The sudden shock to the energy sector caused a dramatic increase in fuel costs and the general cost of living. The economic shock hit the Myanmar people especially hard and exacerbated the already wide disparity of wealth between the military elites and the rest of the population. Monks and nuns who depend on daily gifts of food (dāna) directly from the people in their communities immediately saw the impact and hardship of the military's economic policies. "Monks who receive donations from laymen and who visit households every morning to receive hsoon [cooked rice] witness the deteriorating situation in the predominantly Buddhist country, ruled by a military government" (Schober, 2011, p. 122).

Following the political actions of U Ottama, U Wisara, Saya San (see chapter 3), and the monk's participation in 1974 and 1988, the clerics of the Buddhist firm once again spoke out. Monks of the Buddhist

Figure 6.2. Myanmar Saffron Revolution leader, Buddhist monk Ashin U Gambira attends a ceremony in Yangon, Myanmar, 16 January 2012. *Source*: Htoo Tay Zar

firm spoke their moral truth to power. In saffron-colored robes, thousands of Buddhist monks walked the streets of the country chanting the metta sutta (prayer of loving-kindness). These clerics led a "Saffron Revolution," a nonviolent movement to intervene in a crisis and promote a disruption to the existing social order imposed by the military. Ignoring threats from the government, on September 24, more than 100,000 people (about the seating capacity of the Los Angeles Memorial Coliseum) followed U Gambira and thousands of other monks into the streets of Yangon. The protesters met at the famous Shwedagon pagoda in what turned out to be the largest anti-government protest since the Four Eights Uprising. Led by religious leaders, Myanmar's citizens marched to demand democracy, human rights, and a change to their dire economic situation. The government responded with violence. Government troops sprayed bullets into the crowd and fired tear gas against protesters. The soldiers beat the monks. More than two hundred religious leaders were arrested, many people were injured, and five people were killed. U Gambira declared, "We will march until we bring down the evil government" (Schober, 2011, p. 125).

The Saffron Revolution was led by four Buddhist monks, U Gambira, U Vicitta, U Obhasa, and U Padaka. Their organization, the All Burma Monks' Alliance, provided structure for the movement and was a threat to the military's ruling authority. The monk alliance and the overturned alms bowls undermined the legitimacy of the military rulers. The religious convictions of the Saffron monks helped solidify an important principle of democracy: Political legitimacy comes from the people, who must consent to their government. U Gambira was following John Locke in arguing that the rulers and the ruled have a social contract that defines the powers and responsibilities of the ruler. If the rulers violated their responsibilities and power, as the All Burma Monks' Alliance indicated with evidence of the mistreatment of protesting monks, then the ruler could be replaced. The threat of replacement prompted the military to respond by raiding All Burma Monks' Alliance supporting monasteries in Yangon. The military then accused U Gambira and the All Burma Monks' Alliance of stockpiling weapons (oddly, the military recorded finding eighteen knives, one axe, slingshots, and one bullet) and possessing pornographic material. "It is regrettable that the operation revealed that in some monasteries, women sleep in the buildings where monks reside and forty-two uncensored pornographic VCDs and one uncensored pornographic DVD were found" (Wai Moe, 2007). In October 2007, the Saffron monk leaders, U Gambira, U Vicitta, U Obhasa, and U Adaka, of the All Burma Monks' Alliance, went into hiding.

Religious Convictions of a Saffron Monk

U Gambira was born on Tuesday, June 19, 1979, under the iron fist of General Ne Win (Siochana and Watson, 2020, p. 5). The village where he was born, Pakokku, in northwest Myanmar, was the site of a violent clash between Saffron monks and the government in early September 2007. The police reportedly tied two monks to a pole and beat them (Schober, 2011, p. 124). The violence against revered clerics in Gambira's home prompted the formation of the All Burma Monks' Alliance. Gambira's religious convictions led him to change his country and to Insein Prison, where he was held in solitary confinement, starved, and tortured (Siochana and Watson, 2020, p. 47). In November 2008, Gambira, then a twenty-nine-year-old monk, listened serenely as a Myanmar court handed him a sixty-eight-year prison sentence for his leadership in the Saffron Revolution (Siochana and Watson, 2020, p. 37). A respected religious leader in his community, a peaceful man of deep faith and conviction, Gambira was being sentenced to hard labor in prison for taking up the mantle of leadership for his people and challenging the authority of the military regime.

Following the protests, Gambira went into hiding and wrote an editorial critical of the Myanmar government (Gambira, 2007). Gambira wrote, "The regime's use of mass arrests, murder, torture, and imprisonment has failed to extinguish our desire for the freedom that was stolen from us so many years ago. We have taken their best punch. Now, it is the generals who must fear the consequences of their actions. We adhere to nonviolence, but our spine is made of steel" (Gambira, 2007). The day the *Washington Post* published his editorial, he was arrested. The government stripped him of his robe, announced that he was not a real monk, and sent him to Insein Prison. A decade later, the monk's legal team appealed to a judge for his release based on his mental health; Gambira suffered from acute post-traumatic stress disorder stemming from the torture abuse he suffered at the hands of authorities (Siochana and Watson, 2020, p. 141).

During his imprisonment, Gambira was awarded the Bindmans Law and Campaigning Award in absentia (Allen, 2008).

Beyond leading massive protests, the Saffron monks provided refuge for those who were suffering and being targeted by the military regime for punishment. They established a new organization, the All Burma Monks' Alliance, to respond to the mistreatment of protesting monks. The All Burma Monks' Alliance served organized protests and widely distributed leaflets publicizing the military's brutality (Schober, 2011, p. 124). Following earlier protests, monks once again marched with overturned alms bowls to signal the Buddhist firm's refusal to grant religious or political legitimacy to the military rulers and their families.

The monks who participated in the 2007 protests identify themselves as Saffron monks (Myawaddy Sayadaw, 2016). A Saffron monk typically supports tolerance and interfaith understanding, basic human rights, democratic rule, social justice, and sustainable environmental policies (personal communications, February 2016). The Saffron monks led a direct challenge to the authority, rule, and policies of the military government. The Saffron Revolution began as small rallies against the rising cost of living and rapidly escalated into huge anti-government, pro-democracy demonstrations. The moral convictions of those who participated in the 2007 protests were derived from Buddhist principles and ethics (Gravers, 2013, p. 49; Schober, 2011, p. 127). The Saffron monks' opposition to military rule rests on the Buddhist traditions that empower them to withhold merit and legitimation from underserving members of the society (Schober, 2011, p. 134).

Paralleling political participation by clerics within Christian, Muslim, and Hindu firms, the Saffron monks preached sermons and campaigned for democracy, human rights, and economic development (Schober, 2011, pp. 123–26). The Saffron monks believe that their social protests and actions are consistent with traditional notions of their Buddhist faith, the relief of suffering, and the awakening of human potential. The Buddhist firm supported "the democratization process in the country because democracy is in line with the Buddha's teaching. . . . [The] Metta sutta directly gives attention to the humanitarian approach to democracy. Buddhist monks have a motto in their struggle for democracy, and this is to not tackle each other and not to hurt one another. This is becoming a social ethics base of the democratic struggle of the Burmese monks" (Schober, 2011, p. 126). The Saffron monks pointed to the duties of kings (see Rajadhamma in chapter 1) as evidence of ethical and just responsibilities of the state (Gravers, 2013, p. 48; Schober, 2011, p. 132).

A Preference for the Poor and Oppressed

A Saffron monk from Mingyi Monastery in Mandalay, Ashin Ariya Wun Tha Bhiwun Sa, better known as Myawaddy Sayadaw, regularly shares his religious convictions with the people of Myanmar (Myawaddy Sayadaw, 2016). Myawaddy Sayadaw, a peacemaker who repeatedly called for human rights and democracy, was arrested and disrobed on the first day of the 2021 coup. Before his arrest, Myawaddy Sayadaw was regularly seen with Buddhist, Christian, Muslim, and Hindu leaders at interfaith gatherings across the country. Myawaddy Sayadaw and the Saffron monks have been active participants in interfaith activities throughout the country and vocal supporters of peace, justice, and the rights of minorities. "The role of Buddhist monks is now important as the country is in a transition to democracy," said the monk, and "we need to make our voices louder" (Zaw, 2018). Myawaddy Sayadaw says that monks need to regard it as their duty to publicly criticize those who spread anti-Muslim sentiment. Myawaddy said, "We, the religious leaders, need to play a greater role in promoting harmony among the various religions instead of sowing hatred against minorities" (Zaw, 2018).

In interviews and in his public sermons, Myawaddy Sayadaw applied his religious convictions to support the Myanmar people. Like liberation theologians elsewhere, Myawaddy Sayadaw's preference is for the poor and oppressed and is not aligned with the power and financial support of Myanmar's military regime (Lewis, 2019). In interviews, Myawaddy Sayadaw has called for an end to the oppression of the Myanmar people by the military and Buddhist nationalists, saying, "The dictator misuses and works unjustly to maintain power" (Ariya Wuntha Bhiwunsa, 2020). He argues that the religious principles of the extreme Buddhist nationalist monks "were destroyed by the dictators" (Ariya Wuntha Bhiwunsa, 2020). Before his arrest in February 2021, Myawaddy made it his mission to promote and act to support Myanmar's shaky democracy, to promote social justice, and to end religious and ethnic conflict through direct involvement in political and civic affairs (Myawaddy Sayadaw, 2016). Promoting interfaith dialogue and tolerance, Myawaddy Sayadaw said, "We are very clear that discrimination and hatred are not allowed among us" (Ariya Wuntha Bhiwunsa, 2020). Drawing on his faith and religious convictions, Myawaddy Sayadaw said, "According to the Buddha's loving-kindness practice, we have to share love with all different religions. Buddha taught us about loving-kindness is to live in harmony with each other. As we truly know about loving-kindness, we don't accept anyone who tries to discriminate against others. We fight against the extremist groups that intend to create ethnic and religious conflicts" (Ariya Wuntha Bhiwunsa, 2020).

Myawaddy and many other Saffron monks have strongly condemned the rhetoric of religious nationalists against Muslims under the banner of patriotism. Saffron monks have played an important role in the Peaceful Myanmar Initiative, which was founded in 2016. The Peaceful Myanmar Initiative is urging intensive efforts to promote dialogue for a return to peaceful coexistence and have implemented interreligious activities supporting interfaith dialogue across the country.

The Saffron monks successfully used their traditional Buddhist principles to promote a wider concern for social ethics and justice and to invoke the values and duties of a liberal democracy among the members of the Buddhist firm and the larger Myanmar society. The actions of the Saffron monks pushed the military regime toward democracy. The regime adopted measured (if small) steps toward democracy in 2011. Those steps culminated in a buoyant election in November 2015. The Myanmar people shut down all commerce and traveled or stayed home to vote. The election was a victory for the National League for Democracy party and for Aung San Suu Kyi.

THE BITTER FRUITS OF RELIGION: RELIGIOUS CONVICTIONS AND REPRESSION

The religious convictions, voices, and actions of religious firms have been emancipatory in Myanmar. For the Myanmar people, religious convictions have inspired a way of life and revolution. While their struggle for freedom, democracy, and emancipation continues, religious leaders' convictions and values have guided and shaped the society. Clerics like U Ottama, U Thant, U Gambira, Sister Nu Tawng, and Cardinal Bo were guided by the moral convictions of their religions to act. Those clerics encouraged tolerance, democracy, respect for human rights, and nonviolence. The Saffron monks of Myanmar promote a religious tolerance that calls for the government and others to refrain from persecution and repression of the religious other and to grant them the same rights as their majority religion (Kyaw Phyo Tha, 2013). The Saffron monks' religious convictions hold that all people should hold the right of free exercise of religion. Saffron monks reason that it is important to protect the right of free exercise for those who belong to religions other than their own (personal interviews, 2016).

Conversely, the religious convictions, voices, and actions of religious firms have also been repressive in Myanmar. There are clerics in Myanmar (and worldwide) whose religious convictions promote religious repression, intolerance, discrimination, and the persecution of those with whom they disagree. Factions of the Theravada Buddhist firm in Myanmar have delivered their religious convictions in hate-filled diatribes against Myanmar's Muslim community. These extremist clerics seek to protect and promote their religion. In hate-filled sermons, these monks seek to protect Buddhism from Muslims, who they refer to as "crazy dogs" that are "breeding so fast," "stealing our women, raping them," and "would like to occupy our country" (Beech and Saw Nang, 2019). The same monks instruct their followers to "make your blood boil," and they incite conflict and violence toward Muslims and Christians (Beech and Saw Nang, 2019). These factions of Myanmar's Buddhist monastic community frequently embrace violence against those who practice minority religions and seek government support and protection for their religion.

In 2012, a faction of the Theravada Buddhist firm in Myanmar established an organization called Ma Ba Tha (a Burmese-language acronym for the association) to protect race and religion (Walton and Ma Khin Mar Mar Kyi, 2019). By 2014, the group had become a powerful and vocal political force under the control of the military government. The Ma Ba Tha organization (renamed the Buddha Dhamma Prahita Foundation) was a renaming of the earlier 969 Buddhist nationalist movement (the numeric symbol comes from 9, 6, and 9 attributes or characteristics of Buddha, Dhamma (Buddhist teachings), and Sangha; Walton and Ma Khin Mar Mar Kyi, 2019). In the late 1990s, a Myanmar monk, U Kyaw Lwin, started using the 969 numbers as a direct counter to the Southeast Asian Muslim firm's use of the number 786 (Palatino, 2013). It was long common for South Asian Muslims to display the 786 symbol to identify halal restaurants. For the Muslim firm, the 786 number represents the phrase "In the Name of Allah, the Compassionate and the ever Merciful" (Palatino, 2013; Cockett, 2015, p. 243). The Ma Ba Tha monks sold stickers, flags, and other paraphernalia bearing the 969 symbol and urged consumers to buy only from vendors that displayed the Buddhist nationalist symbol (Jerryson, 2018, p. 39).

The religious convictions of the Ma Ba Tha monks and the organization were radically political (Kyaw Phyo Tha, 2013). A statement released by the organization in 2019 urged voters to reject all candidates from the National League for Democracy party in the 2020 election. The statement read, "We, the Buddha Dhamma Prahita Foundation, which has been protecting race and religion, seriously urge fellow monks and people to oppose by all means—including refusing to vote for—those who are responsible for . . . actions [that] could ruin the country, race and religion" (Htun Htun, 2019). Leading Ma Ba Tha monks regularly gave sermons claiming that Muslims are "wrong believers" (Beech and Saw Nang, 2019).

A Preference for Power, Protection, and Repression

From 2012 to 2017, the Ma Ba Tha organization flourished with significant financial support from top military men and their families. General Min Aung Hlaing, the general who seized power in 2021, made significant donations to the Ma Ba Tha organization (Anonymous, 2019b). When photos of him with Ma Ba Tha monks at a donation ceremony went viral online, the armed forces chief came under public criticism (Anonymous, 2019b). In June 2019, Major-General Zaw Min Tun of the Myanmar military made a public donation to the Buddhist nationalist group, saying "the group is necessary and should be supported in the name of Buddhism" (Anonymous, 2019b). In a public ceremony, the military commander donated thirty million kyats (about US$20k) to the Buddha Dhamma Prahita Foundation as nearly one thousand Ma Ba Tha monks from across the country gathered at the group's headquarters, in Yangon's Insein Township, for their annual meeting. In his speech, General Zaw Min Tun said, "despite the widely-held perception of Ma Ba Tha as an anti-Muslim organization, the organization's only intention is to protect race and religion" (Anonymous, 2019b). A subgroup of "government" monks, who are loyal to the military and directly benefit from the Buddhism-state-military entanglement, have chosen a preference for aligning with state power, the protection of their religion, and the repression of religious minorities.

The "Face of Buddhist Terror"

U Wirathu, a monk who was branded the "Face of Buddhist Terror" by *Time* magazine, has been the most public face of the Ma Ba Tha (Beech, Meikhtila, and Pattani, 2013). Wirathu and the Ma Ba Tha monks are themselves a means of social control used by the Myanmar military. Scholars and journalists have credited Ma Ba Tha with successfully lobbying the Myanmar government for a series of laws that discriminate against women and religious minorities (see chapter 7). For example, in August 2015, Reuters reported, "The measures are part of four 'Race and Religion Protection Laws' that were championed by the Committee for the Protection of Nationality and Religion or Ma Ba Tha" (Hnin Yadana Zaw, 2015). Although Ma Ba Tha monks publicly supported the policy, it was the military government and Myanmar's president Thein Sein who wrote and passed the laws in Myanmar's military-controlled parliament and then signed them into law. The four laws set out a legal structure for discrimination on religious grounds and established the foundation for serious communal tensions. The Ma Ba Tha monks served as a source of legitimacy for the military government. The argument that the monks had the authority to establish an organization and the power to push the military government to pass laws is to misunderstand the actual power and social control the Myanmar military had and still has on the country. Ma Ba Tha was supported and allowed to exist and to grow in a state in which the military regularly arrests and imprisons individuals for Facebook posts they do not like (Kyaw Phyo Tha, 2015). The religious convictions of the Ma Ba Tha monks provided overt political legitimacy to the anti-Muslim narratives that were supported by the military government.

The influence of Ma Ba Tha's religious convictions is supported by highly effective communications. With the support of the Myanmar military, the group produces a range of media: print publications, including a magazine, a cable TV broadcast of sermons throughout the country, and a vast array of social media accounts. For example, Ma Ba Tha regularly publishes a wide range of literature, including printed glossy magazines filled with anti-Muslim hate and propaganda. This literature is widely circulated at an extremely low cost and is frequently given away to people in tea shops in poor villages across the country. The Myanmar government has allowed Ma Ba Tha's political activities to occur without any interference in stark contrast to the lack of freedom afforded to pro-democracy and human rights activists. When the Saffron monk Myanan Sayadaw U Thaddhamma was asked by the Irrawaddy why the government has failed to stop the spread of the violence, the monk replied, "because the authorities concerned haven't taken the necessary action [to stop it]" (Kyaw Phyo Tha, 2013).

After the resounding victory of the National League for Democracy (NLD) in 2015, Ma Ba Tha experienced significant government oversight. The NLD government objected to the organization's hate speech and incitement of violence. In 2016, the NLD-controlled State Mahanayaka Committee (Myanmar's state body that governs the Buddhist firm; see chapter 5) issued a statement distancing itself and the larger Buddhist firm from the organization. The State Mahanayaka Committee stated that Ma Ba Tha was not an official Buddhist organization (Walton and Ma Khin Mar Mar Kyi, 2019). Ma Ba Tha religious convictions took on new significance in 2017 when the military began a genocidal campaign of violence against Muslims in Rakhine State. More than one million Rohingya refugees have since fled to Bangladesh (see chapter 7). The convictions and ideas of the Buddhist nationalist religious organization stirred fears and hatred and provided a legitimate rationale for violence toward the minority Muslim population. In 2017, the State Mahanayaka Committee took another step to regulate the organization's voice by outlawing the group's name. The group promptly renamed itself the Buddha Dhamma Prahita Foundation. The government then outlawed the new name and brought sedition charges against one of the organization's leading monks, U Wirathu. Even as Wirathu was banned and an arrest warrant issued, he continued to widely travel Myanmar and give his anti-Muslim sermons. Soon after the ethnic cleansing campaign began in 2017, Wirathu was pictured in the state news media meeting with children and giving a sermon in the state of Rakhine. In his hate-filled sermons, Wirathu routinely refers to Muslims as "crazy dogs" that are "breeding so fast," "stealing our women, raping them," and "would like to occupy our country" (Beech and Saw Nang, 2019). In July 2019, the State Mahanayaka Committee reaffirmed its ban on Ma Ba Tha and its successor Buddha Dhamma Prahita Foundation, calling both organizations illegal (Htun Htun, 2019).

RELIGIOUS CONVICTIONS IN THE 2021–2022 CIVIL DISOBEDIENCE MOVEMENT

In January 2021, in the weeks leading up to seizing power, General Min Aung Hlaing paid visits and made financial donations to military-friendly Buddhist monasteries (D'Asie, 2021). In the days before General Min Aung Hlaing arrested Myawaddy Sayadaw and other monks and seized control of Myanmar's government on February 1, 2021, monks from one faction of the Buddhist firm demonstrated their support for the military. Carrying banners with claims of election fraud, monks marched through the streets of Yangon, proclaiming the military as the protector of Buddhism (Artinger and Rowand, 2021; D'Asie, 2021). After the coup, General Min Aung Hlaing made sure that he was photographed at pagodas kneeling on the floor while monks, seated on chairs, were elevated above him. This act of photographed and publicized submission was intended to be an expression of authority, legitimacy, and support.

The relationship between Buddhist nationalists and Myanmar's military is symbiotic. The military supports Buddhist nationalists by protecting and promoting their version of Theravada Buddhism. Buddhist nationalists provide the military with religious legitimacy (Artinger and Rowand, 2021). Just days after the coup, General Min Aung Hlaing also visited Cardinal Charles Maung Bo with an offer of medical equipment. As noted above, Cardinal Bo called for the release of all political prisoners and denounced "the brutality of the military dictatorship" (Bo Maung, 2021). Other factions of the Buddhist firm resisted the 2021 military coup. In May 2021, Buddhist monks from Masoeyein monastery in Mandalay held night candlelight prayers for democracy, peace, and for the safety of all civilians, political detainees, and detained leaders (Ohmmar Khine, 2021a). In June 2021, the monks of the Mandalay Sangha Union protest continued without missing a single day since the February 2021 takeover. In the threat of military troops, monks march with banners and three fingers held high to protest (Ohmmar Khine, 2021b). In the fight for democracy, the Buddhist firm was joined by the leaders of nat worship.

The Nats' Will and Spirit Wives Fight for Democracy

Myanmar's powerful nats represented a challenge for King Anawrahta in 1057 and threatened General Min Aung Hlaing in 2021 (Anonymous, 2021). As discussed in previous chapters, the thirty-seven great nats are venerated in Myanmar. Nat worship is part of everyday life for many people in Myanmar who believe that these spirits have dominion over people and land. In short, for many people the powers of the nats rivals those of the military dictators.

Nat worship is centered, in part, on rituals addressed to the thirty-seven performed by spirit mediums—called spirit wives (Brac de la Perrière, 2009b, p. 285). The nat wives (or nat kadaws, as expressed in Burmese) are governed by a spirit possession that is the expression of what is considered to be the "nats' will" (Brac de la Perrière, 2009b, p. 285). Spirit wives are inspired or possessed to express "what a nat has told me he wants here and now" (Brac de la Perrière, 2009b, p. 285).

In February 2021, Achaintan Man Gay Oo and other spirit wives led protests against the military coup and General Min Aung Hlaing (Anonymous, 2021). Ornately dressed spirit wives joined the street protests to denounce the takeover by General Min Aung Hlaing. The nats were displeased with the generals behind the coup. The religious convictions of the spirit wives propelled them to march alongside civil servants, garment factory workers, and students in the commercial capital Yangon to call for the release of ousted leader Aung San Suu Kyi. "Nats do not want military rule," declared Achaintan Man Gay Oo, "They also want the release of Mother Suu" (Anonymous, 2021). Myanmar's military leaders took the threat of nat as seriously as King Anawrahta. After one spirit medium called for the fall of the junta, the police arrested him and took him to Insein Prison. Spirits are not to be underestimated, Achaintan Man Gay Oo said, adding that she feels protected by spirits despite the warnings of the junta of action against protesters (Anonymous, 2021). In April 2021, in the Kyimyindaing township in the western part of Yangon, protesters carried clay pots that are a traditional offering to the nats during an anti-military junta rally (Myanmar Now, 2021a). In the streets of Yangon, anti-regime messages were written on clay pots traditionally used for nat worship (Myanmar Now, 2021a). Myanmar authors underscore that the nats symbolize "the people's struggle against injustice. . . . A wind of revolt blows every year through the nat festivals" (Ho, 2009, p. 278).

CONCLUSIONS

Religious convictions are clearly important in the religious economy of Myanmar. Religious principles and beliefs have served to guide decisions about colonial rule, democracy, human rights, military rule, and even global relations in the United Nations. The fruits of religion have clearly had a significant and important impact on the Myanmar society. Are the fruits of religion emancipatory or repressive? The answer is more complex than simply to say that it is both.

On the one hand, religious convictions helped free the Myanmar people from colonial rule. From ancient times to the present, both majority and minority religions have provided moral guidance for living. During times of crisis, humans often turn to their religious traditions for answers. In Myanmar, this tendency has placed religious leaders in a unique and critical position. Under military rule, clerics (Buddhist monks and others) often find themselves in the position to intervene between the brutality of the state and its citizens. Since 1962, individual clerics and factions of the Buddhist firm have been catalysts for change in Myanmar. Moral judgment guided the Buddhist monks who mobilized for political change. Cleric core values tend (but not always) to transcend the material and immediate issues of the day. This transcendence has allowed religious leaders in Myanmar to act as invaluable mediators between a repressive state and people seeking democracy and respect for human rights. Buddhist monks have been critical actors in the efforts to promote democracy and justice. The religions of U Thant and the Saffron monks supported peace, respect for others, tolerance, human rights, and democracy. Myawaddy Sayadaw's religious convictions serve as the basis for his preference for the poor and oppressed. The religious guidance and convictions of monks such as Myawaddy Sayadaw bring a sweet fruit of emancipation. State repression of religious voices excludes many important ideas.

On the other hand, the religious convictions of the Buddhist nationalist Ma Ba Tha monks have served to support a brutal military regime, to promote hate and intolerance, and perpetrate violence against those with whom they disagree. The mixture of state power with the interests and religious convictions of the Buddhist nationalists leads to a more complex answer about the fruits of religion. Would the fruits of the Buddhist nationalist religious convictions be bitter or as bitter if they were not mixed with the power and authority of the state? The religious convictions of some clerics and religious factions have been distorted or corrupted by the authority and powers of the state. Although Cardinal Bo's religious convictions did not allow him to be controlled by General Min Aung Hlaing's offer of support, there are factions of Buddhist monks who are loyal to the general and support his brutal regime because that regime supports their interests. The principles and religious convictions of the Myanmar religious economy are corrupted by the financial entanglement with the state. Factions of the majority religion in Myanmar are both servant and a tool of state control. The conscience of the state has been altered and corrupted by the power of the state.

The religious convictions of many of the clerics in Myanmar have repeatedly challenged the brutal authoritarian state. Religious convictions shaped U Thant's work in the United Nations and the crisis surrounding his funeral in 1974. Religious convictions provided principles and legitimacy for the Four Eights Uprising, the Saffron Revolution in 2007, and the Civil Disobedience Movement in 2021. In each of these attempts to disrupt the social control of the military, Myanmar's Buddhist firm sought to impress upon the military government that people were suffering from poverty and declining living standards, a brutal repression of fundamental human rights, and political marginalization. Politically engaged clerics succeeded in sharing and promoting liberal causes by clearly stating their moral and religious opposition to military rule. The moral convictions of politically engaged religious leaders made their protests powerful.

Clerics—Buddhist monks, Catholic nuns, and nat spirit wives—challenging the authoritarian state by courageously standing for peace, democracy, and human rights did not immediately change the power structure, but the impact and symbolism of Myanmar's most revered clerics being arrested, disrobed, and violently crushed by the military may well prove to be emancipatory. The religious convictions of Myanmar's clerics have not only had a significant impact on the perceptions of the military government in Myanmar and around the world, but also have shaped the larger religious economy. In the next chapter, the consequences of almost one thousand years of state religion entanglement are explored.

7

✢

The Ashokan Road

The Consequences of a Highly Regulated Religious Economy for the State and Majority Religion

POWER AND CHOICE

The fascinating and often brutal history of religion and the state in Myanmar reveals the use of power in shaping a religious economy. Those who held power in Myanmar used it to control all religions and to limit religious choices and voices. For nearly one thousand years, the Myanmar government has used its authority and power to protect and support one religion—Theravada Buddhism. Theravada Buddhism, in turn, protected and provided the state with varying degrees of legitimacy. Together, these two institutions maintained a specific power structure and social order. That social order favored the Buddhist firm and allowed the state to control the society.

The entanglement of the powers of religion and state and the social order it maintained fundamentally altered and shaped the culture and structure of Myanmar society. The consequences of state and religion entanglement confirm the fears and predictions of Adam Smith, John Milton, John Locke, James Madison, and Thomas Jefferson. One thousand years of state protection of one religious firm has distorted and corrupted nearly every aspect of Myanmar's religious marketplace. In this chapter and in chapter 8 we discuss the six consequences of nearly one thousand years of state religion entanglement. The consequences include (1) a state protected and supported religious monopoly, (2) corruption, regulation, and repression of Theravada Buddhists, and in chapter 8, (3) repression and violence against religious minorities, (4) perpetual conflict and violence, (5) a corrupt religious economy, and (6) a corruption of truth. The most obvious consequence of this history of state-religion entanglement is the Theravada Buddhist firm's monopoly and the depth and breadth of state control and regulation of the religious marketplace.

CONSEQUENCE 1: PROTECTION, CONTROL, AND REGULATION OF THE MAJORITY RELIGION

Centuries of protection, control, and regulation of religion have entrenched a narrative and policy of state support for the majority religion in Myanmar. The historical narrative provides a rationalization of the policy. Since 1057, religion has been supported, highly regulated, and controlled in Myanmar. It is important to note that the Myanmar state regulates all religions, including the majority religion. The Myanmar state not only controls all religious firms, but also discourages religious expression outside of the state-regulated institutions. The history of Myanmar military state–religion policy reveals a policy that is about social control and keeping the Buddhist firm (and minority religions) in check rather than supporting religion. Myanmar's official (legal) religion policy is itself revealing and is an important consequence of centuries of state-religion entanglement.

Understanding of the Spheres of State, Politics, and Religion

One of the consequences of centuries of state religion entanglement is that it has made the difficulty of distinguishing between the spheres of religion and politics an instrument of power. Those who benefit from the entanglement argue that history and culture preclude a clear understanding of the spheres of state authority, politics, and religion in Myanmar. Scholars within and outside Myanmar, as well as state and religious leaders, report that there is no consensus within the country that the state should refrain from entanglement with religious affairs (Fink, 2018, p. 272; personal communications, 2015–2016; Schober and Collins, 2012, p. 159). The history of the entanglement of state, politics, and religion is as contentious in Myanmar as elsewhere in the world. Like many humans, Myanmar's people have difficulty definitively distinguishing between religious and secular spaces (McKay, 2019, p. 17). That difficulty, however, does not preclude the Myanmar society from holding a definitive understanding of the spheres of state authority, politics, and religion.

It is in the interest of some in the Buddhist firm and of some political leaders in the offices of state to promote the narrative of an indistinguishable overlap between culture, religion, and politics. There is power to be had and a social order to maintain in the promotion of a historical and cultural overlap. The interviews of religious and political leaders, conducted in Myanmar in 2015 and 2016 by this author, provided evidence of a broad understanding of the nuances of state and religion overlap. Buddhist monks, Muslim and Christian clerics, and political leaders expressed a robust understanding of both the historical narrative and the debate over the role of the entanglement of religious and secular institutions. While religion and the state have certainly been historically entangled, the people and religious groups in Myanmar view that, and act as if, the two institutions are separate. Evidence of this understanding is found in history since 1947, state–religion policies noted below, in robust internal conversations within the Buddhist firm about monk participation in politics (Walton, 2016a), and in the words in the constitutions adopted in 1947 and 2008. Although survey data are needed to better understand the opinions of the Myanmar people, history and interviews by this author indicate a broad understanding of and general call for religious freedom and a more secular state (personal communications, 2016). In the 1930s, many in the Buddhist firm sought state support for their religion. U Ottama stood against the British colonial state. In 1947, General Aung San and his leadership team promoted a clear separation of state and religion (see chapter 5). The 1947 constitution, abolished by General Ne Win in 1962, served as a guide for the authors of the 2008 constitution and includes concepts of liberal religion-state policies. The authors understood the separation of the spheres of state and religion.

Constitutional Law and Religion

The 2008 Myanmar constitution states that every citizen is equally entitled to freedom of conscience and the right to freely profess and practice his or her religious beliefs. The 2008 constitution forbids "the abuse of religion for political purposes" and does not recognize an official state religion. It does, however, recognize "the special position of Buddhism as the faith professed by the great majority of the citizens of the Union" (Fink, 2018). The Myanmar government has a preferred religion (Fox, 2019c). Although the Myanmar state does not officially endorse Theravada Buddhism, that one religion serves unofficially as the state's religion.

Theravada Buddhism receives unique recognition and benefits, while minority religions receive similar repressive treatment. The Myanmar state supports and substantially controls Theravada Buddhism and generally presents a positive attitude toward the majority religion. The Myanmar constitution favors one religious firm, and the religious marketplace reflects the state's support. The men (and it was largely men) who wrote the 2008 constitution embraced General Aung San's liberal religious marketplace. They declared that every citizen is equally entitled to freedom of conscience and the right to freely profess and practice his or her religious beliefs. But nearly one thousand years of state-religion entanglement has not been erased by constitutional statements about religious liberty. Prime Minister U Nu sought to promote Buddhism in the 1947 constitution by recognizing "the special position of Buddhism" in the country. The 2008 constitution included the favoring of Buddhism and added that "the Union may assist and protect religions it recognizes to it utmost" (Fink, 2018). This constitutional declaration allows that state to control and regulate the entire religious economy and the political leaders of Myanmar have done precisely that.

Myanmar State Support for the Majority Religion

The Myanmar state supports the majority religion directly (for example, financially) and indirectly (for example, symbolic support from top officials). The state also supports the majority religion by limiting and restricting minority religions. Worldwide data indicate that one of the most effective ways to control a religion is to support it (Fox, 2016a, p. 455). Support for Theravada Buddhism has created factions of the religion dependent upon and beholden to the state. Myanmar's military rulers bought the legitimacy that Buddhism offered with gifts, charity, and the construction of religious edifices. The state's support of Buddhism provided the clerics with financial and material assistance, social status, and influence. The Buddhist firm gave the state an ideological legitimacy that ensured continued power and authority. The state's direct support of the Buddhist religion provides the political leaders of Myanmar with influence they otherwise would not have (Grim and Finke, 2010). For example, the posts, titles, awards, lavish gifts, and facilities given to some monks may have allowed the state to successfully pressure the Buddhist firm to alter its official interpretation of the rules in the Vinaya on the issue of monk involvement in politics (Myawaddy Sayadaw, personal communication, 2016). As John Milton predicted, Myanmar state leaders reward monks "they find conformable to their interests and opinions" and those monks in turn "frame themselves to that interest and those opinions which they see best pleasing to their paymasters; and to seem right themselves, will force others as to the truth" (Koppelman, 2009, p. 32 n. 71).

The Religion and State Project (RAS3) has identified fifty-two policies (variables) that governments worldwide employ to support religion (Fox, 2016a, p. 456). The Myanmar state utilizes fifteen (variables were combined here for brevity and clarity) of those policies to support, control, and protect Theravada Buddhism. Each of the following fifteen policy variables were adapted from the RAS3 dataset (Fox, 2020).

Supporting Religious Precepts as Law

- The Myanmar state supports religion with restrictions on interfaith marriages. In 2015, the Myanmar government enacted a series of four laws intended to "protect race and religion." Factions of vocal Buddhist monks supported the enactment of these four laws. These four laws are highly discriminatory against ethnic and religious minorities, as well as against women. The Buddhist Women Special Marriage law stipulates notification and registration requirements for marriages between non-Buddhist men and Buddhist women. The Buddhist Women Special Marriage law includes obligations that non-Buddhist husbands must observe and penalties for noncompliance. To restrict growth in minority religious groups, the Myanmar government enacted the Population Control Law. This act allows for the designation of special zones for which population control measures could be applied, including authorizing local authorities to implement three-year birth spacing. The fourth law, titled the Monogamy Law, bans polygamous practices.
- Supporting religion, the Myanmar state has placed restrictions on conversions away from the dominant religion. Among the four laws passed in 2015, the Religious Conversion Act is the most controversial. To "protect Buddhism," the Religious Conversion law significantly restricts the right to freedom of religion. It regulates an individual's choice of religion by restricting conversion through an extensive application and approval process. The law, though rarely applied, gives the authority to a government Registration Board to review and approve (or not) an individual's decision to convert to a different religion.
- To support religion, Myanmar has enacted laws that specifically make it illegal to be a homosexual or to engage in homosexual sex. These laws have had an impact on nat worship (see below). Since the colonial era, Myanmar has maintained Section 377 of its Penal Code, a provision inherited from British rule that criminalizes consensual same-sex sexual conduct. This provision reads as follows: "377. Whoever voluntarily has carnal intercourse against the order of nature with any man, woman, or animal shall be punished with imprisonment for a term of twenty years, or with imprisonment of either description for a term which may extend to ten years and shall also be liable to fine."
- Supporting religion, the Myanmar state policy restricts a woman's access to abortion. Following Theravada Buddhist precepts, which state that life begins at conception, Myanmar's laws permit abortion only when the woman's life is at risk. Unsafe abortion accounts for nearly 10 percent of all maternal deaths in Myanmar, making it the third leading cause of maternal death. As a direct consequence of

state-religion entanglement, many (246,000 each year) women undergo unsafe procedures that delay seeking help for complications, resulting in greater complications and higher costs for women and the larger public health system (IPAS, 2016, p. 1).
- Supporting religion, the Myanmar state restricts access to birth control. Although contraceptives are available, they can be difficult to obtain, particularly for poor women and women living in rural areas. Among vulnerable populations in Myanmar—such as adolescents, people affected by conflict, and people with disabilities—knowledge of and access to services supporting sexual and reproductive health and rights remain problematic. A consequence of Myanmar's state religion policy is high rates of unmet contraceptive needs and widespread gender-based violence.

Supporting Institutions and Laws That Enforce Religion

- Myanmar supports religion with restrictions on speech about religion. "Blasphemy" laws are part of the Penal Code in Myanmar and are frequently used to criminalize criticism of the majority religion. The Penal Code "blasphemy" provisions include Section 295 (a), which states that "deliberate and malicious intention of outraging the religious feelings" or "insults or attempts to insult the religion or the religious beliefs" will be imprisoned up to two years, or with a fine, or both, and Section 298, which criminalizes the deliberate intention of wounding the religious feelings of any person. In recent years in Myanmar, courts have convicted many individuals under these "blasphemy" provisions. People have been held criminally responsible for written, depicted, or other expressions judged to be at odds with religion and with influential religious or state authorities. In 2014, Htin Lin Oo was sentenced to two and a half years in prison with hard labor for insulting Buddhism at a literary event. Htin Lin Oo was prosecuted under the Penal Code's Articles 295a and 298. Htin Lin Oo expressed criticism of members of the Buddhist clergy. He argued that Buddhist nationalism was being used to discriminate against minority religions (Mann, 2015). "What I said was for love and peace between different communities with different faiths," said Htin Lin Oo outside the court (Mann, 2015).

Funding Religion in Myanmar

- Myanmar's state supports the majority religion with funding for religious education in primary and secondary schools. Theravada Buddhist doctrine remains part of the state-mandated curriculum

in all government-run elementary schools. Students at these schools can opt out of instruction in Buddhism and sometimes do, but all are required to recite a daily Buddhist prayer. Some schools or teachers allow Muslim students to leave the classroom during this recitation, but there does not appear to be a centrally mandated exemption for non-Buddhist students.
- The Myanmar state supports the majority religion with government funding of seminary schools and religious education in colleges or universities. The government financially supports Theravada Buddhist seminaries and missionary activities. The Myanmar state funds two Theravada Buddhist universities. These institutions, one in Yangon and the other in Mandalay, educate Buddhist monks under the direction of the State Sangha Maha Nayaka Committee.
- Supporting religion, the Myanmar government funds religious charitable organizations. In 2019 and again in 2020 (as noted in chapter 6) the then commander in chief of the armed forces, Min Aung Hlaing, made several well-publicized visits to Muslim, Christian, and Hindu—and Buddhist—firms in Nay Pyi Taw, Mandalay, and Yangon. General Min Aung Hlaing made donations of cash, food, and equipment. A military spokesperson characterized the visits as a gesture of "political, social, and religious unity." Some observers said that Min Aung Hlaing's visits were likely to advance his political ambitions (U.S. Department of State, 2019).
- The Myanmar state supports the majority religion by funding the construction, maintenance, and repair of religious sites. From U Nu's building of the Great Cave (see chapter 4) to the present day, the Myanmar state-controlled media frequently report military and government officials and their family members paying respect to Buddhist monks; offering donations at pagodas; officiating at ceremonies to open, improve, restore, or maintain pagodas; and organizing "people's donations" of money, food, and labor to build or refurbish Buddhist religious sites nationwide (U.S. Department of State, 2019).

The Entanglement of Government and Religious Institutions

- The Myanmar state supports religion with an official government ministry that specifically manages the nation's religious affairs. As noted in earlier chapters, the Myanmar Ministry of Religious Affairs Department for the Perpetuation and Propagation of the Śāsana (Buddhist teachings) oversees the government's relations with Buddhist monks and schools. The Ministry of Religious Affairs financially supports the State Sangha Maha Nayaka Committee and religious courts and ceremonies.

- The Myanmar state supports Theravada Buddhism through the hiring practices of government positions. Nearly all senior officials in the military and civil service report to be practicing Theravada Buddhists. Applications for civil service and military positions required the applicant to list their religion. According to one human rights organization, applications by Muslims for government jobs were largely rejected. The government discourages Muslims from enlisting in the military, and Christian or Muslim military officers who aspired to promotion beyond the rank of major were encouraged by their superiors to convert to Buddhism (Humanists International, 2016, p. 2). In effect, adherence or conversion to Buddhism is an unwritten prerequisite for promotion to most senior government and military ranks. Buddhists continued to make up the vast majority of parliamentarians. In 2020, there were no Muslim members of parliament. In 2020, Second Vice President Henry Van Thio, a Chin Christian, continued to serve in his position, and the speakers of the upper and lower houses of parliament were also Christian. The United Nations reported concern about "institutionalized discrimination against Christians in Chin State," particularly in the civil service. Christians hold only 14 percent of state-level senior positions and 25 percent of township administrative officer positions—none are held by women—despite the fact that the state population is 87 percent Christian, 11 percent Buddhist, and 2 percent animist (United Nations, 2013, p. 12).
- The Myanmar state supports the Theravada Buddhist firm with religious education in some public schools (Humanists International, 2016, p. 2). Religious education is mandatory in some public schools; however, upon request, a student may opt out. Religious education is available for only one religion (Theravada Buddhism) although there is a substantial number of students belonging to other religions. The Myanmar government also supports religion with state published and distributed books on Theravada Buddhist instruction. Christian students were required to convert to Buddhism to access "Na Ta La" schools ("border areas national races youth development training school") in Chin state, which were better funded than public schools (United Nations, 2013, p. 12). The Na Ta La schools serve as a "state-sponsored religious and cultural assimilation program" (U.S. Department of State, 2019).
- Myanmar supports the Buddhist firm with official prayer sessions in public schools and prisons. There are official prayer sessions in public schools and, as noted in chapter 5, also in Insein Prison. In the schools and prisons, some students and prisoners are forced to attend sessions in religions other than their own. As in the routine in Insein Prison, teachers in many government schools reportedly

continued to require students to recite Buddhist prayers. Many classrooms displayed Buddhist altars or other Buddhist iconography, as does Insein Prison (Ah Noh, personal communications, 2021). Teaching of anti-Muslim tenets in schools is common throughout the country (U.S. Department of State, 2019).

- The Myanmar state supports religion by listing religion on state identity cards or other government documents that most citizens must possess and complete. Citizens and permanent residents are required to carry government-issued national registration cards. These cards allow holders to access services and prove citizenship. These identification cards often (but not always) indicate religious affiliation and ethnicity. Citizens also are required to indicate their religion on certain official application forms for documents such as passports, although passports themselves do not indicate the bearer's religion. Members of many ethnic and religious minorities, particularly Muslims, face problems in obtaining national registration cards. The card forces a person to be affiliated with a government-defined religious and ethnic group. If a person claims to be Buddhist, their card is commonly noted that their race is either "Bama" or one of the seven major ethnic groups. But if a person is a practicing Muslim, the card must and will also note a "race" from one of three other neighboring countries: India, Bangladesh, or Pakistan. One student reported, "There are some friends of mine who are purely 'Bama' or 'Mon' as race, but since they converted from Buddhism to Islam, they were forced to put those foreign races in their ID card. It doesn't make sense to them that they were pure ethic race when they were Buddhists, but suddenly become 'Indian,' 'Bengali' or 'Pakistani' once they converted to Islam. On my ID card it is written that I am Indian, Sunni, although I was born here in Myanmar and have never been to those countries, never knew about those cultures, and never spoken or understood any of their languages. I am from Myanmar!" (Sterken, 2016, p. 99). Myanmar residents normally apply for a national registration card when they are ten years old and then get a new card when they turn eighteen. Another student reported, "My friend is Mon, he got a card when he turned eighteen. His new card changed him to mixed blood. He is now Mon + India, because he is Muslim" (Sterken, 2016, p. 100). Authorities continued to bar any university students who did not possess citizenship cards from graduating, which disproportionately affected students from religious minorities, particularly Muslim students (U.S. Department of State, 2019). Muslim students could attend classes and take examinations but could not receive diplomas unless they had a citizenship card, the application for which required some religious minorities to identify as a "foreign" ethnic minority (personal communication, 2016).

The consequence of the sum of all this state support for the majority religion is that it allowed (perhaps forced is a better word) Theravada Buddhism to hold a vast majority of the Myanmar religious market. According to state data, Buddhism today holds nearly 90 percent of the Myanmar religious market. The support for Buddhism has not only promoted and protected the Buddhist firm, but has also restricted and repressed minority religions. Following King Ashoka, Myanmar's founding king (as noted in chapter 1) reshaped the entire religious economy. King Anawrahta and his loyal government monk violently eliminated as much of the religious competition as they could, and then they altered what scholars call the most fundamental religion, the general belief in the "animation of all nature" (Peoples, Duda, and Marlowe, 2016, p. 279). Alongside a state-supported Buddhist monopoly, nat worship has flourished in Myanmar.

Figure 7.1. Myanmar's State Saṅgha Mahā Nāyaka Committee, the ruling council of monks, gather during the conclusion of a meeting in Yangon on July 14, 2016, where the Mahana council formally distanced itself from the hardline ultra-nationalist Ma Ba Tha monks. Myanmar's minister of religion warned the ultra-nationalist Buddhist monks over hate speech, as the new civilian government took steps to stem a swell of Islamaphobia across the country. *Source*: Romeo Gacad

THE LADY, LIBERALISM, AND THE PROBLEM WITH BUDDHISM

Since 1988, Aung San Suu Kyi has been one of the most important actors in Myanmar's religious economy. Although her famous father, general Aung San, remains the most important person in the history of modern Myanmar, Aung San Suu Kyi is almost universally revered throughout the country. Like her father's portrait, her image is nearly universally displayed in homes, restaurants, and shops. Under arrest again in 2021, the Nobel Peace Prize–winner's life and political decisions are a consequence of Myanmar's religious economy, and her leadership has shaped the religious marketplace.

Aung San Suu Kyi, the daughter of General Aung San (see chapter 4), is undoubtedly the most famous of all of Myanmar's post-independence leaders. Like her father, U Nu, and U Thant, Suu Kyi is widely respected and revered in Myanmar. She is respectfully referred to as Daw Suu (Aunt Suu) or Amay Suu (Mother Suu) by many in Myanmar. Since the Four Eights Uprising, Suu Kyi has been globally celebrated and widely vilified. She has been praised as an icon of democracy and human rights and rejected as a heartless power-hungry Machiavellian politician (Lubina, 2021, p. 3). Suu Kyi has been a threat to Myanmar's patriarchal power structure and has held at least some power within that structure. From King Anawrahta to modern times, Aung San Suu Kyi is arguably one of the most influential leaders in Myanmar's long history. Since 1988, Suu Kyi's leadership and political struggles have been influenced by and a direct consequence of Myanmar's religious economy. Like U Nu and U Thant, Aung San Suu Kyi's political life reflects her education and religion. Suu Kyi has been a strong advocate for a democratic and secular state–religion policy while drawing and supporting her Buddhist ethos (Schober, 2011, pp. 108–9). Suu Kyi's life and education reflect Buddhist moral convictions and an embracing of liberal democratic structures.

Tuesday's Transnational Child

Aung San Suu Kyi was born on Tuesday, June 19, 1945, in a village in the Irrawaddy Delta region of Myanmar. Suu Kyi, the third of three children, was born in the tumult of world war. Her mother, Maha Thiri Thudhamma Khin Kyi, was a political leader and diplomat, and her father, Aung San, led Myanmar toward a new and inclusive democratic era (see chapter 4). Suu Kyi was two years old when her famous father was assassinated. Suu Kyi's politically active mother raised her in the Theravada Buddhist traditions and provided her with a cross-cultural religious and educational foundation. Like U Ottama (see chapter 3), Suu Kyi was cross-culturally educated. Aung San Suu Kyi was a transcultural or "third culture" child

(Lubina, 2021, p. 17; Poonoosamy, 2018, p. 208). She was educated in several different countries and lived in widely diverse cultural environments for a significant period of time during the formative years of her life. The liberal/neutral state–religion policies of the British had a direct impact on Suu Kyi's education.

British-Era Methodist English High School

Khin Kyi and Suu Kyi's religious educations included Christian ideas that had been freely shared under the liberal/neutral state–religion policies of the British colonial era (see chapter 2). Suu Kyi and her mother both attended Christian schools in Yangon. Khin Kyi attended the American Baptist Mission Kemmendine Girls School (now Basic Education High School No. 1 Kyimyindaing), and she later sent her daughter to the Methodist English High School (present-day Basic Education High School No. 1 Dagon; Ma Thanegi, 2013, p. 14). As noted in chapter 2, during the British colonial era and until Ne Win's coup in 1962, Christian missionaries provided Christian instruction, English-language training, and secular education for children in Myanmar (Hellman-Rajanayagam, 2020, p. 244; Loomis, 1953; Matthews, 1995, p. 301). Baptist and Methodist missionaries as well as her Christian maternal grandfather (Suu Kyi's grandfather, Pho Hnyin, was baptized in a Karen Baptist Church as a young man) opened Suu Kyi to Christian ideas (Lubina, 2021, p. 17; Bengtsson, 2012, p. 49).

Ashoka Road: Influence of India's Cosmopolitan Liberal Thinkers

In 1960, U Nu appointed Khin Kyi to serve as Myanmar's ambassador to India (Ling, 1999, p. 33). During Khin Kyi's tenure in New Delhi, Indian prime minister Jawaharlal Nehru arranged for Ambassador Khin Kyi and Suu Kyi to live at 24 Akbar Road, in a widely diverse colonial-era complex. Ambassador Khin Kyi sent her daughter to the nearby Convent of Jesus and Mary School (to get to her campus every school day, Suu Kyi would travel almost two miles on King Ashoka Road). Established during British rule in 1919, the Convent of Jesus and Mary School is a girls' day school, known for strict discipline and a liberal arts education, and is one of a worldwide network of Roman Catholic schools. Suu Kyi's classmates at the Convent of Jesus and Mary were of widely diverse religious backgrounds, many of them Hindus, but that did not stop the Catholic Jesuit teachers tirelessly teaching Christianity (Popham, 2011, p. 182).

With her home country in political turmoil, Suu Kyi studied political science at Lady Shri Ram College for Women in New Delhi. Lady Shri Ram College for Women is widely recognized as a premier liberal arts institution. In her liberal arts studies, Suu Kyi developed strong critical thinking, problem solving, and communication skills. She learned to approach questions flexibly and to think across multiple disciplines and from a wide range of perspectives. Suu's professors encouraged the study of a wide range of ideas, both Western and Eastern (Popham, 2011, p. 187). Suu was exposed to India's postcolonial pluralistic and global atmosphere (Lubina, 2021, p. 17). In 1962, Nehru won a general multiparty election, and in Myanmar, Ne Win led a coup and propelled his country into violence, turmoil, and poverty. While Suu Kyi was studying power and politics, General Ne Win was violently suppressing student demonstrations, destroying buildings, and sending students home from the university in her home city of Yangon. In 1962, Ne Win's military killed hundreds of students and blew up the Rangoon University Student Union building. While her friends protested in Yangon, Suu Kyi was exposed to a wide range of ideas about power, nationalism, religion, and human rights. Among many others, Suu studied Gandhi, Nehru, Nirad Chaudhuri, and Rabindranath Tagore (Popham, 2011, p. 181).

Suu Kyi was greatly influenced by Tagore's attitudes toward politics and culture, nationalism and transnationalism, tradition, and modernity (Popham, 2011, p. 187). Suu Kyi's work decades later, in *Freedom from Fear and Other Writings*, reflects Tagore's influence (Aung San Suu Kyi, 2010). Tagore's nonfiction and poetry works strongly condemn nationalism and assert the human right of self-determination and to be independent without closing off to the wide range of diverse points of view from abroad (Collins, 2008, p. 2). Tagore wrote, "What is needed is eagerness of heart for a fruitful communication between different cultures. Anything that prevents this is barbarism" (Collins, 2008, p. 1). Suu Kyi adopted and excelled at Tagore's approach to cross-cultural learning. Taking the opposite approach to General Ne Win, Tagore wrote that Indians should learn what is going on elsewhere, they should study how others live, what other cultures and religions value, and remain interested and involved in their own histories, cultures, and heritages (Collins, 2008, p. 3). For Tagore, it was critical that people be free to make their own choices. Tagore's ideal marketplace of ideas is "without fear" and "knowledge is free" and "not broken up into fragments by narrow domestic walls" (Tagore, 1913). Along with the writings of Tagore, Suu Kyi's studies included an in-depth reading of Gandhi's philosophy of nonviolence (Ling, 1999, p. 33; Lubina, 2021, p. 17). Gandhi's nonviolent approach to disrupt the existing social order and to force political change became a central and lifelong component of Aung San Suu Kyi's political philosophy (Lubina, 2021, p. 17; Schober 2011, p. 109). In 1964, she graduated with a degree in political science from Lady Shri Ram College.

After graduation from Lady Shri Ram College, Suu Kyi entered St. Hugh's College of the University of Oxford to study politics, philosophy, and economics. At St. Hugh's she was known as a "highly intelligent and articulate, though quiet and enormously polite" student (Popham, 2011, p. 194). Her studies included the writings on liberty by Adam Smith, John Milton, John Locke, John Stuart Mill, and Thomas Jefferson, which provide the theorical underpinnings of this book (Popham, 2011, p. 194). Following her father, Suu Kyi embraced the ideas of freedom, human rights, rule of law, and democracy (Lubina, 2021, p. 17).

Gandhi, King, and Suu Kyi's Religious Convictions

After graduating from Oxford, Suu Kyi moved to New York to work for three years under U Thant (see chapter 6) in the United Nations. Suu Kyi arrived in the United States just months after the assassination of Dr. Martin Luther King Jr. Living in the United States in the civil rights era, Suu Kyi was placed in a front-row seat to observe Gandhi's nonviolent civil disobedience in action. King's writings ("Letter from Birmingham Jail") and use of Gandhi's nonviolence to prompt change became Suu Kyi's model (*Letters from Burma*) for her own struggle for the rights and freedoms of the people of Myanmar.

During decades under house arrest, Suu Kyi deepened the Buddhist practices instilled by her mother. Years of detention were used to strengthen her spiritual life. Suu Kyi wrote that in detention "I started off on the basis that I would have to be very disciplined and keep to a strict timetable. I must not waste time and let myself go to seed, I would get up at 4:30 and meditate for an hour" (Popham, 2011, p. 292). Ma Thanegi (2013) has noted that during detention Suu Kyi recited a Buddhist mantra every week on Tuesday, the day of the week when she was born. Ma Thanegi wrote, "Lights out and I said to Suu thank God it's not Tuesday. Suu asked why and laughed when I said because on Tuesday, she must tell her beads for 45 rounds. I think at the time she was 44 and every Tuesday which was her birthday she would recite a prayer and tell the 108 beads for 45 rounds" (Popham, 2011, p. 292).

Aung San Suu Kyi and Consequences

Cross-cultural exposure, during Suu Kyi's adolescent and young adult years, allowed her to absorb intellectual, cultural, and behavioral norms that are quite different from those of Myanmar's military leaders. Michael Lubina (2021, p. 26) has aptly labeled Suu Kyi a "hybrid politician." Myanmar's military leaders are hugely different. While Suu Kyi and the Myanmar people came to embrace freedom and democracy, the generals who ruled the country "lived in a hermetically sealed world," where they "lived together, attended the same religious ceremonies, went to the same schools, and told themselves that they were the true patriots and their opponents were traitors" (Thant Myint-U, 2020, p. 132). Modern military leaders have followed the ruling patterns set by authoritarian kings of the past (Maung Maung Gyi, 1983, p. 192). The consequence of this pattern is an enduring authoritarian rule of intimidation, fear, and violence. Myanmar's military leaders have attempted to portray Aung San Suu Kyi as Westernized and foreign. She was often portrayed in Buddhist nationalist campaigns as a leader who was unable to protect religion because she was educated abroad and had married a foreigner. Seeking popular support, Suu Kyi is demonstrative and vocal about her Buddhist beliefs and is frequently photographed with members of the Buddhist firm.

Aung San Suu Kyi, like her father, has had a liberating effect on the Myanmar religious economy. Suu Kyi has done much to promote a liberal democracy for her people. Surveys indicate widespread engagement and citizen participation in politics and in civic activities (Win Nyi Nyi Zaw and Khin Nyein Chan, 2020, p. 26). Suu Kyi remains extremely popular. A 2020 survey by the People's Alliance for Credible Elections found that nearly 80 percent of the Myanmar people had trust in her (Win Nyi Nyi Zaw and Khin Nyein Chan, 2020, p. 41). In 2021, millions of people marched in protest of the military takeover and voiced strong and nationwide support for Suu Kyi and democratic rule. While Suu Kyi has tirelessly promoted a liberal democracy for the people of Myanmar, she has also fostered a deepening entanglement of religion and the state (Lubina, 2021, p. 51).

State Protection of Religion Undermines Legitimacy of Religious Convictions

Suu Kyi's Buddhist religious convictions are strong and frequently outwardly expressed. Her political messages are founded in Buddhism (Schober, 2011, p. 109). Suu Kyi is open about her practice of meditation and views meditation as a foundation for her political actions (Lubina, 2021, p. 51). While Suu Kyi has adopted Gandhi and King's nonviolent path to resistance, like Prime Minister U Nu, she has also advocated socially engaged Buddhism to promote democratic reforms to bring about structural political changes and moral improvement in the Myanmar society (Schober, 2011, p. 109). Suu Kyi, again like U Nu, argues that Buddhist principles and engagement must be used to provide for basic human needs like adequate livelihood, health, and education (Schober, 2011, p. 109). Suu Kyi frequently called for Buddhist principles such as "loving-kindness" to be used to promote Myanmar's democratic transition (Haynes, 2013, p. 173). Suu Kyi's political actions and statements are supported by her Buddhist beliefs, and her reliance on Buddhism is both personal and politically convenient; the Buddhist firm provided her with a very traditional means of legitimacy (Lubina, 2021, p. 51). Like

U Nu, she too is seen by some Buddhists as a near-bodhisattva (Robertson, 2014). Unlike her father (see chapter 4), Suu Kyi does not see the need to keep her religious and political worlds separate. On Facebook and through state-controlled media, Suu Kyi (and top military and government officials and their family members) are frequently depicted paying respect to Buddhist monks. It is common to see Suu Kyi and top officials making donations at pagodas, officiating at ceremonies to open, restore, or maintain pagodas, and organizing "people's donations" of funding to build or refurbish Buddhist shrines.

One of the significant consequences of Myanmar's long history of protecting Theravada Buddhism is that a political leader like Aung San Suu Kyi, who is open about religious convictions, faces a significant historical obstacle. The historical pattern of Buddhist nationalism fosters both xenophobia within sects of the Theravada Buddhist firm and perpetual conflict with those who are labeled as foreign. Buddhist nationalism divides nations and undermines democracy and restricts the sharing of ideas in Myanmar's religious economy.

Suu Kyi's focus on Buddhism (no matter how well intentioned) undermined her attempts to build the foundations of a liberal democracy. In 2019, Aung San Suu Kyi and other senior government officials participated in a conference organized by Myanmar Religions for Peace. In a speech at the event, Suu Kyi urged respect for the country's different religions, but shocked many outside observers when she defended the military's actions against the Rohingya. However, Myanmar's long struggle with Buddhist nationalism and its history of violent repression of religious and ethnic minorities foster mistrust and alienation among religious minorities. Even beloved and well-intentioned leaders like U Nu and Aung San Suu Kyi have faced this divisive problem. U Thant, on the other hand, was able to share and be known for his Buddhist beliefs without significant political problems or conflict while leading the United Nations. The United Nations has no history of protecting and supporting Theravada Buddhism. A direct consequence of the history of Myanmar's state–religion policy of protecting Buddhism is that the expression of religious convictions by its modern leaders carries the divisive burden of Buddhist nationalism.

Attempts to forge a liberal democracy that is open and inclusive of all Myanmar's citizens and religious ideas face the divisive obstacle of centuries of favor for one specific religion. The centuries of favor have nurtured the primordial single story that people who are not Buddhists do not belong in the country and are not real citizens. The single story has significant consequences for the people of Myanmar. It is important to note that religion itself has not created these consequences (Juergensmeyer, 2018, p. 94). It is the centuries of entanglement of state and religion that have generated violent and repressive consequences.

The primordial narrative (promoted by the military, ethnic extremists, and factions of the Buddhist firm) is that certain people have no right to be in Myanmar. This narrative is widely believed and commonly embraced by those seeking power or to promote discord for political gain. Centuries of state promotion and protection of Theravada Buddhism have deeply woven religious prejudices into the Myanmar society. State–religion policies have led directly to the abuse and discrimination against members of minority religious firms and individuals by state and private actors. In 2020, it was common for prominent civilian and religious leaders to promote U Ottama's idea that the Theravada Buddhist firm and culture was under assault by foreigners.

U Nu's government fostered Buddhist nationalism. U Nu's slogan was amyo (only the Burman race), barthar (only the Burmese language), and tharthanar (only the Buddhist religion). This nationalist slogan lies at the heart of Buddhist nationalism, was exploited by General Ne Win, and since March of 1962, the military elite and factions of the Buddhist firm have used religious identity as an instrument and basis for alliance. Ne Win and the military leaders who have followed him used religious identity and the conflict it fosters to hold power. Myanmar's leaders reconstructed memories of the past to fit modern needs. Religious minorities (especially Christians and Muslims) became the scapegoats. All citizens who identify as non-Buddhists are discriminated against simply because they are not Buddhists. Myanmar's leaders harnessed religion, Buddhist nationalism, and the need to protect Buddhism to justify policies, violence, and killing (Juergensmeyer, 1995, p. 382).

CONSEQUENCE 2: CORRUPTION, REGULATION, AND RESTRICTIONS ON THE MAJORITY RELIGION

Theravada Buddhism suffered (1) regulation and restrictions, (2) loss of legitimacy and ability to share religious convictions, (3) corruption of beliefs (violence and truth), (4) and factions of the Sangha have become servants of the state. The Religion and State Project has identified twenty-nine policies that states around the world employ to regulate and restrict the majority religion. The RAS data reveal that the Myanmar government has employed twenty of these policies to restrict and control Theravada Buddhism (Fox, 2020). As above, similar variables have been combined.

Silenced Convictions: Restrictions on Religion's Political Role

- Myanmar law bars members of "religious orders," such as priests, monks, and nuns of any religious group, from running for public office. The constitution bars members of religious orders from voting (see chapter 6). The government restricts by law the political activities and expression of the Buddhist firm. The constitution forbids "the abuse of religion for political purposes."

- The Myanmar state restricts and monitors sermons by Buddhist monks. The government also tightly controls speech, forbids political activity by selected Buddhist monks, and keeps Buddhist temples and monasteries under close surveillance.
- The Myanmar government restricts members and organizations of the majority religion that operate outside the recognized or state-sponsored ecclesiastical framework. The Myanmar government bans any organization of Buddhist monks other than the nine state-recognized monastic orders. Violations of this ban are punishable by immediate public defrocking and harsh criminal penalties. The nine recognized orders are submitted to the authority of the State Sangha Maha Nayaka Committee.
- The Myanmar government officially influences the internal workings and organization of Buddhist religious institutions and organizations. The State Sangha Maha Nayaka Committee, the governing body of monastics appointed by the Myanmar state to oversee and regulate affairs within the Buddhist firm, routinely (but not always) follows state directives (Cockett, 2015, p. 70). For example, in 2016, the State Sangha Maha Nayaka Committee ordered that Ma Ba Tha had been operating unlawfully. The state directly influences the internal workings of the Buddhist firm. When asked if the state changes the rules in the Vinaya (rules governing Buddhist monks), monks said incredulously, "No, they don't change the rules, the government only changes the interpretation of the rules" (personal communication, 2016).
- The Myanmar state harasses, arrests, and imprisons Buddhist religious leaders. There are many examples of this policy. From Ne Win's regime in March 1962 to the present, religious leaders have been questioned, harassed, beaten, imprisoned, disrobed, and killed for expressing their religious convictions. In March 2021, three well-known and widely respected monks, Ashin Ariya Vansa Bivansa (Myawaddy Sayadaw), Ashin Sobitha, and Shwe Nya War, each an outspoken supporter of democracy, a vocal figure standing against toxic Buddhist nationalism and against the human rights violations by the Myanmar military, were arrested, disrobed, and sent to prison on the first day of the coup. Sayadaw Minthonnya of Myanmar's Buddhist University told Radio Free Asia that it is the responsibility of the country's 500,000 monks and 60,000 nuns to secure the release of more than 5,000 people, including monks, held by the junta. "These people have been detained and imprisoned for working for Dharma (Good). Shouldn't we also

fight for Dharma?" he asked. "One of the requirements for the Sangha to stage a boycott is 'cursing and swearing at monks.' But now [the junta troops] not only use blasphemy, but they also kill. In such a situation, we can stage a united boycott. If the military doesn't apologize, if they don't release our Sangha members, we must stop providing religious services to them" (Lipes, 2021).

THE POLITICAL DRIFTS AND OPINIONS OF MYANMAR'S MILITARY RULERS

John Milton warned that state support and protection of religion would elevate the state over religion and subject the religion to the "political drifts or conceived opinions" of the rulers (Milton, 2012). Myanmar's military leaders' control, support, and protection of Theravada Buddhism has divided and reshaped the Sangha (Mendelson, 1975, pp. 66–88). As discussed in early chapters, factions in religions are common. Religions break into sects and often reorganize for many reasons. However, state control in Myanmar has organized Theravada Buddhism into nine sects and purges any sect deemed "deviant" by those in power. Since 1988, state protection and support for Theravada Buddhism have divided the religion along political lines.

Four Political Factions in the Present-Day Buddhist Firm

James Madison expected that the Myanmar government's support of one religion has led to political factions within that religion. Interviews reveal that state control and protection have divided Myanmar's Buddhist monks into four factions (personal communications, Sterken, 2016). While some observers (Lipes, 2021) have defined three groups, interviews revealed that Myanmar's monks tend to divide themselves into one of four distinct and unique groups, (1) government monks, (2) Ma Ba Tha monks, (3) Saffron monks, and (4) pure or passive monks. In interviews, these labels were applied by Myanmar's Buddhist monks to themselves and to other groups of monks.

Government Monks: Pleasing Their Paymasters

"Government monks" are those who are very close to and directly supported by the state. These monks are, as Thomas Jefferson predicted, "servants of the state" (Cousins, 1958, p. 126). As noted in chapter 1, the firebrand monk Shin Arahan presented himself to King Anawrahta as Myanmar's first government monk. In 2021, government monks supported the military coup and accepted the junta rule (Lipes, 2021). Government monks enjoy lavish facilities, government-constructed pagodas, financial support, and titles and awards presented by their military rulers.

In Myanmar's new capital, called Naypyidaw (translated as "seat of the king" or "abode of kings") unveiled in November 2005, sits the gleaming Zay Kone Monastery. In 2021, the monks at Zay Kone Monastery indicated their loyalty to junta leader General Min Aung Hlaing. On February 2, 2021, the day after the general took over the country, the senior abbot, Bhatamda Kavisara, hosted the junta leader for a formal visit that was photographed and widely shared on social media (Maung Maung Swe, 2021). General Min Aung Hlaing paid homage, knelt before the abbot, and presented him with gifts. The general is reported to have explained to the abbot why the military was taking over the country and detailed the regime's plans to restore social harmony and religious traditions. In state-run media, the general also reported that he "listened to instructions from the Sayadaw" (Maung Maung Swe, 2021).

Tragically, the senior abbot, born under British rule in the 1930s, died in a military plane crash on June 6, 2021. The abbot, along with two of his associate government monks, seven donors, and military personnel, were traveling to Pyin Oo Lwin for a ceremony to dedicate the foundation of a new monastery. The military-supported monastery was to be constructed in Pyin Oo Lwin, home to the Myanmar Military's Defense Services Academy, where the military's top officers are trained. Junta leader Senior General Min Aung Hlaing is a graduate of that academy. Support by the government often means government control. Adam Smith wrote that the way for the state to avoid unwanted cleric behavior is "to bribe their indolence, by assigning stated salaries to their profession, and rendering it superfluous for them to be farther active" (Hume, 1985, p. 791). Generals Ne Win and Min Aung Hlaing have lavishly supported loyal government monks. A monk in Mandalay, speaking on the condition of anonymity for fear of reprisal, said that the junta is only paying lip service to religion to legitimize its rule of the country. He said, "No matter how many pagodas they built, how many titles and awards they presented to the monks, it is just a facade" (Lipes, 2021).

Another government monk, Ashin Nyanissara, also known as Sitagu Sayadaw, is a well-known monk in Myanmar. In 2021, he clarified his allegiance to Myanmar's military junta. Quoted in the junta media, Sitagu Sayadaw said, "Human rights are not a law. No country can be controlled. If they do not like it, they will shout that human rights are being violated. Shout as much as you like" (Smith, 2021b). Sitagu Sayadaw enjoys military support to oversee a vast network of projects, including hospitals, clinics, and a Buddhist university in Sagaing, near Mandalay (Walton, 2016b, p. 64). In August of 1988, Sitagu Sayadaw took part in the Four Eights Uprising and gave a famous sermon, criticizing the government for not acting in accordance with the ten duties of the king (see chapter 1). When the military cracked down on the Four Eights protesters, Sitagu Sayadaw fled to the United States. Since his return to Myanmar in the mid-1990s, he has maintained close ties to the military and delivered a sermon attempting to provide religious justification for the military's mass killing of the Rohingya people (Smith, 2021a). Like Abbot Kavisara and Sitagu Sayadaw, government monks make rational choices that result in outcomes aligned with their own interests. As Milton suspected, Myanmar's government monks frame themselves to the interests and opinions that they see as pleasing to their paymasters; and to seem right themselves, attempt force others as to the truth.

Ma Ba Tha Monks: The Degrading of Religion

U.S. Supreme Court Justice Hugo Black argued, "[A] union of government and religion tends to destroy government and degrade religion. [W]henever government allied itself with one particular form of religion, the inevitable result had been that it had incurred the hatred, disrespect, and even contempt of those who held contrary beliefs" (Black, 1961, p. 431). Myanmar's state-supported ultranationalist Ma Ba Tha monks have incurred the hatred, disrespect, and contempt of many. Ma Ba Tha (see chapter 6) monks appear to believe that the welfare of both Buddhism and the state are bound together. According to the monks I interviewed, the state must protect Buddhism. If the state is fulfilling that role, then these ultranationalist monks, in turn, support the state, even if that means loss of control and independence of the Sangha. Thus, Ma Ba Tha monks are typically, but not always, aligned with government monks. Ma Ba Tha monks are not always financially or openly supported by the government, but these monks are often encouraged and supported by the military, are very divisive, and are openly inflammatory and anti-Muslim. Ma Ba Tha monks participate in the Ma Ba Tha (the Burmese language acronym for the Association to Protect Race and Religion) movement that began in 2012. The Ma Ba Tha organization was itself a renaming of the earlier 969 movement; both movements were religious nationalist campaigns that called for the boycott of Muslim-owned businesses and violence against Muslims. As noted above, in June 2019, Brigadier General Zaw Min Tun of the Myanmar military made a public donation to the Buddhist nationalist group, saying "the group is necessary and should be supported in the name of Buddhism." In a public ceremony, the military commander donated thirty million kyats (about US$20k) to the Buddha Dhamma Prahita Foundation—formerly Ma Ba Tha—as nearly one thousand Ma Ba Tha monks from across the country gathered at the group's headquarters, in Yangon's Insein Township, for their annual meeting. In his speech, Brigadier General Zaw Min Tun said, "[D]espite the widely held perception of Ma Ba Tha as an anti-Muslim organization, the organization's only intention is to protect race and religion," and then added that the "donation was to the clergy, not just to U Wirathu" (Anonymous, 2019b). In 2020, Wirathu was sent to Insein Prison for insulting comments about Aung San Suu Kyi. Than Soe Naing, a political analyst, said it was likely Wirathu was being treated well and that the junta wanted to keep him safe until the next time they needed him (Myanmar Now, 2021b). An officer from the Assistance Association for Political Prisoners offered a different perspective: "I think they're keeping him in prison because he's no longer useful to them. They've already used him, and now they're in a situation that could do more harm than good for them if they used him" (Myanmar Now, 2021b). Journalists and scholars have credited Ma Ba Tha with successfully lobbying the Myanmar government for four laws

Figure 7.2. Sayadaw U Ariyawuntha Biwunsa, the abbot of Mandalay's Myawaddy Mingyi monastery, is an outspoken critic of Myanmar's military dictatorship. Known as Myawaddy Sayadaw, in 2021 he commented, "This corrupt political system—'dictatorship' as you call it—will ruin everything. There's a Burmese saying: 'When the sky falls, nobody survives.' You can't have strong economics, education, livelihoods or religion as long as the political system is corrupt. Everything will be in ruins. I don't think those things, let alone religion or the country itself, would survive under such a corrupt system. It really pains me to see that some are destroying the political culture in the name of something sacred." *Source*: Myawaddy Sayadaw

(see above) that discriminate against women and religious minorities. Although it is accurate that the Ma Ba Tha monks very enthusiastically supported the four laws, it was the military government and Myanmar's president, Thein Sein, who passed the laws in Myanmar's military-controlled parliament and then signed them into law. The Ma Ba Tha monks served as a source of legitimacy and a vocal supporter of the military regime. In return, the military government supported the Ma Ba Tha faction of the Buddhist firm by driving competitors (Islam) out of the religious marketplace. The monks of state-supported religion, wrote Adam Smith, "are apt gradually to lose the qualities which gave them authority and influence" (Smith, 1776, p. 608).

Saffron Monks: Democracy, Human Rights, and White Roses

Saffron monks led the 2007 Saffron Revolution (see chapter 6) that helped prompt democratic reforms that were upended by the coup on February 1, 2021. I interviewed Saffron monks who served long sentences in Insein Prison. Saffron monks support democracy, human rights, and interfaith understanding, and reject the military coup. While scholars, such as Matthew Walton (2016a, pp. 71–72), debate monk definitions of democracy and Buddhist support for democracy, the Saffron monks I interviewed in 2015 and 2016 clearly supported the people's right to select the leaders of their government. Additionally, many monks have openly risked their lives to support democracy since the coup in March 2021. Saffron monks tend to focus on Buddhist precepts and not on anti-Muslim hate speech (Walton, 2016b, p. 66). Saffron monks, like Myawaddy Sayadaw, are publicly critical of Buddhist nationalists and Ma Ba Tha (personal communications, 2016). Myawaddy Sayadaw said it is the duty of all monks to publicly criticize misbehaving monks and those who spread hate speech. "Silence is like supporting [misbehavior], so we raise our voices. Open criticism of monks does not mean a divided community—it is an effort to maintain Theravada Buddhism" (Zaw, 2018). "We are fighting for the truth and will challenge nationalist monks openly so that their voices are not louder, and the tone of nationalism is decreased," said Myawaddy Sayadaw (Zaw, 2018). Saffron monks argue that Ma Ba Tha Buddhist nationalist "monks have been behaving irreverently against religious rules. It could tarnish the image of Buddhism and be dangerous for the religion" (Zaw, 2018; personal communications, Sterken 2016). The saffron monks were leaders in the White Rose campaign in 2019. The White Rose Campaign was launched shortly after Muslims' prayer sites were forced to shut down by Ma Ba Tha monks. Hundreds of Buddhist nationalist monks led supporters to three Muslim areas of the South Dagon township in Yangon on the nights of May 14 and 15. On May 17, following the German White Rose Campaign, Thet

Swe Win and Buddhist monk Sayadaw Seindita distributed white roses to Muslims as an act of solidarity (Gindin, 2019). The White Rose Campaign started in Yangon and quickly spread throughout Myanmar. Buddhists, Muslims, Christians, and Hindus gathered and prayed together at an iftar dinner—the meal eaten by Muslims after sunset during Ramadan. The rational choice decision made by the Saffron monks is made in terms of what they consider best for their society. The religious convictions of the Saffron monks (like those of the Ma Ba Tha monks) and individual actions can be explained through rationality. The focus and desired outcomes of these monks' choices differ because they are made according to their personal religious preferences. Saffron and Ma Ba Tha monks, quite obviously, tend to hold different convictions and desired outcomes.

Pure Monks: Passive Loyalty to State Authority

The pure monks are those who stay out of politics. Whereas government monks will compromise with state authority, give up independence, and assume positions of power and privilege, the pure monks are content to remain outside the world of politics altogether. Michael Mendelson labeled these monks "passive" (Mendelson, 1975, pp. 117 and 195). Mendelson noted that the passive part of the Buddhist firm is generally indifferent to civil power struggles and changes (Mendelson, 1975, p. 83). As Matthew Walton notes, monk participation in politics has a long and complex history in Myanmar (Walton, 2016a, p. 129). Walton points out that factions of monks take the position that they are not to participate in politics, while others will identify some limited methods of participation as acceptable (Walton, 2016b, p. 64). Pure monks remain disengaged from all political participation in Myanmar.

Passive or politically disengaged monks are, of course, also participating in politics. The lack of voice, action, and political engagement is a passive stand with the existing power structure (Kertzer, 2022, p. 480). These factions are not new in the Buddhist religion of Myanmar. Mendelson notes that from King Mindon's (see chapter 2) time onward, active groups of monks reacted to government control by forming "miniature Sanghas" with their own observance of Vinaya rules (Mendelson, 1975, p. 195). Several Saffron monks, who were former political prisoners, also stated that since 1962 the fear of Insein Prison has made many monks passive. Passive monks appear to be making the rational decision of staying passive, fearing that they too will be imprisoned.

CONCLUSIONS: THE ASHOKAN ROAD

King Ashoka, King Anawrahta, Shin Arahan, and subsequent rulers established governing precedents that still shape the religion of Buddhism today. King Anawrahta and his self-appointed government monk started a pattern of rulers who held and exercised both secular and religious authority. Myanmar's military rulers continue to employ this powerful tool of social control when they select and reward certain monks and purge others from the religion and larger society. Like ancient kings, if a present-day Myanmar ruler does not like something about a religious community or monastery, he will purge the unwanted and reshape the community to suit his needs and desires.

Since Anawrahta, Myanmar's kings and generals have used Theravada Buddhism to gain legitimacy. Government monks provide Myanmar's generals with much-needed political and religious legitimacy. However, like the relationship between Myanmar's kings and Sangha, there are times when the balance of power has favored the Buddhist firm. A stronger king or ruler could control the Sangha, and a politically engaged Sangha, (see Saffron Revolution in chapter 6) could influence the state (Mendelson, 1975, p. 53). A consequence of the entanglement and of the power and authority of the state and the Buddhist firm is the creation of political factions that have altered the structure of the Buddhist firm. These four political factions indicate that Myanmar's entire Buddhist firm is not as "nationalistic, chauvinistic, and xenophobic" as David and Holliday conclude (2018, p. 200). The simple fact that these political factions exist is evidence of a significant and important consequence of state control of religion in Myanmar. The size and strength of these political factions remain a question to be answered in future research. In the closing chapter, a different Ashokan road and consequences three through six are explored.

8

✛

A Different Ashokan Road

The Consequences for Minority Religions, Religious Competition, and Truth

The historical narrative that Myanmar is a "Buddhist country" is a destructive social construct. It is a social construct that has been nurtured by those who benefit from it. The reality is that the society of Myanmar still hosts a diverse array of religious ideas: Anglicans, Animists (nat worshipers), Baptists, Buddhists, Catholics, Hindus, Jews, Methodists, Panthays, Rohingya, and others. Humans in Myanmar are as religiously pluralistic as humans elsewhere. If not for the state's protection and support of Buddhism, these "minority religious" firms would likely enjoy a greater market share. The Buddhist country myth has protected a version of the majority religion while creating an untenable and hostile situation for the entire society and for minority religious firms and ideas.

The Buddhist country primordial narrative is an imagined reality that enables the state to control and regulate not only the majority religion, as seen in chapter 7, but also the entire religious economy, including minority religions. But it has done something more destructive. The telling and retelling of the myth of the Buddhist country nurtures and supports religious intolerance and xenophobia in the larger society of Myanmar. Non-state actors in Myanmar often act against people who adhere to minority religions (Fox, 2020). The religion and state data indicate that Myanmar society ranks high both in state religious minority discrimination and societal discrimination of minority religions (Fox, 2020). The Buddhist country myth has helped to create a society that is intolerant of minority religions. The consequences have been dire for religious minorities. The consequences include repression, discrimination, violence, and a society that endures perpetual conflict.

MINORITY FIRMS THREATEN BUDDHISM

Competition for believers forces religious firms to promote (some would use the word *glorify*) their ideas. Religious firms nearly always claim that they have the best product. Some, such as the Bahá'í firm, promote the prosperity of all beliefs, but most religious firms claim that their ideas are the true and right ones. Religions that feel threatened by the ideas of another firm sometimes seek the power, authority, and protection of the state. Ma Ba Tha nationalist Buddhist monks have propagated the idea that their religion is under threat. Christianity, Islam, and even Myanmar's ancient nat worship ideas are presented as threats to Buddhism. They may, in fact, be threats. Humans are known to make a wide range of different religious choices when given freedom and opportunity. Some humans will combine various aspects of different religions.

At nat festivals in 2019, Buddhist monks and nuns chastised and bickered with nat worshipers. Nat worship, they argued, is a base superstition and not part of the true Buddhist faith (Anonymous, 2019a). Nat worship, argue some Theravada Buddhists, is not true nor is it part of Buddhism as promoted by King Anawrahta (see chapter 1). Without the intervention of state authority, humans will make a wide array of decisions about religious beliefs. For example, Prime Minister U Nu would have disagreed with the monks and nuns who argue that nat worship is not a component of Buddhism (Nu, 1988). On the other hand, Aung San Suu Kyi would probably have agreed with them. Aung San Suu Kyi wrote, "Nat worship is not strictly in accordance with Buddhist teachings" (Aung San Suu Kyi, 2010, p. 70). However, Suu Kyi went on to explain that "even those who avoid having anything to do with spirit-worship will not do anything which is known to be offensive to nats" (Aung San Suu Kyi, 2010, p. 70). "It is often asked," wrote Suu Kyi,

> why even educated Burmese can sometimes be found taking part in Nat worship. Perhaps the answer lies in two aspects of Burmese life. One is the strong hold that old beliefs from the days before Buddhism still have in the minds of the people. The other is the extreme self-reliance that Buddhism demands from the individual. In Buddhism there are no gods to whom one can pray for favours or help. One's destiny is decided entirely by one's own actions. While accepting the truth of this, most people find it difficult to resist the need to rely on supernatural powers, especially when times are hard. (Aung San Suu Kyi, 2010, p. 71)

CONSEQUENCE 3: REPRESSION, DISCRIMINATION, AND VIOLENCE AGAINST MINORITY RELIGIONS

Myanmar's state religion policy supports a society in which intolerance of religious minorities is tolerated. The state and the larger society engage in egregious intolerance of religious minorities. To promote religious freedom worldwide, the U.S. Congress enacted, and President Bill Clinton signed, the International Religious Freedom Act in 1998. This act, introduced by Senators Don Nickles (R-OK) and Joseph Lieberman (D-CT), responded to the growing concern about religious persecution worldwide. Since 1999, the U.S. Department of State designated Myanmar as a "Country of Particular Concern" for engaging in particularly severe violations of religious freedom. The Myanmar state has engaged in systematic, egregious, and ongoing violations of religious freedom as defined in the International Religious Freedom Act (U.S. Department of State, 2020). Minority religions, especially Animists, Christians, and Muslims, have suffered greatly and the state–religion policy has reshaped the Myanmar society and religious economy. Nat worship is treated by the state as a minority religion, but the religious practice is widespread.

NATS WERE THE GODS OF MYANMAR BEFORE THE BUDDHA ARRIVED

Imagine, for a moment, the community of Taung Pyone Gyi. The Taung Pyone village, located in the Mandalay region, is well known to the Myanmar people. Every August, thousands of people travel the small roads to the village to attend a week-long nat spirit festival. Nat worship is common in Myanmar. Some estimate that as many as 85 percent of the population believe that the nat spirits can bring either grave misfortune or good luck and wealth to humans (Ho, 2010, 255). As noted in previous chapters, nat worship and propitiation have been part of Myanmar's religious culture since the Pye people, or as one Buddhist monk declared, nat worship began "at the beginning of the universe" (Smith, 1965, p. 177). Scholars note that animism is the earliest and most basic religion (Scott, 2009, p. 21). The presence of animist belief predates all other religions and the emergence of belief in an afterlife (Coward, 2016, p. 79; Tylor, 1871). As one early scholar put it, "The nats were the gods of Myanmar, before the Buddha arrived" (Pratt, 1928, p. 127).

Nat worship has not always enjoyed state support in Myanmar. King Mindon (see chapter 2) is said to have not believed in nat worship and ordered that the Taungbyon Festival be canceled (Spiro, 2011, p. 86).

Figure 8.1. Nat deity statues at Kyaik Tan Lan, Kyaikthanlan, Pagoda in Mawlamyine, Mawlamyaing, Burma, Myanmar. *Source*: Petr Svarc/UIG

Shortly after making this declaration, the king's testicles became painfully swollen (Spiro, 2011, p. 86). Unconvinced that his health problem was related to the nats, he charged that if the nats were indeed real, then the swords that their images held at Taungbyon would fall to the ground. Shortly after that, the swords held by the images were reported to have fallen to the ground. The king became convinced of their existence and allowed the festival to continue (Spiro, 2011, p. 86). His health concerns passed.

Modern-Day Nat Worship: The Taungbyon Brothers

Although more research is needed to determine the full extent of nat worship today, there is evidence of widespread nat belief among the people of Myanmar. In the branches of large trees or in small wood structures near the streets of any city or village in Myanmar, there are many tiny wooden "houses." Some contain Buddha images, but most contain small figures of nats. In addition, many Myanmar people attend annual festivals to propitiate the nats (Spiro, 2011, p. 116). The annual Taungbyon Festival is one of the most exciting and entertaining events of the year in Myanmar. During this festival, the people of Myanmar honor two of the thirty-seven nats, the brothers Shwepyingyi and Shwepyingge, who are known as the Taungbyon Brothers (Spiro, 2011, p. 113).

The story of the Taungbyon Brothers (also called brothers Min Gyi and Min Lay) began nearly one thousand years ago. It is itself a testament to the resilience of nat worship in a highly regulated religious economy. Nat worship has endured and remained an essential part of Myanmar's religious economy, even as the worship of the thirty-seven nats has been denigrated and regulated by the state and other religious firms. The story of the Taungbyon Brothers began in 1038 when the ship of a Muslim merchant from Malabar sank off the coast of Myanmar. The wealthy merchant did not survive the shipwreck, but his two sons drifted ashore near Thaton, a village on the coast of the Gulf of Martaban (Spiro, 2011, p. 113). The boys were rescued by a Buddhist monk, who raised them in his monastery. The monk kept a preserved corpse of a hermit magician for medicinal purposes, and one day he discovered that the brothers had eaten the corpse and acquired supernatural powers (Spiro, 2011, p. 113). The king was concerned about the powers of these two brothers and ordered their capture. The elder brother was captured when he walked under the garments of the mother of his sweetheart. He lost all his powers when he walked under the garments (Spiro, 2011, p. 113).

Women's Garments and Lost Powers in 2021

Power lost by walking under women's garments became a widespread belief in Myanmar (Spiro, 2011, p. 114). Beginning with this ancient nat story, the tradition holds that a man's hpone, or masculine essence, can be lost if he passes under a woman's lower clothing items (Lusan, 2021). This belief is so ubiquitous that in March 2021, it was used to hinder the Myanmar military and protest the government's junta takeover (Lusan, 2021). Pro-democracy protesters strung up women's garments on lines over streets across the country. Twitter and Facebook photos showed groups of soldiers stopped and waited for the lines of women's garments to be cut down before continuing down the street (Khinny, 2021).

After his older brother lost his powers due to women's garments, the younger brother, called Byatta, is said to have escaped into the forest. In the forest, Byatta happened to join the soldiers sent by King Anawrahta (see chapter 1) to obtain Buddhist scriptures from another city. Byatta managed to secure the desired scriptures and deliver them to King Anawrahta. The king rewarded Byatta with a royal post (flower officer). Byatta married and had two sons, Shwepyingyi and Shwepyingge, who became the famous Taungbyon brothers. The brothers were raised on Mount Popa by their mother. Promoting Buddhism, King Anawrahta ordered the boys to go to China to retrieve the Buddha's relics (Spiro, 2011, p. 114). Their mother refused to let them go, so King Anawrahta sent an officer with a magic wand, who forced the mother and her sons to roll down Mount Popa. The boys were seized, and their mother is said to have died of a broken heart. She is now a nat called Popa Medaw or the mother of Popa (Spiro, 2011, p. 114). The brothers succeeded in securing Buddhist relics for King Anawrahta. On the return journey, the elephant carrying the relics stopped and knelt at the site of the Taungbyon village. King Anawrahta, again promoting Buddhism, built a pagoda at the site where the elephant knelt. The king ordered each soldier to participate by contributing a brick to the construction of the pagoda. The two brothers refused to participate and instead played with marbles in the shade of a tree. Because they did not participate in the construction project, two bricks were missing from the pagoda (the missing bricks are still pointed out to those who visit the pagoda; Spiro, 2011, p. 115). Upset with the unfinished pagoda, King Anawrahta had the brothers killed. In death, the brothers became the Taungbyon nats (Spiro, 2011, p. 115). The Taungbyon nats communicate with the living through "nat wives" who are engaged in sacred marriages with the nat-brothers (Brac de la Perrière, 2009b, p. 285).

Nat Wives and Legitimacy

When properly propitiated, the nats communicate via spirit wives to provide guidance, heal illnesses and infertility, reveal the future, and provide prosperity. Since the 1980s, most of the spirit wives have been gay or transgender (Taylor, 2017). In a country where gay relationships are illegal, the nat spirit wives (nat-kadaws) are given adoration and respect. Nat worship and festivals provide the LGBTQ community with respect and legitimacy (Taylor, 2017). During the festivals, the spirit-wives set up shrines for their nat, dance, and accept offerings of food, alcohol, and money in exchange for advice and blessings from their nat. "My nat likes to drink beer, wine, Johnny Walker, and champagne," says Mg Mg Kyi, who has been a spirit-wife for forty years, since he was thirteen (Taylor, 2017).

Protecting Religion: Consequences for Nat Worship

State regulation of religion has had significant consequences for nat worship. As noted in chapter 1, King Anawrahta added his own nat to the pantheon of nats for political reasons. State authority created a new nat (and thus changed the religion) by adding a new spirit to the existing thirty-six (Aung Htin Muang, 1958). The king announced that this new spirit, Thagymin, would be the guardian god of Buddhism and act as the head spirit (Smith 1965, p. 14). The Myanmar state/king then promoted nat worship and Buddhism by allowing nat worship in Buddhist places of worship.

Nat worship remained unregulated and unsupported during the British colonial period but was then strongly supported and promoted under Prime Minister U Nu. Nu's religious faith clearly included a belief in nats (Nu, 1988, p. 8; Butwell, 1963, p. 61; Spiro, 2011, p. 138). Prime Minister Nu regularly retired to Mount Popa, the ancient center of the nats, for long retreats to meditate and make policy decisions based on his nat beliefs (Spiro, 2011, p. 61). In 1961, Nu reported that while meditating on Mount Popa, Popa Medaw, the nat mother of the Taungbyon nats, gave him copies of Buddhist scriptures (Spiro, 2011, p. 277). Prime Minister Nu and his cabinet leadership team, including the president and his entire cabinet, made annual official ceremonial offerings to nats (Spiro, 2011, p. 61). Nu also ordered the state construction of two national shrines of the Mahagiri nats, one for upper and one for Lower Myanmar (Spiro, 2011, pp. 60–61). Nat worship was supported during the early post-independence years, but that changed with the military coup in March of 1962.

Figure 8.2. The thirty-seven nats of Myanmar, all put up in a row inside the holy shrine of Mt Popa. People place money into the hands of the nats, to make them benevolent. *Source*: Emily Khine

Suppression, Denigration, and Embarrassment of Nat Worship

In the 1960s, scholars and elites worldwide theorized that "modernization" would lead to secularization (Fox, 2018, p. 12; Haynes, 2013, p. 171). Toft and colleagues (2011, p. 74) stated, "By the late 1960s, everyone (a term we do not use lightly) believed that the widespread aspiration of political secularism was rapidly becoming a reality in virtually all parts of the world." In 1966, Anthony F. Wallace predicted that "Belief in supernatural powers is doomed to die out, all over the world" (Fox, 2018, p. 12). Elites in Myanmar (including military elites) were swept up in the becoming modern theory. Writing in the 1960s, Melford Spiro (2011, p. 62) noted that skepticism and disbelief in nat worship were found in urban areas among the intellectual and military elite. The military elite, concerned with "modernization and economic development," actively opposed nat worship because it promoted "magical habits of thinking" and encouraged the spending of resources in nonproductive ways (Spiro, 2011, p. 62). As discussed in chapter 5, General Ne Win canceled Prime Minister U Nu's state-built nat shrines and launched a public campaign to eradicate and denigrate nat worship. Ne Win issued a decree to "criminalize the supernatural," and all films depicting nats were banned (Ho, 2010, p. 306).

The consequences of the state's nat-worship policies in the larger Myanmar religious economy are significant. Modernization did not lead to secularization. Animist beliefs remain in modern-day Myanmar and are legitimated and accepted, although some people attempt to explain them as traditional, rural, and unsophisticated (personal communications, August 2016; Spiro, 2011, p. 62). The suppression and denigration of nat worship did not end the practice of the religion; it only drove it from official reporting and made some people ashamed to admit the practice (personal communications, December 2015; Spiro, 2011, p. 62). The government's public campaign of denigration of nat-worship created a situation in which many people who believed in the nats were (and are) "embarrassed" to admit that belief to outsiders (including researchers; personal communications, August 2016; Spiro, 2011, p. 62).

NATS, ACCEPTANCE, AND RESPECT FOR PEOPLE IN MYANMAR'S LBGTQ COMMUNITY

The suppression and denigration of nat worship also had a positive and emancipatory effect on Myanmar's LBGTQ community. In the Ne Win years, the denigrated and marginalized religion became a refuge for those rejected by the existing power structure. The role and respect for the "spirit wives," especially during the nat festival season, have elevated members of the LBGTQ community to a position of prestige. The widespread belief in the nats has altered the way women, gay, and trans people are perceived (Ho, 2010, p. 256). Nat worship "enables Myanmar women and sexual minorities to access transgressive opportunities, personas, and behaviors that defy the normative scripts of heteropatriarchy and the dominance of abusive centralized authority" (Ho, 2009, p. 277; Ho, 2010, p. 256). Although some monks in the Buddhist firm denigrate nat worship, the religion has become a means to gain acceptance and respect, and to avoid discrimination for people in the LBGTQ community (Baker, 2017). Anthropologists have shown that nat worship (in contrast to the Buddhist firm's patriarchy and hierarchies of power) functions as an economically and psychologically inclusive institution (Ho, 2009, p. 277). In a religious economy dominated by centralized state authority and the Buddhist firm's masculinist, heteropatriarchal, and hierarchical powers, nat worship has survived, thrived, and supported an acceptance of the feminine, plural, and transgendered.

MYANMAR'S RELIGIOUS DISCRIMINATION AGAINST MINORITY RELIGIONS

In the spring of 2011, the religious convictions and demands of the Saffron monks, along with the desperate needs of the Myanmar people, began to be addressed by the military leaders in a so-called democratic transition (Thant Myint-U, 2020, p. 138). The steps taken by the military failed to address the questions of identity and belonging. Myanmar's marketplace of ideas (religious and other) had been completely closed since March 1962. Generations of Myanmar students had been taught the Buddhist nationalist narrative; they do not know any other history (see chapter 1). The military leaders ignored or did not understand the fact that Myanmar is a diverse and pluralistic society. As Myanmar opened to reforms under President Thein Sein, centuries of state protection of Theravada Buddhism supported a rebirth of Buddhist nationalism.

Under President Thein Sein, Buddhism and belonging once again became a divisive and repressive factor in the Myanmar religious economy. As society and military government lurched toward openness and a liberal democracy, questions about belonging once again became part of the national political conversation. Seeking protection and political advantage, factions of the Buddhist firm and political leaders once again used the narrative of a primordial religious identity as an instrument of legitimacy and set one community against another. Buddhist nationalism, fear, and intolerance undermined Saffron monks' and others' visions of Myanmar as a tolerant, inclusive, and religiously pluralistic society, and it fostered disunity and violence (Thant Myint-U, 2020, p. 188; Skidmore, 2004, p. 98). Buddhist nationalism turned violent, and the protection of Buddhism and religious identity became policy in the above discussed four laws designed to "protect race and religion" (Lehr, 2018, p. 157).

As noted in chapter 5, the Myanmar military's extreme version of Buddhist nationalism defined religious minorities as foreign threats to race and Buddhism. Driven by Buddhist nationalism, the Myanmar military systematically and brutally attacked Muslims and Christians (Habiburahman, 2019; Ibrahim, 2016; Cheesman and Farrelly, 2016). In 1959, 1966, 1967, 1971, 1973, 1974, 1978, 1991, and again in 2017, Myanmar's military conducted ethnic cleansing operations against the Rohingya (McKay, 2019). One of the most tragic and direct consequences of the religion–state entanglement in Myanmar is that the Rohingya people are one of the most persecuted minorities in the world. The "othering" of the Rohingya citizens who do not claim to be Buddhist has had severe consequences (Lee, 2021).

The Othering of the Rohingya: Call It Genocide

The history of government-established religion in Myanmar reveals the consequences of hatred, disrespect, and contempt for those who hold beliefs contrary to the majority religion. The violence against the Muslim Rohingya people is well documented (Fortify Rights, 2020b; Holt, 2019; Ibrahim, 2016). As noted in earlier chapters, significant waves of violent attacks were orchestrated against the Muslim Rohingya by the Myanmar military in 1978, 1991–1992, 2012, 2016, and 2017. Following the violence in 2017, more than 720,000 Rohingya fled to Bangladesh (Rohingya Language Preservation Project, 2022, p. 17). The Rohingya people have been killed, raped, and subjected to forced labor, extortion, and police harassment, and had their land and homes confiscated or destroyed (LeBlanc and Simmons, 2021, p. 147). Professor William Schabas describes life for Rohingya in Myanmar:

> It's analogous to some of the ghettos that existed for Jews in Nazi-occupied Europe. It did have the effect of isolating and depriving people of fundamental rights, such as the right to free movement within a state, the right to leave the country. However, people could get in and out illegally by crossing the border into Bangladesh. Indeed, that may have been one of the things that was hoped for all along. (Fortify Rights, 2020a)

In 2016 and 2017, General Min Aung Hlaing led a campaign of massacres, mass rape, and mass arson, displacing more than 800,000 Rohingya men, women, and children to Bangladesh. In November 2019, The Gambia filed a case at the International Court of Justice (ICJ) in The Hague against Myanmar for failing to prevent or punish the genocide against the Rohingya. On January 23, 2020, the ICJ ruled unanimously in favor of The Gambia's request for provisional measures of protection for Rohingya in Myanmar.

The plight of the Rohingya and the origins of the conflict are complex. The treatment of the Rohingya is, in part, a direct consequence of centuries of state protection and promotion of Theravada Buddhism in the Myanmar religious economy. The Buddhist nationalist narrative fosters the othering of those who practice faiths different from the majority. The Buddhist belonging narrative excludes all who practiced other religious beliefs. The xenophobic society cultivated by Myanmar's generals led to a law, the Citizenship Act of 1982. As noted in chapter 5, this law sanctioned discrimination based on religion. A consequence of this xenophobic law is that about two million Rohingya Muslims and Chinese descendants are stateless and cannot obtain passports or even identity cards (Cockett, 2015, p. 59). Supported by the state, many Myanmar people have adopted a xenophobic view that has led to widespread conflict, discrimination, human rights violations, and cultural genocide against the Rohingya and other minority groups (Rohingya Language Preservation Project, 2022, p. 17).

In 2020, it was common for leaders of factions of the Buddhist firm to make pejorative and hateful statements against Muslims in sermons and on Facebook. In July 2020, an anti-Muslim campaign in Mandalay included the distribution of stickers reading "We don't want the NLD [Suu Kyi's party the National League for Democracy] to make Myanmar a kalar country" (U.S. Department of State, 2020). Kalar is

Figure 8.3. Aung San Suu Kyi gives speech to supporters at Hlaing Thar Yar Township in Yangon, Myanmar on November 17, 2011. *Source*: Htoo Tay Zar

a pejorative term in the Burmese language used to describe Muslims, Indians, or those of South Asian descent (Cockett, 2015, p. 38; Sterken, 2016, p. 95). Kala literally means "alien," but in Burmese, it holds a broader meaning: something between "unwanted, hated, and despicable" (Lubina, 2016, p. 435).

The conflict between Buddhist nationalists and the Muslim community in Rakhine is complex and best characterized by a "web of grievances" (Aron, 2018, p. 3). The violence is over historical tensions, power, and belonging. Religious nationalism has burdened the country with violence and conflict. Buddhist nationalism has long been a central component of the conflict within the Rakhine state. A consequence of the ancient narrative of Buddhism and belonging is that even among otherwise tolerant individuals, an anti-Muslim and anti-Christian sentiment remains. Christians, Hindus, and Muslims are perceived as not belonging in the country, irrespective of citizenship status, and are too commonly viewed as foreign.

Myanmar Policies of Religious Discrimination against Minority Religions

The Religion and State Project has identified thirty unique policies of religious discrimination and restrictions against minority religions around the world (Fox, 2020). The Myanmar state has employed twenty-seven of those discrimination and restriction policies identified in the RAS database. While the Myanmar government imposes restrictions on all religions, the state specifically discriminates and restricts minority religions. As a result, minority religions are treated differently from the majority religion. The Myanmar government "openly practices discriminatory policies against religious minorities in Burma" (U.S. Department of State, 2020).

Myanmar State Restrictions on Religious Practices

- Myanmar's government policies restrict the public and private observance of religious services, festivals, and holidays, including the Sabbath. Religious communities that register with government authorities are entitled to practice and manifest their religions, but the government imposes restrictions on the religious activities of minority groups. Non-Buddhist minority groups, including Christians, Hindus, and Muslims, said that authorities restricted religious practice, denied freedom of movement to members of religious minority groups, and closed places of worship. Authorities in Rakhine state prohibit Rohingya from gathering publicly in groups of more than five persons (U.S. Department of State, 2020).

- The Myanmar state places restrictions on the ability to write, publish, or disseminate religious publications and to make/obtain materials necessary for religious rites/customs/ceremonies. Government officials rarely allow local printing or photocopying of copies of minority groups' religious texts and materials. The Ministry of Religion required that teaching materials, including Islamic materials printed in Arabic, be in the Burmese language and submitted to the ministry in advance for approval. State policies also restrict minority religions from importing religious publications (Fox, 2020).
- Government policies place restrictions on observing dietary laws or access to food appropriate for religious dietary requirements. Government authorities granted limited permission to slaughter cows during Eid al-Adha. Local government authorities in some villages restricted the licensing of and butchering of cattle by slaughterhouses, the vast majority owned by Muslims. These restrictions negatively affected the ability of Muslim communities to celebrate Islamic holidays (U.S. Department of State, 2020).
- The Myanmar state has placed restrictions on the observance of religious laws concerning marriage and divorce. Myanmar law does not carry penalties for men who commit adultery. Women who commit adultery risk divorce and loss of property. Myanmar law permits a man to take more than one wife; a woman cannot. Myanmar law places restrictions on Buddhist women who marry non-Buddhist men. This policy seeks to ensure the primacy of Buddhist religious law over the application of Islamic law (Crouch, 2016b, p. 85).
- Myanmar's state policies place restrictions on the observance of religious laws on burial. Shan Buddhist monks were prohibited from holding their traditional funeral arrangements and ceremony for a famous monk (Fink, 2013, p. 241). Since 2012, the authorities of Kalaymyo (a village in Sagaing Region where many Chin live) have taken land from fourteen Christian cemeteries (Fleming, 2016, p. 14). The land confiscation orders came from Tha Aye, chief minister of the Sagaing Region, a former major general in the Myanmar military (Fleming, 2016, p. 14). Christian communities held public protests and took their complaints to the highest levels of government but did not receive a response (Fleming, 2016, p. 15).
- The Myanmar state policies restrict religious firms and individual clergy. Myanmar law bars members of "religious orders" such as priests, monks, and nuns of any religious group, from running for public office. The constitution bars members of religious orders from voting. The government restricts by law the political activities and expression of the Buddhist clergy.
- The Myanmar government restricts building, leasing, repairing, and maintaining places of worship. Religious groups throughout

the country, including Buddhists, Christians, Hindus, and especially Muslims, report difficulties and delays that could last for years in getting permits to allow construction of and repairs to religious buildings. Buddhist leaders said obtaining such permission was more difficult for non-Buddhist groups (U.S. Department of State, 2019).
- The Myanmar state places restrictions on access to existing places of worship. In response to communal Buddhist-Muslim violence in 2012 in Rakhine state, the government closed more than forty mosques throughout the country. In December 2019, fifty-one Baptist churches were closed, and every church was limited to no more than four families together in some areas. Hindu leaders also reported authorities limiting access to religious sites (U.S. Department of State, 2019). Since the coup in 2021, the Myanmar military has destroyed ninety-seven religious buildings throughout the country, including seventy-six Christian churches, twenty Buddhist monasteries, and one mosque (ALTSEAN-Burma, 2022).
- The Myanmar state restricts ordination of and access to the clergy. To become a pastor in most Christian denominations in Chin State, women must have fifteen years of experience and be unmarried. On the other hand, Chin men need only five years of experience and are free to marry (Smith, 2013).
- The Myanmar government restricts both proselytizing and conversion. Conversion of religious minorities to the majority religion through coercion, bribes, or threats is not uncommon. The Chin Human Rights Organization reported that local officials in Ann Township in southern Rakhine State forced three ethnic Chin Christians, including a pastor, to convert to Buddhism or face expulsion from the village and a fine of 100,000 kyat ($68) for Christian activities. Some local Christians were verbally harassed and physically assaulted by local authorities because of their faith and moved to nearby villages (U.S. Department of State, 2019).
- The Myanmar state restricts the running of religious schools and religious education in general. The Myanmar military has destroyed or damaged more than three hundred churches and one hundred Christian schools in Kachin State since 2011. The government and Buddhist nationalists used their influence and resources to build Buddhist infrastructure in majority Christian areas, including in Kachin and Chin, against the local population's wishes. Minority religious communities said they perceived these efforts to be part of a process of "Burmanization" (U.S. Department of State, 2019).
- The Myanmar state fails to protect religious minorities against violence and does not punish the perpetrators. There are many examples of this restriction on minority religions. In 2016, for example, a violent assembly of Buddhist nationalists destroyed a Muslim prayer

hall in Lone Khin village, Kachin state. Later in the same year, a similar group destroyed a mosque in Thaye Thamain village, Bago Region. In each of these cases, the authorities failed to stop the destruction and hold the perpetrators responsible (Fortify Rights, 2016).
- The Myanmar state engages in surveillance of minority religious activities not placed on the activities of the majority (Fox, 2020). In 2016, the Ministry of Home Affairs issued orders to monitor Christian and Muslim religious activities, such as how they are funded and with whom religious leaders are meeting (Fleming, 2016, p. 13).
- The Myanmar state and military fund anti-religious propaganda in official or semi-official government publications. The military is deeply involved in propaganda distributed as ordinary books, magazines, and entertainment (Cockett, 2015, p. 100). In the early 2000s, the military circulated a book that propagated lies and myths about Islam (Cockett, 2015, p. 101). Called Myo pyauk hma so yauk teh (Fear of Losing Our Race), this work was full of footnotes and references to simulate authenticity and was made widely available for free. The book was patterned after the notorious and widely distributed antisemitic publication *The Protocols of the Elders of Zion*. The book distributed by the Myanmar military was intentionally written to blame Muslims for a variety of ills and portray followers of Islam as conspirators against the state. Religious leaders and civil society activists report that government and military officials use anti-Rohingya and anti-Muslim rumors and hate speech at official events. With the support of the Myanmar military, Buddhist nationalist groups produce a variety of media and print publications, including a magazine, a cable TV broadcast of sermons throughout the country, and a vast array of social media accounts. For example, Ma Ba Tha (see chapter 6 and below) regularly publishes a wide range of literature, including printed glossy magazines, filled with anti-Muslim hate and propaganda. This literature is widely circulated at very low cost and is frequently given away to people in tea shops in poor villages across the country.

Violence, regulation, and restrictions against religious minorities committed by Buddhist nationalists and the Buddhist-dominated military have corrupted the religious marketplace. The entanglement of state power and Buddhism has led to scores of deaths, the burning of Christian and Muslim villages, and an exodus of hundreds of thousands of people into neighboring countries. Moreover, the linking of Buddhism to citizenship and belonging has entrenched the nation in conflict. Between 2012 and 2020, waves of violence left many people dead or injured, and more than 1,300 buildings—mainly mosques, churches, schools, and the homes of Muslims and Christians—were destroyed. Following the February 2021 coup, the military stepped up attacks in regions that are majority Christian. The military has specifically targeted Christian religious leaders. On February 27, 2021, the military raided the Hakha Baptist Church in the capital of Chin State, arresting the pastor, and then the next day, the military raided a Kachin Baptist Church in Shan State twice, arresting eleven members (Greenwalt, 2021, p. 3). On March 17, 2021, in Kalay township in Sagaing Region, the military shot and killed twenty-five-year-old pastor Cung LianCeu and three other civilians (Greenwalt, 2021, p. 3). The Myanmar military continued to attack and destroy churches. On May 24, 2021, the military attacked a Catholic church near Loikaw, the capital city of Kayah state. On June 7, airstrikes struck and damaged another Catholic church in Kayah state. The minority community was not alone in its suffering. The larger Myanmar religious economy has also suffered under centuries of state support and protection.

CONSEQUENCE 4: PERPETUAL CONFLICT IN A DISTORTED RELIGIOUS ECONOMY

A distorted religious economy lacks freedom, justice, and fairness. A consequence of this distortion is perpetual conflict and violence. Myanmar has been in a perpetual state of war since independence. Clearly, not all conflicts in society are related to religion, but the underlying injustices of the state-supported religious monopoly and the political othering of religious minorities have been a significant and key factor in Myanmar's perpetual conflicts. A society's prospects for avoiding conflict increase significantly with the political system's fairness. The restriction of religious freedoms in the Myanmar state and the persecution of religious minorities has led to conflict and violence. The protection of the Buddhist firm has undermined the essential elements of a liberal peace. Individual rights, liberty, equality, and the rule of law have all been sacrificed by the Myanmar state. Myanmar's citizens are not treated with equal respect and are not accorded freedom of conscience. Minority religions face violence, denigration, and disrespect. Individuals in Myanmar are not free to leave or change their religion. Myanmar's state does not uphold the rule of law or respect all human rights and freedoms, and has failed to gain the consent of the governed through free and fair elections. Myanmar does not have a free marketplace for ideas and religions. The lack of religious freedoms, othering, violence, and persecution has led to injustice and perpetual violence. The protection of religion has led to injustices. Muslims and Christians have suffered greatly. Suffering and injustice make violence more likely.

In Myanmar's religious history and culture, the concepts of justice, liberty, human rights, and fairness have been largely absent. The result is that the entire society has suffered. Violence is not only inflicted on minorities. Violence also harms the perpetrators and everyone else. The people of Myanmar know and desperately want the elements of a liberal peace. In 2021, they and many of Myanmar's religious leaders loudly called for a liberal democracy and protested in the face of brutal violence from the military junta.

CONSEQUENCE 5: LACK OF COMPETITION IN MYANMAR'S DISTORTED RELIGIOUS ECONOMY

The state's policy of linking religion with belonging has distorted Myanmar's religious economy. The religious makeup of the people of Myanmar has been altered from its original (before 1057) and natural state. Religious consumers in Myanmar have not had a choice in religious ideas and institutions. As illustrated in earlier chapters, the religious marketplace has been largely closed and tightly regulated by the state since 1057. Like the example of Shan-style rice in the introduction of this book, state control, protection, and oversight have limited the marketplace to all but a particular version of Theravada Buddhism (Hayek and Bartley, 1989, p. 137).

Given freedom in an open religious market, an individual may identify as Animist, Buddhist, Christian, Hindu, Jew, Muslim, or any number of religions and subsects of religions. Religious beliefs tend to be personal. Like humans worldwide, the religious identities of the people of Myanmar are pluralistic and ever changing (Carstens, 2018, p. 128). However, the state protection of religion in Myanmar has outwardly manufactured a Buddhist identity that cannot be altered beyond the limits imposed by those in power in the Buddhist firm and the government. Official census data reflect a distorted marketplace. Rohingya are not counted as citizens, and the government has worked to minimize the importance of the Muslim and Christian communities, both numerically and spiritually. Since 1962, the number of Muslims has been deliberately underreported. The official 2014 national census reports that 89 percent of the Myanmar population has chosen to follow Buddhism, while only 6 percent have opted for Christianity, 4 percent Islam, and only 0.2 percent have selected the Hindu religious firm; 0.2 percent fall into the "other" category, and a tiny fraction (0.1 percent) report no religion at all. Only 0.8 percent report being animists. This data reflects the distortion of nearly one thousand years of state protection of Theravada Buddhism.

There are two significant distortions reflected in the official state religion data. First, people in Myanmar report being Buddhists who are *not* practicing Buddhists. Charles Carstens (2018, p. 127) noted that religion, belonging, nationalism, and "othering" are all entangled with race and citizenship in Myanmar. State protection of Theravada Buddhism has tied belonging and citizenship to religion, making non-Buddhists reluctant to disclose their individual religious choices to the state (Carstens, 2018, p. 127). The Myanmar government's support and protection of Theravada Buddhism created a society in which non-Buddhists are outsiders. Non-Buddhists are not seen (by themselves or others) as legitimate members of the larger political community. Conversely, Buddhists (or those who claim to be Buddhists) are insiders and are the real and favored members of the political community. The state has made Theravada Buddhism the only rational choice for official reporting and documents.

Second, the official data indicate historical state manipulation of the religious choices of the Myanmar population. The state has sharply limited consumer choices of religious ideas. Religious ideas (be they Animist, Christian, Islam, Hindu, or others) were largely forced out of the Myanmar marketplace. The Theravada Buddhist firm was promoted, selected, and has held a monopoly in the Myanmar market because of state protection. Other religions were simply not realistic choices for the people of Myanmar.

Supply-side theory predicts that the more a government supports a religion, the less religious the population will be (Fox, 2018, p. 85). Less freedom of choice is believed to lead to less overall religious participation. This does not appear to be the case in Myanmar. Evidence of robust religious participation in the form of nat and Buddhist shrines and attendance does not support this supply-side argument. Myanmar's Buddhist firm is supported by government funding and generous donations from the population. Every day, lines of monks, nuns, and novices find their alms bowls filled by the generous Myanmar people.

As noted above, Buddhist monks in Myanmar regularly declare that the state must protect their religion, or the people of Myanmar will choose different religions. For example, the Buddhist Abbot, Venerable Ambalangoda Sumedhananda Thero, said, "Think of what used to be Buddhist lands: Afghanistan, Pakistan, Kashmir, Indonesia. They have all been destroyed by Islam" (Beech, 2019). A brief look at neighboring India seems to confirm his fears of some in the Buddhist firm. Today the Buddhist King Ashoka's India is largely Hindu. However, large populations of Indians have also chosen to be Buddhists, Christians, Muslims, Sikhs, Jains, and Animists. Today, India's population includes the vast majority of the world's Hindus and the second-largest group of Muslims within a single country, behind only Indonesia. According to Pew Research Center projections, many of India's citizens are choosing Islam (Majumdar, 2018). By 2050, the Muslim population in India is expected to grow to 311 million, making it the largest Muslim population in the world. India is religiously pluralistic and, like Myanmar, a multi-ethnic society. The religious choices of the people of India reflect that diversity. India's religious marketplace is not without government regulation, but the religious choices made by Indians reflect a religious economy that supports freedom of conscience and the right to profess, practice, and propagate religion. On the other hand, Myanmar's religious economy reflects nearly one thousand years of state promotion and protection of one religion, limited freedom of conscience, and few options to practice a religion other than the one chosen by Myanmar's founding king. In Myanmar, all citizens and all religious firms (Animists, Buddhists, Christians, and Muslims) have suffered distortion and corruption under state protection and regulation of religion.

CONSEQUENCE 6: INCOMPETENT PERVERSION OF TRUTH?

In 1689, in *A Letter concerning Toleration*, John Locke argued that state authority over religion corrupted religion. Locke argued that the state would be incompetent in the administration of religion. Has nearly a thousand years of state control and protection of versions of Theravada Buddhism distorted and/or altered the "truth"? Is true Buddhism peaceful, tolerant, nonviolent, and pacifist? Perhaps monk-led violence is acceptable in Theravada Buddhism? Perhaps, as King Ashoka argued, truth is found in all creeds? What is the truth? According to John Stuart Mill, religious liberty is necessary for discovering our "truth" (personally finding what is true). Mill argued that humans could only discover their truth in circumstances in which different beliefs and religious ideas are permitted to flourish (Leiter, 2014, p. 20). Mill argued that state-mandated beliefs do not allow for the discovery of truth. Toleration of divergent beliefs and practices, Mill argued, would facilitate an understanding of "truth" (Leiter, 2014, p. 21). Our understanding of truth, our values, and the lives we lead might be found in different beliefs that themselves capture components or parts of the truth. The moral truths found in Theravada Buddhism, for example, are truths about how we ought to live. There are, of course, many different understandings of truth. In Myanmar, however, the protection of religion has limited and corrupted the expression of religious convictions and truths. Nat worship has been denigrated. Islam and Christianity have been violently repressed. The state has purged many sects and versions of Buddhism since 1057. State-mandated intolerance has nurtured its own singular and likely distorted version of truth.

In the 1980s, under the Ne Win regime, a monk named U Nyana studied Theravada Buddhism for many years at several different universities and monasteries in Myanmar (Nyi Nyi Kyaw, 2019, p. 184). After some time in his studies, U Nyana stated that he had reached the stage of ariya or holiness by seeing the "truth." U Nyana felt that he understood the truth. The young monk then took steps to inform the State Sangha Maha Nayaka Committee that he had seen the truth. The State Sangha Maha Nayaka Committee promptly disapproved. The committee stated that U Nyana had violated a cardinal Buddhist rule by revealing that he had seen the truth. U Nyana could not accept the Buddhist leadership's decision to reject his claim, and he publicly disowned both Theravada Buddhism and the monkhood (Nyi Nyi Kyaw, 2019, p. 184). His truth was different from the state-mandated truth. U Nyana stopped wearing saffron robes, started wearing blue clothing, and preached a new vada or doctrine. U Nyana had many followers. In 1984, 1986, and again in 1991, U Nyana was imprisoned for spreading false news while knowing that it was not true. After being released from prison, U Nyana once again returned to share his version of the truth. In 2010, he was sentenced to another twenty years in prison for conflicts with the Rules of the Buddhist Order.

Like King Anawrahta's purging of the Ari monks, the State Sangha Maha Nayaka Committee was intolerant of U Nyana's "deviant" sect and his version of the truth. For centuries, the power of the Myanmar state has shaped and reshaped Theravada Buddhist versions of the truth and repressed all other faiths and versions. A consequence of state-mandated intolerance and repression of religious ideas is a distortion or repression of "truth." The truth, wrote Thomas Jefferson, "is too personal, too sacred, too holy, to permit its unhallowed perversion by a civil magistrate" (Cousins, 1958, p. 125). We will never know what truths and ideas have been lost to the perversion of the state in Myanmar. However, in 2021 it was apparent that the Myanmar people support tolerance and liberal policies that will allow an open and free religious economy in which different beliefs and religious ideas are allowed to flourish.

CONCLUSIONS: THE ASHOKAN ROAD?

Nearly one thousand years of state protection of religion has corrupted Myanmar's religious economy. King Ashoka and the Myanmar kings who followed his example ruled with brutal force and promoted, protected, and controlled Theravada Buddhism as an atonement for their brutal actions. Myanmar's military leaders since 1962 have followed the same Ashokan road. The consequences have been stark:

1. An established state-supported religious monopoly
2. Corruption, regulation, and restrictions on the majority religion
3. Repression, discrimination, and violence against minority religions

4. Perpetual conflict
5. A distorted religious economy and competition
6. A perversion and corruption of truth

State and religion policy decisions made by kings and military leaders have contributed to making Myanmar a battlefield of civil war and a society of perpetual violence. As a result, Myanmar has suffered the longest civil war in the world. The coup d'état on February 1, 2021, was a step back into the ancient and destructive narrative that the people of Myanmar know far too well.

The Ashokan pattern of king law and king protection of Buddhism was briefly interrupted by a British neutral state–religion policy. New religions and ideas grew throughout the country during the British era. General Aung San attempted to adopt the same neutral policies toward religion but was tragically cut short. Prime Minister U Nu promoted a divisive state–religion policy during a short-lived parliamentary democracy that General Ne Win abruptly ended in a coup in 1962. Ne Win and the military leaders who followed him violently plunged the newly independent nation into a pattern of brutal repression and violence. The liberal democratic ideals promoted by Aung San, U Nu, and U Thant were crushed by Ne Win's "Burmese Way to Socialism." Ne Win's regime was hostile to all minority religions while defining and reinforcing the narrative that being a Myanmar citizen meant being Buddhist. From 1962 to 1987, Ne Win controlled and regulated religion with the same brutal and heavy-handed methods he used on the larger macroeconomy. By 1987, the nation was one of the poorest on earth, and the only religion allowed (Theravada Buddhism) was made an instrument of control for Ne Win's regime.

The Myanmar people resisted. The Four-Eights Uprising revealed the convictions and the desire of the people of Myanmar to bring down Ne Win's dictatorship. Aung San Suu Kyi emerged as an icon of liberal democracy but was placed under house arrest. In 2007, the religious convictions of the nation's monks in the Saffron Revolution pushed the nation toward democratic reforms. The military brutally suppressed the voices of the protesting Saffron monks, but their message was loudly and forcefully expressed and widely accepted by the people of Myanmar. Under military leaders trained in the narratives of "king law," inequalities and injustices ensued. Atrocities were systematically perpetrated against the Chin, Karen, Kachin, Mon, Rakhine, and Shan peoples. The ethnic cleansing operations against the Rohingya Muslims finally captured international attention in 2017. Myanmar's military leaders attempted to "Burmanize" ethnic minorities and repeatedly defined and reinforced a national identity based on religion. Non-Buddhists became foreign and were portrayed as enemies of the state and Buddhism. Following the Buddhist nationalists of the 1930s, the military employed religion as a polarizing instrument of "us versus them." Seeking legitimacy, the military cast themselves as the protectors of race and religion; under the guise of protecting race and religion, the military-led systematic massacres of religious minorities were supported by the Ma Ba Tha Buddhist nationalists.

The military's narrative and policy of linking citizenship to religion divided the nation. Still, the foundation planks of tolerance, religious freedom, respect for all, and democracy were clearly present in the nationwide reaction to the 2021 coup. The generals may temporarily hold power with guns and bloodshed, but the people of Myanmar (including most of the religious leaders of all firms) are united in their determination to move forward with a liberal democracy founded on the principles of a liberal peace. The brutal and divisive policies of the military since 1962 have bonded marginalized ethnic and religious minorities with the majority Buddhist and nat worshipers. Nevertheless, the Myanmar people are poised to embrace liberty and rebuild their society without king law and the protection of religion.

Perhaps the Myanmar people are following a different Ashokan road? After choosing the Buddhist faith, King Ashoka recommended that his people act according to the principle of tolerance. The English philosopher Bernard Williams wrote that the principle of toleration includes "the moral good involved in putting up with beliefs one finds offensive" (Leiter, 2014, p. 8). The Ashokan road led India toward toleration and an open religious economy. Expressing the need for the moral good of toleration, Ashoka said, "Acting thus, we contribute to the progress of our creed by serving others. Acting otherwise, we harm our own faith, bringing discredit upon the others" (Krishnaswami, 1960, p. 1). King Anawrahta and Shin Arahan's closing of the Myanmar religious economy was indeed a critical turning point in the history of Theravada Buddhism, but Myanmar's founding king was not following the Ashokan road. Ashoka, the model king of Buddhism, declared,

> One should not honor only one's religion and condemn the religions of others, but one should honor others' religions for this or that reason. So doing, one helps one's own religion to grow and renders service to the religions of others too. In acting otherwise, one digs the grave of one's own religion and also does harm to other religions. Whosoever honors his own religion and condemns other religions, does so indeed through devotion to his own religion, thinking "I will glorify my own religion." But on the contrary, in so doing he injures his own religion more gravely. So, concord is good: let all listen and be willing to listen to the doctrines professed by others. (Rahula, 1974, pp. 4–5)

King Ashoka suggested "that all creeds be illumined as they all profess pure doctrines" (Krishnaswami, 1960, p. 1). The Ashokan model is not one of a closed religious economy. Ashoka, like Milton, Smith, Locke, and Jefferson after him, saw value and wisdom in a liberal and open religious economy. The people of Myanmar, all people, deserve liberal institutions that embrace and promote justice and fairness and provide all citizens with equal respect and freedom of conscience.

Glossary

Ava Kingdom: The capital of Burma off and on from 1364 to 1881. The kings of Ava restored Burmese supremacy in the region, which had disintegrated after the collapse of Pagan, which ended the First Burmese Empire founded by King Anawrahta in 1044.

Burmese Road to Socialism: This was the official ideology of Myanmar's military regime between 1962 and 1988.

Cetana: Cetana translates to intention or will; it is the driving force behind any action that generates a future effect.

Chin: A Tibeto-Burman speaking group in the lower western Myanmar border area, in the Chin Hills. Traditionally, the Chin peoples were animists. However, in the British era, the first Christian missionaries arrived in the Chin state. Due to the work of the Baptist and Methodist missionaries, today the majority of Chin are Christians. The military government has persecuted the Chin people for religious reasons.

Dhamma: The Buddhist law.

Dobama Asiayone: We Burmans Association, commonly known as the Thakhins, was a Buddhist nationalist group formed in the 1930s. Drawing their name from the way in which the British were addressed during colonial times, the association brought together traditionalist Buddhist nationalist to stir up political consciousness in Myanmar.

Firm: See *religious firm* below.

Government monk: A monk who is loyal, close to, and often directly supported by the state.

Kachin: The term Kachin people is used in Myanmar for a group called the Jingpo people in China. The Burmese Kachin are three times more numerous than the Jingpo in China. Since Myanmar's independence, animist and Buddhist beliefs have been replaced by Christianity.

Kala/Kalar: Many Myanmar people did not distinguish in their language between Europeans and Indians. Europeans and Indians were frequently called "Kala," meaning foreigners. Later in the colonial era, Europeans were called Ingaleit Kala (English Kala). They were also called thosaung Kala, or "sheep-wearing kala," a reference to their thick woolen clothes. Today, kala is a derogatory term used to refer to Muslims in Myanmar.

Karen: The Karen people are a major Tibetano-Burman speaking group who reside primarily in Kayin State, southern and southeastern Myanmar. With a population of approximately five million people, account for approximately 7 percent of the Myanmar population. Many Karen have migrated to Thailand, having settled mainly on the Thailand-Myanmar border. The majority of Karens are Theravada Buddhists who also practice animism. Approximately 15 percent of the Karen are Christian.

Kings of Buddhism: The men who have ruled Myanmar, from King Anawrahta to King Thibaw Min, to modern military dictators, have assumed the role of protectors and promoters of one specific school of Buddhism, Theravada Buddhism. Modern rulers of Myanmar, like Generals Ne Win and Min Aung Hlaing, have cast themselves as Buddhist kings and have courted and controlled Buddhist clerics and Buddhism. In 2021, Min Aung Hlaing portrayed himself as the next in the long line of just and good Buddhist kings and monarchs who protect Buddhism. Soon after his coup, General Min Aung Hlaing undertook major construction projects to insert himself into the Buddhist king lineage. In 2022, he built three enormous statues of Buddhist kings in northern Shan state. The statues aim to amplify the image of the Buddhist kings while not-so-subtly allowing the general to associate himself with them.

Ma Ba Tha: acronym for the Association for the Protection of Race and Religion in Myanmar. The association is an ultra-Buddhist nationalist group. Established in January 2014, the association's mission is defending Theravada Buddhism in Myanmar.

Ma Ba Tha Monk: A Buddhist nationalist monk who believes that the state must protect Buddhism. These monks are sometimes but not always financially or openly supported by the government; they are often encouraged and supported by the military, are very divisive, and are openly inflammatory and anti-Muslim and anti-Christian.

Mahayana: School of Buddhism practiced predominantly in China, Japan, Korea, Tibet, and Vietnam.

Mandalay: The second largest city in Myanmar after Yangon. Located on the east bank of the Irrawaddy River, north of Yangon. Mandalay was founded in 1857 by King Mindon. It was Burma's final royal capital before the kingdom's annexation by the British Empire in 1885. Mandalay is Myanmar's cultural and religious center of Buddhism, having numerous monasteries and more than seven hundred pagodas.
Metta Sutta: Loving-kindness, a Buddhist virtue.
Mon: The Mon people inhabit Lower Myanmar's Mon State, Kayin State, Kayah State, Tanintharyi Region, Bago Region, and the Irrawaddy Delta. The Mon were one of the earliest to reside in Southeast Asia and were responsible for the spread of Theravada Buddhism in Mainland Southeast Asia.
Nats: Myanmar's animist religion refers to the animistic and polytheistic religious worship of nats. Nats are spirits that communicate with the living. The thirty-seven great nats are widely worshiped or propitiated in Myanmar.
Panthay: Term used to refer to a group of Muslims of Chinese descent in Myanmar.
Pongyi: A Buddhist monk.
969 Movement: A loose faction of extreme Buddhist nationalist monks that became Ma Ba Tha. The organization is responsible for anti-Muslim and anti-Christian violence.
Religious firm: A religious organization that shares religious ideas. Religious ideas are the fundamental answers to the questions of life. Following the work of William Bainbridge, Roger Finke, Tony Gill, Rodney Stark, and many others, I use the term *firm* to refer to religions and religious groups as competing entities that vie for customers. A religious firm is an organization that shares religious ideas with people who make rational choices among the available products (religious ideas) that are shared in a given society. The use of the word *firm* is not meant to be disrespectful. Rather, it is meant to place all religions and religious groups in an equal light.
Religious liberty: Represents the degree to which the state regulates the religious economy.
Religious marketplace or **religious economy:** The social arena or society (in this book, it is the state of Myanmar) where religious firms compete for members and resources.
Pure (passive) monks: Those Buddhist monks in Myanmar who stay out of politics.
Saffron monks: Participated in the 2007 Saffron Revolution. These monks (and those who have adopted their ideological and philosophical approach) support democracy, human rights, and interfaith understand-

ing, and reject the military regime. Saffron monks tend to focus on the Buddhist precepts and not on anti-Muslim hate speech.

Saffron Revolution: The name given to the 2007 uprising against the military regime.

Sangha: A Sanskrit word that means association or community. In this book, Sangha is used to broadly refer to the Theravada Buddhist religious community or the Buddhist religious firm. The word *sangha* was first used for popular assemblies that governed many South Asian cities during the Buddha's lifetime—roughly the fifth century BCE. Early Buddhist texts state that the Buddha was inspired by the example of republics and the importance of convening full and frequent public assemblies. Early Buddhist Sanghas were meticulous in their demands for all monks to gather to reach unanimous decisions on matters of general concern, resorting to majority vote only when consensus broke down (Graeber and Wengrow, 2021, pp. 319–20).

Śāsana: The Buddha's teaching, practice, doctrine, or "the teaching of the Buddha."

Shan: A Tai-speaking group living primarily in the Shan State, but they also inhabit parts of the Mandalay Region, Kachin State, and Kayin State. The majority of Shan are Theravada Buddhists and animists. Shan-style rice is a must-try Myanmar dish.

State Sangha Maha Nayaka Committee: Often called Mahanayaka, or Mahana for short, a government-appointed body of high-ranking Buddhist monks that oversees and regulates the Sangha (Buddhist clergy) in Myanmar. The committee or council of forty-seven Buddhist monks all appointed by the state, to set policy for the Buddhist firm. The Mahana's structure and allocated authority has been replicated in regional divisions and at township levels throughout the country.

Stupa: A monument containing the remains of an enlightened person, often a pilgrimage destination.

Synretism: Occurs when more than one religion or culture combines to create a new or blended belief or practice that incorporates elements of the original religious ideas.

Tatmadaw: The official name of the armed forces of Myanmar.

Theravada: A school of Buddhism practiced in Cambodia, Laos, Myanmar, Sri Lanka, and Thailand. Theravada translates to "teachings of the elders."

Vinaya: Contains the rules of the Buddhist monastic community, conduct, and discipline.

Wa: People who reside in the China-Myanmar-Laos-Thailand border area. Many of the Wa are animists, and a small proportion of the population follows a derivative of either Buddhism or Christianity.

Bibliography

Abeysekara, A. (2002). *Colors of the robe: Religion, identity and difference*. University of South Carolina Press.
Adas, M. (1974). *The Burma delta: Economic development and social change on an Asian rice frontier 1852–1941*. University of Wisconsin Press.
Ahdar, R. (2006). The idea of "religious markets." *International Journal of Law in Context*, 2(1), 49–65.
Ahdar, R., and Leigh, I. (2013). *Religious freedom in the liberal state*. Oxford University Press.
Albert, E., and Maizland, L. (2020). *The Rohingya crisis*. Council on Foreign Relations. https://www.cfr.org/backgrounder/rohingya-crisis.
All Burma Young Monks Union. (1991). *The Buddha Sāsana and Burma military regime*. Revolutionary Area, Burma.
Allen, T. (2008, April 22). Bindmans Law and Campaigning Award honors Burmese monk. https://www.bindmans.com/news/bindmans-law-and-campaigning-award-honours-burmese-monk.
Altbach, P. G., and Gavin, P. K. (1991). *Education and the colonial experience*. Advent Books, Inc.
ALTSEAN-Burma. (2022). [@Altsean]. (2022, April 22). "Since the coup, junta forces have destroyed 97 religious buildings across #Myanmar #Burma Including 76 churches 20 Buddhist monasteries 1 mosque Destroying religious buildings is a violation of international law. Religion is NOT a target." #WhatsHappeningInMyanmar [Tweet]. Twitter. https://twitter.com/Altsean/status/1517422761551056898?s=20&t=SEoO6Ky7_BEranEiY7brWA.
Anderson, B. (1991). *Imagined communities: Reflections on the origins and spread of nationalism*. Verso.
Anderson, C. (1956). *To the Golden Shore: The life of Adoniram Judson*. Little, Brown.

Anderson, K., Rausser, G., and Swinnen, J. (2013). Political economy of public policies: Insights from distortions to agricultural and food markets. *Journal of Economic Literature, 51*(2), 423–77.

Andrews, M., Squire, C., and Tamboukou, M. (Eds.). (2008). *Doing narrative research*. Sage.

Anonymous. (2019a). Nat guilty. *The Economist, 433*(9169), 50–51. https://www.economist.com/asia/2019/11/14/monks-in-myanmar-have-a-new-target.

Anonymous. (2019b). Yangon military chief donates nearly $20,000 to Buddhist nationalist group. *Irrawaddy*. https://www.irrawaddy.com/news/yangon-military-chief-donates-nearly-20000-buddhist-nationalist-group.html.

Anonymous. (2021). Myanmar spirit mediums take aim at military coup. *Bangkok Post*. https://www.bangkokpost.com/world/2068035/myanmar-spirit-mediums-take-aim-at-military-coup.

Ariya Wuntha Bhiwunsa. (2020, January 17). Interview with Myawaddy Sayadaw. https://www.facebook.com/100043951938822/videos/134069758068088/.

Aron, G. (2018). *Reframing the Crisis in Myanmar's Rakhine State. Peace Brief no. 242*. United States Institute of Peace.

Artinger, B., and Rowand, M. (2021). When Buddhists back the army: Many monks in Myanmar are supporting the military coup. *Foreign Policy*. https://foreignpolicy.com/2021/02/16/myanmar-rohingya-coup-buddhists-protest.

Asad, T. (1999). Religion, nation-state, secularism. In C. W. Gailey (Ed.), *Civilization in crisis: Anthropological perspectives*. University Press of Florida.

Ashin, J., and Crosby, K. (2017). Heresy and monastic malpractice in the Buddhist court cases (Vinicchaya) of modern Burma (Myanmar). *Contemporary Buddhism, 18*(1), 199–261.

Association of Myanmar Architects. (2012). *Thirty heritage buildings of Yangon: Inside the city that captured time*. Serindia Publications.

Atkinson, C. (1972). *Jeremy Bentham: His life and work* (Books for college libraries, BCL-10). Methuen and Co.

Aung Htin Muang. (1958, February). Folk-elements in Burmese Buddhism alchemy, spirits, and ancient rituals. *The Atlantic*. https://www.theatlantic.com/magazine/archive/1958/02/folk-elements-in-burmese-buddhism/306833/?utm_source=share&utm_campaign=share.

Aung Htin Muang. (1962). *Folk elements in Burmese Buddhism*. U Myint Maung Religious Affairs Department Press.

Aung Htin Muang. (1967). *A history of Burma*. Columbia University Press.

Aung San Suu Kyi. (1991). In quest of democracy. In M. Aris (Ed.), *Freedom from fear and other writings* (pp. 167–79). Viking Press.

Aung San Suu Kyi. (1996, September). The benefits of meditation and sacrifice. *Bangkok Post*, 1A.

Aung San Suu Kyi. (1996, September 9). Faith eases the mind in times of political turmoil: Letters from Burma 40. *Mainichi Daily News*, 1A.

Aung San Suu Kyi. (1997). *Letters from Burma*. Penguin Books.

Aung San Suu Kyi. (2010). *Freedom from fear and other writings* (M. Aris, Ed.; Rev. ed.). Penguin Books.

Aung-Thwin, M. (1979). The role of Sasana reform in Burmese history: Economic dimensions of a religious purification. *Journal of Asian Studies, 38*(14), 671.

Aung-Thwin, M. (1985). *Pagan: The origins of modern Burma*. University of Hawai'i Press.

Aung-Thwin, M. (2005). *The mists of Ramanna: The legend that was lower Burma*. University of Hawai'i Press.

Aung-Thwin, M. (2009). *Of monarchs, monks and men: Religion and the state in Myanmar* (Working Paper Series No. 127). National University of Singapore's Asia Research Institute.

Aung-Thwin, M. (2011). *The return of the Galon king: History, law, and rebellion in colonial Burma*. Ohio University Press.

Aung-Thwin, M. (2012). *A history of Myanmar since ancient times: Traditions and transformations*. Reaktion Books.

Aung, W. Y. (2019). 65 years since thousands of monks began the sixth Buddhist Council in Yangon. *Irrawaddy*. https://www.irrawaddy.com/specials/on-this-day/65-years-since-thousands-monks-began-sixth-buddhist-council-yangon.html.

Aung, W. Y. (2020). Jubilee Hall: From colonial social hub to hotbed of Myanmar independence activity. *Irrawaddy*. https://www.irrawaddy.com/specials/places-in-history/jubilee-hall-colonial-social-hub-hotbed-myanmar-independence-activity.html.

Aung, Z. (2007, September 11). Burmese monks in revolt. *Irrawaddy*, 1A. https://www2.irrawaddy.com/opinion_story.php?art_id=8581.

Aye, K. (1993). *The voice of young Burma*. Cornell University Press Southeast Asia Program Publications.

Ba, Yin. (2007). *Sayadaw U Ottama: Sower of seed of independence movement* (in Burmese). Yangon.

Badgley, J. (1962). Burma's military government: A political analysis. *Asian Survey*, 2(6), 24–31.

Badgley, J. H. (1963). Burma: The nexus of socialism and two political traditions. *Asian Survey*, 3(2), 89–95.

Baker, N. (2017). How Myanmar's paranormal spirit wives escape LGBTQ persecution. *Vice*. https://www.vice.com/en/article/43axew/how-myanmars-paranormal-spirit-wives-escape-lgbtq-persecution.

Basedau, M. (2017, August). The rise of religious armed conflicts in sub-Saharan Africa: No simple answers. *GIGA Focus Africa*, 4.

Basedau, M., Strüver, G., Vüllers, J., and Wegenast, T. (2011). Do religious factors impact armed conflict? Empirical evidence from sub-Saharan Africa. *Terrorism and Political Violence*, 23(5), 752–79.

Basu, R. C. S. (2018). *The Rohingya in South Asia: People without a state*. Routledge.

Bates, R. H., Greif, A., Levi, M., Rosenthal, J. L., and Weingast, B. R. (1998). *Analytic narratives*. Princeton University Press.

Bechert, H. (1970). Theravada Buddhist Sangha: Some general observations on historical and political factors in its development. *Journal of Asian Studies*, 29(4), 761–78.

Bechert, H. (1973). Sangha, state, society, "nation": Persistence of traditions in "post-traditional" Buddhist societies. *Daedalus*, 102(1), 85–95.

Beech, H. (2019). Buddhists go to battle: When nationalism overrides pacifism. *New York Times*. https://www.nytimes.com/2019/07/08/world/asia/buddhism-militant-rise.html.

Beech, H., Meikhtila, and Pattani (2013, July 1). The face of Buddhist terror. *Time*. https://content.time.com/time/subscriber/article/0,33009,2146000,00.html.

Beech, H., and Saw Nang. (2019, May 29). He incited massacre, but insulting Aung San Suu Kyi was the last straw. *New York Times*. https://www.nytimes.com/2019/05/29/world/asia/myanmar-wirathu-monk-buddhism.html.

Bengtsson, J. (2012). *Aung San Suu Kyi: A Biography*. Amaryllis.

Beneke, C. (2010, Spring). The free market and the founders' approach to church–state relations. *Journal of Church and State*, 52(2), 323–52.

Berzin, A. (1996, June). *Buddhism and its impact on Asia* (Asian Monographs, no. 8). Cairo University, Center for Asian Studies.

Beyer, J. (2016). Houses of Islam: Muslims, property rights, and the state in Myanmar. In E. Crouch (Ed.), *Islam and the state in Myanmar: Muslim–Buddhist relations and the politics of belonging* (pp. 127–56). Oxford University Press.

Bhattacharya, S. (2004). A close view of encounter between British Burma and British Bengal [Unpublished manuscript]. https://www.scribd.com/document/394035346/A-Close-View-of-Encounter-between-British-Burma-and-British-Bengal-By-Dr-Swapna-Bhattacharya-Chakraborti.

Bigandet, P. A. (1995). An outline of the history of the Catholic Burmese Mission from the year 1720 to 1857. White Orchid Press.

Black, D. (1976). *The behavior of law*. Academic Press.

Black, H. L., and Supreme Court of the United States. (1961). U.S. Reports: Engel v. Vitale, 370 U.S. 421.

Blackburn, A. (2007). Writing Buddhist histories from landscape and architecture: Sukhothai and Chiang Mai. *Buddhist Studies Review*, 24(2), 192–225.

Blackburn, A. (2014). *Locations of Buddhism: Colonialism and modernity in Sri Lanka*. University of Chicago Press.

Bo Maung, C. (2021). [@cardinal_bo]. (2021, May 25). "An Earnest Appeal—With Special Reference to the attack on the Sacred Heart Church in Kayanthayar near Loikaw in Eastern Myanmar on 23rd May 2021 that killed four and wounded many (25th May 2021) [Tweet]. Twitter. https://twitter.com/cardinal_bo/status/1397229937325662223?s=20.

Bond, G. (1988). *The Buddhist revival in Sri Lanka: Religious tradition, reinterpretation, and response*. University of South Carolina Press.

Booth, A. E. (2007). Colonial legacies: Economic and social development in East and Southeast Asia. University of Hawai'i Press.

Borchert, T. (Ed.). (2018). *Theravada Buddhism in colonial contexts*. Routledge. https://doi.org/10.4324/9781315111889.

Boswell, J. (2013). Why and how narrative matters in deliberative systems. *Political Studies*, 61(3), 620–36.

Boyd, K. (1999). *Encyclopedia of historians and historical writing*. Fitzroy Dearborn.

Brac de Perrière, B. B. (1989). The Taungbyone festival. In M. Skidmore (Ed.), *Burma at the turn of the twenty-first century* (pp. 65–89). University of Hawai'i Press.

Brac de La Perrière, B. B. (2005). The Taungbyon Festival: Locality and nation-confronting in the Cult of the 37 Lords. (A. Dilidon, trans.). In M. Skidmore (Ed.), *Burma at the turn of the 21st century* (pp. 65–89). University of Hawai'i Press.

Brac de la Perrière, B. B. (2009a). An overview of the field of religion in Burmese studies. *Asian Ethnology*, *68*(2), 185–210.

Brac de la Perrière, B. (2009b). "Nats' Wives" or "Children of Nats": From spirit possession to transmission among the ritual specialists of the cult of the thirty-seven lords. *Asian Ethnology*, *68*(2), 283–305.

Brackney, W. (1998). The legacy of Adoniram Judson. *International Bulletin of Missionary Research*, *22*(3), 122–27.

Braun, E. (2013). *The birth of insight: Meditation, modern Buddhism, and the Burmese monk Ledi Sayadaw*. University of Chicago Press.

Brockman, D. R. (2020). *Christian Americanism and Texas politics since 2008*. Baker Institute. https://www.bakerinstitute.org/media/files/files/3c850d0b/rel-pub-americanism-030220.pdf.

Brown, David. (1994). *The state and ethnic politics in Southeast Asia*. Routledge.

Brown, R. G. (1921, June). The pre-Buddhist religion of the Burmese. *Folk-Lore: The Transactions of the Folk-Lore Society*, *32*(2), 77–100.

Brubaker, R. (2012). Religion and nationalism: Four approaches. *Nations and Nationalism*, *18*(1), 2–20.

Butwell, R. (1962). The four failures of U Nu's second premiership. *Asian Survey*, *2*(1), 3–11.

Butwell, R. (1963). *U Nu of Burma*. Stanford University Press.

Butwell, R. (1972). Ne Win's Burma: At the end of the first decade. *Asian Survey*, *12*(10), 901–12.

Cady, J. F. (1953, February). Religion and politics in modern Burma. *Far-Eastern Quarterly*, *12*(2).

Cady, J. F. (1958). *A history of modern Burma*. Cornell University Press.

Callahan, M., and American Council of Learned Societies. (2005). *Making enemies: War and state building in Burma*. Cornell University Press.

Carstens, C. (2018). Religion. In A. Simpson, N. Farrelly, and I. Holliday (Eds.), *Routledge handbook of contemporary Myanmar*. Routledge.

Chain, Tun Aung. 2015. Inscriptions and chronicles of the historiography of Myanmar. In S. Fraser-Lu and D. M. Stadtner (Eds.), *Buddhist art of Myanmar*. Yale University Press with the Asia Society Museum. https://www.academia.edu/14578590/ Buddhist_Art_of_Myanmar_Asia_Society_New_York_exhibition_catalogue.

Chancey, K. (1998). The star in the East: The controversy over Christian missions to India, 1805–1813. *Historian*, *60*(3), 507–22.

Charney, M. W. (2006). *Powerful learning: Buddhist literati and the throne in Burma's last dynasty, 1752–1885*. University of Michigan, Centers for South and Southeast Asian Studies.

Charney, M. W. (2009). *A history of modern Burma*. Cambridge University Press.

Cheesman, N. (2003). School, state and Sangha in Burma. *Comparative Education*, *39*(1), 45–63.

Cheesman, N. (2015). *Opposing the rule of law: How Myanmar's courts make law and order*. Cambridge University Press.

Cheesman, N. (2019). Routine impunity as practice (in Myanmar). *Human Rights Quarterly*, *41*(4), 873–92.

Cheesman, N., and Farrelly, N. (Eds.). (2016). *Conflict in Myanmar: War, politics, and religion*. ISEAS Publishing.

Chen, J. (2014). Money and power in religious competition: A critique of the religious free market. *Oxford Journal of Law and Religion*, 3(2), 212–34.
Cockett, R. (2015). *Blood, dreams and gold: The changing face of Burma*. Yale University Press.
Coedes, G. (2015). *The making of South East Asia*. Routledge.
Collins, M. (2008). *Rabindranath Tagore and nationalism: An interpretation*. Working Paper No. 42. University of Heidelberg: South Asia Institute. http://archiv.ub.uni-heidelberg.de/volltextserver/8844/1/HPSACP_COLLINS.pdf.
Coşgel, M., and Miceli, T. (2009). State and religion. *Journal of Comparative Economics*, 37(3), 402–16.
Cousins, N. (1958). *In God we trust: The religious beliefs and ideas of the American founders*. Harper Press.
Coward, F. (2016). Scaling up: Material culture as scaffold for the social brain. *Quaternary International*, 405, Part A.
Cox, J. (2009). *The British missionary enterprise since 1700*. Routledge.
Crouch, M. (2016a). *Islam and the state in Myanmar: Muslim–Buddhist relations and the politics of belonging*. Oxford University Press.
Crouch, M. (2016b). Promiscuity, polygyny, and the power of revenge: The past and future of Burmese Buddhist law in Myanmar. *Asian Journal of Law and Society*, 3(1), 85–104.
Crouch, M. (2018). Dictators, democrats, and constitutional dialogue: Myanmar's constitutional tribunal. *International Journal of Constitutional Law*, 16(2), 421–46.
Dahl, R. A. (1956). *A preface to democratic theory*. Chicago University Press.
D'Asie, E. (2021). Buddhist monks divided over Myanmar resistance movement. *UCA News*. https://www.ucanews.com/news/buddhist-monks-divided-over-myanmar-resistance-movement/91803.
David, R., and Holliday, I. (2018). *Liberalism and democracy in Myanmar*. Oxford University Press.
De, P., and Chirathivat, S. (Eds.). (2018). *Celebrating the third decade and beyond: New challenges to ASEAN–India economic partnership*. Routledge.
DeCaroli, R. (2004). *Haunting the Buddha: Indian popular religions and the formation of Buddhism*. Oxford University Press.
Demerath, N. J. (2001). *Crossing the gods: World religions and worldly politics*. Rutgers University Press.
Diamond, L. (2004). What is Democracy? https://diamond-democracy.stanford.edu/events/lecture/what-democracy.
Dingrin, L. (2009). Is Buddhism indispensable in the cross-cultural appropriation of Christianity in Burma? *Buddhist–Christian Studies*, 29, 3–22.
Dizikes, P. (2019). Bringing figures in anticolonial politics out of the shadows. MIT News Office. https://news.mit.edu/2019/sana-aiyar-history-politics-1210.
Dorn, W. A. (2007). U Thant: Buddhism in action. In Kent Kille (Ed.), *The UN secretary-general and moral authority: Ethics and religion in international leadership*. Georgetown University Press.
Duncan, J. S. (1990). *The city as text: The politics of landscape interpretation in the Kandyan Kingdom*. Cambridge University Press.
Eberle, C. (2002). *Religious conviction in liberal politics*. Cambridge University Press.

Edwards, P. (2006). Grounds for protest: Placing Shwedagon pagoda in colonial and postcolonial history. *Postcolonial Studies, 9*(2), 197–211.

Egreteau, R. (2011). Burmese Indians in contemporary Burma: Heritage, influence, and perceptions since 1988. *Asian Ethnicity, 12*(1), 33–54.

Elster, J. (2000). Analytic narratives by Bates, Greif, Levi, Rosenthal, and Weingast: A review and response / Rational Choice history: A case of excessive ambition. *American Political Science Review, 94*(3), 685–95.

England, J. C. (1998). *The hidden history of Christianity in Asia: The churches of the East before the year 1500*. ISPCK and CCA.

Enno, S. P. K. (1994). Nat worship: A paradigm for doing ecumenical theology in Myanmar. *Asia Journal of Theology, 8*, 42–55.

Epstein, R. A. (2018). The nature of the religious firm. *Journal of Markets and Morality, 21*(1), 141–66. https://ezproxy.uttyler.edu/login?url=https://search-proquest-com.ezproxy.uttyler.edu/docview/2091167911?accountid=7123.

Farrelly, N. (2016). Muslim political activity in transitional Myanmar. In *Islam and the state in Myanmar: Muslim-Buddhist relations and the politics of belonging*. Oxford University Press.

Farry, J. (2000). John Stuart Mill on liberty and control. *Perspectives on Political Science, 29*(2), 120.

Fink, C. (2013). *Living silence in Burma: Surviving under military rule.* (2nd ed.). Silkworm Books.

Fink, C. (2018, June). Myanmar: Religious minorities and constitutional questions. *Asian Affairs, 49*(2), 259–77.

Finke, R. (1990, Summer). Religious deregulation: Origins and consequences. *Journal of Church and State, 32*(3), 609–24.

Finke, R., and Starke, R. (1992). *The churching of America: Winners and losers in our religious economy*. Rutgers University Press.

Firestone, B. (2013). Failed mediation: U Thant, the Johnson administration, and the Vietnam War. *Diplomatic History, 37*(5), 1060–89.

Firestone, B. (2019). Thant, U, United Nations, 1961–1971. *Biographical dictionary of secretaries-general of international organizations*. http://www.ru.nl/fm/iobio.

Fleming, R. (2016). *Hidden plight: Christian minorities in Burma*. U.S. Commission on International Religious Freedom. https://www.uscirf.gov/sites/default/files/Hidden%20Plight.%20Christian%20Minorities%20in%20Burma.pdf.

Ford, E. (2017). *Cold War monks: Buddhism and America's secret strategy in Southeast Asia*. Yale University Press.

Ford, G. R. (1974). *Statement on the death of U Thant*. Online by Gerhard Peters and John T. Woolley, The American Presidency Project: https://www.presidency.ucsb.edu/node/255988.

Fortify Rights. (2016). Investigate destruction of religious buildings: Hold perpetrators accountable, ensure protection for religious minorities. https://www.fortifyrights.org/mya-inv-2016-07-05/.

Fortify Rights. (2020a). Previously unpublished interview with Myanmar government lawyer details international crimes against Rohingya. https://www.fortifyrights.org/mya-inv-2020-03-06/.

Fortify Rights. (2020b). RE: Call it genocide—Act for the Rohingya. https://www.fortifyrights.org/downloads/Join%20Petition%20-%20Call%20it%20Genocide.pdf.
Foucault, M. (1995). *Discipline and punish: The birth of the prison*. Vintage.
Fox, J. (2008). *A world survey of religion and the state*. Cambridge University Press.
Fox, J. (2016a). Comparative politics. In D. Yamane (Ed.), *Handbook of religion and society*. Springer.
Fox, J. (2016b). *The unfree exercise of religion: A world survey of religious discrimination against religious minorities*. Cambridge University Press.
Fox, J. (2018). *An introduction to religion and politics: Theory and practice* (2nd ed.). Routledge.
Fox, J. (2019a). A world survey of secular–religious competition: State religion policy from 1990 to 2014. *Religion, State and Society*, 47(1), 10–29.
Fox, J. (2019b). The correlates of religion and state: An introduction. *Religion, State and Society*, 47(1), 2–9.
Fox, J. (2019c, February 10). *The religion and state project, round 3*. ARDA. http://www.thearda.com/internationalData/countries/Country_37_1.asp.
Fox, J. (2020, April 12). *The religion and state project, minorities module, round 3*. https://www.thearda.com/data-archive?fid=RAS3.
Fox, J., Finke, R., and Mataic, D. R. (2018). New data and measures on societal discrimination and religious minorities. *Interdisciplinary Journal of Research on Religion*, 2(14).
Franklin, B. (1997). From Benjamin Franklin to Richard Price, 9 October 1780. In B. B. Oberg (Ed.), *The papers of Benjamin Franklin, July 1 through November 15, 1780* (Vol. 33). Yale University Press.
Friedrichs, R. (1985). The uniquely religious: Grounding the social scientific study of religion anew. *Sociological Analysis*, 46(4), 361–66.
Furnivall, J. S. (1929). *Christianity and Buddhism in Burma: An address to the Rangoon Diocesan Council*. People's Literature Committee.
Furnivall, J. S. (1946). *Colonial policy and practice*. New York University Press.
Gagarin, Michael. (2009). *The Oxford encyclopedia of ancient Greece and Rome* (Vol. 7). Oxford University Press.
Gambira, U. (2007, November 4). What Burma's Junta Must Fear. *Washington Post*.
Geis, G. J. (1894). Myitkyina. *The Missionary Magazine: The American Baptist Missionary Union*, LXXVII. https://archive.org/stream/baptistmissiona04socigoog/baptistmissiona04socigoog_djvu.txt.
Gellner, E. (1983). *Nations and nationalism*. Cornell University Press.
Gheddo, P. (2014). Raised to the altars, Isidoro Ngei Ko Lat, first Burmese Blessed. *AsiaNewIt*. http://www.asianews.it/news-en/Raised-to-the-altars,-Isidoro-Ngei-Ko-Lat,-first-Burmese-Blessed,-and-Mario-Vergara,-19th-PIME-martyr-30915.html.
Ghosh, D. (2016). Burma–Bengal crossings: Intercolonial connections in preindependence India. *Asian Studies Review*, 40(2), 156–72.
Gill, A. (2001). Religion and Comparative Politics. *Annual Review of Political Science*, 4, 117–38.
Gill, A. (2007). *The political origins of religious liberty*. Cambridge University Press.

Gill, A. (2017). Christian democracy without romance: The perils of religious politics from a public choice perspective. *Perspectives on Political Science, 46*(1), 35–42.

Gillman, I., and Klimkeit, H. J. (1999). *Christians in Asia before 1500*. Routledge.

Gindin, M. (2019). *A white rose for Myanmar: Buddhists in Myanmar are pushing back against the country's nationalist monastics and trying to shift public opinion on the Rohingya crisis*. Tricycle. https://tricycle.org/trikedaily/white-rose-for-myanmar/.

Girke, F. (2015). The Yangon court buildings: Between thick and thin heritage. *Sojourn, 30*(1), 72–104.

Goldstein, W. (2020). What makes Critical Religion critical? A response to Russell McCutcheon. *Critical Research on Religion, 8*(1), 73–86.

Gomes, R. (2021, March 4). US bishops express solidarity with people of Myanmar. *Vatican News*. https://www.vaticannews.va/en/church/news/2021-03/myanmar-usccb-solidarity-message-sister-nu-tawng-courage.html.

Government of Burma. (1868–1941). *Catalogue of books and pamphlets published in Burma*. Government of Burma.

Graeber, D., and Wengrow, D. (2021). *The dawn of everything: A new history of humanity*. Farrar, Straus and Giroux.

Gravers, M. (1999). *Nationalism as political paranoia: An essay on the historical practice of power*. Curzon.

Gravers, M. (2013). Spiritual politics, political religion, and religious freedom in Burma. *The Review of Faith & International Affairs, 11*(2), 46–54.

Gravers, M. (2015). Anti-Muslim Buddhist nationalism in Burma and Sri Lanka: Religious violence and globalized imaginaries of endangered identities. *Contemporary Buddhism, 16*(1), 1–27.

Green, N. (2011). *Bombay Islam: The religious economy of the West Indian Ocean, 1840–1915*. Cambridge University Press.

Green, N. (2015). Buddhism, Islam and the religious economy of colonial Burma. *Journal of Southeast Asian Studies, 46*(2), 175–204.

Greenwalt, P. (2021, November). *United States Commission on International Religious Freedom: Country Update Burma*. https://www.uscirf.gov/sites/default/files/2021-11/2021%20Burma%20Country%20Update.pdf.

Grim, B. J., and Finke, R. (2010). *The price of freedom denied: Religious persecution and conflict in the twenty-first century*. Cambridge University Press.

Grzymala-Busse, A. (2015). *Nations under God*. Princeton University Press.

Grzymala-Busse, A. (2016). The difficulty with doctrine: How religion can influence politics. *Government and Opposition, 51*(2), 327–50.

Gurr, T. R. (1993). *Minorities at risk*. United States Institute of Peace.

Habiburahman, H. (2019). *First, they erased our name: A Rohingya speaks*. Scribe.

Hall, D. G. E. (1955). *A history of South-East Asia*. St. Martin's.

Hall, D. G. E. (1956). *Burma*. Hutchinson's University Library.

Hall, T. L. (1992–1993). Religion and civic virtue: Justification of free exercise. *Tulane Law Review, 67*(1), 87–134.

Harmon, N. B. (1974). *The encyclopedia of world Methodism by World Methodist Council* (Publication No. MARCXML). U.S. United Methodist Church,

Commission on Archives and History. https://archive.org/details/encyclopedi aofwo01harm.
Harris, E. J. (2006). *Theravāda Buddhism and the British encounter: Religious, missionary and colonial experience in nineteenth century Sri Lanka*. Routledge.
Harris, I. (2007). *Buddhism power and political order*. Routledge.
Harvey, G. E. (1925). *History of Burma: From the earliest times to 10 March 1824*. Frank Cass.
Harwood, H. J. (1955). *Methodism in Burma* (Publication No. MARCXML). Joint Section of Education and Cultivation, Board of Missions, U.S. Methodist Church.
Hayami, Y. (2018). Karen culture of evangelism and early baptist mission in nineteenth century Burma. *Social Sciences and Missions, 31*(3–4), 251–83.
Hayek, F., and Bartley, W. (1989). The fatal conceit: The errors of socialism. University of Chicago Press. https://www.mises.at/static/literatur/Buch/hayek-the-fatal-conceit.pdf.
Haynes, J. (2011). *Religious actors in the public sphere: Means, objectives, and effects*. Routledge.
Haynes, J. (2013). Religion, democracy and civil liberties: Theoretical perspectives and empirical ramifications. *European Political Science, 12*(2), 171–83.
Hayward, S. (2015). The double-edged sword of "Buddhist Democracy" in Myanmar. *Review of Faith & International Affairs, 13*(4), 32.
Hayward, S., and Frydenlund, I. (2019, October). Religion, secularism, and the pursuit of peace in Myanmar. *Review of Faith & International Affairs, Taylor & Francis Journals, 17*(4), 1–11.
Hellman-Rajanayagam, D. (2020). From Rangoon College to University of Yangon—1876 to 1920. In S. Kurfürst and S. Wehner (Eds.), *Southeast Asian Transformations* (pp. 5–6). Transcript-Verlag.
Hnin Yadana Zaw. (2015). Myanmar's president signs off on law seen as targeting Muslims. Reuters. https://news.yahoo.com/myanmars-president-signs-off-law-seen-targeting-muslims-113700783.html.
Ho, T. C. (2009). Transgender, transgression, and translation: A cartography of nat kadaws: Notes on gender and sexuality within the spirit cult of Burma. *Discourse, 31*(3), 273.
Ho, T. C. (2010). Review of the film *The Legend of Lady Hill* (Pan Dandayi) (2005). *Visual Anthropology, 23*(3), 254–57.
Holt, J. (2019). *Myanmar's Buddhist-Muslim crisis: Rohingya, Arakanese, and Burmese narratives of siege and fear*. University of Hawai'i Press.
Htun Htun. (2019). Religion ministry done leaving Sangha to govern Ma Ba Tha. *Irrawaddy*. https://www.irrawaddy.com/news/burma/religion-ministry-done-leaving-sangha-govern-ma-ba-tha.html.
Htun, Khaing. (2016). Rites and raucous fun at the Taung Byone nat festival. *Frontier Myanmar*. https://www.frontiermyanmar.net/en/rites-and-raucous-fun-at-the-taung-byone-nat-festival/.
Hudson, B. (2008). Restoration and reconstruction of monuments at Bagan (Pagan), Myanmar (Burma), 1995–2008. *World Archaeology: Debates in World Archaeology, 40*(4), 553–71.

Humanists International. (2016). *Freedom of thought report: Myanmar (Burma)*. https://fot.humanists.international/countries/asia-south-eastern-asia/myanmar-burma/.

Hume, D. (1985). *The history of England*. Lippincott.

Hunt, R. H. (2005). *Bless God and take courage: The Judson history and legacy*. Judson Press.

Hurd, Ian. (1999). Legitimacy and authority in international politics. *International Organization*, 53(2), 379–408.

Huxley, Andrew. (2007). Rajadhamma confronts leviathan: Burmese political theory in the 1870s. In E. Harris (Ed.), *Buddhism Power and Political Order* (pp. 26–51). Routledge.

Hylton, K. N. (2011). Church and state: An economic analysis. *ALER*, 13(402), 404–6; *Metallo*, 3, 499.

Ibrahim, A. (2016). *The Rohingya: Inside Myanmar's genocide*. Hurst.

Ikeya, C. (2011). *Refiguring women, colonialism, and modernity in Burma*. University of Hawai'i Press.

Ingersoll, J. (2015). *Building God's kingdom: Inside the world of Christian reconstruction*. Oxford University Press.

IPAS. (2016). Ipas in Myanmar: Reducing unsafe abortion, improving care, saving lives. *IPAS*. https://www.ipas.org/wp-content/uploads/2020/07/IPASMYAE16_IpasInMyanmar.pdf.

James, H. (2002). Adoniram Judson and the creation of a missionary discourse in pre-colonial Burma. *Journal of Burma Studies*, 7, 1–28.

Jefferson, T. (1779). A bill for establishing religious freedom. https://founders.archives.gov/documents/Jefferson/01-02-02-0132-0004-0082.

Jerryson, M. (2018). *If you meet the Buddha on the road: Buddhism, politics, and violence*. Oxford University Press.

Jerryson, M., and Juergensmeyer, M. (2010). *Buddhist warfare*. Oxford University Press.

Jordt, I. (2003). From relations of power to relations of authority: Epistemic claims, practices, and ideology in the production of Burma's political order. *Social Analysis*, 47(1), 65–76.

Jordt, I. (2007). *Burma's mass Lay meditation movement: Buddhism and the cultural construction of power*. Ohio University Press.

Judson, A. (1823). *An account of the American Baptist mission to the Burman Empire*. J. Butterworth & Son. https://ia802605.us.archive.org/18/items/anaccountameric01judsgoog/anaccountameric01judsgoog.pdf.

Juergensmeyer, M. (1995). The new religious state. *Comparative Politics*, 27(4), 379–91.

Juergensmeyer, M. (2018). The global rise of religious violence. *Nordic Journal of Religion and Society*, 31(2), 87–97.

Kawanami, H. (2016). *Buddhism and the political process*. Palgrave Macmillan.

Keck, S. (2016). Reconstructing trajectories of Islam in British Burma. In E. Crouch (Ed.), *Islam and the state in Myanmar: Muslim-Buddhist relations and the politics of belonging*. Oxford University Press.

Keenan, P. (2011). *Discrimination, conflict, and corruption: The ethnic states of Burma*. Chang Mai, Ethnic Nationalities Council, Union of Burma.

Kennedy, R. (1969). *Thirteen days: A memoir of the Cuban Missile Crisis*. W. W. Norton.

Kenny, P. (2018). *Populism in Southeast Asia: Elements in politics and society in Southeast Asia*. Cambridge University Press. https://doi.org/10.1017/9781108563772.

Keown, D. (2000). *Contemporary Buddhist ethics*. Routledge.

Kertzer, D. I. (2022). *The pope at war: The secret history of Pius XII, Mussolini, and Hitler*. Random House.

Keyes, C. (2007). Monks, guns and peace: Theravada Buddhism and political violence. In J. K. Wellman (Ed.), *Belief and bloodshed: Religion and violence across time and tradition*. Rowman & Littlefield.

Khinny. (2021). [@Myia_K]. (2021, March 4). "Ruthless Myanmar security force is terrified to pass under women's Longyi (sarong) as they believe this'll cause them lose their 'hpon,' spiritual power/male superiority. Longyi movement as a way of women's resistance and fight against the dictatorship. #WhatsHappeningInMyanmar" [Tweet]. Twitter. https://twitter.com/Myia_K/status/1367702244368338949?s=20.

Kin, A. (1983). Burma in 1982: On the road to recovery. *Southeast Asian Affairs*, 87–101. http://www.jstor.org/stable/27908475.

King, M. L. (1963). *A knock at midnight*. https://kinginstitute.stanford.edu/king-papers/documents/knock-midnight.

Kitiarsa, P., and Whalen-Bridge, J. (2013). *Buddhism, modernity, and the state in Asia: Forms of engagement*. Palgrave Macmillan.

Knowles, J. D. (1854). *Memoirs of Ann H. Judson, missionary to Burma*. Gould & Lincoln.

Kongrut, A. (2016). A different kind of prison, Ma Thida is fighting for freedom through literature. *Bangkok Post*. https://www.bangkokpost.com/life/social-and-lifestyle/1088157/a-different-kind-of-prison.

Koppelman, A. (2009). Corruption of religion and the establishment clause. *William and Mary Law Review, 50*, 1831–2215.

Krishnaswami, A. (1960). *Study of discrimination in the matter of religious rights and practices*. United Nations. https://www.ohchr.org/Documents/Issues/Religion/Krishnaswami_1960.pdf.

Kyaw, N. (2016). Islamophobia in Buddhist Myanmar: The 969 movement and anti-Muslim violence. In E. Crouch (Ed.), *Islam and the state in Myanmar: Muslim-Buddhist relations and the politics of belonging*. Oxford University Press.

Kyaw Phyo Tha. (2013). Two Sides of the Sangha. *Irrawaddy*. https://www.irrawaddy.com/in-person/interview/two-sides-of-the-sangha.html.

Kyaw Phyo Tha. (2015). Man arrested for Facebook post denied bail, moved to Insein Prison. *Irrawaddy*. https://www.irrawaddy.com/news/burma/man-arrested-for-facebook-post-denied-bail-moved-to-insein-prison.html.

Lammert, C. (2021). *Buddhist law in Burma: A history of Dhammasattha texts and jurisprudence, 1250–1850*. University of Hawai'i Press.

Lamotte, E. (1988). *History of Buddhism: From the origins to the Saka era*. Université Catholique de Louvain, Institut Orientaliste.

Lang, G. (2004). Challenges for the sociology of religion in Asia. *Social Compass, 51*(1), 99–110.

Larkin, E. (2003). The self-conscious censor: Censorship in Burma under the British, 1900–1939. *Journal of Burma Studies, 8,* 64–101.
Larkin, E. (2011). *Finding George Orwell in Burma.* Penguin/Random House.
Lat, K. (2010). *Art and architecture of Bagan, and historical background.* Mudon Sarpay.
Laycock, D. (2007). Substantive neutrality revisited. *West Virginia Law Review, 110*(1), 51–88.
LeBlanc, J. R., and Simmons, W. P. (2021). Terror, nihilism, and joy: Reconsidering Camus's confrontation with political violence. In N. Susan Laehn and Thomas R. Laehn (Eds.), *Welcoming the other: Student, stranger, and divine.* Lexington.
Lee, R. (2019). Myanmar's citizenship law as state crime: A case for the international criminal court. *State Crime Journal, 8*(2), 241–79.
Lee, R. (2021). *Myanmar's Rohingya genocide: Identity, history and hate speech.* I. B. Tauris.
Lehr, P. (2018). *Militant Buddhism: The rise of religious violence in Sri Lanka, Myanmar and Thailand.* Palgrave Macmillan.
Leider, J. (2009). Relics, statues, and predictions: Interpreting an apocryphal sermon of Lord Buddha in Arakan. *Asian Ethnology, 68*(2), 333–64.
Leigh, M. D. (2011). *Conflict, politics and proselytism.* Manchester University Press.
Leight, I., and Ahdar, R. (2004). Is establishment consistent with religious freedom? *McGill Law Journal, 49*(3), 635–81.
Leiter, B. (2014). *Why tolerate religion?* Princeton University Press.
Leopold, A. M., and Jensen, J. S. (2005). *Syncretism in religion: A reader.* Routledge.
Lewis, C. (2019). Buddhist monk stands firm against hatred and violence in Myanmar. *Global Buddhist Door.* https://www.buddhistdoor.net/news/buddhist-monk-stands-firm-against-hatred-and-violence-in-myanmar.
Lewy, G. (1972). Militant Buddhist nationalism: The case of Burma. *Journal of Church and State, 14*(1), 19–41.
Lewy, G. (1974). *Religion and revolution.* Oxford University Press.
Lieberman, V. (1980). The political significance of religious wealth in Burmese history: Some further thoughts. *Journal of Asian Studies, 39*(4), 753–69.
Lieberman, V. (2003). *Strange parallels: Southeast Asia in global context, c. 800–1830, studies in comparative world history.* Cambridge University Press.
Ling, B. (1999). *Aung San Suu Kyi: Standing up for democracy in Burma.* Feminist Press.
Lintner, B. (2009). The resistance of monks: Buddhism and activism in Burma. *Human Rights Watch.* http://www.hrw.org.
Linz, J. (2004). The religious use of politics and/or the political use of religion: Ersatz ideology versus ersatz religion. In H. Maier (Ed.), *Totalitarianism and political religions: Concepts for the comparison of dictatorships.* Routledge.
Lipes, J. (2021). A dozen dead in Myanmar military plane crash, including prominent senior monk: A Buddhist group has called on the junta to release nearly 20 activist monks. https://www.rfa.org/english/news/myanmar/crash-06102021214123.html.
Locke, J. (1689). A Letter concerning toleration. https://link.springer.com/content/pdf/bfm%3A978-94-011-8794-7%2F1.pdf.

Loomis, H. (1953). *On the road to Mandalay: A visit to Burma*. Woman's Division of Christian Service, Board of Missions, the Methodist Church.

Lubina, M. (2016). Overshadowed by kala: India-Burma Relations. *Politeja*, 13(40), 435–54.

Lubina, M. (2021). *A political biography of Aung San Suu Kyi: A hybrid politician*. Routledge Publishing.

Luce, G. H., and Ba Shin, B. H. (1970). Old Burma: Early Pagán [Supplemental issue]. *Artibus Asiae*, 25, 5–467.

Lusan, N. N. (2021). Sarong revolution: Women smash gender taboos to fight Myanmar junta. *Vice World News*. https://www.vice.com/en/article/bvxej5/sarong-revolution-women-smash-gender-taboos-to-fight-myanmar-junta?utm_source=viceasiatw.

Lynch v. Donnelly, 465 U.S. 668, 687 (1984). (O'Connor, J., concurring).

Ma Thanegi. (2013). *Nor iron bars a cage*. Things Asian Press.

Madison, J. (1785). *Memorial and remonstrance against religious assessments*. https://founders.archives.gov/documents/Madison/01-08-02-0163.

Madison, J. (2003). The federalist, no. 10. In V. Hodgkinson and M. W. Foley (Eds.), *The Civil Society Reader* (pp. 70–75). Tufts University Press.

Majumdar, S. (2018). *Five facts about religion in India*. Pew Research Center. https://pewrsr.ch/2lJYGmh.

Mang, P. (2020). Ethnicity, war, and peace in Burma. *Journal of Church and State*, 62(2), 269–93.

Mann, Z. (2015). 2 years hard labor for Htin Lin Oo in religious offense case. *Irrawaddy*. https://www.irrawaddy.com/news/burma/2-years-hard-labor-for-htin-lin-oo-in-religious-offense-case.html.

Martin, M. F. (2002). Adoniram Judson and the creation of a missionary discourse in pre-colonial Burma. *Journal of Burma Studies*, 7(1), 1–28.

Masuzawa, T. (2005). *The invention of world religions: Or how European universalism was preserved in the language of pluralism*. University of Chicago Press.

Mataic, D. R., and Finke, R. (2019). Compliance gaps and the failed promises of religious freedoms. *Religion, State and Society*, 47(1), 124–50.

Ma Thida. (2017). *Prisoner of conscience: My steps through Insein*. University of Washington Press.

Matthews, B. (1993). Buddhism under a military regime: The iron heel in Burma. *Asian Survey*, 33(4), 408–23.

Matthews, B. (1995). Religious minorities in Myanmar: Hints of the shadow. *Contemporary South Asia*, 4(3), 287–308.

Maung Kaung. (1930). The beginnings of Christian missionary education in Burma, 1600–1824. *Journal of Burma Research Society*, 20(2), 59–75.

Maung Maung. (1969). *Burma and General Ne Win*. Asia Publishing House.

Maung Maung. (1980). *From Sangha to laity: Nationalist movements of Burma (1920–1940)*. South Asia Books.

Maung Maung. (1989). *Burmese nationalist movements (1940–1948)*. Kiscadale Publishing.

Maung Maung Gyi. (1983). *Burmese political values: The socio-political roots of authoritarianism*. Praeger.

Maung Maung, L. (2007). Study on Chinese Muslims in Burma: Emergence of the Panthay community in Mandalay. *Southeast Asian Affairs, 129*, 50–55.

Maung Maung Swe. (2021). Senior General Min Aung Hlaing pays homage to presiding monk of Zay Kone Buddhist Monastery. *Myanmar Digital News.* https://www.mdn.gov.mm/en/senior-general-min-aung-hlaing-pays-homage-presiding-monk-zay-kone-buddhist-monastery.

Maung Shwe Wa. (1963). *Burma Baptist chronicles.* (Vol. 1). Burma Baptist Convention Board of Publications.

McCarthy, S. (2008). Overturning the alms bowl: The price of survival and the consequences for political legitimacy in Burma. *Australian Journal of International Affairs, 62*(3), 298–314.

McConnell, M. W. (2000). Why is religious liberty the "first freedom"? *Cardozo Law Review, 21,* 1243–55.

McConnell, M. W., and Goodrich, L. W. (2016). On resolving church property disputes. *Arizona Law Review, 58,* 307–541.

McKay, M. (2019). *The religious landscape in Myanmar's Rakhine state.* United States Institute of Peace. https://www.usip.org/sites/default/files/2019-09/20190829-pw_149-pw.pdf.

McKinnon, A. M. (2013). Ideology and the market metaphor in rational choice theory of religion: A rhetorical critique of "religious economies." *Critical Sociology, 39*(4).

McLaughlin, T. (2021, February 11). Why Did It Take a Coup? *The Atlantic.* https://www.theatlantic.com/international/archive/2021/02/myanmar-military-coup-joe-biden/617997/?utm_source=share&utm_campaign=share.

Mende, J. (2021). Are human rights western—And why does it matter? A perspective from international political theory. *Journal of International Political Theory, 17*(1), 38–57.

Mendelson, E. M. (1961). A messianic Buddhist association in upper Burma. *Bulletin of the School of Oriental and African Studies, 24*(3), 560–80.

Mendelson, E. M. (1963). Observations on a tour in the region of Popa, central Burma. *France-Asie, 19,* 780–807.

Mendelson, E. M. (1975). *Sangha and state in Burma: A study of monastic sectarianism and leadership.* Cornell University Press.

Metcalfe, D. (2021). [@davidmetcalfe]. (2021, February 15). "Otherworldly forces are displeased with the generals behind Myanmar's coup, according to the ornately dressed spirit mediums joining street protests . . ." Myanmar Spirit Mediums Take Aim at Military Coup | @BangkokPostNews [Tweet]. Twitter. https://twitter.com/davidbmetcalfe/status/1361348176842805248?s=20.

Metro, R., and Aung Khine. (2022). Putting down our weapons when we talk about history: Using primary sources documents to teach multiple perspectives on Burma's past. In M. S. Wong (Ed.), *Teaching for peace and social justice in Myanmar.* Bloomsbury Press.

Methodist Church. (1964). *Burma, Methodist work, from kings and commonwealth, people, Christianity, education and literacy, challenge of Buddhism, Methodist church in Burma* [Pamphlet]. Editorial and Literature Department, Joint Commission on Education and Cultivation, Board of Missions, U.S. Methodist Church.

Milton, J. (2012). *John Milton prose: Major writings on liberty, politics, religion, and education*. Wiley Publishing.
Mitchell, J. (2007). Religion is not a preference. *Journal of Politics*, 69(2): 351–62.
Moe, David Thang. (2015). Nat-worship and Paul Tillich: Contextualizing a correlational theology of religion and culture in Myanmar. *Toronto Journal of Theology*, 31(1), 123–36.
Moe Moe Nyunt. (2008). Burmese reactions to Christianity. *MIT Journal of Theology*, 9, 104.
Moffett, S. H. (2005). *A history of Christianity in Asia, 1500–1900*. (Vol. 2). Orbis.
Mon, Y. (2015). Sayadaw refuses to halt stupa construction. *Myanmar Times*. http://www.mmtimes.com/index.php/national-news/16516-sayadaw-refuses-to-halt-stupa-construction.html.
Mon, Y. (2016). Provocations mount in stupa saga. *Myanmar Times*. http://www.mmtimes.com/index.php/national-news/20127-provocations-mount-in-stupa-saga.html.
Mon, Y., and Aung Kyaw Min. (2016, May 11). Minister apologises to Christians in Kayin State. *Myanmar Times*. http://www.mmtimes.com/index.php/national-news/20224-minister-apologises-to-christians-in-kayin-state.html.
Moore, E. (2009). Place and space in early Burma: A new look at "Pyu culture." *Journal of the Siam Society*, 97, 101–28.
Morrow, A. (2008). *Shin Arahan's legendary Sangha purification*. http://avery.morrow.name/studies/shin-arahan.
Moscotti, A. (1974). *British policy and the nationalist movement in Burma, 1917–1937*. University of Hawai'i Press.
Munger, M. C., and Munger, K. M. (2015). *Choosing in groups: Analytical politics revisited*. Cambridge University Press.
Myanmar Now. (2021a). [@Myanmar_Now_Eng]. (2021, April 13). "Anti-regime messages are written on clay pots placed on the streets of Yangon on Tuesday to welcome Myanmar's New Year. The pots are a traditional offering to the 'nat' or spirit of the New Year Water Festival in what is this year being called #RevolutionaryThingyan" [Tweet]. Twitter. https://twitter.com/Myanmar_Now_Eng/status/1381852702519402496?s=20.
Myanmar Now. (2021b). [@Myanmar_Now_Eng]. (2021, July 10). "VIDEO—U Wirathu, known as a nationalist monk who said soldiers must be worshipped like people worship Buddha, is still in Insein Prison, an official from the Department of Prisons told Myanmar Now. 'He's no longer useful to them'–junta leaves Wirathu in prison after freeing other extremists" [Tweet]. Twitter. https://twitter.com/Myanmar_Now_Eng/status/1413848731414302722?s=20.
Myat Htoo Razak. (2007). U Razak of Burma: A teacher, a leader, a martyr. OS Printing House Co., Ltd. https://www.burmalibrary.org/sites/burmalibrary.org/files/obl/docs4/U_Razak_of_Burma.pdf.
Myawaddy Sayadaw. (2016). Personal communication.
Myo Myint. (1987). The politics of survival in Burma: Diplomacy and statecraft in the reign of King Mindon [Doctoral dissertation, Cornell University].
Nash, J. C. (1960). *Living with nats: An analysis of animism in Burman village social relations*. University of Chicago Press.

Nemoto, K. (2015). Burma's (Myanmar's) "exclusive" nationalism. In J. Kingston (Ed.), *Asian nationalisms reconsidered*. Taylor & Francis.

Neo, J., Jamal, A., and Goh, D. (Eds.). (2019). *Regulating religion in Asia: Norms, modes, and challenges*. Cambridge University Press.

Nietzsche, F. (1919). *The genealogy of morals*. Modern Library.

Niharranjan, R. (1946). *Theravada Buddhism in Burma*. (2nd ed.). Orchid Press.

Nu, U. (1975). *U Nu, Saturday's son*. (U Kyaw Win, Ed.; U Law Yone, Trans.). Yale University Press.

Nu, U. (1988). Nats. *Crossroads: An Interdisciplinary Journal of Southeast Asian Studies*, 4(1), Special Burma Studies Issue (Fall 1988), 1–12.

Nyi Nyi Kyaw. (2016). Islamophobia in Buddhist Myanmar: The 969 movement and anti-Muslim violence. In M. Crouch (Ed.), *Islam and the state in Myanmar: Muslim-Buddhist relations and the politics of belonging* (pp. 184–211). Oxford University Press.

Nyi Nyi Kyaw. (2019). Regulating Buddhism in Myanmar: The case of deviant Buddhist sects. In J. Neo, A. Jamal, D. and Goh (Eds.), *Regulating religion in Asia: Norms, modes, and challenges*. Cambridge University Press.

Nyunt, K. M. (1970, February). The "shoe question": Or the loss and regaining of our independence. *Guardian*, 26.

Obadia, L. (2011). *Economics of religion: Anthropological approaches*. (Research in Economic Anthropology Ser). Emerald Publishing Limited.

Obama, B. (2012). *Remarks by President Obama at the University of Yangon*. White House. https://obamawhitehouse.archives.gov/the-press-office/2012/11/19/remarks-president-obama-university-yangon.

Oldham, W. F. (1918). *Thoburn—Called of God*. Methodist Book Concern.

Ohmmar Khine. (2021a). [@kk36980591]. (2021, May 12). "Last night // light Candlelight strike of buddhist monks from Masoeyein monastery praying for the peace of Myanmar and safety of all civilians, political detainees and our detained leaders. #WhatsHappeningInMyanmar #May13Coup #WhiteCoatStrike" [Tweet]. Twitter. https://twitter.com/kk36980591/status/1392647896214827009?s=20.

Ohmmar Khine. (2021b). [@kk36980591]. (2021, June 8). "Mandalay Sangha Union Strike never skips a day to oppose military dictatorship despite tight security of Junta troops everywhere in Mandalay. #WhatsHappeningInMyanmar #RejectCoupRejectASEAN #June8Coup" [Tweet]. Twitter. https://twitter.com/kk36980591/status/1402249076096180227?s=20.

Ono, T. (1981, March). The development of education in Burma. *East Asian Cultural Studies*, 20 (1–4), 107–33.

Ottama, U. (1931). *The case against the separation of Burma from India: A statement by Ottama Bhikkhu of Burma*. Carmichael Medical College Hospital.

Pace, E. (1995). U Nu, first premier of independent Burma and democracy advocate, dies at 87. *New York Times*. https://www.nytimes.com/1995/02/15/obituaries/u-nu-first-premier-of-independent-burma-and-democracy-advocate-dies-at-87.html.

Palatino, M. (2013). The politics of numerology: Burma's 969 vs. 786 and Malaysia's 505. *Diplomat*. https://thediplomat.com/2013/05/the-politics-of-numerology-burmas-969-vs-786-and-malaysias-505/.

Peacock, D. H. (1932). The University of Rangoon. *Nature*. https://www.nature.com/articles/130283a0.pdf.

Pearn, B. R. (1962). *Judson of Burma*. Edinburgh House Press.

Pe Maung Tin and Luce, G. H. (1921). *The glass palace chronicle of the kings of Burma*. Oxford University Press. https://www.burmalibrary.org/docs20/Glass_Palace_Chronicle_Of_The_Kings_Of_Burma.pdf.

Peoples, H. C., Duda, P., and Marlowe, F. W. (2016). Hunter-gatherers and the origins of religion. *Human Nature*, 27(3), 261–82. https://doi.org/10.1007/s12110-016-9260-0.

Perrin, R. (2001). When religion becomes deviance: Introducing religion in deviance and social problems courses. *Teaching Sociology*, 29(2), 134–52.

Pham, J. (2005). J. S. Furnivall and Fabianism: Reinterpreting the "plural society" in Burma. *Modern Asian Studies*, 39(2), 321–48.

Philpott, D. (2012). *Just and unjust peace: An ethic of political reconciliation*. Oxford University Press.

Philpott, D. (2015). Reconciliation, politics, and transitional justice. In R. S. Appleby, A. Omer, and D. Little (Eds.), *The Oxford Handbook of Religion, Conflict, and Peacebuilding*. Oxford University Press.

Poe, S. C. (1928). *Burma and the Karens*. Elliot Stock.

Poonoosamy, M. (2018). Third culture kids' sense of international mindedness: Case studies of students in two International Baccalaureate schools. *Journal of Research in International Education*, 17(3), 207–27.

Popham, P. (2011). *The lady and the peacock: The life of Aung San Suu Kyi*. Experiment Publishing.

Pratt, J. B. (1928). *The pilgrimage of Buddhism and a Buddhist pilgrimage*. Macmillan.

Prebish, C. S. (2004). *Encyclopedia of Buddhism*. Routledge.

Purser, W. C. B. (1911). *Christian missions in Burma*. Society for the Propagation of the Gospel in Foreign Parts.

Rahula, W. (1974). *What the Buddha taught*. Grove Press.

Rajshekhar. (2006). *Myanmar's nationalist movement (1906–1948) and India*. South Asian Publishers.

Rambo, L. R. (1993). *Understanding religious conversion*. Yale University Press.

Rieffer, B.-A. J. (2003). Religion and nationalism: Understanding the consequences of a complex relationship. *Ethnicities*, 3(2), 215–42. Sage.

Reiss, S. (2015). *The 16 strivings for God: The new psychology of religious experiences*. Mercer University Press.

Riley, J. (2015). *Routledge guidebook to Mill's* On liberty. Taylor & Francis.

Robertson, T. (2014). Aung San Suu Kyi: Colluding with tyranny. *Diplomat*. https://thediplomat.com/2014/11/aung-san-suu-kyi-colluding-with-tyranny/.

Rogers, B. (2007). *Carrying the cross: The military regime's campaign of restriction, discrimination and persecution against Christians in Burma*. Christian Solidarity Worldwide.

Rogers, B. (2008). The saffron revolution: The role of religion in Burma's movement for peace and democracy. *Totalitarian Movements and Political Religions*, 9(1), 115–18.

Rogers, B. (2012). *Burma: A nation at the crossroads*. Random House.

Rogers, B. (2015). The contribution of Christianity to Myanmar's social and political development. *Review of Faith & International Affairs: Religion, Law, and Society in Myanmar*, 13(4), 60–70.

Rohingya Language Preservation Project. (2022). *"First they targeted our culture and language:" Threats to Rohingya language, culture, and identity in Myanmar and Bangladesh*. https://static1.squarespace.com/static/60bf6286f8727b345cf75b1b/t/6371eec6f9e44173e6fb96b7/1668415615840/First-They-Targeted-Our-Culture-and-Language-RLPP-Report.pdf.

Rousseau, Jean-Jacques. (2003). *On the social contract* (G. D. H. Cole, Trans.). Dover.

Rozenberg, G. (2010). *Renunciation and power: The quest for sainthood in contemporary Burma* (J. Hackett, Trans.). Yale University Southeast Asia Studies.

Ruppell, G. (1999). The hidden history of Christianity in Asia: The church in the East before 1500. *International Review of Mission*, 88(351), 435.

Rush, E. (2015). *Still lifes from a vanishing city*. Global Direction Press.

Sakhong, L. H. (2003). *In search of Chin identity: A study in religion, politics and ethnic identity in Burma*. NIAS Press.

Samuel, N. L. (1998). *The meeting of Christianity and Buddhism in Burma: Its past, present and future perspective* [Doctoral dissertation, Tokyo International Christian University].

San Yamin Aung. (2020, July 9). Myanmar president tells officials to control hate speech ahead of election. *Irrawaddy*. https://www.irrawaddy.com/news/burma/myanmar-president-tells-officials-control-hate-speech-ahead-election.html.

Saw Mra Aung. (2015, September 7). Sayadaw U Ottama. *The global light of new Myanmar*. https://www.gnlm.com.mm/sayadaw-u-ottama.

Schissler, M., Walton, M. J., and Phyu Phyu Thi. (2017). Reconciling contradictions: Buddhist–Muslim violence, narrative making and memory in Myanmar. *Journal of Contemporary Asia*, 47(3), 376–95.

Schmidt-Leukel, P., Grosshans, H., and Krueger, M. (2021). *Ethnic and religious diversity in Myanmar*. Bloomsbury Press.

Schober, J. (1997, February). Buddhist just rule and Burmese national culture: State patronage of the Chinese tooth relic in Myanmar. *History of Religions*, 36(3), 218–43.

Schober, J. (2004). Burmese spirit lords and their mediums. In M. N. Walter and E. J. Neumann-Fridman (Eds.), *Shamanism: An encyclopedia of world beliefs, practice and culture* (pp. 803–6). ABC-CLIO.

Schober, J. (2005). Buddhist visions of moral authority and civil society: The search for the post-colonial state in Burma. In M. Skidmore (Ed.), *Burma at the turn of the twenty-first century* (pp. 113–32). University of Hawai'i Press.

Schober, J. (2007). Colonial knowledge and Buddhist education in Burma. In I. Harris (Ed.), *Buddhism, power and political order* (pp. 52–70). Routledge.

Schober, J. (2011). *Modern Buddhist conjunctures in Myanmar: Cultural narratives, colonial legacies, and civil society*. University of Hawai'i Press.

Schober, J. (2018). To be Burmese is to be Buddhist. In T. Borchert (Ed.), *Theravada Buddhism in colonial contexts*. Routledge. https://doi.org/10.4324/9781315111889.

Schober, J., and Collins, S. (2012). The Theravāda civilizations project: Future directions in the study of Buddhism in Southeast Asia. *Contemporary Buddhism*, 13(1), 157–66.

Scott, J. (2009). *The art of not being governed: An anarchist history of upland Southeast Asia* (JSTOR eBooks). Yale University Press.

Seekins, D. M. (2002). *The Disorder in order: The army-state in Burma since 1962*. White Lotus Press.

Seekins, D. M. (2011). *State and Society in Modern Rangoon* (1st ed.). Routledge. https://doi.org/10.4324/9780203610794.

Seekins, D. M. (2013). Sacred site or public space? The Shwedagon Pagoda in colonial Rangoon. In P. Kitiarsa and J. Whalen-Bridge (Eds.), *Buddhism, Modernity, and the State in Asia: Forms of Engagement*. Palgrave Macmillan US.

Selth, A. (2018). *Death of a hero: The U Thant disturbances in Burma, December 1974*. Griffith Asia Institute. http://www.griffith.edu.au/asiainstitute.

Semple, J. (1993). *Bentham's prison: A study of the Panopticon Penitentiary*. Clarendon Press.

Sharot, S. (2002). Beyond Christianity: A critique of the rational choice theory of religion from a Weberian and comparative religions perspective. *Sociology of Religion*, 63(4), 427–54.

Silverstein, J. (1992). Burma: 30 years under an iron fist. *New York Times*. https://www.nytimes.com/1992/03/28/opinion/IHT-burma-30-years-under-an-iron-fist.html.

Simba Shani Kamaria Russeau. (2013, May 3). *Myanmar: Rohingyas at home and nowhere*. Global Information Network.

Simpson, A., Farrelly, N., and Holliday, I. (Eds.). (2018). *Routledge handbook of contemporary Myanmar*. Routledge. https://doi.org/10.4324/9781315743677.

Siochana, M., and Watson, R. (2020). *Naraka: The U Gambira Story*. Amazon Thorpe Press.

Skidmore, M. (2004). *Karaoke fascism: Burma and the politics of fear*. University of Pennsylvania Press.

Sladen, E. (1849). *Papers of Col Sir Edward Sladen, Madras army 1849, British Burma Commission 1856–86*. British Library, Asian and African Studies.

Slater, R. L. (1951). *Paradox and nirvana: A study of religious ultimates with special reference to Burmese Buddhism*. University of Chicago Press.

Smith, A. (1776). An inquiry into the nature and causes of the wealth of nations. https://www.ibiblio.org/ml/libri/s/SmithA_WealthNations_p.pdf.

Smith, D. E. (1965). *Religion and politics in Burma*. Princeton University Press.

Smith, M. (1999). *Burma: Insurgency and the politics of ethnicity*. Zed Books.

Smith, M. (2013). Myanmar's economy needs human rights reforms. *Fortify Rights*. https://www.fortifyrights.org/mya-inv-oped-2013-11-27/.

Smith, M. (2021a). [@matthewfsmith]. (2021, March 9). "Coincidentally, human rights *are* law, protected in some of #Myanmar's own laws. Not to mention this is the same monk who delivered a sermon attempting to provide religious justification for the mass killing of #Rohingya. He's an insult to #Buddhism. #WhatsHappeningInMyanmar." [Tweet]. Twitter. https://twitter.com/matthewfsmith/status/1369315540045561856?s=20.

Smith, M. (2021b). [@matthewfsmith]. (2021, March 9). "#Myanmar monk Sitagu Sayadaw once again clarified his allegiance to the military, quoted today in junta media: "Human rights are not a law. No country can be controlled. If they do not like it, they will shout that human rights are being violated. Shout as much as you like . . ." [Tweet]. Twitter. https://twitter.com/matthewfsmith/status/1369315538674061314?s=20.

Smith, S. D. (1990). The restoration of tolerance. *California Law Review, 78*(2), 305–56.

Snyder, J. L. (2000). *From voting to violence: Democratization and nationalist conflict*. W. W. Norton.

Snyder, J., and Ballentine, K. (1996). Nationalism and the marketplace of ideas. *International Security, 21*(2), 5–40.

Solomon, R. L. (1969). Saya San and the Burmese rebellion. *Modern Asian Studies, 3*(3), 209–23.

South, Ashley. (2008). *Ethnic politics in Burma: States of conflict*. Routledge.

Spiro, D. A. (1987). The creation of a free marketplace of religious ideas: Revisiting the establishment clause after the Alabama secular humanism decision. *Alabama Law Review, 39*(1), 13.

Spiro, M. E. (1982). *Buddhism and society: A great tradition and its Burmese vicissitudes*. University of California Press.

Spiro, M. E. (2011). *Burmese supernaturalism*. Routledge.

Stargardt, J. (1991). *The ancient Pyu of Burma: Vol. 1. Early Pyu cities in a manmade landscape*. PACSEA, in association with ISEAS, Singapore.

Stargardt, J. (2016, October). From the Iron Age to early cities at Sri Ksetra and Beikthano, Myanmar. *Journal of Southeast Asian Studies: Singapore, 47*(3), 341–65.

Stark, R. (2007). *Discovering God: The origins of the great religions and the evolution of belief* (1st ed.). HarperOne.

Stark, R., and Finke, R. (2000). *Acts of faith: Explaining the human side of religion* (1st ed.). University of California Press.

Stark, R., and Bainbridge, W. (1997). *Religion, deviance, and social control*. Routledge.

Steinberg, D. I. (2001). *Burma: The state of Myanmar*. Georgetown University Press.

Sterken, R. E., Jr. (2016). *Teaching barefoot in Burma: Insights and stories from a Fulbright year in Myanmar*. YSPS Publishing.

Sterken, R. E., Jr. (2019). Religion and the state: The politics of social control in Myanmar and the United States. In C. E. Rabe-Hemp and N. S. Lind (Eds.), *Political authority, social control and public policy* (Vol. 31.), *Public Policy and Governance* (pp. 109–22). Emerald Publishing Limited.

Stevenson, H. C. (1944). *The Hill Peoples of Burma*. Burma pamphlets no. 6. Longmans, Green.

Strong, J. (1983). *The legend of King Aśoka: A study and translation of the Aśokavadana*. Princeton University Press.

Suzuki, S. (2020). *Zen mind, beginner's mind*. Shambhala Publishing.

Symes, M. (1827). *An account of an embassy to the kingdom of Ava, in the year 1795* (Vol. 1). Constable & Co.

Symes, M. (1955). *Journal of his second embassy to the court of Ava in 1802*. Allen and Unwin.

Tagore, R. (1913). *Gitanjali 35*. https://www.poetryfoundation.org/poems/45668/gitanjali-35.

Tambiah, S. (1976). *World conqueror and world renouncer: A study of religion and polity in Thailand against a historical background*. Cambridge University Press.
Taylor, G. (2017). Taung Pyone spirit festival: Inside Burma's unofficial gay pride. *Independent*. https://www.independent.co.uk/travel/asia/taung-pyone-spirit-festival-burma-myanmar-gay-pride-august-lgbt-rights-it-legal-dates-a7860856.html.
Taylor, J. (1993). *Forest monks and the nation-state: An anthropological and historical study in northeastern Thailand*. Institute of Southeast Asian Studies.
Taylor, R. H. (1976). Politics in late colonial Burma: The case of U Saw. *Modern Asian Studies*, 10(2), 161–94.
Taylor, R. H. (1987). *The state in Burma*. University of Hawai'i Press.
Taylor, R. H. (2005). Do states make nations? The politics of identity in Myanmar revisited. *South East Asia Research*, 13(3), 261–86.
Taylor, R. H. (2006). *The state in Myanmar* (Rev. ed.). University of Hawai'i Press.
Taylor, R. H. (2015). *General Ne Win: A political biography*. ISEAS-Yusof Ishak Institute.
Temple, R. C. (1991). *The thirty-seven nats: A phase of spirit worship prevailing in Burma*. Kiscadale Publications.
Tegenfeldt, H. G. (1968). *Through deep waters*. Foreign Mission Society.
Tha, K. P., and San Yamin Aung. (2016, July 13). State-backed monks' council decries MaBaTha as "unlawful." *Irrawaddy*. https://www.irrawaddy.com/news/burma/state-backed-monks-council-decries-ma-ba-tha-as-unlawful.html.
Than Htun, (Ed.). (1989). *Royal orders of Burma, A.D. 1598–1885*. Center for Southeast Asian Studies, Kyoto University.
Than Tun. (1978). History of Buddhism in Burma A.D. 1000–1300. *Journal of the Burma Research Society*, 61(1 and 2).
Thant Myint-U. (2001). *The making of modern Burma*. Cambridge University Press.
Thant Myint-U. (2008). *The river of lost footsteps: A personal history of Burma*. Farrar, Straus and Giroux.
Thant Myint-U. (2020). *The hidden history of Burma: Race, capitalism, and the crisis of democracy in the 21st century*. W. W. Norton.
Thapar, R. (2004). *Early India from the origins to A.D. 1300*. University of California Press.
Thoburn, J. M. (1892). *India and Malaysia*. Cranston & Curts.
Toft, M. D., Philpott, D., and Shah, T. S. (2011). *God's century: Resurgent religion and global politics*. W. W. Norton.
Trager, F. (1961). U Thant of Burma: A biographical note. *Asian Survey*, 1(10), 32–34.
Tuckness, A. (2020). Locke's political philosophy. *Stanford encyclopedia of philosophy* (Winter Ed.; E. N. Zalta, Ed.). https://plato.stanford.edu/archives/win2020/entries/locke-political.
Turner, A. (2014). *Saving Buddhism: The impermanence of religion in colonial Burma*. University of Hawai'i Press.
Turner, A., Cox, L., and Bocking, B. (2020). *The Irish Buddhist: The forgotten monk who faced down the British Empire*. Oxford University Press. https://oxford.universitypressscholarship.com/view/10.1093/oso/9780190073084.001.0001/oso-9780190073084.
Tylor, E. B. ([1871] 1958). *Religion in primitive culture*. Harper.

Urquhart, B. (2013). *U Thant: Character sketch.* https://news.un.org/en/spotlight/character-sketches-u-thant-brian-urquhart.
United Nations. (2013). *Situation of human rights in Myanmar: Note by the Secretary-General.* https://www.ohchr.org/Documents/Countries/MM/A-68-397_en.pdf.
U.S. Department of State. (2019). *2019 report on international religious freedom: Burma.* Office of International Religious Freedom. https://www.state.gov/reports/2019-report-on-international-religious-freedom/burma/.
U.S. Department of State. (2020). *2020 report on international religious freedom: Burma.* Office of International Religious Freedom. https://www.state.gov/reports/2020-report-on-international-religious-freedom/burma/.
VanAntwerpen, J. (2014). Reconciliation as Heterodoxy. In J. J. Llewellyn and D. Philpott (Eds.), *Restorative Justice, Reconciliation, and Peacebuilding.* Oxford University Press.
Van Der Veer, P. (2001). *Imperial encounters: Religion and modernity in India and Britain.* Princeton University Press.
Von Der Mehden, F. (1961). Buddhism and politics in Burma. *Antioch Review,* 21(2), 166–75.
Von Der Mehden, F. (1963). *Religion and nationalism in southeast Asia: Burma, Indonesia, and the Philippines.* University of Wisconsin Press.
Wade, F. (2017). *Myanmar's Enemy Within: Buddhist violence and the making of a Muslim "Other."* Zed Books.
Wah, Htoo Htoo. (personal communication, May 4, 2021).
Wahlrab, A., Sass, S. M., and Sterken, R. E. (2019). The need to disrupt social control. In C. E. Rabe-Hemp and N. S. Lind (Eds.), *Political authority, social control and public policy* (pp. 245–58). Public Policy and Governance, Vol. 31. Emerald Publishing. https://doi.org/10.1108/S2053-769720190000031016.
Wai Moe. (2007). Burma media claims monks possessed weapons, pornography. *Irrawaddy.* https://www2.irrawaddy.com/article.php?art_id=8936.
Walton, M. (2008). Ethnicity, conflict, and history in Burma: The myths of Panglong. *Asian Survey,* 48(6), 889–910.
Walton, M. (2016a). *Buddhism, politics, and political thought in Myanmar.* Cambridge University Press.
Walton, M. (2016b). Buddhist monks and democratic politics in contemporary Myanmar. In H. Kawanami (Ed.), *Buddhism and the political process.* Palgrave Macmillan.
Walton, M., and Hayward, S. (2014). Contesting Buddhist narratives: Democratization, nationalism, and communal violence in Myanmar. *Policy Studies,* 71, 1–51, 53–65, 67.
Walton, M., and Ma Khin Mar Mar Kyi. (2019). Is this the end of Ma Ba Tha? *Tea Circle.* https://teacircleoxford.com/2019/12/02/is-this-the-end-of-ma-ba-tha/.
Washington, G. (1796). Farewell address. https://avalon.law.yale.edu/18th_century/washing.asp.
Wayland, F. (1853). *The memoir of the life and labours of the Reverend Adoniram Judson.* (Vol. 1). Philips & Sampson.
Weber, M. (2001). *The Protestant ethic and the spirit of capitalism.* Routledge.

Wells, T. (2016). Making sense of reactions to communal violence in Myanmar. In N. Cheesman and N. Farrelly (Eds.), *Conflict in Myanmar: War, politics, religion*. ISEAS, Yusof Ishak Institute.

Whitehead, A. L., and Perry, S. L. (2020). *Taking America back for God: Christian nationalism in the United States*. Oxford University Press.

Whitman, A. (1974). U Thant is dead of cancer at 65. *New York Times*.

Wilcox, C., Wald, K., and Jelen, T. (2008). Religious preferences and social science: A second look. *Journal of Politics*, 70(3), 874–79.

Wilson, P. J. (1988). *The domestication of the human species*. Yale University Press.

Win Kanbawza. (1988, October). Colonialism, nationalism and Christianity in Burma: A Burmese perspective. *Asia Journal of Theology*, 2(2), 270–81.

Win Nyi Nyi Zaw and Khin Nyein Chan. (2020). Citizens' political preferences for 2020. *People's Alliance for Credible Elections*. https://drive.google.com/file/d/1gHp1VzwzVbtHRC9cpTToLzqDhjUWVE1B/view?usp=sharing.

Woodward, M. (1988). When one wheel stops: Theravada Buddhism and the British Raj in upper Burma. *Crossroads: An Interdisciplinary Journal of Southeast Asian Studies*, 4(1), 57–90.

Yaw Mingyi U Hpo Hlaing. (2004). Rajadhammasangaha (L. E. Bagshawe, Trans.). Sape U Publishing House (Original work published 1979). https://www.burmalibrary.org/en/the-rajadhammasangaha.

Yazawintawyi, H. N. (1960). *Glass palace chronicle of the kings of Burma* (Pe Maung Tin and G. H. Luce, Trans.). Rangoon University Press. (Original work published 1923).

Ye Mon and Aung Kyaw Min. (2016). Minister apologises to Christians in Kayin State. *Myanmar Times*. https://www.mmtimes.com/national-news/20224-minister-apologises-to-christians-in-kayin-state.html.

Yegar, M. (1966). The Panthay (Chinese Muslims) of Burma and Yunnan. *Journal of Southeast Asian History*, 7(1), 73–85.

Yi, K. (1988). *The Dobama movement in Burma, 1930–38*. Cornell University Press.

Young, L. A. (1997). *Rational choice theory and religion*. Routledge.

Young Men's Buddhist Association. (1994). *The illustrated history of Buddhism*. Theravada Buddhist Society of America. (Original work published 1951).

Za Mang, P. (2017). Religion, ethnicity, and nationalism in Burma. *Journal of Church and State*, 59(4), 626–48.

Zakaria, F., Norén-Nilsson, A., and Bourdier, F. (2019). Religion, mass violence, and illiberal regimes: Recent research on the Rohingya in Myanmar. *Journal of Current Southeast Asian Affairs*, 38(1), 98–111.

Zaw, J. (2018). Buddhist body urged to discipline Myanmar's unruly monks. *UCA News*. https://www.ucanews.com/news/buddhist-body-urged-to-discipline-myanmars-unruly-monks/81624#.

Index

8888 generation. *See* Four Eights Movement

'Abd al-Khaliq, xxvii, 23, 49, 58–63, 70
All Burma Monks Alliance (ABMA), 147–148
Alms Bowl Boycott, 144–145
Anawrahta, xxvii, xxix, 28, 37–40, 44–46, 53, 71, 73, 99, 123, 134, 155, 168–169, 177, 183, 190, 205
animism, xii, 2, 8, 23, 31, 43, 56, 115, 187
Anti–Fascist People's Freedom League (AFPFL), 89, 101
Arakan, 56, 57, 77, 101, 125
Ari monks, 35–36, 38–39
Ashoka, xvii, xxviii, 23, 29, 33–37, 40, 45–46, 134, 168, 170, 183, 203–204, 205–208
Ashokan spirit (road), xvii, 183, 207–208
Ava, 61–62
Aung San, General (father of Aung San Suu Kyi), xxviii, 3, 24, 89–94, 102–103, 107, 112, 119–120, 137, 139, 144, 161, 206; religious liberty and, 90–92
Aung San Suu Kyi, xxviii, 20, 42–43, 128, 132, 134, 136, 144–145, 151, 155, 169–175, 180, 186, 195–196, 206; king law, statement about, 30, 42–43, 134, 145; nats, beliefs in, 186; religion and beliefs, 171–174
Aung-Thwin, Maitrii, 80

Bagan, 28, 32, 71
Bagyidaw, King, 61
Bahá'í religion in Myanmar, 67
Baptists in Myanmar, xvii, xxviii, 22, 28, 48–49, 58–67, 103, 116–117, 131–135, 170, 185, 199, 201
Bentham, Jeremy, 110–111
Black, Hugo, 17, 179
Bo, Charles Maung Cardinal, 132–133, 151, 155, 157
bogus Buddhist, 106–108, 115
Bogyoke Market (also Scott Market), 3
British colonial rule, xiii, xiv, xxv, 9, 24, 41, 46–88, 89, 90–93, 107, 110, 116–119, 123, 131, 137, 170, 206; British professors influence, 78, 117, 137–139, 171; state religion policy, 9, 48–87
Buchanan, Claudius, 60
Buddha Sasana Council (BSC), 106
Buddha's tax, 124–125

Buddhism: as a state religion, 1–43; national identity, 71, 83–87
Buddhist country, xi–xii, 11, 56, 87, 101, 119–122, 125, 154, 185, 195, 197
Burmese Way to Socialism, 113, 128, 139, 143, 206
Butwell, Richard, xxii
Cady, John, 30, 40, 67–68, 71, 80
Calcutta, 60, 78, 138
Carstens, Charles, 7, 30, 202–203
Catholics in Myanmar, 48, 59–69, 109, 116–119, 131–132, 157, 170, 185, 201
Charney, Michael, 8
Cheesman, Nick, 9–10, 121
Christians in Myanmar, xiii, xix, xx, xxviii, 8, 18, 28–29, 43, 50–78, 86–90, 102–105, 113–135, 170, 175, 182, 186–187, 194, 197–204; missionaries, 2, 3, 23, 47, 49, 170–175; nationalists, xiii, 84; Chin people, 55, 59, 65, 87, 104, 116–117, 126, 166, 199, 201; Kachin people, 55, 59, 65, 87, 103, 116, 120, 131, 200–201; Karen people, 6, 55, 59, 65, 87, 90, 116, 206
citizenship issues, xv, 9, 18, 86, 102, 108, 114, 119–129, 167, 195, 197, 202–203, 207
Civil Disobedience Movement 2021, 155
Cochrane, Archibald Douglas, 75
consequences of state and religion entanglement, xiv, 1–4, 159, 185, 205–206
Craddock, Sir Reginald, 89
Crouch, Melissa, xxii, 51

David, Roman, xxii, 20–21, 183
deviance and religion, 13, 46, 204–205
Dhammaraja, 30, 34, 41–43, 149
Dobama, 112

education, religious, 39, 49, 52, 60, 65–68, 76–79, 93, 113, 139, 164–166, 169–173, 180, 199

Fink, Christina, 10
Finke, Roger, xxii, xxvi, 5, 18–19

Fortify Rights, xxi, 194, 200
Four Eights Movement Uprising, xx, xxix, 128, 137, 143–147, 157, 169, 178–179, 206
Fox, Jonathan, xxii, 14–15
Franklin, Benjamin, 69
Furnivall, J.S., 39, 138–139
Fytch, Albert, 54–55

Gambira, Ashin, xxix, 23, 147–149, 151
Gandhi, Mahatma, 77–79, 82, 146, 171–173
genocide, 26, 194–195
Gill, Anthony, xxii
Gravers, Mikael, 10
Green, Nile xxii, 58–59
Government monks, 17, 38–39, 124, 136, 145, 153, 168, 177–179, 183

Hand, Learned, 70
Hayek, Friedrich, 19
Hayward, Susan, xxii
Hindu, xii, 8, 31–38, 43–45, 48–49, 55–59, 67, 78, 84, 87, 96, 99, 102–103, 117, 125, 131, 149, 165, 170, 182, 185, 197, 199, 202, 203
Holliday, Ian, xxii, 20–21, 183
Human rights, xxi, xxiii, xxix, 12, 18, 64, 78, 104, 106, 110, 120–122, 129, 135, 136–139, 141–149, 156–157, 164, 166, 169, 171–172, 176, 178, 181, 195, 199, 201; sovereign cetana and, 120–121

identity cards, 121, 167, 195
Insein Prison, xx, 109–111, 118, 124, 128, 137, 144, 148, 155, 166, 167, 180–182
interfaith marriages, 12
Irrawaddy River, 27, 31–32, 47–48, 131, 138
Islam in Myanmar, xi, xii, xxvii, 8, 23, 47, 53, 55–59, 67–69, 90, 97–99, 102–106, 117, 121–125, 131, 167–168, 186, 198–204
Isodore Ngei Ko Lat, 65

Jefferson, Thomas, 15–17, 44, 159, 172, 177, 205–208
Jewish communities in Myanmar, 67, 185, 195, 202
Jubilee Hall, 75, 89–92
Judson, Adoniram, xxviii, 49, 60–70, 116
Judson, Ann Hasseltine, xxviii, 49, 60–62
Judson Research Institute, xix, 21

kala, 69, 195, 197
Karen Baptist Theological Seminary, 60
keeper of the religion. *See thathanabaing*
King Law. *See* Ten Duties of Kings, 29, 42, 149, 179
King, M. L., 134, 172
Konbaung dynasty, 56

laws for the protection of race and religion, 86, 117–118, 120–122, 151–154, 163–166, 167, 179, 194, 202
Lee, Ronan, xxii
legitimacy of Myanmar government and religion, xxvi, 12–13, 16, 37, 39, 44–45, 49–52, 84–87, 96, 99–100, 111, 123, 129, 133–136, 142–148, 154–159, 162, 174–175, 181–183, 194, 207–208
LGBTQ community in Myanmar, 2, 191
Lubina, Michał, xxii
Luce, G. H., 138
Locke, John, 15–16, 44, 147, 159, 172, 204, 208
Lwin, Sein, (General, known as the "Butcher of Rangoon, 143

Ma Ba Tha and, 152–154, *168*, 179–181
Madison, James, 15–18, 53, 159, 177
Mahagiri nats, 31–32, 94–99, 191. *See also* nats
Mandalay, xvii, 21–23, 28, 30–31, 41, 45–48, 58, 64, 69, 76, 101, 105, 115, 117, 144, 150, 155, 165, 178, 180, 187
Mendelson, Michael E., 26, 66, 182
Methodists in Myanmar, xxi, 22, 48–49, 59, 63–67, 103, 117–118, 131, 170, 185

Min Aung Hlaing, xxvii, xxviii, xxix, 41, 128, 152, 155–156, 157, 165, 178, 195–196
Mindon, xxviii, 41–47, 182, 187
Milton, John, 15–16, 44, 159, 162, 172, 179, 208
Ministry of Religious Affairs, 28, 55–56, 98, 106, 114, 118, 126, 165, 198
Mitchell, Derek (US Ambassador), xxi, 22
monks and political factions, 177–182
Moulmein, 63, 81
Mount Popa, 32, 94, 116, 190–192
Muslims in Myanmar, xxviii, 3–4, 43, 51–59, 74–78, 83–87, 103, 119–129, 143, 150–155, 166–167, 175, 179–182, 182, 187, 194–206
Myanmar Institute of Theology, xix, xxiii, 21–22, 60, 109, 120
Myawaddy Sayadaw. *See* Sayadaw Ashin Arriyawuntha Biwunsa
Myat Thu, xx, xxi
Myitkyina, 120, 131–132
Myint-U, Thant, xxv–xxvi, 30, 41, 120, 141, 194

National League for Democracy, 132, 144–145, 151, 152, 154, 195–196
nationalism, xxix, 1–2, 9–10, 24, 49, 65, 70; 969 Movement, 152, 179; Buddhist, 70–87, 97–100, 108, 114–124, 139, 164, 171–176, 181, 194, 197, 202; Christian, xiii–xiv
nats, 2, 31–33, 35–45, 81, 87, 92–99, 103, 107, 115–116, 142, 155–156, 186–193; festivals, 2, 35, 115–116, 156, 186–193; kadaws (spirit wives), 191, 193; LBGTQ and, 193; Thirty-Seven nats, 31, 37–38, 155, 189, 191–192;
nats, specific: Mahagiri Siblings, 31–33; Taungbyon Brothers, 189–190; Thagymin, 37–38
Naypyidaw, 41, 42, 178
Nehru, Jawaharlal, 93, 96–97, 170–171
Ne Win, xxvii, xxix, 9, 13, 15, 17, 23, 108, 110–130, 137–138, 140, 141–144,

170–172, 175–178, 204–206; nats and, 115–116, 192–195
Northern Illinois University, and Center for Burma Studies, 94–95
Nu Tawng, Ann Rosa (Catholic Sister), 132
Nu, U, xxx, 89–122; emerging Buddha, 95–96; minority religions and, 102–105; nats and, 94–95; promoting religion, 96–98
Nyanissara, Ashin U (also Sitagu Sayadaw), xxix, 178–179
Nyi Nyi Kyaw, xxii, 13,

Obama, Barak, and Yangon University, 139
O'Conner, Sandra Day, 129
Ottama, U, xxix, 77–89, 97–98, 108, 134, 146, 151, 161, 169, 175

pagodas, 29, 34, 40, 42–47, 71–76, 82–83, 89, 98–99, 106, 123–125, 142, 147, 165, 174, 178, 188–190
Pali Canon, 34–35, 45–47, 100
Pakokku, 148
Panthay or Chinese Muslims, 47, 57, 185
passive (pure) monks, 25, 177, 182
political factions in the Buddhist firm (Sangha), 177–182
pongyis (monks) and political, 79–80
prison. *See* Insein
Protocols of the Elders of Zion, 200
Pyu people, 31

Rangoon University (also Yangon University), 67, 78, 79, 93, 138–139, 142, 171
Razak, U, 90, 120
relics, Pyu and, 31; Buddha and, 34, 44, 71, 123, 190
Religion and the State Project, 14–15, 175–178, 197–199
religious economy, 3–6
restrictions on religion's political role in Myanmar, 175–177

Rohingya, xi, xiii, xxv, xxviii, xxix, 9, 26, 55–56, 73, 120–125, 154, 179, 185, 194–206
Rogers, Benedict, 63–64

Sachsenhausen concentration camp, 110
Saffron monks and, xx, 137, 146–156, 181–182
Saffron Revolution, xxix, 137, 145, 146–158, 181–183, 193–194, 206
Sangha (Buddhist monkhood): negative side of, 150–154; positive side of, 136–150
Sangha Mahanayaka Committee, 2, 13, 16, 126–127, 143, 145, 154
Sayadaw Ashin Arriyawuntha Biwunsa (also known as Myawaddy Sayadaw), xx, xxvii, xxix, 150–157, 162, 176, 180–181
Saya San, U, 77–87, 97, 108, 111, 120, 123, 146
Schober, Julian, xxii, 8
secularism, 5, 30, 44, 49, 54, 65–66, 77, 84, 90, 92, 107, 114, 127, 160–161, 169–173, 183, 192
Sepoy Rebellion, 50
Shan people, xxvii, 55, 57, 73, 78, 87, 90, 103, 128, 198, 201–202, 206
Shan-style rice, xxii, 3–4
Shin Arahan, xxix, 28, 37–43, 53, 183, 207
shoe question, 71, 73–76
Shwedagon Pagoda, 82–83, 89, 106, 142, 147
Shwe Hpi (Muslim writer), 83
Shwesandaw Pagoda, 71–72
Sixth Buddhist Synod, 100
Sladen, Edward Bosc, xxix, 48, 52, 55, 70
Smith, Adam, 15–19, 34, 159, 172, 178, 181
Smith, Donald, E., xxii, 8–10
Smith, Matthew, xxi
socially engaged Buddhism, 173, 182–183

state establishment of religion in Myanmar, xiii, 17, 30, 39–41, 49, 55
State Law and Order Restoration Council, 145
State (Myanmar) restrictions on religious practices, 197–201
stupa, 27–29, 34, 43–47, 71, 99, 125
syncretism, 36

Tagore, Rabindranath, 171
Taungbyon, 189–191. See also festivals
Ten Duties of Kings, xxix, 42–43, 149–150, 179
thakin, xxx, 90
Thant, U., xxx, 23, 137–142; funeral crisis and, 140–143
thathanabaing, xxix, 39, 50, 54–55, 58–59, 86, 97
Thein Sein, 153, 181, 194
Thibaw, King, xxvii, xxix, 40–50, 65, 81, 116
Thirty Comrades, 112
Thoburn, James Mills (Methodist Bishop), 63–66

tolerance of intolerance, xii, xv, 3, 18, 136, 141, 151, 157, 185, 187, 194, 204–205
truth, perversion of, 204–205
Turner, Alicia, xxii, 9

under garments women, 190

Vinaya, 34, 40, 47, 50, 52–53, 69, 81, 96, 127, 162, 176, 182

Walton, Matthew, 22, 9–10, 181–182
Washington, George, 133
Weber, Max, 134
White Rose movement Myanmar, 181–182
Wirathu, Ashin, 22, 29, 153, 154, 180
Wisara, U, xxx, 77–87, 98, 146

Yangon School of Political Science, xii, xx, 22,
Young Men's Buddhist Association, 75–78

About the Author

Robert Edward Sterken Jr. is a professor of political science at the University of Texas at Tyler. Sterken's research is focused on religion and the state in Southeast Asia. He is the author of *Teaching Barefoot in Burma*, *Bill Ratliff: A Profile of Courage and Leadership in American Politics*, and numerous articles and chapters. In 2015–2016, Sterken was a Fulbright Scholar at Yangon University and the Myanmar Institute of Theology. As a Fulbright Specialist in 2018, Sterken taught religion and politics at Jilin University in Changchun, China, where he was awarded Jilin University's Distinguished Visiting Professor Award.

Sterken argues that religious liberty or the lack thereof results from rational interest-based calculations of both religious and state actors. Using insights dating back to Adam Smith, John Locke, and Thomas Jefferson, Sterken argues that centuries of state support for Theravada Buddhism has corrupted the Myanmar religious marketplace. At the expense of religions and society, Myanmar's military leaders have protected and regulated religion to enhance their own political survival. The consequences of stated religion entanglement include (1) a state-supported religious monopoly; (2) corruption, regulation, and repression of Theravada Buddhists; (3) repression and violence against religious minorities; (4) perpetual conflict and violence; (5) a corrupt religious economy; and (6) a corruption of truth. The consequences of state control are stark and should serve as a warning to all who would seek to entangle religion and the state.

www.ingramcontent.com/pod-product-compliance
Lightning Source LLC
Chambersburg PA
CBHW070236240426
43673CB00044B/1810